W9-ATD-442

RITUALS
OF BLOOD

Also by Orlando Patterson

Nonfiction

The Sociology of Slavery: Jamaica, 1655–1838

Ethnic Chauvinism: The Reactionary Impulse

Slavery and Social Death: A Comparative Study

Freedom in the Making of Western Culture

*The Ordeal of Integration: Progress and Resentment
in America's "Racial" Crisis*

Ecumenical America (forthcoming)

Fiction

The Children of Sisyphus

An Absence of Ruins

Die the Long Day

RITUALS
OF BLOOD

Consequences of Slavery in Two American Centuries

ORLANDO PATTERSON

CIVITAS
COUNTERPOINT
Washington, D.C.

Library of Congress Cataloging-in-Publication Data
Patterson, Orlando, 1940–
Rituals of blood : consequences of slavery in two American
centuries / Orlando Patterson.
p.   cm.
Includes bibliographical references and index.
1. United States—Race relations.   2. United States—Ethnic
relations.   3. Sex role—United States.   4. Afro-Americans—Social
conditions.   5. United States—Social conditions.   I. Title.
E185.615.P353   1999
305.8'00973—dc21   98-47778
CIP

ISBN 1-887178-82-1 (alk. paper)

Printed in the United States of America on acid-free paper that meets the
American National Standards Institute Z39-48 Standard.

CIVITAS/COUNTERPOINT
P.O. Box 65793
Washington, D.C. 20035-5793

Counterpoint is a member of the Perseus Books Group.
10 9 8 7 6 5 4 3 2

CONTENTS

INTRODUCTION

As we approach the end of the twentieth century, the time is ripe to examine just how far we have come since the historical sociologist W. E. B. Du Bois made his famous prediction that this would be the century of the color line. By now, it is stating the obvious to say that Du Bois's prophecy was correct. This has been a century torn by the often murderous imposition of ethnic, including so-called racial, boundaries, and by the struggles to overturn them.

There have already been many such assessments, and there are undoubtedly more to come. In *The Ordeal of Integration: Progress and Resentment in America's "Racial" Crisis*, the first volume of this trilogy, I assayed our recent progress on the journey toward social justice, paying special attention to changes in ethnic and racialist attitudes and to the socioeconomic condition of Afro-Americans. My bottom line assessment was that, overall, remarkable progress had been made in both areas, especially over the past half century, but that major problems still remained and new ones shadowed the horizon. It is these persisting problems, and the paradoxical ways in which ethnic changes take place and are differentially perceived, that, I argued, explain the growing chorus of pessimism about relations between people on different sides of the color line.

The aim of this second volume of the trilogy is to take a closer look at the most critical of these persisting problems by means of three original, interlocking essays. If *The Ordeal of Integration* took stock, with guarded optimism, of where we are now, the task of this volume is to examine soberly just how far we still have to go by investigating the major obstacles to further and faster progress. Of necessity, the tone and mood of this volume are very different from those of its predecessor. The problems I appraise are acute, and in the course of delineating and explaining them, I have some shocking tales to tell.

The change of tone is quite appropriate and I make no apologies for it. Sociologists or policy analysts, if they are to practice their craft responsibly, behave like good internists. If a patient has been horribly sick, as America has been for most of its history in its ethnic relations and treatment of its Afro-American citizens, it is appropriate that any general assessment of its ethnic body politic should isolate and emphasize all indicators of progress. Optimism, when justified, itself becomes a good part of the cure. But when the analyst turns to the task of diagnosing persisting ailments, the responsible one examines with a wary eye, anticipating the very worst.

This change of focus and mood also requires a change in relation to time. By this, I mean not only that my analysis will be written in another key but that my temporal orientation is different. A stocktaking of the sort conducted in *The Ordeal of Integration* projects into the future the trends leading up to the present. An analysis of persisting problems, especially for a historical sociologist, must return to the past in completing the search for causes.

A distinction is often made between the internal and external causes of Afro-America's problems, the former being those originating within the group's social behaviors and cultural patterns; the latter, those arising from a socioeconomic environment dominated by racism. Sharp ideological cleavages hinge on this distinction. The distinction is provisionally useful but should be used with care because, in the final analysis, internal and external causes are closely linked not so much as in a causal chain as in a layered net. Consider, for example, the etiology of psychic disorders. A person suffering from agoraphobia may seem to be experiencing an external problem with a very internal source, but while the proximate cause of his incapacity to venture outdoors is indeed internal, deeper analysis would in all likelihood find that the agoraphobia itself originated in an earlier, externally induced trauma. Conversely, an internal problem such as low self-esteem can be shown to have both internal and external causes.

The parallels with the problems of Afro-Americans (or the working class or whatever one's problematic group of interest) should already have been apparent. The internal and external problems of the group are inextricably linked. For the purposes of analysis, we often focus on one or the other area and level of the causal net, but when people insist, as conservatives are wont to do, that only the proximate internal cultural and behavioral factors are important ("So stop whining and pull up your socks, man!"), or as liberals and mechanistic radicals are inclined to do, that only the proximate external factors are worth considering ("Stop blaming the victim, racist!"), they are playing tiresome and obfuscating ideological games. This second volume, like the first, attempts to go beyond these unrewarding squabbles.

In the first essay in this volume, "Broken Bloodlines: Gender Relations and the Crisis of Marriages and Families Among Afro-Americans," I argue that the main persisting problems of Afro-Americans congeal around the set of social issues we have in mind when we speak of gender and gender relations. I use the term *gender* in its broad sociological sense to mean all aspects of human relations involving people's identities, attitudes, and behaviors as males and as females. To be more specific, I contend that the fundamental problem now facing Afro-Americans pertains to (1) the ways they *define* their roles and identities as men and as women and the ways in which others have defined—and, in the process, twisted and distorted—these roles both today and in the past; (2) the nature of the *relations* between Afro-American men and women in their roles as fathers, mothers, sons, and daughters; and especially (3) the nature of their intimate relations as lovers, cohabiting partners, wives, and husbands. These roles, identities, and relations embrace and overlap with what is commonly called "the family." I refrain from speaking about *the* family for reasons to be explained in the first essay. For now, let me just say that terms like "*the* family," and, even worse, "family values" are misleading sociologically and have been all but obfuscated politically.

I do not know what Dan Quayle and his liberal critics mean by the term "family values" in their culture wars, beyond the sociological tautology that it has to do with values pertaining to familial relations, and beyond the moral platitude that these values are good and should be respected. What I do know is that the professional social scientists who are most qualified to speak on this subject—sociologists who specialize in the study of gender, including familial, relations—have been conspicuously absent from public debates on these issues. This is partly a reflection of the impoverished state of public discourse in America today, especially on social issues. But it is equally a sad reflection on the public timidity and intellectual hermitage of academic sociology, which is ironic given the fact that, contrary to popular misconception, sociology has emerged from its methodological disputes of the seventies and eighties in the best shape it has ever been in as a discipline. The sociology of gender and familial relations is now among the most vigorous and productive areas of the discipline. And if it has demonstrated anything, it is that any understanding of familial matters requires an analysis of the underlying gender roles and relations that make them up and the broader socioeconomic and historical context in which they are situated.

Thus it is not possible to make sense of modern American families or so-called family values without understanding the revolution in gender roles that came with the rapid growth of women's participation in the workforce over the past half century. When women work, they become more independent economically. If they are more independent economically, they are less willing to put up with unhappy marriages. And if they divorce more frequently, their attitudes and values about marriage and divorce change accordingly.

No group of people and no experience illustrates this more vividly than those of Afro-Americans. There is a crisis in nearly all aspects of gender relations among all classes of Afro-Americans, and it is getting worse. Before it became de rigueur for academic and other advocates of Afro-Americans to deny behavioral and cultural problems, the crisis was widely acknowledged and deplored by all thoughtful Afro-Americans. When the sociologist and jazz musician Charles Keil wrote in 1966, "For the vast majority of Negroes, the battle of the sexes is no mere figure of speech. In the ghetto, men and women are considered to be separate and antagonistic species, and this division 'overrides the minor distinctions of creed, class and color.'"[1] The remark, for all its exaggeration, went unchallenged largely because most Afro-American men at the time acknowledged the seriousness of the problem. Afro-American women were even more emphatic in recognizing and lamenting the problem. The 1970 observation of the distinguished novelist and feminist Toni Cade Bambara was typical: "One of the most characteristic features of our community is the antagonism between our men and women."[2]

Not long after that, however, the tide turned with the rise of Afro-American chauvinism and, in its service, a feel-good social science that condemned any and all explorations of the group's behavioral problems as racist or, when coming from Afro-Americans, reactionary. For nearly two decades, serious examination of this social wound was largely censored, with only a few literary figures and the occasional scholar daring to take it on. Fortunately, by the late eighties the tide began to turn again, thanks in good part to the works of Afro-American women writers and scholars.

I have found that Afro-Americans are today as isolated internally from each other as they are isolated externally, as a group, from other Americans. However, while their external isolation is still serious, yet declining (as I demonstrated in *The Ordeal of Integration*), their internal isolation is getting worse. The root cause of this internal isolation, I argue, is the sorry state of relations between men and women. Afro-Americans have the lowest rate of marriage in the nation, and those who do get married have the highest rate of divorce of any major ethnic group. The result is that most Afro-Americans, especially women, will go through most of their adult lives as single people.

My analysis belies two myths that are often offered up by apologists in their attempt to deny and obscure this tragedy. One is that Afro-Americans have developed alternate forms of lasting and viable gender relations and alternate modes of child rearing. While such alternate institutional arrangements may have existed in the rural South and among the earliest generation of migrants north—although always precariously, as Richard Wright and Ralph Ellison, among others, disclosed[3]—there is now no evidence for them. As I will show, alternatives to marriage such as cohabitation are even more volatile, and are disrupted at an even greater rate, than marriages. Nor is there a shred of evidence that male kinsmen and friends of single mothers provide alternate male role models for Afro-American boys and girls.

Which brings me to the second popular piece of folklore among modern Afro-Americans, what may be called the myth of the "hood," the belief that viable informal friendship patterns and communities exist, compensating for the breakdown or absence of more formal institutions. Through sheer, baseless repetition, and through nonrepresentative case studies of a few Afro-American housing projects by urban anthropologists, it has become an accepted belief that large networks of support and natural neighborhood communities are out there waiting to be developed and built on. Would that this were so. But my own analysis of representative samples of national network surveys confirms what other scholars have found: The typical Afro-American has a much smaller network of friends and kinsmen than other Americans do. And, what was most unexpected, the proportion of the members of this attenuated network who are kinsmen is smaller than in other Americans' networks. There are no "hoods" out there, which is precisely why murderous gangs, like opportunistic social cancers, rush in to fill the vacuum.

Not only has there been censorship and denial of this problem, but a great deal of fantastic hype has asserted the very opposite of the grim social realities. Afro-Americans have convinced themselves and nearly everyone else that, whatever their socioeconomic condition, their gender relations are blessed with a special warmth and vivacity, when, as we will see, these relations are fraught with distrust and conflict. The presumed vitality of Afro-Americans' sexual relations is celebrated in endless popular love songs and is the envy of Norman Mailer and other bemused Euro-Americans who yearn for soul, when the truth, as we will see, is that Afro-American men and women profoundly disagree over sexual attitudes, practices, and behaviors. Nearly a third of Afro-American women are dissatisfied with their present sexual partners. Over 40 percent report a loss of interest in sex during the course of the previous year, and one in six abstain completely. Afro-Americans celebrate family, kinship, and roots like no other group of Americans, often meeting in media-covered reunions down home, when in fact they have the fewest numbers of *active* extended kin relations. An Afro-American actor, Bill Cosby, has become the nation's symbol of fatherhood—the celebrated Dr. Huxtable—when in fact 60 percent of Afro-American children have been abandoned by their fathers. For all the hype, for all the defensive, compensatory ethnic bombast, the simple, sad truth is that Afro-Americans are today the loneliest of all Americans—lonely and isolated as a group; lonely and isolated in their neighborhoods, through which they are often too terrified to walk; lonely as households headed by women sick and tired of being "the strong black woman"; lonely as single men fearful of commitment; lonely as single women wary of a "love and trouble" tradition that has always been more trouble than love.

In delineating the problem and its proximate socioeconomic sources and correlates, I draw upon current census data and on several recent national surveys. However, while paying full attention to current social and economic factors, I argue strongly that the roots of the problem go back, first, to the two and a half centuries of slavery and, then, to its aftermath, the neoslavery of Jim Crow. In so doing, I go against the prevailing revisionist view that slavery had little or nothing to do with present gender and familial problems. This revisionist denial, I insist (and I hope I will have shown), is not just an academic absurdity. It is an intellectual disgrace, the single greatest disservice that the American historical profession has ever done to those who turn to it for guidance about the past and the etiology of present problems. Indeed, in many ways this denial of the consequences of slavery is worse than the more than two centuries of racist historiography that preceded it, culminating in the writings of U. B. Phillips, for many years during the first third of this century Sterling Professor of History at Yale. At least Phillips took slavery and its consequences seriously, even if he felt, perversely, that these consequences were largely benign.

The other two essays in this volume narrow the focus to one crucial area of the problem: the reality, images, and conception of Afro-American masculinity both now and in the past. Racist oppression took many forms and damaged Afro-American men and women in numerous ways, but the single greatest focus of ethnic domination was the relentless effort to emasculate the Afro-American male in every conceivable way and at every turn. The second essay, "Feast of Blood: 'Race,' Religion, and Human Sacrifice in the Postbellum South," examines the most brutal episode in this long history of "racial" gender-destruction. It shows how there emerged in the post-Reconstruction South a neoslavery system in which religion, politics, and economics fused in the rituals of the lynch mob. In a substantial minority of lynchings, those rituals partook of a cult of human sacrifice, focused on the literal and symbolic castration of Afro-American males. The worshipers castrated and then immolated their victims alive, as burnt offerings to a Southern Christian God whom they felt they had to assuage and propitiate after their humiliating defeat in the Civil War and their trauma of losing a cherished way of life. As with similar cults of human sacrifice in other periods and places—most notably those of the Aztecs and Tupinamba of pre-Columbian Mexico and northeastern Brazil, respectively—there was, I will show, a strong element of ritual and literal cannibalism associated with these rites.

That essay was not easy to write. It will be even less easy to read, especially for Southerners and practicing Christians. On several occasions, analyzing the materials for it literally made me sick. I still get queasy on the rare occasions that I attempt to eat roasted meat. Nonetheless, I am convinced that a subset of the lynchings of Afro-Americans went well beyond, and cannot be explained by, vigilante terror and mob rule. The Ku Klux Klan, the culmination of this sacrificial cult, especially in the Klan's second, twentieth-century phase, was not a mob. It was a highly organized and extremely successful cult that counted thousands of ministers of religion among its membership, and an even higher proportion in its leadership. Its leaders and many of its members were drawn from the most educated and respected citizens of their communities. At its height, in states from Georgia to Colorado and Indiana, it powerfully influenced governors, senators, congressmen, and most of the mayors where its Klaverns were located. Further, it drew heavily on fundamentalist ritual and theology to devise its own anthropologically very sophisticated ritual practices. "Clothed in the symbols of Protestantism," writes the historian Robert Goldberg, "the Klan promised to unite Protestants in a crusade that would combat the teachings of evolution and restore faith in God, the Bible, and the Christian fundamentals."[4] And it did. Indeed, cult leaders such as Imperial Wizard Simmons, himself a former preacher, rightly insisted that the Klan was as much a religion as a secular cult. Its icon of the burning cross was a powerful symbolic instrument that appealed directly to the religious impulses of its adherents. It was the KKK that formalized the cult of human sacrifice of Afro-American men that had spontaneously emerged in the lynching rituals of the post-Reconstruction South. By the mid-1920s, the Klan had become not the Protestant church's main competitor in the South but a major force in the religious revival of the period. And its focus, it can never be too frequently repeated, was the emasculation and sacrifice of Afro-American males, preferably those who were most successful, with consequences that we are still living with today.

In attempting to understand how and why so gruesome and barbaric a cult could thrive in what had already emerged as the major economy, political order, and Christian nation of Western civilization (Woodrow Wilson, one of the most learned men to hold the office of president, actually enjoyed a private showing in the White House of the movie *Birth of a Nation*, which celebrates the cult), I was led not only into the deeper recesses of postbellum Southern culture but also into the darker side of Christian sacrificial symbolism and theology. If researching the practices of human sacrifice in the South made me physically sick, exploring its religious roots brought me close to spiritual nausea. How in heaven's name could Christianity, which worships as the one, true living God a swarthy-skinned, working-class Semite from the sticks of ancient Roman Palestine who preached a doctrine of love and fellowship, end up as a sacrificial cult that legitimized and celebrated the genocidal torturing and burning alive, by its most ardent believers, of helpless males from a wretchedly exploited ex-slave minority?

I was brought up a Christian by a rather too devout mother. I went to an Anglican grammar school founded and headed by a celebrated churchman, the Right Reverend Percival Gibson, who throughout my school days doubled as the suffragan bishop of Kingston, Jamaica's capital city. Until my voice broke, I was a choirboy. I sang the solo "Oh, Perfect Love" at Old Boys' weddings. And I believed. Even after college, and Marx, and London in the sixties, and intellectually discarding every word of Scripture, I still believed. The liturgical order encoded in the *Book of Common Prayer* still moves me. The Anglican communion remains, for me, the most compelling sacred ritual that a congregation can perform.

> This is my body, which is given for you . . .

I ate.

> This is my blood . . . which is shed for you . . .

I drank.

Therein lies the problem. Christianity is quintessentially a sacrificial creed. In committing their barbarities, Southern lynchers instinctively drew on this defining element of the creed. I was led to wonder, is there an inherently brutal impulse in this religion? The history of inhumanities committed in its name is long, ghastly, and riddled with paradox. Hardly a decade after the burning cross first appeared, drenching the South with blood and consecrating it with the burnt offerings of Afro-American male bodies, it rose again with even greater terror in the form of the Nazi iron cross. And if the butchery of Afro-Americans in the name of a dark-skinned God is perplexing, the two thousand years of pogroms against the group that gave us this very God, culminating in their mass destruction in the Second World War, will forever defy understanding. What is it about the cross that so easily turns people on to genocide? That so frequently makes bloodthirsty brutes and cannibals of ordinary men and women? Of what earthly or heavenly value is a creed that can so easily justify good and evil, humanity and inhumanity, life and death?

And yet this creed turns the heads and hearts not only of princes and the ruling classes, but of the oppressed everywhere it takes root, and nowhere more than in the Deep South. There we find the seemingly frightful paradox that the more Afro-Americans were tortured and crucified by Christians in the name of their God and under the banner of the cross, the more Afro-Americans renewed their faith in this very same religion, seeking solace from this very same cross. Furthermore, it is this same Christian faith that inspired the revolutionary abolitionist zeal of a William Lloyd Garrison—in his fanatical mother's words, "a complete Baptist as to the tenet," as Henry Mayer reminds us in his glorious new biography.[5]

For most of my intellectual life I have been grappling with two contradictory creeds: the creed of freedom and the creed of Christianity. Eventually, I came to realize that the two are intimately linked, that indeed they are merely two aspects of a single sublime contradiction. My reasons for so thinking were given in my book *Freedom in the Making of Western Culture*.[6] In the course of writing that book, I came to understand existentially what I had already known intellectually, and what is common knowledge among historians of religion: that Christianity is not the religion of Christ, the Jewish religious *and* social militant, but the religion about Christ and, more perversely, the religion about his lynching. Christ did not know Christianity. Not a single statement he made anticipated such a creed or, even less, a church. Many of his most authentic sayings suggest that he believed and practiced just the opposite of what was eventually preached, made, and destroyed in his name. The Christianity that prevails today is really the creed of Paul, a devious and possibly disturbed religious genius who stole and reinvented the creed of the Jew Jesus as surely as nineteenth-century Euro-American minstrels stole and misrepresented Afro-American folk art and reconstructed out of it a whole new tradition that ended up demonizing its original creators.

The analogy with the cultural "love and theft" that was blackface minstrelsy—as Eric Lott calls it in his brilliant treatment[7]—is apt for yet another reason. For all the perversions, the mockery, the caricature, and the burlesque of Afro-American art and life that were the explicit intent of minstrelsy, there nonetheless remained, stubbornly, miraculously, core elements of the original, so much so that in the end it was still possible for Afro-Americans to reclaim it. Similarly, for all the theological and organizational reconstruction and downright perversion of the original preaching of Jesus, core elements of his doctrine and his religious being-in-the-world remained. Throughout the Pauline ages, bold spirits have attempted to reclaim the original. However, all but one such attempt have failed to make a significant dent on their societies. I suggest, in the last part of the second essay, that that one successful case occurred within the lifetime of most of us: it is none other than the religion of the Afro-American Southern Christian Leadership Conference and other strivers toward the "beloved community." By reclaiming the nonsacrificial religion of the original Jesus movement, this revitalized Afro-American Christianity ushered in a political revolution in America not unlike the revolution that Jesus sought for his own colonized ethnic group.

From the nadir at the turn of this century, when the lynching cult was rampant, I move, in the final essay, to the ambiguities at the turn of the next. Things change, things remain the same, or so they seem. Today, once again, we find the image of the Afro-American male's body dominating the popular culture and imagination of America out of all proportion to the size of his group, in much the same way that in the nineteenth century his distorted, minstrel image dominated the popular culture of the North, and the lust for his crucified body dominated that of the South. How do we explain the national obsession with O. J. Simpson? Surely not by the ghastliness of his alleged crime, since hardly a week passes in which some horror of equal or greater magnitude is not reported in the press. How do we explain the fact that a presidential candidate in this great polity was able to eliminate a thirty-point disadvantage in the polls and come back to win the presidency mainly through the use of the image of an Afro-American rapist? And, as if those conundrums were not enough, how do we explain the fact that, in this same nation, the closest thing to a demigod is Michael Jordan, and the likely hero of the typical Euro-American boy or man is an Afro-American male star? This is a cultural quandary, a sociological enigma like none other in the history of mass societies.

I try to solve the riddle in the last essay, "American Dionysus: Images of Afro-American Men at the Dawn of the Twenty-First Century." By examining the cultural role of the Afro-American male today, a century after the nadir of the lynching cult, we can gauge just how far we have come as a nation in this regard. There is good news and bad news. The sacrificial cult of the lynch mob is finished, as my comments on the recent lynch-like murder in Jasper, Texas, suggest. Contrary to the racism-forever school of social analysts, I maintain that the adulation for Afro-American heroes in the entertainment and sports world is genuine. It is now possible, and indeed commonly happens, that Afro-American men cross the color line—which is exactly what O. J. Simpson had done—and there is no gainsaying the fact that the "racial" attitudes and values of the great majority of Euro-Americans have gone through a sea change.

But something quite disturbing has emerged along with all this. The Afro-American male—the image of his body and the stereotypes of his behavior, stereotypes which, tragically, are increasingly self-fulfilling—has come to play a new role in American culture: that of an archetypal Dionysian counterweight to the Apollonian impulses of America's overworked, postindustrial civilization. There had been hints of this before, but for reasons explained in the essay, only with the changes of recent decades has this role become possible. Ironically, these changes involved the very same positive developments that I examined and lauded in *The Ordeal of Integration*. However, in the ancient bacchanalian fields as in the ghettos of today, Dionysus is a "badass" god, as dangerous as he is necessary—a transvestite seducer and dissembler with a nasty attitude. The god of masks and reversals, he is a hunter and trapper who ensnares from without and within with "nets of iron." I argue that there are signs everywhere that Afro-American men are being ensnared, with consequences wonderfully cathartic for the audience of the wider culture, but disastrous for those playing this cultural role. For, like Agave and her fellow revelers, those Afro-American men are destroying themselves, destroying each other, despoiling those who love them, while imagining that they are blessed with the "cool pose" of soul. We may already have lost a whole generation of young men. The nets were cast originally from outside, and their catch still serves the needs of the wider culture, but the hunter now is his own prey and the nets tighten from within.

OVER THE YEARS, I have used three approaches to analyze and express my sociological and historical ideas. The first is the positivist method of quantitative sociology, which attempts to provisionally validate statements about the social world with sampled data analyzed statistically, the various types of the mean being the primary methodological tool. The second is the sociohistorical approach, which uses the comparative and ideal-type case methods to arrive at general statements either about broad macrosociological processes, about the nature and functions of social institutions, or about the meaning and significance of cultural practices, my model here being the great German historical sociologist Max Weber. The third is the interpretive sociological essay, which blends literary methods with social analysis and draws cn real and mythic archetypes as interpretive pathways into the human condition and into particular social patterns and situations. Nietzsche's and Freud's more sociological essays and those of Georg Simmel, one of sociology's founders, are the great exemplars of this approach. Among contemporary social scientists, the essays of Levi-Strauss, David Riesman, and Daniel Bell have been my models. Mean-type, ideal-type, and archetype—there are, to be sure, other arrows in their quivers, but these are the distinctive instruments of the three methods of sociology.

Usually, I have employed these methods separately, depending on the subject. I am convinced that certain aspects of the social world are best understood and articulated in certain ways and that attempts to analyze and talk about them with inappropriate methods only end up doing violence to the subject.

In this volume, I have used all three approaches, while continuing to observe the principle of methodological appropriateness. I was able to do so because each of the three essays required a different one of the three approaches. Thus, the first employs the analytic strategies and techniques of modern quantitative sociology. As I indicated earlier, the sociological study of the family exhibits some of the finest work in contemporary sociology, and I have situated that essay very much within this tradition of scholarship. A great deal of the nonsociological writings on Afro-American gender and family relations rely heavily on autobiographical or anecdotal sources, which is perhaps the main reason why the crisis in these relations has been either misinterpreted, underestimated, swept under the rug, or denied altogether. In the first essay, I draw on four major sources: the most current census data and three representative national surveys. One of the latter is the National Health and Social Life Survey (NHSLS), conducted in 1991 by a team of researchers led by the sociologist Edward O. Laumann of the University of Chicago. This survey is simply the best and most representative national examination of sexuality ever conducted in America. In the course of studying sexuality, the researchers inevitably accumulated a vast body of data on broader issues of gender and familial relations. Of special interest to me is the fact that the Afro-American population was oversampled, making this study also the best source of detailed information on Afro-American sexual and related practices. I was given access to these data in 1994, within weeks of the first major publication to come from this survey,[8] and have been analyzing them ever since.

The second survey upon which the first essay draws was conducted by a research team in the latter half of 1997 under the auspices of Harvard

University's School of Public Health, the *Washington Post,* and the Kaiser Family Foundation. It is one of the most detailed national surveys ever conducted on gender relations, gender roles, and attitudes toward women's participation in the economy. This survey (hereinafter, the HWPK survey) also oversampled the Afro-American, as well as the Latino, populations. Preliminary basic statistics from this study were published in a series in the *Washington Post,* but mine is the first detailed analysis of these data; the findings reported here are being published for the first time. The third data set I used was selected from the annual General Social Survey (GSS) of the National Opinion Research Center at the University of Chicago.

Logistic modeling was the main statistical tool I used in the analysis of these data, supplemented where necessary by OLS regressions and other techniques. Since this book is intended as much for the general reader as for the professional social scientist, I have taken the advice of my editor and reported only the results of these statistical procedures and not the detailed computer models from which they were drawn. Whenever possible, I have recast the results in the form of charts and tables to make them more easily understandable. Professional sociologists who wish to see the more detailed computer printouts on which my reports are based can write me at my Harvard address.

The second essay uses the sociohistorical method mentioned above. The data on lynching came from those compiled over the years by the Tuskegee Institute and the NAACP and from newspaper accounts collected and republished by several editors, especially Ralph Ginzburg. I also drew on a growing body of excellent monograph-length case studies of lynching. I have used the Tuskegee data in spite of recent questions about their accuracy. For now, I should note only that they are still the sole national compilation of these data and it is likely that the Tuskegee Institute erred on the conservative side in underestimating the actual number of lynchings.

The third essay is a cultural study that employs the interpretive techniques of the sociological essay. I draw on symbolic anthropology and on classical and literary studies in my attempt to understand what is happening to the image and cultural role of Afro-American men in America at the end of the twentieth century. Where the sociohistorical method of the second essay uses comparisons and ideal-type cases, the third essay unapologetically uses the archetype of the Greek myth of Dionysus as an interpretive tool. My sociological colleagues are almost certain to be distressed by this. Too bad. With this approach, I think I have come much closer to an unriddling of the mystery of the Afro-American male role in American culture than any positivistic strategy would have permitted.

As in the first volume of this trilogy, I prefer to use the terms "Afro-American" and "Euro-American" instead of "black" and "white" to describe Americans of African and European ancestry. I do so both because I take the literal and figurative meaning of words seriously and know it to be true that words fashion and refract meanings and experience as much as they express them. According to the unabridged version of *Webster's New Twentieth Century Dictionary* the following are among the main meanings of the word "black":

> 1. figuratively, dismal, gloomy, sullen, forbidding, or the like; destitute of moral light or goodness; mournful; calamitous; evil; wicked; atrocious; thus Shakespeare speaks of *black* deeds, thoughts, envy, tidings, despair, etc. 2. soiled; dirty. 3. disgraceful. 4. without hope, as a *black* future. 5. inveterate, confirmed, deep-dyed, as a *black* villain. 6. humorous or satirical in a morbid, cynical or savage way, as *black* comedy.

And the following are among the main meanings of the term "white":

> 1. having the color of pure snow and milk . . . opposite of black. 2. morally and spiritually pure; spotless; innocent. 3. free from evil intent; harmless; as white magic; a white lie 4. happy; fortunate; auspicious. 5. (a) having a light colored skin; Caucasian; (b) of or controlled by the white race; as *white* supremacy; (c) [from notions of racial superiority.] [Slang.] honest; honorable; fair; dependable. 6. favorite.

It is preposterous to assume that when Americans call each other "white" and "black" they are somehow able to mentally bracket the historically and culturally ingrained and dictionary sanctioned meanings of these terms. The decision of Afro-American leaders and their Euro-American allies (no doubt gleefully, if quietly, abetted by the nation's racists) to insist on a return to these terms during the sixties was linguistically naïve, culturally obtuse, socially inept, and politically stupid.

I refuse to call any Euro-American or Caucasian person "white," and I view with the deepest suspicion any Euro-American who insists on calling Afro-Americans "black."

The term African-American, which has been growing in use lately, is certainly more acceptable but, as I noted in *The Ordeal of Integration,* the term mutes the Americanness of Afro-Americans (which is culturally and politically unwise) and fails to distinguish the growing number of immigrants from Africa who, whatever sentimentalists and mythmakers may think, are far more culturally different from Afro-Americans than are Afro-Americans from any group of Euro-Americans.

one

BROKEN
BLOODLINES

&

Gender Relations and the Crisis of Marriages and
Families Among Afro-Americans

2

AFRO-AMERICAN GENDER RELATIONS, and consequently their marital and familial relations, have always been in crisis. This crisis has changed its shape with each new environment Afro-Americans have found themselves in, although, as we will see, there have been important continuities going back to the distant past. Over the past three or four decades these problems have assumed new and alarming forms, leading many ill-informed persons to look nostalgically back to some supposedly golden period that is the stuff of myth.

This crisis is the major internal source of the wider problems of Afro-Americans. It is the main means by which the group ends up victimizing itself. For, without consistent and lasting relations between men and women, and without a durable, supportive framework within which children are brought up, a group of people is in deep trouble. Even more tragically, this internal wound is the main means by which the externally originating problems of Afro-Americans are magnified and transmitted.

Two single, unskilled, and unemployed individuals receiving minimum welfare payments in any of the larger cities of the nation are in dire poverty and run the risk of homelessness. These same two individuals, living together in a mutually supportive, loving union, by pooling their resources can provide themselves with some kind of shelter; more important, they can emotionally support each other and more effectively ward off the threat of poverty.

Afro-Americans are the most unpartnered and isolated group of people in America and quite possibly in the world. Unlike any other group of Americans, most of them will go through most of their adult lives without any deep and sustained attachment to a non-kin companion. Sixty percent of Afro-American children are now being brought up without the emotional or material support of a father. This is so because the great majority of Afro-American mothers have been seduced, deceived, betrayed, and abandoned by the men to whom they gave their love and trust.

The most common response among Afro-Americans to this tragedy has been to sweep the problem under the rug with talk about not washing dirty linen in public. As the legal scholar Emma Coleman Jordan caustically observes: "The 'dirty linen' charge has special irony because it depends upon an absolute prohibition against violating the pseudo-intrafamilial expectation of private conversations about sensitive matters. But this dysfunctional pseudo-family doesn't talk about the taboo subject in private either."[1]

From time to time, however, the issue bursts on the scene in sudden gusts of very angry talk usually stimulated by some artistic or literary event. The debates surrounding Ntozake Shange's play *For Colored Girls Who Have Considered Suicide*, Michele Wallace's book *Black Macho and the Myth of the Superwoman*, the movie version of Alice Walker's novel *The Color Purple*, and, more recently, Terry Macmillan's novel *Waiting to Exhale* are a few examples.[2] A growing number of Afro-American feminists have begun to find the celebration of the "black family" and especially "black motherhood" a little bogus, especially coming from Afro-American men. "Far too many black men who praise their own mothers," writes Patricia Hill Collins, "feel less accounted to the mothers of their own children."[3] She is equally acerbic in her views on the "love and trouble" tradition of Afro-American gender relations.[4]

A small but growing number of academic works have also documented various aspects of the problem. In a study of 256 mainly working- and lower-middle-class Afro-American students at Temple University, Noel Cazenave and Rita Smith asked respondents for their views on Michele Wallace's assertion that there was "distrust, even hatred, between black men and women." Only 34 percent of the men, and 26 percent of the women, disagreed with this statement. What is more, the majority of respondents, men and women, agreed that "black women seem to have many more opportunities than black men."[5] And Castellano Turner and Barbara Turner, in their study of Afro-American evaluations of future marital relations, found that most Afro-American women considered "most men" less responsible, reliable, trustworthy, and happy. While most Afro-American men considered Afro-American women "trustworthy," the researchers were forced to conclude that "black females' views of relationships with black men were laced with the anticipation of disappointment."[6] I will have much more to say on this later.

This andecdotal and limited survey evidence has recently been buttressed by some remarkable results coming from the national sample of the *1996 General Social Survey,* conducted by the National Opinion Research Center of the University of Chicago. The survey that year probed the frequency and degree to which Americans experienced feelings of anger toward persons at work and in their families. Asked if they had felt "really angry" about something that happened at work within the past months, only 23 percent of Afro-American women answered in the affirmative, compared with 35 percent of Afro-American men, 37 percent of Euro-American women and 43 percent of Euro-American men. However, when people were asked if they had felt "really angry" with someone in their family during this period the ethnic and gender responses went in the opposite direction. Afro-American women were the sub-group with the highest percentage of persons who had gotten really angry (46.4%), in contrast with Afro-American men (28.6%), Euro-American women (38%), and Euro-American men (18%). Not only did Afro-American women get angry more often with a family member than other groups of persons but the anger lasted longer among them than others. Nearly 40 percent said that they felt angry either continuously or for several days, compared with a third of Euro-American women and 24 percent of the men of both ethnic groups. Furthermore, over two-thirds of Afro-American women said they had refused to accept the situation that had occasioned their anger, again in sharp contrast not only with Euro-American women, half of whom said they had been prepared to accept it, but with Afro-American and Euro-American men, who differed little from each other: 54 and 55 percent respectively said they were prepared to accept it and carry on.

Why is home the site of such anger for Afro-American women, in striking contrast with their relative calmness at work? The answer, according to the survey, is clearly the "love and trouble" tradition that beset intimate relationships among Afro-Americans. Asked how much they liked or disliked the person or people who made them angry or annoyed, 44 percent of Afro-American women responded that they liked the person in question "a great deal," compared with 36 percent of Euro-American women and 20 percent of Euro-American men. Interestingly, almost exactly the same percent of Afro-American men (43) claimed that they liked the person who made them angry "a great deal." So while they did not get angry as often and intensely as Afro-American women, when they did get angry it was as frequently with a loved one. These results rather strongly suggest that Afro-American men are the source of the trouble since the relative calmness of Afro-American women at work indicates that they are less prone to get annoyed. Whoever the source of the trouble, the facts are that Afro-Americans of both genders are getting angry with loved ones to a far greater degree than other people, and women are 62 percent more likely to be the ones feeling the pain.

Sadly, the survey also indicated that there was little chance of resolving the sources of conflict eliciting the experience of anger since, to an unusual degree, Afro-American men and women were likely to blame each other fully for the problem. In a follow-up question, people were asked how responsible was the person they were angry at for the problem causing their anger. On a scale of 0 to 10, with 0 meaning that the other person was in no way responsible and 10 that they were "completely responsible," only 43 percent of Euro-American men and 47 percent of Euro-American women claimed that the other person was fully responsible for getting them angry. In other words, a substantial majority of Euro-Americans allowed for a range of joint levels of responsibility for the problem causing the anger even though, as might be expected, most attributed more blame to the other person. The Afro-American responses, however, were strikingly different from Euro-Americans and other ethnic groups. Fully 64 percent of men and women insisted that the other person was completely responsible for the problem leading to their anger. Interestingly, when the question was turned around and people were asked how responsible *they* were for the problem generating anger, two-thirds of Afro-American women insisted that they were in no way to be blamed (giving themselves a score of zero on the responsibility scale) while somewhat fewer Afro-American men claimed that they were completely blameless (46 percent scoring themselves zero). There is little hope for compromise here. The problems that lie behind all this anger and lack of compromise and their tragic consequences in terms of marital and relational disruption will be examined at some length later in this essay.

Two aspects of the gender crisis must be distinguished: the external problems, or those that Afro-American men and women face in their relations with Euro-Americans, the majority ethnic group; and the internal gender problems that arise in their relations with each other. Both men and women have had to cope over the centuries with negative ethnic stereotyping of their respective genders. The external Euro-American environment has also created peculiar obstacles and provided different opportunities for Afro-Americans based partly on their gender.

One of my main arguments is that in recent decades the external gender environment has grown somewhat better for Afro-American women while it has stagnated for Afro-American men; at the same time, the internal gender environment—that between Afro-American men and women—has grown markedly worse for Afro-American women, partly resulting from the conservatism of certain domains of Afro-American male gender attitudes but also partly the result of the very improvement in their external gender environment.

This essay is divided into nine parts. In the next section I delineate the external gender environment of Afro-Americans, focusing on the growing disparity in the educational and economic performance of men and women and its troubling demographic and social consequences. Part two identifies the origin of the problem in the socio-cultural depredations of slavery, contra the prevailing school of revisionist historians of slavery, and the third part traces its continuation and consolidation through the Jim Crow era. In the fourth part I move to a detailed statistical analysis of the problems of marriage, cohabitation and divorce based on the National Health and Social Life Survey (NHSLS) and U.S. census data. Part five explores current Afro-American gender attitudes and ideologies in relation to those of other Americans, drawing mainly on the 1997 Harvard University School of Public Health/ *Washington Post*/Kaiser Family Foundation (HWPK) survey. Next I examine the sexual practices and related intimate relations of Afro-Americans, the first such detailed analysis of Afro-American sexual behavior based on data from a national sample, the NHSLS. Part seven searches, in admittedly speculative ways, for the proximate sources of the problems previously discussed in the broader familial and socio-cultural contexts of Afro-American life, drawing freely on available anthropological, psychological, and sociological accounts. The eighth part of the essay focuses on the two major consequences of Afro-Americans' low marriage rate: their internal isolation from each other and their external isolation from other groups of Americans. I strongly question the conventional view that Afro-Americans have well-developed informal networks among themselves based on extended kin ties and close friendships in their neighborhoods by examining the most important body of data, drawn from a national sample on this subject, namely the General Social Survey on network ties conducted in 1985. I then examine what I call the external isolation of Afro-Americans by analyzing available census data on inter-ethnic marriages. The essay closes with a reprise of the main themes and arguments and a brief indication of what is required to solve the problem.

THE EXTERNAL GENDER ENVIRONMENT:
Aspects of the Double Burden

AFRO-AMERICAN women writers and leaders have long claimed that they share a double burden, being victims of both their gender and their ethnicity. This sociological trope originated in the middle of the nineteenth century with the ex-slave writer Harriet A. Jacobs when she wrote of Afro-American women in general: "Superadded to the burden common to all, *they* have wrongs, and sufferings, and mortifications peculiarly their own."[7] In today's terms, added to the burden of racism is the "double jeopardy" of mainstream gender discrimination.[8] All this is well taken.

My only problem with this view is the assumption that it applies exclusively to Afro-American women. It was always the case in America that "superadded" to the burden of being a male slave or a male laborer was the burden of the assault on Afro-American men's integrity and identity as men. As we will see in the next essay, racist oppressors were virulently obsessed with the maleness of the Afro-American male and brutally sought to extinguish any hint of manhood in him.

With the remarkable changes in the attitudes of Euro-Americans and the condition of Afro-Americans over recent decades, the situation has now become rather more complex. When we examine the facts carefully, we find that Afro-American men are now, by many indicators, the gender at greater risk among Afro-Americans, while by others Afro-American women clearly continue to bear the greater burden. These factors affect the lives of Afro-Americans separately and interactively in complex ways. We must attempt to sort them out prior to our examination of the history and present internal problems of gender relations between Afro-American men and women.

There can be no denying what has been called the feminization of poverty for a large minority of Afro-American women.[9] As Figure 1.1 shows, in both individual and familial terms, women of all ethnic groups experience higher levels of poverty than men. As is well known, households headed by single women, which now constitute the single largest category among Afro-Americans, are at high risk of poverty compared with other kinds of households: 46.4 and 53.5 percent for Afro-American and Latino ethnicities, respectively. There is no doubt that there is a gender burden here, but whether an added "racial" burden can be claimed is questionable.

As I argued in *The Ordeal of Integration*, while "race" is obviously the decisive factor in explaining the origins of the acute problems of the Afro-American poor, it is not at all clear that it has much to do with explaining contemporary poverty levels among either men or women. Latinos were never enslaved here; the majority of them are of European ancestry; and a substantial minority descended from slaveholders—uncomfortable facts too often glossed over in multicultural rhetoric—yet, as Figure 1.1 shows, their poverty levels are higher than Afro-Americans'.

What about the majority of Afro-American women, who are not poor? In terms of equal pay for equal work and qualifications, how do they fare in the labor market when compared with men and Euro-American women? This is a complex issue. In most respects Afro-American women share with their Euro-American counterparts a persistent burden of gender prejudice. In one or two areas there is also an ethnic discrepancy. However, in most respects there is little evidence of a double burden of gender and ethnic prejudice. When current trends are projected, there is every reason to believe that Afro-American women will soon surpass Afro-American men in median income. Indeed, when we take account not just of median income but of the numbers and proportions of Afro-American women in desirable occupations, it is already the case that they have outperformed Afro-American men in absolute terms and Euro-American women in relative terms.

Figure 1.2 shows an unambiguous pattern of gender discrepancy in annual earnings for both groups of women at every educational level. This, of course, is not necessarily proof of gender prejudice; much depends on the

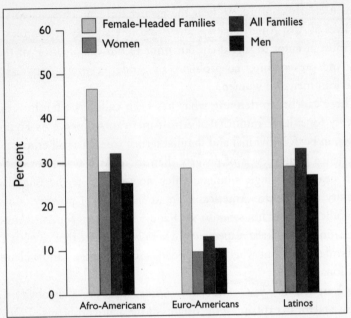

FIGURE 1.1. Percentages of Individuals and Families in Poverty by Gender, March 1997. SOURCE: Author's tabulation of data from U.S. Bureau of the Census (Internet release, June 26, 1997).

work histories, as well as the occupational and industrial locations, of men and women. However, there is now good reason to believe that even after controlling for these factors, substantial gender discrepancies remain between the earnings of equally educated full-time working men and women.

We see also that for each educational level there is a discrepancy between the earnings of Afro-American and Euro-American women, albeit much smaller than the gender discrepancy for either group. Figure 1.3 recalculates, in terms of income ratios, the absolute figures given in Figure 1.2. Is this evidence of a double burden? Seen in static terms, the answer is "yes." But the discrepancy between the incomes of the two women's groups is largely a reflection of past ethnic prejudices in favor of Euro-American women, especially at the higher educational levels. The proportion of Euro-American women with college degrees who are now at or near their maximum earning capacity is much larger than that of Afro-American women. The impressive growth in the numbers and proportions of Afro-American women with "some college" or "bachelor's degree or more" levels of education, discussed below, is a post–1970 phenome-

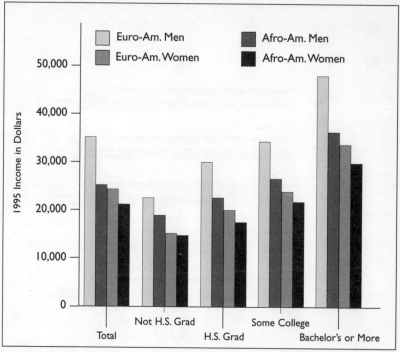

FIGURE 1.2. Median Earnings by Educational Attainment, Ethnicity, and Gender, 1995. SOURCE: Author's tabulation of data from U.S. Bureau of the Census (Internet release, June 26, 1997).

non. In fact, young Afro-American female college graduates now earn more than their Euro-American counterparts.

Comparing the economic returns to women of different groups is difficult because of important differences in their economic activities. Thus, Afro-American women have traditionally had higher labor-force participation rates, but higher unemployment rates, than Euro-American women; they work more hours per week but roughly the same number of hours per year.[10] A lot depends on what measures one uses to make comparisons between the two groups. Using mean, rather than median, earnings, one can show that there is no remaining gap. Emphasizing income rather than earnings reveals persisting ethnic differences. On yet another measure, estimated lifetime earnings, the gap has nearly vanished. On the whole, it is safe to say that ethnic differences in the economic experiences of Afro-American and Euro-American women have either disappeared or are on the verge of becoming insignificant. Afro-American women continue to suffer serious gender biases in the economy, but they suffer them

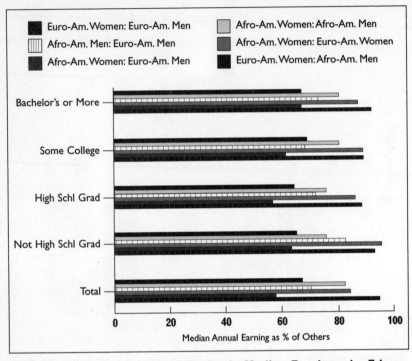

FIGURE 1.3. Gender and Ethnic Ratios in Median Earnings, by Educational Attainment, March 1996. NOTE: Includes only year-round, full-time workers, ages 25 or older. SOURCE: Author's tabulation of data from U.S. Bureau of the Census (Intenet release, June 26, 1997).

equally with Euro-American women. Appearances to the contrary, there is no double burden of race and gender in economic matters.

Life, however, is a great deal more than economic activity. When we compare the life-chances and actual experience of Afro-American men and women in recent years, we are forced to question the conventional wisdom that Afro-American women are somehow more destructively burdened by the system than their male counterparts. It cannot be denied that when it comes to evaluating life's burdens, vital statistics are the ultimate tests. How long we live, the rate at which we can expect to die at given years of life, and the rate of survival—all are bottom-line assessments of just how well or badly a given group is doing in relation to others. On every one of these indicators, Afro-American men are not only far behind their Euro-American counterparts but also significantly worse off than Afro-American women. In contrast, Afro-American women not only

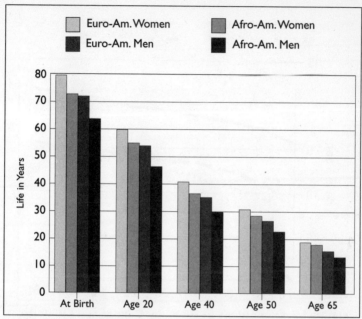

FIGURE 1.4. Average Expectancy at Birth, by Gender and Ethnicity, 1994. SOURCE: Author's tabulation of data from U.S. National Center for Health Statistics, "Births and Deaths: United States, 1996," *Monthly Vital Statistics Report* 46:1, Suppl. 2 (Sept. 1997).

have far better life-chances than Afro-American and Euro-American men but are fast catching up with Euro-American women on most indicators, and in a few cases are doing better.

Thus, as Figure 1.4 shows, in 1994 (the most recent data available), Afro-American male life expectancy at birth was 64.9 years, which was 8.4 years less than for Euro-American men, 9 years less than for Afro-American women, and 14.7 years less than for Euro-American women. This figure is not only shocking for an advanced industrial society, it is, in fact, significantly lower than that for men of several Third World societies such as Cuba and the Afro-Caribbean states of Jamaica, Barbados, and Trinidad—all with populations that originated in exactly the same regions of West Africa, and with almost identical Afro-European levels of miscegenation, as Afro-Americans. Furthermore, while this vital rate has been improving over the years for all other groups in the United States, it has remained flat for Afro-American men since 1985 (see Figure 1.5).

Equally distressing are the differences in expected death rates per year. For every 1,000 live male Afro-American births in 1990, almost 20 were

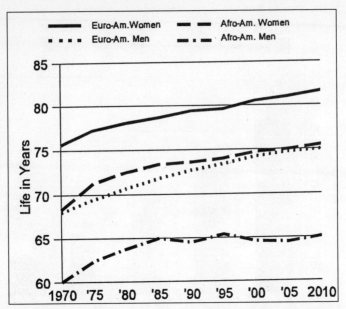

FIGURE 1.5 Expectancy at Birth, by Gender and Ethnicity, 1970–1995, and Projections for 1995–2010. SOURCE: Author's tabulation of data from National Center for Health Statistics, "Births and Deaths, United States, 1966," *Monthly Vital Statistics Report* 46: 1, Suppl. 2 (Sept. 1997).

expected to die by 1991, compared with 16 Afro-American females, between 8 and 9 Euro-American males, and between 6 and 7 Euro-American females. At age twenty the differences are even greater; 3.8 times as many Afro-American men as Afro-American women could expect to die within the year.[11] A major factor contributing to both the low life-expectancy rates and the high death rates is the much higher rate of death from violence and accidents among Afro-American men. Frequent public commentary has tended to focus attention on violence among youth, but as Figure 1.6 demonstrates, Afro-American men die from violent and accidental causes at disproportionately greater levels throughout all age categories. Note, in contrast, that the gap between Euro-American and Afro-American women is negligible for most age groups and virtually disappears after age sixty-five.

Among the causes of death, suicide is often singled out as especially indicative of social anomie and despair, and there has been anguished recent

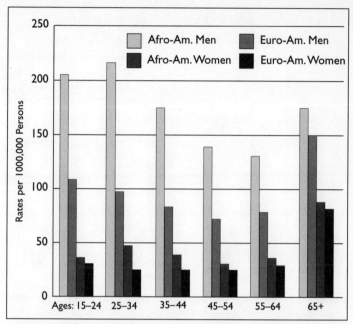

FIGURE 1.6. Death Rates from Accidents and Violence, by Age Group, Gender, and Ethnicity, 1990. SOURCE: Author's tabulation of data from Center for Health Statistics, "Report of Final Mortality Statistics, 1995," *Monthly Vital Statistics Report* 45: 11, Suppl. 2 (1997): Table 7.

commentary on the growing rate among young Afro-American men. However, suicide rates, as all sociologists know from one of the discipline's founding fathers,[12] are complex and must be treated with great caution. In nearly all Western societies, more prosperous classes have tended to experience higher suicide rates than less prosperous ones. Because they have less to lose and make fewer demands on themselves, poorer people tend to experience catastrophic feelings of failure and despair less often. Partly for this reason too, men have typically experienced much higher rates than women. Nonetheless, even after taking all these factors into account, the suicide rate for Afro-American men is unusually high. Figure 1.7 shows that in 1994 the Euro-American male rate was 4.3 times that for Euro-American females, while Afro-American men committed suicide at 6.2 times the rate at which Afro-American women did. What is more, Afro-American men are the only group for whom the rate is rising steadily. As dismal as these figures are, it is likely that the situation is actually much worse, not only because of underreporting for Afro-American

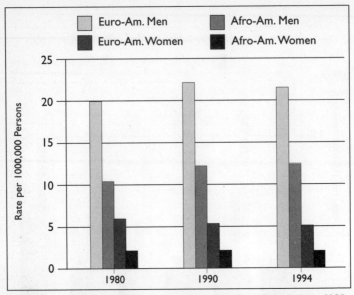

FIGURE 1.7. Suicide Rates, by Gender and Ethnicity, 1980-1994. SOURCE: Author's tabulation of data from U.S. National Center for Health Statistics, "Report of Final Mortality Statistics, 1995," *Monthly Vital Statistics Report,* 45: 11, Suppl. 2 (June 1997).

youth, which according to J. T. Gibbs and A. M. Hines may be as high as 82 per 100,000,[13] but because of the masking effect of what R. H. Seiden calls "victim precipitated" homicide, in which young Afro-American men commit suicide the "macho" way by inciting violence against themselves.[14] The gender difference, according to specialists on the subject, stems from the much greater involvement of women with institutions in the Afro-American community, such as church organizations, other support networks, and remaining kin ties. Indeed, the suicide rate for Afro-American women is among the lowest in the nation.

Beyond these vital statistics, we find that in almost every area of educational and skills acquisition Afro-American women are far outperforming Afro-American men. It is well known that females do better than males in the primary, secondary, and, more recently, undergraduate levels of the educational system. However, the gender differences between Afro-American men and women now bear little comparison with those in other groups. Between 1977 and 1995, Afro-American women almost doubled the gender gap in bachelor's degrees conferred, from 12,300 to

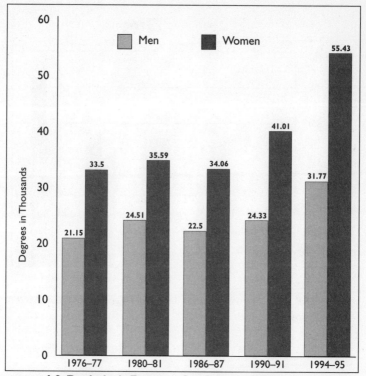

FIGURE 1.8. Bachelor's Degrees Conferred on Afro-Americans, by Gender, 1976–1995. SOURCE: Author's tabulation of data from U.S. Dept. of Education, National Center for Education Statistics (HEGIS) (Internet data release, 1997).

23,600 (see Figure 1.8). In all other ethnic groups, women have been catching up with, and surpassing, men in the acquisition of bachelor's degrees since about the early eighties. Afro-American women had passed this milestone years earlier and simply widened the gap with the enhanced opportunities that came with the seventies.

There are many other respects in which the Afro-American gender differences in education depart from those of other ethnic groups. Thus, Afro-Americans are the only ethnic group in which women outperform men in most of the hard sciences, especially physics, math, and computer science; engineering is an exception, but Afro-American women are fast catching up. Of even greater significance for the future gender composition of the Afro-American middle class is the unusual trend in the acquisition of first professional degrees. In 1977 Afro-American men received twice as many professional degrees as women (see Figure 1.9). A decade

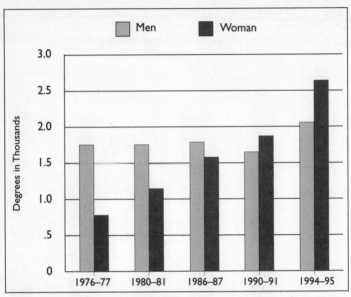

FIGURE 1.9. First Professional Degrees Conferred on Afro-Americans, by Gender, 1976–1995. SOURCE: Author's tabulation of data from U.S. Dept. of Education, National Center for Education Statistics (HEGIS) (Internet data release, 1997).

later, women took the lead, and since then the gap has been widening substantially each year. Figure 1.10 indicates that this trend is unique among ethnic groups. With the exception of Asian Americans in the legal profession, where both genders are near parity, only among Afro-Americans do we find men substantially below parity in the fields of medicine, dentistry, law, and business.

The same trends hold for the acquisition of doctorates between 1977 and 1995. Afro-American women are at the head of a trend toward gender parity in the attainment of doctorates. Their situation is unique in two respects. First, in 1987 they became the first women to outperform the men of their group in achieving doctorates. Second, the Afro-American gender gap comes not only from women gaining more doctorates but, as Figure 1.11 shows, from men gaining fewer such advanced degrees. Between 1977 and 1987 there was a 37 percent fall in the number of Afro-American men gaining doctorates, a disastrous decline from which Afro-American men are yet to recover fully; in 1995 they still obtained 35 fewer doctorates than they did in 1977.

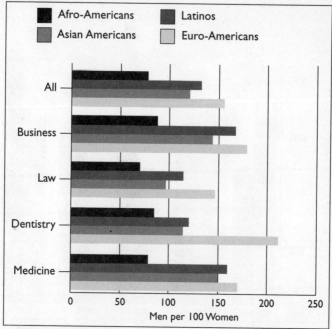

FIGURE 1.10. Male/Female Ratios in Attainment of Selected Professional Degrees, by Ethnicity, 1995. SOURCE: Author's tabulation of data from U.S. Dept. of Education, National Center for Educational Statistics (IPEDS) (Internet data release, 1997).

HOW DO WE EXPLAIN ALL THIS? Why are the fortunes of Afro-American men declining so precipitously while those of Afro-American women are getting better? Why, in particular, are Afro-American women now poised to assume leadership in almost all areas of the Afro-American community and to outperform Afro-American men at middle- and upper-middle-class levels of the wider society and economy? Has the double burden been eliminated for Afro-American women?

It clearly has not, but it is perhaps time to think again, more carefully, about the nature of the burdens that each gender has had to face. Being burdened, having to work harder than others, is not in itself a necessarily bad thing, as the workaholic behavior of the nation's Fortune 500 executives attests. From the days of the Puritan founders, Americans have always prided themselves on being hardworking; people have competed with each other for the privilege of being burdened with great responsi-

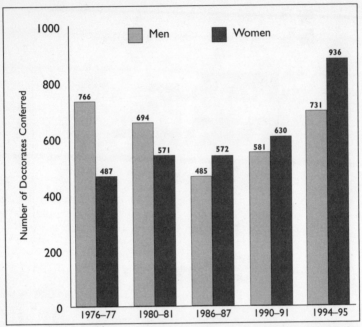

FIGURE 1.11. Doctorates Conferred on Afro-Americans, by Gender, 1976–1995. NOTE: Includes Ph.D., Ed.D., and comparable degrees at the doctoral level. SOURCE: Author's tabulation of data from U.S. Dept. of Education, National Center for Education Statistics (IPEDS) (Internet data release, 1997).

bilities and with the necessity to work long hours. Some burdens, in other words, we not only welcome but consider generative and empowering.

Without in any way underplaying the enormous problems that poor Afro-American women face, I want to suggest that the burdens of poor Afro-American men have always been oppressive, dispiriting, demoralizing, isolating, and soul killing, whereas those of women, while physically and emotionally no doubt as great, have always also been at least *partly* generative, empowering, and humanizing. Furthermore, as I will document later, the experience of Afro-American women during both the past and the present has nearly always entailed their incorporation into the norms, values, and work habits of the dominant culture, while the experience of Afro-American men has been until recently one of unmitigated exclusion.

Take, first, the role of mother. As Patricia Hill Collins correctly observes: "Some women view motherhood as a truly burdensome condition that stifles creativity, exploits their labor, and makes them partners in their own oppression. Others see motherhood as providing a base for self-actualization, status in the Black community, and a catalyst for social activism."[15] One of the great tragedies of Afro-American men was that for the great majority of them, for most of their history, fatherhood was rarely a "base for self-actualization." Indeed, to the degree that slavery, and later racial discrimination in the employment sector, prevented them from meeting their material obligations as providers, and to the degree that their own inner failings and distorted masculine values (on which more later) prevented them from meeting their social and emotional obligations to their offspring, to that extent was fatherhood a site of shame and humiliation.

Second, even under slavery and Jim Crow, the Afro-American woman, in her roles as domestic, nanny, nurse, and clerk, has always had greater access to the wider, dominant Euro-American world. As Fran Sanders has written, with little exaggeration, "For two hundred years it was she who initiated the dialogue between the white world and the African American."[16] Today, Afro-American scholars and intellectuals are inclined to speak contemptuously about the job of domestic, but it is clearly wrong to project such attitudes onto the past. In spite of its unpleasant association with slavery and the often exploitative terms of employment, what Afro-American and Euro-American domestics always hated was not the job itself but live-in domestic work. When done on a regular basis with civilized employers and a decent wage in both kind and money, the job was a modestly secure one in which the Afro-American woman, unlike her male counterpart in the fields or factories, to quote Jacqueline Jones, "wielded an informal power that directly affected the basic human services provided within the white households."[17]

Domestic and other employment in the service sector also brought the Afro-American woman into direct contact with the most intimate areas of the dominant culture. This intimacy was sometimes deepened by another factor peculiar to women: that in America, as in most human societies, women of different statuses and ethnic groups can and often do establish close relationships, where men so separated cannot or will not. The knowledge thus acquired was valuable cultural capital, a point explicitly stated by many of the domestics interviewed by Bonnie Thornton Dill; these women "saw work as an ability rather than a burden. Work was a means for attaining [their] goals; it provided [them] with the money [they] needed to be an independent person, and it exposed [them] and [their] children to 'good' things—values and a style of life which [they] considered important."[18]

It has been suggested that this cultural capital was selectively transmitted only to daughters and not to sons, for reasons that were complex but may have had to do with the differing realistic expectations Afro-American mothers had of their daughters and sons in light of the dominant labor market and its gender and ethnic biases. The less successful daughter could be expected to pursue a job as a domestic; the more successful daughter, to become a schoolteacher or nurse. In both cases, the cultural skills acquired from the dominant culture would be an asset. No such transmissions were considered important for lower-class boys, who had few prospects beyond manual work. Some ethnographic and psychological studies suggest that this pattern continues today among the lower classes.[19] However, the most recent survey data I have analyzed indicate that, at least in expressed attitudes, this is no longer the case. When asked in the HWPK survey conducted in the fall of 1997 whether parents should have different expectations for boys and girls, the great majority of Afro-Americans responded that parents should have the same expectations. Men did respond positively to this question nearly twice as often as women (22 percent versus 11.8 percent), but the difference was not statistically significant in this sample. However, the question whether boys and girls should be raised differently yielded a significant difference in responses according to income group. A third of the poorest Afro-Americans thought they should be raised differently, while nearly all better off Afro-Americans thought they should be raised alike.[20] The responses of the poorest Afro-Americans may well be a vestige of a time, not so long ago, when all Afro-American parents raised boys and girls with different sets of expectations.

The attitudes and prejudices of the dominant group have also played an important role in generating gender disparities among Afro-Americans. Euro-Americans have always been more willing to accept Afro-American women than Afro-American men. Greater fear of Afro-American men, induced by racist sexual attitudes,[21] and greater familiarity with Afro-American women in the course of growing up made it much easier for Afro-American women to find jobs in clerical, and later in professional, Euro-American settings.

There is good evidence that these attitudes and expectations persist toward all classes of Afro-Americans. The economist Harry J. Holzer recently documented a marked preference for Afro-American women over Afro-American men among suburban and inner-city employers. This preference is most striking where noncollege jobs require cognitive-interactive skills. The difference in employment cannot be explained solely in terms of qualifications (although this is indeed a factor) because less skilled and educated Afro-American women and Latino men are persistently placed ahead of Afro-American men in urban job queues.[22] In middle-class occupations this preference may well be interacting with affirmative action to reinforce the traditional bias in favor of Afro-American women. It is not simply that firms under pressure to meet affirmative action guidelines can achieve both gender and ethnic targets when they employ Afro-American women. Even more important, it has been found that in the professional and corporate world the intersection of "race" and gender benefits Afro-American career women, when compared not only with Afro-American men but with Euro-American women. Corporate Euro-American men are less inclined to view Afro-American women as sex objects, as women "out to get a husband," and are therefore more inclined to take them seriously as fellow professionals. The highly successful Afro-American women interviewed by sociologist Cynthia Epstein in the early 1970s almost all agreed that being female "reduced the effect of the racial taboo" against Afro-Americans in corporate positions and that the combination of being Afro-American, female, and educated created a unique social space for them, enhancing their self-confidence and motivation.[23]

In the quarter of a century since Epstein's study, Afro-American women have expanded that social space impressively, in the process not only catching up with Euro-American women in many important areas but numerically surpassing Afro-American men in all the top occupational categories (see Figure 1.12). Among executive, administrative, and managerial workers, there are now 127 Afro-American women for every 100 Afro-American men; among professionals, 151 for every 100. By way of contrast, there are, respectively, only 64 and 85 Euro-American women for every 100 Euro-American men in these two categories of occupations.

From what has been said, it should now be clear that the claim that Afro-American women peculiarly and uniquely suffer a double burden in this society both misleads and obscures the realities of the Afro-American condition. For some Afro-American women, especially among the poor, the assertion is correct; but it is equally true that for an equally substantial minority of Afro-American men, a similar double burden can be claimed. As we have seen, the intersection of ethnicity and gender has deadly consequences for a large and growing minority of lower-class Afro-American men, reflected in the Third World levels of their vital statistics.

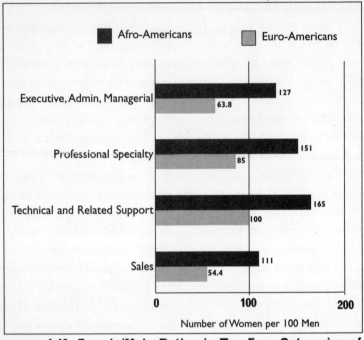

FIGURE 1.12. Female/Male Ratios in Top Four Categories of Occupations of Longest Job, by Ethnicity. SOURCE: Author's tabulation of data from U.S. Bureau of the Census (Internet release, 1997).

Afro-American women, like their Euro-American counterparts, suffer serious gender discrimination. But, ironically, when gender and ethnicity interact, this sometimes works to the benefit of Afro-American women, especially those of the middle classes, as their increasing outperformance of Afro-American men in higher learning, white collar occupations, and the professions attests.

But as I suggested earlier, the very success of Afro-American women in the wider world exacerbates what is their greater gender problem—that between them and Afro-American males in all their sex roles and at all periods of the lifespan. Parts four to six will explore these internal problems at some length. However, before doing so I wish to step back in time in order to locate the crucible of the crisis during the holocaust of slavery and to excavate its historical lineaments through the neo-slavery of Jim Crow and Northern racial segregation, a period that began in 1617 and came to an end only in the middle of this century.

THE ORIGINS OF THE CRISIS:
Bringing Slavery Back In

CONTRARY TO WHAT ADVOCATES and historically misinformed social scientists think, these problems are not new and cannot be *sufficiently* explained by current social and economic conditions or those of the recent past. Poverty, as we will see, is an important facilitator and conditioning factor, but it cannot be the whole or even the main explanation. Most of the world's peoples are poor, far poorer than Afro-Americans, but do not experience the marital and familial problems that Afro-Americans do. Millions of chronically unemployed men live, on the verge of starvation, in urban squalor all over Asia and Latin America without abandoning their wives and children. In America itself, the three-quarters of a century of urban semighetto poverty experienced by the postfamine Irish, and the present condition of most of the Latino minority, who now have higher levels of poverty than Afro-Americans, have not resulted in men's massive abandonment of their wives and children. Similarly, living in urban ghettos as a persecuted minority among a racist majority cannot explain such instability, as the experiences of the Jews of Europe and the overseas Chinese all over Southeast Asia attest. I have no doubt that urban ghetto life and economic deprivation are *necessary* factors contributing to an explanation of the Afro-American problems of gender and family relations. But they cannot be sufficient.

Something else must be at play. Something that runs deep into the peculiarities of the Afro-Americans' own past. In searching for it, we are inevitably led back to the centuries-long holocaust of slavery and what was its most devastating impact: the ethnocidal assault on gender roles, especially those of father and husband, leaving deep scars in the relations between Afro-American men and women.

Between the seventeenth and eighteenth centuries, approximately 600,000 Africans were brought in chains to work as slaves in what would become the United States. Nearly all came from the Guinea Coast area of West Africa.[24] In spite of considerable variations in languages and cultural practices, there were certain common underlying patterns of gender and familial relations in this part of Africa.[25] Most important of all was the fact that these were all kin-based societies. With the exception of a few bilateral societies, kinship systems were organized into unilineal descent groups, membership in which was determined either through the mother's line (matrilineal systems) or the father's line (patrilineal systems).[26] These lineages were corporate entities that determined individuals' statuses and roles in their society and the rights and privileges to which they were entitled. Kinship was pervasive and indeed became the idiom by means of which all social relations were structured, so that even if two people were not related by blood, there was a strong tendency to reinterpret their relationship in fictive kinship terms should they have a close bond with each other.

Marriages, which were polygamous for a minority of high-status and older men, were important in these societies not only for the creation of unions and the formation of families but for the linking of lineages in a complex web of alliances that, in effect, constituted the entire society. In the typical family compound, women shared in the socialization of children up until their initiation into adulthood. As in all other free societies, the father's role was decisive in the training of children for adulthood and in determining their status in society, their competence as adults, and their inheritance.

Gender relations in these societies had distinctive features. Women played a major part in the economic life of their communities. While men cleared, burned, and prepared the land for planting, women did the major part of planting and tending the crops.[27] Markets were a vital part of the economic and social life, and women were prominent as traders.[28] The unusually important role of women in economic life accounts for their relatively independent status in these societies. There is general agreement among anthropologists that women played a greater role in the economic, social, and religious life of West African societies than in any other part of the preindustrial world that enjoyed similar levels of socioeconomic development.[29]

Slavery had a traumatic impact on both genders and on all aspects of life for the Africans brought over to America. However, its impact varied with each gender and with different areas of culture. The problem of the transferability and adaptation of African cultural patterns to the New World slave environment is a complex issue that cannot be entered into here. Suffice it to say that the organizational aspects of West African life, especially its elaborate, finely tuned lineage systems, simply could not be replicated in any form under the gulaglike prisons of the slave plantations. What were more likely to survive the Middle Passage were the belief systems and the values of West Africans. The degree to which these beliefs and values were actualized in transformed adaptations to the New World environment depended on the nature of the slave regime and the geographical environment.

Of three things we are certain. First, that throughout the New World slave systems, Africans and their descendants tenaciously held on to the strong valuation of kinship and to the fundamental West African social tendency to use kinship as the idiom for the expression of all important relationships and rankings. I have shown in an earlier work that this process began even on the slave ships of the Middle Passage. Slaves who survived the trauma of the crossing redefined themselves in fictive kinship terms as ship brothers and sisters, and this extended to their progeny, if any.[30] Pathetically, this principle extended even to the slave owner— though not the despised overseer—in places such as Jamaica where absentee owners were addressed as "Tata," or father.

The second certain consequence of slavery was that it was most virulent in its devastation of the roles of father and husband. The reason is obvious. Slavery was quintessentially about one person assuming, through brute force and the legalized violence of his government, absolute power and authority over another. The slave was reduced in law and civic life to a nonperson. He or she was socially dead as a legal entity (a person with independent capacities or rights or powers) and as a civic being (a recognized member of the sociopolitical order). As a person in law and civil society, the slave did not exist but instead was a mere surrogate of the master. Hence, the status and role of husband could not exist under slavery, since it meant having independent rights in another person and, in both the U.S. South and West Africa, some authority over her. Fatherhood could also not exist, since this meant owning one's children, having parental power and authority over them. Both infringed upon the power of the master and were therefore denied in law and made meaningless in practice.

Clearly, this does not mean that slaves could not have regular sexual relations or reproduce children whom they loved and by whom they were loved. Nor does it mean that they could not have informal social relations. They could and they did. What is more, to the degree that such informal relations added to the master's property and reduced social tensions and the constant temptation to flee the horror of his enslavement, to that degree did the slaveholder encourage such informal relations. But it is patently absurd to confuse these informal relations with the roles of fatherhood, husbandhood, and civic membership in one's community, all of which carried weighty obligations and rights that were utterly critical for men's definition of their very beings as men and as persons. West Africans, in particular, were sticklers for the formalities of the rules, roles, relations, and obligations that came with membership in social groups, as almost every anthropologist of the area has attested. They were acutely conscious of the principle of legitimacy and as litigious in their own traditional legal systems as are modern Americans. Indeed, slavery was actually well established in the societies from which West Africans came—which in no way justifies their enslavement by Europeans—and in those societies, the main thing about slaves and their progeny was their utter illegitimacy. Slaves had children and relatives but no legitimate kin; therefore, they did not belong in their own right to any lineage. They were kinless, which in effect meant that they were socially dead and were so defined in the laws, rituals, and customs of West Africa. More than for any other group of people, then, the experience of being denied legitimate claims in one's spouse, one's children, and one's place in society would have weighed traumatically on the minds and souls of West Africans and their descendants.

But there is a third point to note about the forced adaptation to slavery. In some cases preexisting norms, practices, and values were congruent with the interests of the slaveholder and the exigencies of the plantation gulag. Among these, as we will see, was the important role of women in farming. Furthermore, throughout the Americas, the slaves as property were legally defined as persons either bought as slaves or born to a slave mother.[31] For this reason, slave motherhood had legal status and was jealously guarded by the slaveholder. Hence, while slavery and the slave master decimated the roles of father and husband and indeed all other significant male roles—which, by their very nature, were preoccupied with the power and authority of officeholding, and with honor, status, and dignity—they strengthened the bond between mother and child and reinforced the preexisting agricultural roles of women.

What resulted from this monstrous cultural and human transmission was not chaos or a social vacuum. Human society, like nature, abhors vacuums, and this was true even of the slave gulags of the Caribbean archipelago, arguably the worst nightmares of human brutality in the history of the world. Rather, the forced adaptations to the unnatural state of slavery over two and a half centuries resulted in patterns of interaction between men and women that, while precariously functional within the plantation slave regimes, were later to prove tragically disruptive for Afro-Americans in their postdulotic history.

During the 1970s, a revisionist literature emerged in reaction to the earlier scholarship on slavery that had emphasized the destructive impact of the institution on Afro-American life.[32] In their laudable attempt to demonstrate that the slaves, in spite of their condition, did exercise some agency and did develop their own unique patterns of culture and social organization, the revisionists went to the opposite extreme, creating what Peter Parish calls a "historiographical hornet's nest," which "came dangerously close to writing the slaveholder out of the story completely." Or as Kolchin more bluntly puts it, the old myth of decimated Sambos and Aunt Jemimas with no social life of their own was replaced by a new myth: "that of the utopian slave community."[33]

The excesses of this revisionist literature on slavery have been sharply challenged by a younger generation of counterrevisionists, many of whom, significantly, are women scholars; and several of the revisionists have qualified their earlier positions. Counterrevisionist scholars have questioned the many methodological flaws of the revisionists, such as the bias toward the large plantations in the selection of sources; the overemphasis on the nuclear household type; the relative neglect of the distribution of children across household types and the nature of children's socialization; the failure to take account of the abundant evidence on violence and compensating patriarchalism in gender relations among slaves and freedmen; and the underplaying of the negative impact of the slaveholder class.[34]

For me, there are at least two important flaws in the revisionist literature on slavery. First is the revisionists' neglect or ignorance of the conceptual issues that their focus on the family as a unit posed for their work and findings. They compounded this flawed focus with their implicit assumption that what they called "the family" meant only one thing: the suburban, nuclear unit to which they were accustomed. With these assumptions, they then went in search of the thing they called "the family." Upon finding something that looked vaguely like "the family unit" to which they were accustomed, they emerged triumphant with the academic news that slavery had had no damaging impact on the Afro-American family, that indeed the Afro-Americans had emerged from two and a half centuries of powerlessness, sexual degradation, male emasculation, childhood neglect, legal nonexistence (in which being raped by anyone Euro-American was not a crime), and general racist oppression with their nuclear families intact, their gender relations unsullied, and their communities tightly knit and harmonious.

The revisionist focus on the family as a unit is perhaps forgivable in light of a similar emphasis among sociologists and demographers during the seventies. However, as the Brazilian demographer Maria Coleta De Oliveira points out, family studies have been going through something of a theoretical crisis precisely because of this long established tendency to analyze relations between men, women, and their children in terms of a single unit called the family. "Focusing on the family," she writes, is based on "the supposition that it is possible to take the behavior of the familial group as univocal and consistent. This supposition has often led to concealment of conflicts, tensions, and inequalities that are inherent to the family unit. *The family is often selected as a unit for analysis to the detriment of the individual and even the possibility of comprehending the dynamics of the family itself*" (emphasis added).[35] She further points out that it is important not to confuse the conjugal, consanguineous, and coresidential dimensions of a group's relationships, all of which intersect in various ways to define various kinds of families but are not themselves the same thing as "the family." Most important, she endorses the view of those who insist on looking beneath the structure of "the family" "into such dyadic relationships as husband/wife, mother/child, father/child, or brother/sister."[36]

This is precisely the position I take in this essay. However, the revisionist historians of slave family life do just the opposite. They have relentlessly focused on the family unit and have been able to show that a unit consisting of man, woman, and child existed in about two-thirds of the cases of slave unions during the last decades of slavery on the large plantations in the Southeast. As Paul David and Peter Temin point out in their critique of Robert William Fogel and Stanley Engerman's revisionist work, *Time on the Cross:* "Instead of examining the functions fulfilled by slave families, [it] concentrates on revising our notions about [their] form."[37] What Fogel and Engerman had in fact found was a nuclear *reproductive* unit facilitated by the slave owner, who wanted his slaves to breed as many children as possible but was, as we will see, unwilling to invest in an adequate diet for these children. But a reproductive unit is not necessarily a social unit. And, more important, these units tell us nothing about the gender relations that constitute families.

A second major flaw of the revisionists, especially the late Herbert Gutman, was their disregard for variations in the conditions of slave life both in regional and structural terms. Structurally, slaves toiled on small and medium-sized farms and on large plantations. Large plantations, because they had greater numbers of slaves and relatively fewer Euro-

Americans, allowed for more reproductive units and even genuine unions, although the proportion and stability of even these have been exaggerated. The large plantations also kept the best records. Herbert Gutman, Eugene Genovese, and their followers found these sources irresistible, but by concentrating on the large plantations during the last decades of slavery while neglecting the medium and small farms, they very badly understated the true effects of slavery on gender and familial relations.

Most of the revisionist studies also failed to take account of important regional differences in the kind of slave environment that Afro-Americans encountered. As Ira Berlin has forcefully reminded us, there were profound differences over time and place in the slave systems of the United States. Northern, domestic, and family-farm-type slavery differed radically from the tobacco-based system that developed in the Chesapeake Bay region; the latter differed again from the rice-plantation systems of the Carolina and Georgia low country; and the cotton belt of the south-central and southwestern states also had distinctive modes of exploitation that challenged the survival skills of Afro-Americans in unique ways.[38] Thus, slaves were far more isolated in the Northern states and more open to the influence of Euro-Americans, although their sexuality was less at risk due to the stronger constraints of Puritanism. In the Chesapeake Bay area, they were at far greater risk of sexual abuse from slave owners and from lower-class Euro-Americans, both on and off the plantation. The absence of slave quarters of significant size would also have negatively affected their ability to form stable unions. Allan Kulikoff, a leading specialist on Chesapeake slavery, wrote of the region generally:

> Slave men had to search their neighborhood to find a compatible spouse because even the largest quarter contained few eligible women. Some of the potential mates were sisters or cousins, groups blacks refused to marry. When they were excluded, few choices remained on the quarter, and youths looked elsewhere. . . . Most planters owned too few slaves, on too few quarters, to permit a wide choice of spouses within their plantations; furthermore, they could not afford to purchase the husband or wife. Inevitably, a majority of slave couples remained separated for much of their married life.[39]

In the low country, a more complex system emerged, in which patterns of sexual and gender relations differed markedly within and between Afro-Americans and Euro-Americans depending on whether Afro-

Americans were located in the urban or rural areas. On the plantations, the large numbers of slaves and the provisioning system allowed for more stable reproductive unions, although even here the term *marriage* remains inappropriate. In the urban areas, a distinctive system of concubinage between Euro-American men and light-skinned freed women developed, along with greater sexual contact of the slaves with freed Afro-Americans and Euro-American men. This pattern, which was also found in Louisiana, resembled the loose system of color-class gender relations found in the Caribbean, and indeed was directly influenced by that region, since so many of the early planters in the Carolinas came with their slaves from the British islands.

But even if we confine ourselves to the revisionists' own highly selected turf, we find that most of their arguments collapse under closer scrutiny. The revisionists were largely silent on the question of whether the adult male slave could perform the minimum requirements of the roles of husband and father as found in all human societies except for a couple of museum-piece polyandrous communities of concern only to anthropological theorists: Could he monopolize his partner's sexual services and guarantee that her progeny were in fact his own? Could he protect her from the sexual predation of other men? Could he at least partly provide for her materially? Could he prevent her from being brutalized and physically punished by other men? Could he prevent her from being torn from the place where she was brought up, bundled like cargo, and sold away from him, her children, her kinsmen, and her friends? If the answer to any of these questions is "No," the role of husband did not exist. If the slave could do none of these things, then the role of husband had been devastated.

The evidence is overwhelming that just such a devastation of his role happened regularly to the adult male Afro-American over two and a half centuries in the United States. Against the Euro-Americans, both on and off the plantations and farms, he could offer the offspring he had bred (and who were explicitly stated not to be his own in the courts of the land) and his partner no security, no status, no name, no identity.

While this male emasculation did not lead to "matriarchy," it did change the position of women in relation to men, a change already set in motion by the peculiar circumstances of socialization on the plantation, where "most slave girls grew up believing that boys and girls were equal."[40] The slave regime did restrict the role of mother in a manner that had lasting consequences, and I will return to this later. But as Deborah Gray White demonstrates in her study of the female slave, "giving birth was a life-affirming action. It was, ironically, an act of defiance, a signal to the slave owner that no matter how cruel and inhumane his actions, Afro-Americans would not be utterly subjected or destroyed."[41] However, for the legal and reproductive reasons mentioned earlier, it was simply not in the slave owner's interest to completely undermine the role of mother as he did that of father and husband.

True, the slave woman was doubly burdened with the tasks of being both reproducer and worker, not to mention "the malevolence that flowed from both racism and sexism."[42] However, with regard to her role as worker, while it was exploitative, as it was for Afro-American men, it is a mistake to argue, as James Oliver Horton and others have done, that it "affronted [the] femininity" of the Afro-American woman. As I pointed out earlier, the plantation emphasis on the woman as field-worker merely reinforced a preexisting pattern of work and gender roles. The opposite was true for Afro-American men, who experienced a devastating break with preexisting patterns of work and gender roles.[43]

There was certainly strong cultural resistance to the degradation of gender and familial relations during the period of slavery. The evidence from interviews with ex-slaves, along with demographic data analyzed by cliometricians, strongly suggests that they did everything possible to maintain familial and kinship ties.[44] But this brings me to another important feature of Afro-American familial relations that revisionist historians have misapprehended.

A good part of the revisionist work on slavery is really just a demonstration that slaves cared deeply for their kinsmen and went to great lengths, in spite of the restraints of the slaveholders, to maintain ties with their kin and, after slavery, to find long lost relatives. As one disciple, Charles Wetherell, triumphantly concluded after his reanalysis of the kinship data on a large slave plantation originally studied by Herbert Gutman: "The average Good Hope slave could walk out of his or her cabin, look around slave row, and more than three-quarters of the buildings there would house kin, or the kin of those kin."[45] I am in no doubt about the veracity of all this, and revisionist scholarship deserves some credit for emphasizing this component of slave life. However, there were two important aspects of slave kinship relations that the revisionists have failed to take account of.

The first is the severe attenuation of the legal rights and obligations of kinship—as normally understood and practiced all over the world, especially in Africa—that came from being slaves. The anthropologist Stephen

Gudeman expresses this well: "For the slaves, kinship was founded on blood. . . . What we call legal ties—legal in the triple sense of official law, socially recognized obligations, and relationships conceived to be created by volition and not nature—were not an important part of slave kinship patterns."[46] This, in effect, deprived kinship relations of much of their significance.

The second distinctive feature of slave kinship patterns is the fact that consanguineal ties often came in conflict with conjugal or affinal ones, and with the formation and functioning of households or coresidential units. Thus, it never occurred to Wetherell that walking out of one's cabin and realizing that three-quarters of all the other huts in "slave row" housed kinsmen would have been a deeply depressing thought for any young slave in search of a partner, especially since "slave row" was a virtual prison that one could leave only after getting the slave master's permission, and since one's sexual values prohibited intercourse with even distant cousins.

Because men had no legitimate ties to, or rights in, their female partners, they tended to emphasize the ties that they were certain of, namely, those they had acquired by "blood" through their mothers. Women, for their part, knew that their men could not protect them. Their men were liable to be either sold away or, in the not uncommon case of "abroad husbands" living on other plantations, simply forbidden from seeing them by new owners or overseers. Hence, women turned to the only people they could really trust, their own maternally linked kinsmen.[47]

What is more, the uterine kin tie far outweighed paternal kin ties. It also weakened, rather than complemented, the conjugal or cohabitational ties between men and women. There is some evidence that slave owners recognized and reinforced this uterine bias with a gender bias in the separation of siblings and children. Thus, Cheryll Ann Cody, in her study of a South Carolina slave plantation over the period 1786 to 1833, found that "separation from kin was an ever-present threat" for all the slaves, but the owner had a policy of separating sons "from their parents and their younger siblings, while daughters more frequently remained with them." She adds that "Daughters were more likely to stay with their sisters than were their brothers. This pattern of dispersal resulted in a family structure in which matrifocality was reinforced."[48] I found a very similar pattern in my studies of slavery in the Caribbean, a pattern that led during slavery to a system of residential kin communities that I called the matri-deme.[49]

The tendency to emphasize uterine and female kin continues today. Although Carol Stack points out that it would be inaccurate to say that

Afro-American lower-class children "derive all their kin through females," her own research shows clearly that there is a strong uterine bias in these relations. Not only do young mothers almost always turn to their own mothers and uterine kin for help, but after being abandoned by the fathers of their babies, should they ever seek help from his side of their children's relatives, it is not to the father but to the father's uterine kin that they turn.[50]

If paternal kin ties were weak under slavery, affinal ones were virtually nonexistent. The slaves' emphasis on blood excluded affines, or in-laws, as part of their kinship group. Clearly, the idea of an "in-law" made no sense when one's relationship with one's sexual partner had no basis in law. Significantly, although slaves made a point of naming their children in honor of kinsmen, affines were never honored in this way.[51]

It was during the period of slavery, too, that many of the deep-seated gender attitudes and tensions between Afro-American men and women that I mentioned in the introduction and will discuss at greater length later were first established. Slavery almost certainly bred distrust in gender relations, especially on the part of men. One of the main reasons for marriage all over the world is that it provides security to men that their partners' children are in fact their own biological offspring. In the absence of any legally recognized marriage rights in his partner; and in the presence of both predatory Euro-American men, who could rape or otherwise sexually manipulate slave women with impunity, and a large minority of other young, unattached slave men; and further, with severe restrictions placed on his ability to conduct a mate search that would lead to the selection of someone whom he felt confident he could trust, the male slave was placed in an impossible situation, one bound to reduce him to a state of chronic jealousy and insecurity about women.

Slave women, especially on the large plantations, were only too aware of these male anxieties. They and their mothers responded in the same manner that human societies all over the world employ to allay male fears about female sexuality:[52] They strongly emphasized norms of sexual faithfulness and chastity. That a majority of slave women adhered to Victorian standards of sexual rectitude has now been widely confirmed by historians.[53] While this had the effect of stabilizing women's behavior, it was only partly successful with men.

In an important qualification of his earlier position, Nobel laureate Robert William Fogel argued in his last work on slavery that the restrictions that masters of large plantations imposed on cross-plantation unions may have made family life more stable, but at devastating costs to Afro-American gender relations: "If requiring slaves to marry within the plantation increased family stability, that boon was achieved at a heavy cost to the slaves. A significant proportion of adults who could not find mates on their own plantation were forced to remain single for large parts, if not all, of their lives. Thus slavery tended to destabilize slave marriages in a variety of ways, some of which were inherent in the system."[54]

Fogel remains silent on the issue of just how these slave men, forced to remain single, satisfied their sexual needs. Nor has anyone asked similar questions about so-called abroad husbands, forced to spend long periods of time away from their "wives," who lived on plantations very far away. These two categories of men would, in fact, have constituted the majority of male slaves on most plantations. Given the hardness and long hours of plantation labor, and given the tedium of living in a virtual prison, sex would have been the only thing that made life worth living for these men. The suggestion of the cliometricians and other revisionists that these men remained chaste is preposterously naive, if not downright disingenuous. No one who has grown up in the sugar-plantation belt of an ex-slave society, as I have, and has heard firsthand, in vivid details, the sexual exploits of the young cane workers who swarm into the region to harvest the crop, work backbreaking hours during the day, ravage the local women at night, then leave a legion of broken hearts and pregnant women when the crop is over, can take this inane revisionist assumption about the sexuality of unattached male slaves seriously.[55] I grew up in the market towns of Lionel Town and May Pen, in Clarendon parish, Jamaica, which is located in the heart of the island's sugar growing estates. Ask anyone from the region about the sexuality of cane-cutters and they will tell you tales to make even the most jaded person of color blush crimson. So how were their sexual needs met? We know it wasn't by the white women. We know there were no brothels on the plantation, and even if there were, the slaves had nothing to pay with. The answer was given long ago by W. E. B. Du Bois, who very sensibly argued that a dual system of gender and familial relations had existed.[56] Most slave women adhered to stable sexual norms, as did, in all likelihood, that minority of male slaves fortunate enough to find compatible spouses on their own plantation. But a substantial minority of slave women must have had multiple partners and have led more freewheeling sexual lives, and it must have been these women who met the sexual needs of the majority of slave men who were either completely without regular partners or were forced to stay away from their "abroad" spouses for long periods of time. Some of these women, too, would have met the sexual needs of single Euro-American men. It is they who lent a core of truth to the Euro-American accounts of promiscuous slave women, in much the same way that today the disproportionate number of Afro-American prostitutes in many of the nation's large cities sustains execrable Euro-American stereotypes about Afro-American women.

It would be naive to assume, however, that slavery had no negative effects on the more stable gender relations between men and women living together on the same plantation. There is good evidence that slave men, emasculated by the slave owner, compensated for this by abusing their partners. In her detailed study of slave families in Louisiana, Ann Patton Malone found frequent "reports of domestic violence in planters' records involving slave men against their wives" and attributed them to the "overwhelming sense of powerlessness and impotence which threatened the male's concept of his manhood and fatherhood."[57] She could also have attributed them to the brutality and pervasive violence of slavery itself, which corroded all human relations, especially those of stronger to physically more vulnerable persons, including slaveholders' relations with their Euro-American wives.[58]

More generally, slavery divorced motherhood from the sexual and conjugal union as surely as it did fatherhood. As White observes:

> The nature of plantation life required that marital relationships allow slave women a large degree of autonomy. Marriage did not bring the traditional benefits to female slaves. As we have seen, slave women could not depend on their husbands for protection against whipping or sexual exploitation. Slave couples had no property to share, and essential needs like food, clothing, and shelter were not provided by slave husbands. Thus slave men could not use the provision of subsistence goods as leverage in the exercise of authority over women. In almost all societies where men consistently dominate women, their control is based on male ownership and distribution of property and/or control of certain culturally valued subsistence goods. The absence of such mechanisms in slave society probably contributed to female slave independence from slave men.[59]

Even today, Afro-American women's unexpectedly strong valuation of mothering as the most fulfilling role for women, so seemingly out of tune with their other, highly modern gender views, can only be explained in terms of the long years of struggle during slavery and its aftermath. Sheer survival under the concentrated horror of the slave plantation entailed, both culturally and socially, an extreme preference for mothering and security, independent of any support from the dishonored roles of "husband" and "father." Inevitably, White concludes, the mother-child relationship "superseded [that] between husband and wife. Slaveholder practices encouraged the primacy of the mother-child relationship, and in the mores of the slave community motherhood ranked above marriage."[60] White shows, too, that it was under the impact of slavery that romance, though cherished, as often as not had to give way to "pragmatic considerations."[61]

We find these gender attitudes already fully developed in the life of the early-nineteenth-century slave, freedom fighter, and feminist Harriet Jacobs. Jacobs ("Linda," in her *Incidents in the Life of a Slave Girl*) never sexually consummated her relationship with her only "love-dream," the freeborn "young colored carpenter" who courted her, but instead established a companionless concubinage of convenience with the Euro-American attorney Samuel Tredwell Sawyer ("Mr. Sands"), by whom she had two children, expecting "security" for them and the ultimate "boon" of freedom. Her moving struggle for freedom, first for herself, then for her children, was counterpoised by her deep filial love for her mother-substitute—she was a "grandmother's child"—and her devotion to her children, especially her daughter, Louisa Matilda. It is striking that Jacobs, an intelligent, beautiful woman who must have had many suitors, never married, even though she was freed at the age of thirty-nine and lived for another forty-five years. It is also noteworthy that, in contrast to Louisa Matilda, with whom she had a strong, lifelong bond, both Jacobs's brother, Joseph, and her son of the same name were lost to the family.

In this regard, Jacobs was not unusual. In the early nineteenth century, there was already a marriage squeeze for free, middle-class Afro-American women of both the South and the North. Quite apart from the shortage of free Afro-American men with adequate incomes, it was not unusual for the Afro-American women of Petersburg "to refrain from marriage, thereby retaining their legal autonomy." Those who did marry often regretted doing so: "There was a relatively high degree of open antagonism between the sexes," writes Susan Lebsock. "Free black women had relatively little cause to defer to their men, and the result may have been a substantial amount of conjugal conflict." One husband terminated an argument over who should preside at the table by hitting his wife over the head with an iron bar.[62] In the North during this same period, according to Horton, "many black women remained single or postponed marriage while they pursued a career in business or reform." Middle-class Afro-American aunts, in striking contrast with their Euro-American counterparts, rather than cajoling their nieces into marriage, would condemn the institution as "a waste of time." And those nieces who did marry were sometimes bitter about their lot, one of them complaining about the "grievous trials" and "painful results" of her mistake.[63] Harriet Jacobs, then, like her counterparts today, had good reason to remain single.

Finally, there is the tragic impact of slavery on the socialization of children, which is perhaps one of its most devastating legacies. The main reason for families is the reproduction and rearing of children—an obvious point that has to be restated since one of the statistical tricks of the revisionists is to include childless couples in their count of "stable slave families." If parents were unable to raise their children, then the "unit" they participated in was not a family but a reproductive union. The evidence is overwhelming that, as Richard Steckel concludes, slave "parents had little time to spend with their young children. Working slaves ate breakfast and lunch in the fields and probably had dinner after the non-working children had eaten in the evening. Mealtime was not an activity during which parents shared food and discussion with their younger children."[64] Mothers were torn from their infants long before the period of lactation was over, in order to return full-time to the fields. Wilma King considers this to be one of "the most unsettling events in the lives of [slave children]," who, on plantations of more than twenty slaves, were placed in "nurseries where their care was in the hands of slaves either too infirm, too old, or too young to work elsewhere."[65] Usually, these old slaves, tired and overwhelmed with too many infants, simply neglected their wards or else beat them with switches when they became unruly. As soon as they were able to, children were put to work, which, according to King, "can be rightly called the thief who stole the childhood of youthful bond servants."[66]

Children, of course, will somehow find time for play even under these brutal circumstances, as King ably documents. And parents, especially mothers, tried their best to protect their children from slavery's worst horrors. However, several consequences flowed from this nightmarish environment. The first, documented by Steckel,[67] is that young children were horribly malnourished. Owners hedged their bets, not wanting to invest resources in the offspring of their slaves until they were certain that they would become productive adults. An unusual pattern of growth emerged in which those children who survived this Malthusian hurdle were then well fed from their adolescence onward. Steckel has correctly pointed out that this would have had disastrous consequences for the personalities of the slave children. Like malnourished children today, they are likely to have been "apathetic, emotionally withdrawn, less aggressive, and more dependent."[68]

Another feature of slave childhood was the added psychological trauma of witnessing the daily degradation of their parents at the hands of the slaveholders. King finds that the ordeal of seeing their parents whipped, and especially seeing their mothers stripped naked and beaten raw, made slave children prematurely old. To the trauma of observing their parents' humiliation was later added that of being sexually exploited by Euro-Americans on and off the estate, as the children grew older.[69] Though we hear only of the rape and sexual abuse of girls, it is hard to believe that slave boys were not raped by homosexual slaveholders.[70]

The third aspect of the socialization of slaves that I want to emphasize bears directly on the question of the meaningfulness of speaking of "fathers" and "husbands" during slavery. Willie Lee Rose cites the case of the slave child, Jacob, who was being trained to become a jockey and whose trainer took to beating him mercilessly. When the boy turned to his father for help, he was devastated by his progenitor's advice: "Go back to your work and be a good boy, for I cannot do anything for you."[71] Rose's comment on this incident, which every slave child must have experienced frequently, is apt: "Unfortunately, the effort to overturn the prevailing monolithic view of family life under slavery offers a temptation to exaggeration. Clearly there were limits placed upon the father's role in the family. The historian must recall enforced separations and the father's pitiful ineffectuality to protect his family in the face of plantation authority. These problems bore upon both parents."[72]

And they bore most of all upon the slave children, who, in addition to being disciplined by sadistic Euro-Americans, were often horribly whipped by their parents in much the same way that the parents themselves were disciplined by those in charge of them. Tragically, the inherently violent nature of slavery resulted in the most vulnerable being the most punished. Brenda Stevenson finds:

> The violence and brutality that whites imposed on their slaves undoubtedly influenced the ways in which bondsmen and bondswomen reared their own children. The ability to beat someone, to hold that kind of physical control over another

human, was a sadistic expression of power that blacks learned
repeatedly from their interaction with, and observation of,
white authority figures.[73]

The beatings, she adds, were meant to show the children just who was in
control and, as such, could be seen as a pathetic defiance of Euro-
American authority. The same held for spousal abuse by men. This chain
of violence, according to the testimony of the slaves, extended right down
the pecking order to children themselves, who, in their games with each
other, often simulated, and sometimes actually performed, the whipping
of playmates, girls no doubt, like their adult counterparts, getting the bitter end of the stick.[74] As we will see, this tradition of corporal punishment
of children persists among the Afro-American lower and working classes,
reinforced by their fundamentalist creed.

The conclusion children drew would not have been that their fathers
did not love or care for them, for there is evidence that fathers did what
they could for their children in the little time they were permitted with
them;[75] nor was it that they themselves did not love the man that had so
little power to protect them. Rather, the conclusion drawn was that fatherhood was a marginal role among Afro-Americans.

To summarize and conclude this part of the essay, after two hundred
fifty years of forced adaptation to the extreme environment of slavery,
Afro-American men and women developed a distinctive set of reproductive strategies in their struggle to survive. Tragically, the strategies that
were most efficient for survival under the extreme environment of slavery
were often the least adaptive to survival in a free, competitive social order.

Given the high infant and maternal mortality rates and the slaveholder's venal practice of delaying the provision of adequate sustenance
until the midadolescent years when he was certain that the slave's life expectancy justified the higher investment in food, the most sensible reproductive strategy for a woman was to delay her first birth until the period
of adequate provision, which began at age seventeen or so. Attempting to
bear children before this not only would have increased the risk of mis-
carriage and infant mortality but would have put the still wretchedly malnourished mother at risk of death also, especially given the murderously
short leave from the fields that the slaveholders allowed immediately before and after delivery.

For adolescent slave women, this most adaptive reproductive strategy
required the separation of the conjugal from the maternal roles. Young

slave women who insisted on linking these roles too closely would be asking for a great deal of emotional and physical pain. They knew only too well that the young men who might be interested in becoming the fathers of their children were those at greatest risk of being sold or hired out. And even if these young men were not sold, there was a high probability that they would be living on another plantation, under an entirely different authority figure who would be making profit calculations that could devastate the couple's lives at any time. Slaves did not need courses in probability theory to calculate that adding an extra all-powerful figure to their lives—which is what the very common "abroad marriages" did—multiplied the probability of the disruption of their union.

Finally, the U.S. slave environment, by reducing to zero—and thereby equalizing—the resources controlled by both genders, would have drastically influenced the criteria slave women used for mate selection. The anthropologist and reproductive specialist Jane B. Lancaster has observed, in reference to all human populations, that "female preference for a man with resources should not be expected in social groupings where there is low male variance in resource access or independent female access to resources."[76] If not a man's access to resources, what, then, would women emphasize in mate choice? Lancaster argues that "under conditions where the most that men can offer are their good genes and fit physical condition, women should be more interested in indicators such as handsomeness, masculinity, and athletic ability but not particularly in youthfulness because male reproductive potential deteriorates much more slowly and is not limited by menopause."[77] King's account of courting behavior among the slaves suggests that this may well have been the case. There is no mention of male capacity to command resources as a factor in courtship. Instead, men who could walk great distances between plantations, who were brave and tough enough to risk being beaten by their owners and by Euro-American patrollers, and who could do so after a long day's labor in the field were admired, as were good dancers and men good at "sweet talk."[78]

Slave men, for their part, developed a reproductive strategy with two distinctive features. First, a man's having as many children as possible would have made most sense, in order to ensure that he would leave progeny who would survive to adulthood. In many respects, this was true of all populations at the time, given the high infant mortality rate, but the practice would have been reinforced not only by the planters but by the even greater mortality rate among slave children. In the absence of any other meaningful ways of expressing manhood, becoming a progenitor would have acquired special value. For those many slave men who were unattached or who were forced to live away from partners they did not entirely trust, impregnating as many women as possible would have been the most rational reproductive strategy. Since they either could not secure a regular mate or could not be sure that the children of their partners on other plantations were their own, their best hope of satisfying the fundamental biological need to leave some progeny in the world would have been to plant their seed whenever and wherever they could. This was not promiscuity. Under the severe environmental exigencies of slavery, it would have been supremely rational male reproductive behavior. The fact that some masters persistently, and nearly all masters at some time, actively encouraged young unattached male slaves to act as human studs would simply have reinforced this reproductive strategy.

This tendency would also have been encouraged by the second distinctive feature of male slaves' reproductive behavior, namely, that control over resources did not enter into the decision to have a child. The unusual nature of this strategy cannot be overemphasized. In every other known form of human society, from the most primitive to the most advanced, men's decision to take on the responsibility of fatherhood, and hence their age of marriage, is critically linked to their capacity to provide for their offspring. In some European societies such as those of traditional Britain, men would sometimes delay marriage, and often sex, until well into their thirties as they waited to inherit the family farm.[79] After two and a half centuries in which this linkage was forcibly severed, however, Afro-American male slaves, and their descendants, *like male slaves and their descendants all over the Americas*, developed a reproductive strategy in which these two aspects of life were no longer necessarily or normatively linked. Bringing a child into the world became a virtual obligation of manhood and of ethnic survival that did not entail any consideration of the means whereby one would support it. Afro-Americans, and American society at large (like Afro-Caribbean and Afro-Latin societies), are still living with the devastating consequences of this male attitude toward reproduction. In all of these ex-slave societies, male descendants of slaves firmly believe that "birth control is a plot to kill the Negro race." And in all of them, men bear children whom they have no resources to support and whom they, in the majority of cases among the lower classes, simply abandon.

The upshot of all this was the dual pattern of gender and familial relations that Du Bois identified a hundred years ago, which astonishingly is still very much with us. An interesting feature of the quantitative studies

of slave relations and unions is that they suggest a distribution very similar
to what prevails today; that is, roughly two-thirds of all reproductive units
had two progenitors present, exactly two-thirds of ex-slave interviewees
born before 1851 said they were in unions, and about the same proportion of children grew up in these two-adult households.[80] It is very likely
that these reproductive units were the models for what became families
after emancipation. If we look only at the sociohistorical abstraction
called the "family unit," we will, along with the legion of revisionists clad
in white armor who truly believe that they have handed back to Afro-
Americans their pride and historical claim to agency, applaud the transmission of this Trojan horse. Now that we know what gendered misery
lies inside the Trojan unit, we are better prepared to understand what
follows.

UP FROM SLAVERY

THE END OF SLAVERY posed new challenges for Afro-Americans. The
Thirteenth Amendment abolished the individual ownership of one person by another but did not remove the culture and institutional system of
slavery. Indeed, as we will see in the next essay, in many respects these
were compensatorily reinforced, making life more precarious and fright-
eningly oppressive for Afro-Americans.

After an initial attempt to force the ex-slaves into semiservile gang labor
on the plantations failed, the system of farm tenancy, or sharecropping,
emerged by the end of the century. The vast majority of Afro-Americans
were to toil under this regime for most of the first half of the twentieth
century. Also during this period, a minority moved to the cities, where
they faced, in the North, racist resistance and ultimate exclusion from the
emerging industrial order.

In adapting to these new environments, Afro-Americans drew upon
two sets of cultural resources: those they had developed during the period
of slavery, and those of the Euro-American majority. What worked under
slavery were not necessarily the best strategies for these new environments; and what worked for Euro-Americans were not necessarily what
most adequately met the extreme exigencies of life in the sharecropping
South or in urban areas. Emerging from this process were changed patterns of gender and familial behaviors that partly reflected the past and its
problems, and partly reflected the proximate socioeconomic realities.

The census data for the period between 1850 and 1910 have been a valuable source of information for our understanding of this tradition. In regard to family composition, whatever it may mean sociologically, the census data show clearly that the dual pattern of familial and gender relations established during the period of slavery continued, although in modified form. Thus in 1880, 31 percent of all Afro-American households were headed by a single person; of those, 25.3 percent were headed by women and 5.9 percent by men. This pattern differed significantly from those of other ethnic groups at that time. The proportion of Afro-American households headed by women was exactly twice that of the Irish, over three times that of the German Americans, and slightly less than twice that of native-born Euro-Americans.[81] Herbert Gutman, persisting in his quixotic mission to prove that slavery had no negative impact on Afro-American gender and family life, completely misrepresented the census data of the period by including couples without children in his total count of households, thereby greatly decreasing the proportion of households headed by women.[82] For this attempted statistical sleight of hand he was sharply upbraided by Frank Furstenberg Jr. and his colleagues, who pointed out that the inclusion of childless couples not only grossly underestimated the proportion of female-headed households but introduced an irrelevant factor, since "the assumption that underlies the association of the female-headed household with a set of negative social consequences is that the absence of the father adversely affects the socialization of the young."[83]

Unfortunately, Furstenberg and his colleagues then went on to introduce their own biases in attempting to explain the relatively high proportion of female-headed households among Afro-Americans during the late nineteenth and early twentieth centuries. Dutifully toeing the revisionist line of the 1970s, which was more obsessed with intellectually flagellating Daniel Patrick Moynihan's 1965 report on the Afro-American family than with ascertaining the truth about the dynamics of racial oppression and survival in Afro-American history, Furstenberg and his colleagues argued against any legacy of slavery and instead for "the primacy of urban economic and demographic factors." They attributed the relatively high proportion of female-headed households among Afro-Americans to widowhood, which, they claimed, "overwhelmingly predominate[d] among female household heads."[84]

Now, there is no doubting the fact that Afro-American men had unusually high mortality rates at the turn of the century, due to the dangerous nature of the work they were obliged to do as well as their vulnerability to illnesses and stress resulting from their extreme impoverishment. There were therefore significantly more widows among Afro-American women than other Americans. However, as Samuel Preston, possibly the nation's leading sociological demographer, and his colleagues have definitively shown, this can in no way explain the higher proportion of female-headed households.[85]

From as early as 1904, the U.S. Census Bureau issued official warnings that a significant proportion of Afro-American women whose husbands had abandoned them, or who had never been married, had misrepresented themselves as widows to census enumerators. In 1939, E. Franklin Frazier properly took account of these warnings in his treatment of the census data when preparing his classic study, *The Negro Family in the United States*,[86] a favorite target of revisionist historians. Revisionists, however, fearful of attacking an Afro-American scholar directly, pilloried Frazier through the surrogate target of the unfortunate Daniel Patrick Moynihan. Then, in 1992, Preston and his colleagues were able to take advantage of the recently released public-use sample from the census of 1910 to show that there had been serious flaws in the reports on the marital status of Afro-Americans in the census data, flaws that completely undermine the claims of Gutman and other revisionists about the Afro-American family in the nineteenth century and the sociological innocence of slavery in explaining later developments. What Preston found with the more detailed public-use samples was that "too many widows [had been] reported, and at least some of the discrepancy appears to reflect a propensity to legitimate birth outside marriage. Furthermore, by using data on the reported duration of the current marriage, [Preston's team found] that marital turnover [had been] faster than could be explained by actual widowhood or formal divorce." Their findings vindicated Frazier's work and, by implication, the dual familial and gender thesis first stated by W. E. B. Du Bois. They write: "In general, our results support Frazier's claim that marriage for many African-American women early in this century was more fluid than direct census reports on current marital status would imply. In turn, the results suggest that patterns of marital instability among blacks show greater historical continuity than is suggested by some current discussions."[87]

Preston's study is valuable not only for its revelation that the 1910 census data underestimated the proportion of single mothers but for its findings on gender relations; more particularly, for its estimate of the duration and distribution of first marriages of women in different age groups. A substantial number of cohabiting women reported that they were married, and on the termination of their old unions and the beginning of new ones, they reported the new unions as first marriages. Many of the earlier unions were reproductive. Thus, almost 14 percent of Afro-American women in their late twenties had a child that was older than the reported duration of their first marriage, as did almost 16 percent of those in their early thirties.[88]

It was not the intention of Preston and his colleagues to deny or underplay the role of changing socioeconomic forces in the evolving patterns of Afro-American gender and familial relations. Indeed, they make it clear that the "enormous burden of mortality clearly played havoc with the stability of black marriages" at the turn of the century and that it was precisely because the "true incidence" of widowhood was so "extraordinarily high . . . that the label was overused in other situations." Their point, rather, is that "underestimating past marital instability exaggerates the amount of observed change" and, at the same time, downplays the role of cultural factors in explaining Afro-American life, both those derived from Africa and those that emerged in Afro-Americans' forced adaptation to the slave environment.[89]

Slavery is important not only for our understanding of the high proportion of female-headed households resulting from fragile unions and male abandonment of their spouses and children but also for any explanation of other gender and familial patterns, including those that from the "family unit" perspective may seem to have been stable two-parent households. Nowhere is this more true than in our attempts to make sense of the patterns that evolved under the impact of the sharecropping farms where the great majority of Afro-Americans were to be found for the first four decades of the present century.

By the start of the century, a distinctive pattern had emerged among Southern rural Afro-Americans trapped in farm tenancy: that of very early marriage and extremely high fertility. By 1900 the typical rural Afro-American couple had about eight children, and the mean age of marriage for Afro-American women in the rural South was 21.69 years, whereas the Euro-American rural population had far fewer children and much later ages of marriage.[90]

If one is concerned only with family forms and familial units, all this may seem like a happy development. However, this pattern was a recipe for chronic and persistent poverty, which is precisely why almost all other rural groups in the Western world were moving in a diametrically opposite demographic direction. Stewart Tolnay has persuasively argued that a major factor was the entrapment of Afro-Americans in farm tenancy, rather than farm ownership. This "created a social environment in which early marriage and rapid childbearing were rational behavioral responses, but these in turn socially and economically handicapped the tenant class."[91] Tenancy obviated the need to postpone marriage until land and other resources were acquired. It made wives and children essential assets for the male tenant, who needed their labor. "Landownership was an economic advantage relatively denied southern rural blacks," Tolnay writes.

> Therefore, the personal "sacrifice" of delayed and slowed family formation often associated with establishment of households in agricultural economies was not only *unnecessary* for rural blacks but was also largely *futile*. Alternative economic opportunities were also restricted because of the relative unavailability of nonagricultural employment opportunities for blacks and the generally hostile racial atmosphere after the Civil War.[92]

Perhaps the most unfortunate consequence of this development was its effects on the education of children. The widespread use of child labor by Afro-American tenants prevented children from making use of what educational opportunities were available. Parents saw little need to educate children when their main asset as children and adults would be their labor power in the fields. Uneducated adults, in turn, could function only as tenant farmers.

Now, what is interesting about all this is that it is also partly explained by continuities with the previous slave system. Recall that the most rational reproductive strategy for slave men was to have as many children as possible, given their lack of rights in their partners and the fact that they had no need to consider the availability of resources in making the decision to start a family. We now see that tenancy similarly created a disincentive to postpone starting a family and a strong incentive to produce as many children as possible. The really fascinating sociohistorical issue here is whether farm tenancy and its demographic consequences were wholly independent developments, bearing only a coincidental resemblance to what had existed during the period of slavery, or whether the reproductive strategy developed under slavery, and which had certainly become normative after two hundred fifty years, strongly primed the ex-slave male population to fall into the trap of tenancy.

Tolnay never mentions this possibility, so I assume that he favors a purely contemporaneous socioeconomic explanation. Indeed, he states explicitly that "rural blacks were locked in tenancy with little potential for escape."[93] There can be no doubt that opportunities for Afro-Americans were limited and that farm tenancy was something of a trap. But how deep was the trap? And how completely circumscribed were their chances of escape? It is possible to exaggerate the degree to which Afro-Americans were constrained by the sharecropping system. More precisely, if the ending of slavery meant one thing to the ex-slave, it was his or her ability to move from one employer or landowner to another. The economic historian Gavin Wright has shown that Afro-Americans could and did frequently change landowners and that being indebted was not a decisive factor in their decision to move.[94] We also know that while the Great Migration was to come into full flow only in the late 1920s, from the last quarter of the nineteenth century there was a not insignificant flow of migrants from the rural areas to the urban South and North.

As constraining and exploitative as the sharecropping system was, then, it must be admitted that Afro-Americans exercised some agency in their decision to stay in it. Thus the question is, what motivated them to make this ultimately disastrous choice? My answer is that the reproductive and familial strategies of slavery predisposed male Afro-Americans to go with the sharecropping arrangement. It proved to be a terrible choice, like a sociological quicksand: Once they got in, it became harder and harder to get out. To the degree that their reproductive and familial heritage from slavery induced them to make this choice in the first place, to that extent did slavery continue to adversely influence Afro-American family life.

It should further be noted that the farm tenancy system, while congruent with male reproductive interests as they had emerged on the slave plantation, offered no such correspondences with reinforcements of women's reproductive strategies. Women had nothing to be gained by marrying too young, except more years of labor on the farm and more children. Women did have opportunities that men did not, especially if they had some education: as clerks, schoolteachers, nurses, hospital orderlies, and so on.

These differing reproductive interests by themselves would have generated a good deal of gender tensions in marriage. But there was another lingering pattern from slavery that greatly complicated women's lives: the dualism in family form and gender relations that Du Bois spoke of, and especially the double standard in sexual morality that had emerged under the peculiar circumstances of plantation life. Although Samuel Preston and his colleagues have taken us "beneath the surface of census" data to reveal dimensions of marital relations that were not apparent in earlier published reports, there are still aspects of these relations that even the most detailed census data cannot portray. What is needed are fine-grained ethnographic materials. Fortunately, these do exist.

What they show is that the ex-slave population did indeed make remarkable efforts to overcome the worst aspects of the systematic assault on gender roles, especially those of father and husband. Slavery left all Afro-Americans with gender attitudes and reproductive strategies that were vulnerable to socioeconomic circumstances; hence, the dualism laid down during slavery would continue as a result of varying economic circumstances.

As early as 1937, on the basis of his detailed psychoethnographic studies of a typical Southern town, the psychologist John Dollard could write:

> It is unmistakable that middle-class Negroes have different conceptions of their roles from lower-class Negroes, and that these conceptions are nearer to the dominant American middle-class pattern. . . . However it may be among lower-class Negroes, in the life histories of the middle-class group the father plays a considerable role and the mother does not seem to play a disproportionately important one. The father seems to appear regularly as disciplinarian and as one who stresses restrictive aspects of the culture. It is very likely that families whose children emerge into the middle class have already a tradition and discipline which is superior to the mine run of lower-class Negroes, and, further, that the family form tends to approximate the white patriarchal type."[95]

In this passage we read a world of progress and effort, but we also detect the lingering shadows of the past. Afro-American men reacted in two ways to the sociological mutilation of slavery. The lower-class reaction, which Dollard clearly distinguished and delineated in the thirties, and which is still very much with us, was to embrace, both defiantly and tomishly, the very role the Euro-American aggressor had forced upon them. The resulting anger and self-loathing found expression inwardly in the high incidence of depression among lower-class Afro-American men, both in the rural

South and in the modern ghetto,[96] and outwardly in violence against other Afro-American men as well as sexual aggression against women. Significantly, the sexual aggression against women did not stop at mere compulsive sexuality; rather, we find throughout the decades of the rural South, and throughout the underclass today, the vicious desire to impregnate and abandon women, as if Afro-American men were unable to shake off the one gender role of value (to the master) thrust upon them during slavery, that of progenitors. Dollard, so much closer to the period of slavery than we are, was in no doubt that the aggressive and "disproportionate" sexuality of the lower-class Afro-Americans he observed and interviewed in the South was "a feature of [their] permissive slave culture."[97] Recent historical work has supported Dollard's viewpoint.

Why would lower-class men—and a not insignificant number of men from other classes—perpetuate a tradition of sexuality that had such horrible origins and associations? One can only speculate that there is something in this self-destructive pattern of sexual behavior that smacks of the counterphobic attraction of a drug addict to the drug he once deeply feared and loathed. As Heinz Kohut wrote: "He cannot overcome the original fear, and so he continuously covers it up, to himself and to the judging social surrounding, by proving not only that he is not afraid of it but that, on the contrary, he loves it. Little Hans has become a jockey."[98] The sexually predatory under- and lower-class Afro-American men studied as early as the 1880s by W. E. B. Du Bois would appear to idealize what once dehumanized them, to internalize what once externalized them as mere sexual objects, and to invest their manhood in the very thing that once emasculated them. Little Black Sambo had become a "badass" dude.

But working- and middle-class Afro-Americans did not escape unscathed. From Dollard's observations in the thirties, it was already obvious what one of the problems inherited from the past would be: Afro-American male-dominance ideology. Where the lower-class Afro-American reacted to the trauma of the past by pathologically internalizing the perverse role assigned him, with all its destructive consequences, the middle-class Afro-American reacted in two ways. One was a healthy venting of his anger against the Euro-American oppressor in social and political action, on both the individual and the collective levels, often at great risk to himself, since he was always outnumbered and outgunned. Afro-American radicalism and the achievement of civil rights, full citizenship, and racial dignity against all odds, by men as well as women, must rank as one of the greatest episodes in the modern history of freedom.

The other kind of reaction was more problematic. In casting off the hateful gender role assigned to the Afro-American man, middle-class Afro-Americans both positively and negatively identified with the Euro-American paternalistic male role. This is understandable since the latter role was the only other cultural model available. The more conservative, positive identification took the form of an internalization of the Southern Euro-American male's ideal for his relationship with Euro-American women. The middle-class Afro-American strove to outdo the "best" that Euro-American elite men had to offer their own women. That "best" ideology, of course, was to spell trouble for Afro-American women, as it had for Southern elite Euro-American women, for it was nothing other than the courtly tradition of genteel male dominance. The Afro-American woman was to be protected, to be cherished, even to be placed on a pedestal; and Afro-American men could graciously pay lip service to equality as long as women knew and kept their place in the exercise of power both in and out of the household. But as we will see, unlike Euro-American women, Afro-American women have refused to conform to this genteel paternalistic tradition either in their attitudes or in their behavior.

It is remarkable that this pattern of imitative patriarchal behavior and the resulting gender conflicts with independent-minded Afro-American women were already evident among the free Northern Afro-Americans of the early nineteenth century. As Horton shows, Afro-American women were systematically excluded from the public spheres of politics and religious leadership by their Afro-American male counterparts, who slavishly modeled gender attitudes on Euro-American bourgeois norms. As with the majority Euro-American group, "manhood and freedom were tied to personal power," which within the household meant power over wives, who were expected to be models of female rectitude:

> All women were expected to defer to men, but for Afro-American women deference was a racial imperative. Slavery and racism sought the emasculation of Afro-American men. Afro-American people sought to counter such effect. Part of the responsibility of Afro-American men was to "act like a man," and part of the responsibility of Afro-American women was to "encourage and support the manhood of our men. . . . [She must] never intimidate him [the black man] with her knowledge or common sense, [but] let him feel stable and dominant."[99]

Then, as now, gender realities were inconsistent with these patriarchal ideals. Not only did early-nineteenth-century Afro-American women vigorously protest their exclusion from positions of public leadership, but their relatively greater economic independence then, as now, meant that middle-class Afro-American women could effectively prevent men from actualizing their gender stereotypes. To the degree that they conformed to the role expectations of the times, it was largely of their own choosing, and one doubts how emotionally attached they were to these outward shows of bourgeois female behavior.

But there was also a negative assimilation of the Euro-American oppressor's gender ideal. Here, the middle-class Afro-American man angrily rejected that ideal as a model, claiming that nothing good could come from an oppressor so vile. What replaced the Euro-American paternalistic ideal, however, was not a counterideal of genuine gender equality, but the male-dominance ideology and double standard to be discussed later.

Sometimes male dominance has been rationalized as part of a nationalistic ideology of "nigrescence" or Africanness, sometimes as a dangerous pseudoradical expression of unity with the lower-class brothers through a glorification of their pathological hip-hop sexuality. This tragic embourgeoisement of lower-class promiscuity has been encouraged, on the one hand, by the fact that many of the leading figures in the Afro-American radical movement themselves came up from the lower classes—Eldridge Cleaver and his execrable *Soul on Ice* is the most notorious case in point— and, on the other hand, by the fact that Afro-American "race"-leaders of middle- or solidly working-class backgrounds have, in their partly guilt-driven, partly self-interested desire for solidarity with the most oppressed Afro-Americans, found it psychologically only too easy to reject the courtly paternalism of their own fathers. Whatever its source, the ideology of masculinity has spelled even more trouble and contradiction for middle-class Afro-American women.

THE PRESENT CRISIS OF MARRIAGE AND DIVORCE

MARRIAGE OR A STABLE PARTNERSHIP is the most important gender relationship for all adult Americans, including Afro-Americans. It is necessary to repeat this seemingly obvious fact because of the number of misguided statements to the contrary coming from defensive advocates of single parents and of those pursuing alternate lifestyles. Without implying any judgment about these alternative modes of behavior, it will be useful to begin by stating in clear sociological terms the reasons for the centrality of marriage and marriagelike gender relations for society. I can do no better than to quote at length from an important 1977 study of the subject by the sociologists Paul Amato and Alan Booth:

> Establishing satisfying long-term intimate relationships is one of the main challenges of early adulthood. Emotionally close and supportive relationships are critical because they contribute to people's sense of well-being and mental health. In the United States, as well as in a variety of other societies, married individuals report greater happiness, exhibit fewer signs of depression and anxiety, engage in less risk-taking behavior, and live longer than do single individuals. Marriage is advantageous because people provide emotional support to their spouses and discourage their spouses from engaging in risky behavior. Marriage also provides economic benefits to men as well as to women; compared with single people, married people have higher household incomes and benefit from economies of scale. Although people with a high level of psychological and economic well-being are more likely to be selected into marriage, research strongly suggests that marriage *causes* many of these benefits."[100]

Americans still strongly value the institution of marriage. In the Harvard/ *Washington Post*/Kaiser Family Foundation (HWPK) national survey conducted late in 1997, people were asked how they evaluated the importance of having a "successful marriage." Eighty-six percent of Americans responded that this was either "the most important" or a "very important" goal in their lives. By wide margins, marriage ranked above all but one other goal as the "most important" in people's lives, that being the desire to be a "good parent." This should surprise no one. However, what I want to emphasize is that there were no significant gender or ethnic differences in responses to this question; 82 percent of Afro-Americans, like 88 percent of Euro-Americans, reported that having a successful marriage and being a good parent were their two most important goals. There was virtually no difference between Afro-American men and women on this score; 83 percent of men and 82 percent of women agreed.

Acknowledging and even strongly and sincerely believing in a goal or ideal is one thing; actualizing and living by it quite another. It is when we consider the realities of marriage that we find enormous conflict and even turmoil, especially among Afro-Americans. As most Americans know by now, marital and broader familial patterns underwent considerable change following the Second World War. While remaining fully committed to marriage, Americans have increasingly had problems confining themselves to the same marital partners. The result has been what sociologist Andrew Cherlin refers to as "the roller-coaster pattern of rapid change in marriage and divorce" since the fifties, bringing in its wake dramatic shifts in the composition of households and families and the structure of kinship and affinal ties.[101]

It is important to view the crisis among Afro-Americans within this broader national context. As in so many other respects, the problems of Afro-Americans are partly what may be called trend setting, partly group specific, and partly an interaction between these two. This point is fundamental for the argument that follows, so let me elaborate. When I say that the problems of Afro-Americans are partly trend setting, what I mean is that in many respects they are similar to those found among Euro-Americans except that they tend to be at the extreme leading end of emerging problem trends in the society.

Marriage, household, and fertility patterns well illustrate this. The declining marriage rate, increasing divorce rate, increasing rate of female-headed families, and rising rate of teenage pregnancy that are beginning to beset and alarm Euro-Americans have long been experienced by Afro-Americans. Indeed, the Euro-American trend seems to trail the Afro-American by about fifteen years or so. To take one example to which I will return later, during the late sixties, within two years of the dissolution of their first marriages, 52 percent of Euro-American women had remarried (see figures 17A and 17B). By then, however, Afro-American women were already experiencing a marriage-gap crisis, in that it took them five years for 52 percent to remarry. Fifteen to twenty years after the mid-sixties, during the period 1980–1984, we found Euro-American women in almost exactly the same position as Afro-American women were during the late sixties; it now took five years for 50 percent of them to remarry. We could illustrate the same point from data on teenage fertility and out-of-wedlock trends, as well as trends in the proportion of households headed by single women. Most other analysts have found the same similarities.[102]

Having emphasized the error of identifying a problem as peculiarly Afro-American when it is not, I must now point to the equally serious error of failing to recognize group-specific dimensions of Afro-American problems where they exist: those arising from the very distinctive history of ethnic persecution and centuries-long economic discrimination suffered by the group. Here are some of the distinctively Afro-American features of these trends over the course of this century.

First, the timing of marriage among Afro-Americans has always differed from that among Euro-Americans. As we already pointed out, during the half a century between the last decade of the nineteenth century and 1940, Afro-Americans tended to marry at earlier ages than Euro-Americans. All this changed during the forties. After about 1950, Euro-American women began to marry earlier while Afro-American women married later, resulting in a post-sixties reversal in which the proportion of single Afro-American women significantly exceeded that of single Euro-American women.[103]

Second, there has been a sizable decline in the marriage rate of Afro-American men since the forties. In 1940 the overall marriage rate of Afro-American men under twenty-four exceeded that of their Euro-American counterparts, as did the percentage of Afro-American men under thirty who were married. After 1950 the rate at which Afro-American men married plunged, although it still remains significantly higher than that for Afro-American women.[104]

Third, marital disruption rates have always been unusually high among Afro-Americans, a phenomenon to which I will return later.

Perhaps the most important group-specific problem of Afro-Americans is the fact that the roles of father and husband are very weakly institutionalized, possibly the worst heritage of the slave past. This is not to say that Afro-Americans do not value or idealize marriage and parenting; as I already pointed out, they do. But to repeat what was said then, idealizing something does not mean that one has the means or commitment to achieve it. We all cherish the ideal of altruism but rarely behave accordingly. As already explained, Afro-Americans had their cultural scripts for the roles of father and husband destroyed and were never quite able to redefine them.

Marriage and Cohabitation

Just how bad is the present crisis in marital relations? Let us be candid right up front. The situation is already grim, but it is certain to get worse before improving.

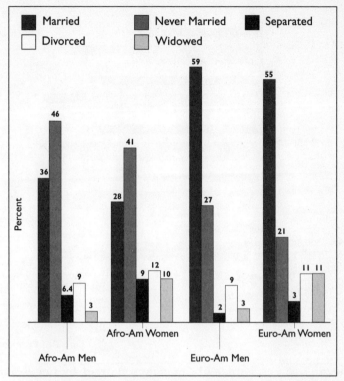

FIGURE **1.13. Marital Status of Persons over 15, by Gender and Ethnicity, March 1997.** SOURCE: Author's tabulation of data from U.S. Bureau of the Census (Internet release, July 1998).

Figure 1.13 summarizes the most recent gross data on the overall pattern for the entire population over fifteen as of March 1996. What strikes us most is the unpartnered state of the Afro-American population. The majority of both men and women are single. Among those who are single, the percentage who have never married is unusually high. Afro-American men are the most likely never to have been married, and Afro-American women are more than twice as likely as Euro-American women never to have been.

As disturbing as these figures are, they actually understate the extent of the problem, as we see when we turn to Figure 1.14, which reports age-specific rates for 1996. During the critical years in the life cycle from the mid-twenties to the mid-thirties the majority of Americans have already entered marital relationships, some more than once. However, fewer than 32 percent of Afro-Americans of either sex are married during this period.

An important difference between Afro-American men and women emerges during their forties. Starting in the mid-forties and for the re-

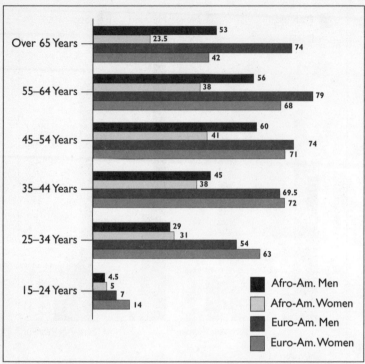

FIGURE 1.14. Percentage of Americans Married, by Age Group, Ethnicity, and Gender, 1996. SOURCE: Author's tabulation of data from U.S. Bureau of the Census (Internet release, July 1998).

mainder of their lives, a majority of Afro-American men are married, although in ratios still well below those of other groups in the population. During this period, however, a declining proportion of Afro-American women are married. A similar decline occurs among Euro-American women, although their marriage rates remain some twenty to thirty percent higher than those of Afro-American women. These trends are partly due to the demographic fact that women survive men at growing rates during these later years and to the higher marriage rates of older men, but these are only a part of the explanation, especially among Afro-Americans.

The unmarried state of Afro-American women in the prime of life is the end result of a trend that emerged earlier in the century but escalated from the sixties onward. Figure 1.15 shows that nearly two-thirds of the Afro-American women born as late as the second half of the 1940s had husbands when they were between forty and forty-four years old. The no-

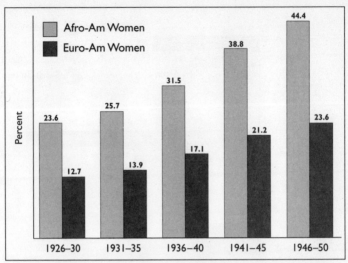

FIGURE 1.15: Percentage of Unmarried Women at Age 40–44, by Birth Cohort and Ethnicity. NOTE: Unmarried women are defined as "single, widowed, and divorced." SOURCE: Author's tabulation of data from J. J. Ventura, "Births to Unmarried Mothers: United States 1980–1992," U.S. National Center for Health Statistics, *Vital and Health Statistics,* Series 21, No. 53 (Washington, D.C.: Center for Disease Control, 1995).

ticeable decline seen in Figure 1.14 came with generations born in the sixties and after.

How do we explain these changes? In purely demographic terms, they are obviously the joint result of changes in the propensity of Afro-Americans to marry in the first place, of the growing rate at which marriages are disrupted when Afro-Americans do get married, and of the declining tendency to remarry after separation and divorce. Robert Mare and Christopher Winship attribute most of these changes to the declining marriage rate (including the rate of remarriage).[105] While this is correct, it is important to be aware that the rate of marital disruption among Afro-Americans is easily underestimated for two reasons. The first is that Afro-Americans tend, to a far greater degree than Euro-Americans, to terminate their marriages with separation rather than divorce, partly because of the expense of the divorce process. A second reason is that, as we have already seen, historically Afro-American women have tended to disguise their divorces as widowhood.

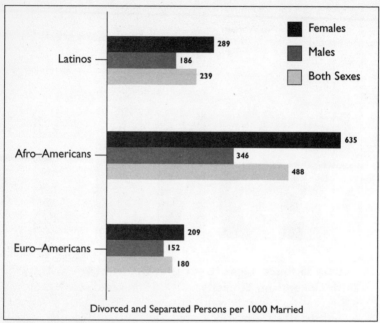

FIGURE 1.16. Marital Disruption Ratios, by Gender and Ethnicity, 1995. SOURCE: Author's tabulation of data from U.S. Bureau of the Census, *Current Population Reports: Marital Status and Living Arrangements, March 1995* (Update) (P20-491, 1996).

In Figure 1.16 I have calculated the marital disruption rate as the number of divorced and separated persons for every one thousand married persons, a popular measure recently adopted by the U.S. Census Bureau. Overall, the Afro-American rate is twice that of Latinos and 2.7 times that of Euro-Americans. The gap is even higher for women.

The really important difference between Afro-Americans and the majority population, however, is less in their rates of divorce and more in their disinclination to remarry when their marriages dissolve. Figure 1.17a shows that for all Euro-American women, remarriage rates after the dissolution of first marriages have been going down appreciably since the mid-sixties, but as we observed earlier, the percentages have been much lower, and the rate of change much greater, among Afro-Americans. As shown in Figure 1.17b, as late as the latter half of the sixties, 81 percent of Afro-American women whose first marriages collapsed were eventually remarried, half of them within five years. By the early eighties, only 20 percent of those whose first marriages failed could expect to remarry, and it took many years to do so; after five years, 85 percent of first divorcees remained unmarried.

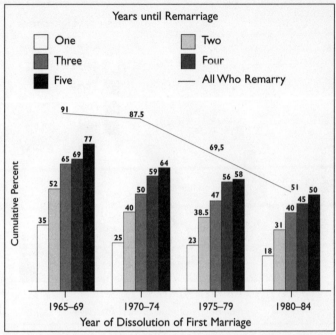

FIGURE 1.17a. First Marriage Dissolution and Years until Remarriage for Euro-American Women, 1988. SOURCE: Author's tabulation of data from National Center for Health Statistics, *Advance Data from Vital Health Statistics, No. 194* (Washington, D.C.: Center for Disease Control, 1997).

It has been estimated that a Euro-American woman can now expect to spend 43 percent of her lifetime in one or more viable marriages, a modest 11-point reduction from the lifetime proportion prevailing at mid-century. The typical Afro-American woman, however, can expect to spend only 22 percent of her lifetime being married.[106] As Andrew Cherlin observes, this is the same proportion of life that the average college-educated person spends at school. He adds: "Marriage has become just a temporary stage of life for blacks, preceded by a lengthening period of singlehood and followed by a long period of living without a spouse. Some of that time is commonly spent in cohabiting relationships, but these relationships tend to be relatively short."[107]

Demographic explanations of these troubling developments merely beg the question. We want to know why Afro-Americans are refusing to get married even while insisting with all sincerity that they highly value the relationship; why, when they do get married, their marriages collapse at such unusual rates; and why they choose to remain single when the social,

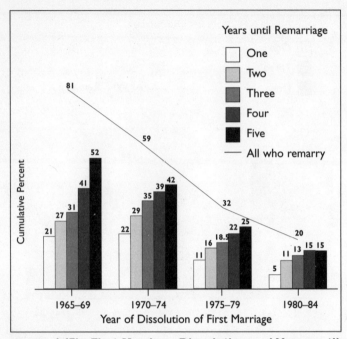

FIGURE **1.17b. First Marriage Dissolution and Years until Remarriage for Afro-American Women, 1988.** SOURCE: National Center for Health Statistics, *Advance Data from Vital and Health Statistics, No. 194* (Washington, D.C.: Center for Disease Control, 1997).

psychological, and economic rewards of marriage or stable partnering are, especially in their case, so substantial.

The most frequently cited explanations for both the present state of affairs and the trends leading up to it are summarized by Mare and Winship under three heads: the "male marriage pool" argument of William Julius Wilson; the "female independence" thesis; and their own "school enrollment" hypothesis.[108] Wilson's by now familiar argument is that the Afro-American marriage rates have deteriorated since the seventies because of the declining job prospects of Afro-American men, especially young Afro-American men, at a time when most Americans are entering their first marriages. Low labor-force participation has also encouraged illegal behavior, which results in high rates of incarceration and homicide. These forces, which Wilson ultimately attributes to the unemployment crisis, have created a severe shortage of marriageable men for Afro-American women.[109]

The "female independence" thesis argues that the improved economic situation of women since the fifties, expressed in greater labor-force participation, growing absolute income, and a decline in the wage gap with males, has made all women more independent of men. Women delay marriage in order to pursue their careers or because they do not feel as pressured to secure a marriage early, and when they do get married they are less reluctant to walk away from unhappy circumstances. These changes have been especially marked among Afro-American women, as we have already documented above.[110]

Mare and Winship hypothesize that increased school enrollment accounts for the delay of marriage. Younger Afro-Americans are pursuing their education instead of going directly into the work force and getting married, as they might have done during earlier periods when there were fewer educational opportunities.

As persuasive as they may appear at first sight, none of these explanations adequately accounts for the low and declining marriage rates. Educated and prosperous Afro-American men are no more likely to marry than their poorer counterparts. As for Afro-American women, their improved labor-market prospects tend to work in opposite directions: these prospects make Afro-American women more attractive to potential husbands, but by making them more independent they reduce their inclination to marry or to remain in trying marriages. Both influences seem to cancel each other out. Finally, Mare and Winship were unable to support their own hypothesis regarding increased school enrollment.[111]

My reanalysis of the National Health and Social Life Survey (NHSLS) data not only strongly questions Wilson's economic claims but indicates that the relationship between income and marriage is far more complex than previously thought. There is a modest relationship between individual personal income and the likelihood of ever being married. For Afro-American men, each increase in a seven-category income scale increases the likelihood of ever being married by 53 percent; for Afro-American women, by 77 percent. However, the true relationship between income and the likelihood of ever marrying is curvilinear rather than linear; that is, the two extremes of the income curve behave alike, in contrast with people whose incomes fall in between.

Much to my surprise, I found among all Americans, especially Afro-American men, a strong and significant relationship between being poor and ever being married. Poverty increases the odds of ever marrying almost sevenfold for Afro-American men, and 3.3 times for Afro-American women. Among Euro-Americans I found a similar tendency, although the gender impact is reversed; poverty increases the odds 4.6 times for Euro-American women and by a little over 3 times for Euro-American men.

At the same time, being very well off—with a personal income at least six times the individual poverty level in 1992, when the survey was conducted—has a powerful impact on Afro-American women's likelihood of ever being married; it increases their odds tenfold. High income also strongly influences Euro-Americans, although less dramatically, increasing women's odds nearly sixfold and men's odds two and a half times. The major exception here are Afro-American men; high personal income has no significant impact on their odds of ever being married, just the opposite of Wilson's prediction.

In light of all this, Mare and Winship's basically negative, but important, conclusions make sense: that socioeconomic factors fail to account for all but a small amount of the changes in rates of marriage. Just as important, these already modest effects are relevant only within given years. When residual trends over time are considered (by including the additive effect of time itself), the explanatory power of socioeconomic factors is reduced to near zero. In other words, socioeconomic factors, to the degree that they have any explanatory power, are applicable mainly in cross-sectional analysis within each given year, and are reduced to nonsignificance in explaining changes over time.[112]

How, then, do we explain the changes in marriage rates that have been taking place in the latter half of this century? There are many issues involved, and they interact in complex ways. No wholly sufficient explanation is possible at this time, for the simple reason that marriage and gender relations seem to be still going through significant changes due to powerful cultural shifts that are periodic in nature.[113] However, six sets of factors are necessary for any understanding of these changes. These factors often operate differently for men and women.

FIRST, THERE IS WHAT MAY BE CALLED the opportunity structure of marriage. Obviously, the availability of mates sets limits on the possibilities of marriage, although this varies with age and gender. Mate availability is itself largely determined by the sex ratios of different age groups and by the mobility patterns of the different genders.

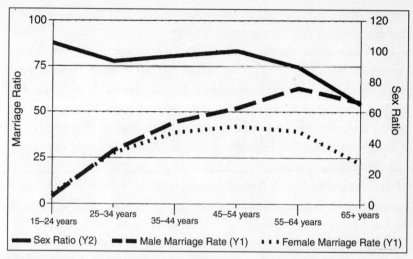

FIGURE 1.18. Age-Specific Sex Ratios and Marriage Rates for Afro-American Men and Women, 1996. NOTE: Sex ratio is number of men per 100 women. The marriage rate here is simply the percent married in a given age-category. SOURCE: Author's tabulation of data from U.S. Bureau of the Census (Internet release, July 1998).

The impact of sex ratios on spouse availability for each age group, but especially the earliest cohort, is influenced by the tendency of women to marry earlier than men. Even so, Figure 1.18 reveals a surprising feature in the relationship between intercohort trends in the sex ratio (the number of men per 100 women) and the marriage rate (measured here simply as the percentage of men or women married in the age group) of Afro-Americans. The high death rate of young Afro-American men (due mainly to homicide) has led many to imagine that there is a low sex ratio in the Afro-American population between ages fifteen and twenty-four. In fact, just the opposite is the case. For the fifteen-to-twenty-four-year cohort, not only is the sex ratio the highest of all cohorts of Afro-Americans—there are 105 men for every 100 women—but it is also the only age group where the ratio is higher than that of Euro-Americans.

The misapprehension about the dearth of young Afro-American males springs from the fact that when we refer to a high death rate for a particular age group, we are always speaking in relative terms. The death rate for young Afro-Americans is indeed inordinately high when compared with those for other American subpopulations and other Afro-American age groups. In 1995 there were 249.2 deaths for every 100,000 youths aged fifteen to twenty-four, which was a little over twice the Euro-American death rate of 122.3 for that age group.[114] Even so, we should not forget that all this means, in more familiar percentile terms, is that under a quarter of 1 percent of young Afro-American men in this age group died that year, compared with about an eighth of 1 percent of Euro-American youths. Idle talk about Afro-American young men being "an endangered species" is mischievous nonsense. And it is simply irresponsible coming from academic social scientists.

Now, what is striking about the marriage rate for this youngest cohort is not the fact that it is low but that it is one in which the marriage rate of Afro-American women is greater than that of Afro-American men (5 percent compared with 4.5 percent). This might suggest that the sex ratio is a factor explaining marital behavior. However, the fact that the female marriage rate remains slightly above the male in the 25–34 age group implies that other factors are at work.

The high sex ratio, in conjunction with the earlier age of entry into vaginal intercourse by Afro-American youth, explains another aspect of Afro-American teenage behavior that has been of great concern to social analysts: the growth of out-of-wedlock births. The median age of first vaginal sex for Afro-American men is fifteen, compared with age seventeen for women. What this combination of factors—more men who start sex earlier and engage in it more frequently—means is that Afro-American women of this youngest cohort have the best marital opportunities of their lives as well as the greatest pressure to engage in sex. A few take advantage of the opportunity to get married, resulting in the higher rate of marriage among young women of this cohort. Others enter into short-term cohabitation, with the inevitably greater risk of pregnancy, while others delay entry into sex. We will return to this subject later, when we consider the intimate relations of Afro-Americans in more detail.

Another major factor determining marital opportunities—class mobility—comes into greater play in these later ages. Wilson, as we have already noted, has, along with others, pointed out the imbalance in mate availability for Afro-American women. We have seen that neither male unemployment nor low income is the major factor explaining this imbalance. Rather, it is the greater mobility, via educational attainment, of

Afro-American women. Since greater educational attainment begins to pay off for women in later years, we find that age, class, and demography interact with gender values to depress both the propensity to marry and the spousal market for women beyond the mid-twenties.

I am not quite sure why the Afro-American sex ratio declines so sharply after age twenty-five, in strong contrast with the Euro-American ratio, which remains above or near parity until the middle of the sixtieth year. This could be the delayed cohort effect of a male mortality surge during the decade between the 1960s and early 1980s, brought about by the higher Afro-American mortality rates in the Vietnam War and later by the scourge of crack, homicide, and the AIDS epidemic. If so, we have already discussed the good news: that there has been full demographic recovery from this earlier decline, reflected in the robust sex ratio of the *current* fifteen-to-twenty-four-year age group.

The bad news is that this demographic bust is having *some* negative effects on the marriage market for older Afro-American women. The greater educational attainment of Afro-American women begins to pay off in their thirties, just when the male demographic decline starts to work its way through the adult life cycle. Thus age, class, demography, and differential gender mobility all interact with negative consequences for the marriage rate.

It is very important, however, not to exaggerate the role of purely demographic or compositional factors in explaining the declining marriage rates among Afro-Americans, especially among the great majority who belong to age groups older or younger than those in their late twenties and early thirties. The question is, just how much do these imbalances explain? In an important study of the best available data sources for answering this question, the sociologists Robert Schoen and James R. Kluegel have persuasively demonstrated that these compositional factors account for only a quarter of the differences between Euro-American and Afro-American marriage rates, that they only apply to women's marriage rates, and that they account "for little to essentially no part of the change in black marriage rates between 1967–1971 and 1979–81."[115] Instead, Schoen and Kluegel explain the differences largely in terms of Afro-Americans' changing propensity, or inclination, to marry. Put in simpler terms, Afro-Americans are getting married less and less because they find available marital options unattractive, or because of incompatible "sex-role ideologies" and expectations between men and women, issues to be considered at greater length later. These factors also apply to Euro-

Americans, but to a much lesser degree. In this sense, Afro-Americans are societal trend-leaders. But the authors rightly conclude that there are also group-specific factors involved, stating that "we must look to forces unique to blacks to account for the large and increasing gap between black and white marriage propensities."[116]

The interactions discussed above frame, but do not determine, the second set of factors to be considered in our explanation of the crisis of marriage and partnering, namely, the expected benefits from marriage.

Two 1992 studies have gone a long way toward filling the previous gap in our knowledge of the perceived benefits of marriage for Afro-Americans.[117] Both found Afro-American men and women to have remarkably different expectations about marriage, which partly explain both the declining tendency to enter it and its fragility when Afro-Americans do marry. Shirley Hatchett partly confirmed earlier claims that Afro-Americans were more instrumental in their attitudes toward marriage than other groups. However, she found that, on average, Afro-American women tended to place emphasis on the instrumental and security aspects of marriage, while Afro-American men expected emotional and expressive rewards from it. It is striking that more than two and a half times as many men as women gave companionship as the main reason for having a relationship: 49 percent of men as against only 19 percent of women. "All in all," comments Hatchett, "black women seem to value the instrumental aspects of marriage—particularly financial security—more than black men. Black men . . . place more emphasis on the socio-emotional aspects of living with the opposite sex."[118] Hatchett believes that this "contradiction," or "lack of fit," between the attitudes of Afro-American men and women exacerbates the marriage squeeze, or shortage of marriageable men.

This contradiction, however, is strongly qualified by age, which was a major finding of Scott J. South's study of the determinants of expected benefits from marriage. At all age levels, Afro-American unmarried men have lower expectations of marriage than do women. Especially when young, they expect less improvement in their general state of happiness, but they grow somewhat more positive on this dimension with age.[119] Younger Afro-American women have far greater expectations than do men about improvement in their standard of living, in their freedom to do what they want, in their level of emotional security, in their sex lives, and in their relations with parents and friends. However, by about their mid-thirties Afro-American women increasingly become disillusioned. Their expectations of happiness from marriage decline steeply, although they never reach the level of pessimism of Afro-American men, whose expectation of overall happiness begins low and stays low throughout their lives.

By their mid-thirties, South found, Afro-American women come to expect less improvement in their standard of living than Afro-American men expect as a result of marriage, reflecting Afro-American women's relatively greater performance in the labor market. Even before reaching thirty, they readjust their expectations of personal freedom, expecting less from marriage beyond this age than do Afro-American men. The same appreciable shift away from optimism is found in their expectations of improved friendships and parental relations. South quite reasonably interprets these findings to mean that "the low rates of marriage among black women appear to be as much a function of black males' reticence to marry as of black females' inability to find attractive mates."[120]

More speculatively, he suggests that the strong gender contrasts in younger Afro-Americans' expectations of marriage may be attributed to their experience growing up in female-headed households. Young women come to value marriage highly, he argues, in order to avoid repeating the hardships of their mothers, whereas young men, having had no male role models, come to see few benefits from marriage. Father-absence certainly has important implications for Afro-American children, but it operates in complicated ways, as we will see shortly.

I have already suggested the main reason why young Afro-American women are more enthusiastic about marriage: the high sex ratio during the fifteen-to-twenty-four-year age group creates a good partner market for them. In addition, young men who drop out of school and begin working, however unpromising their long-term prospects, are financially better off during these early years than women who stay in school and earn little or no income. Young women feel good about marriage during this period because they are in demand sexually, have not yet economically outpaced their male counterparts, and may even be having a good time. By their late twenties, everything changes, and they become more skeptical of both men and marriage.

A surprising omission in South's study is his failure to consider what is perhaps the most important expected benefit of marriage: bearing and rearing children. Shirley Hatchett found that a large percentage of Afro-American respondents (69 percent) felt that marriage was very important for raising children. Afro-American men tended to place a slightly higher emphasis on the reproductive aspect of marriage than did women. This does not mean that Afro-American women valued childbearing less; quite the contrary. Rather, it would seem from Hatchett's study that they were less inclined to give this as a primary reason for marriage. Marriage and childbearing are simply not as closely tied among Afro-American women as they are among other groups.

My analysis of the HWPK data generally supports Hatchett's findings. Afro-American men and women both highly value having children, 99 percent of Afro-American women ranking it as one of the most important activities, or *the* most important activity, in life. And while one finds important differences, depending on marital status, in the value Afro-Americans attribute to marriage, no such differences are to be found in the value they attribute to childbearing.

A third set of factors influencing the marriage rate among Afro-Americans is their premarital behavior. Three kinds of such behavior would seem to influence the likelihood of ever marrying: a person's frequency and pattern of early sexual relations; the experience of cohabitation; and having one or more out-of-wedlock children.

It seems plausible that a pattern of early entry into sex and frequent changes of partners would reduce the tendency to marry. Men and women who have had multiple sexual partners and numerous short-term sexual relationships would appear likely to find marriage too confining. At the same time, those who most desire marriage and the stability it brings may find persons with a too varied or promiscuous past unappealing as potential spouses. There was a fair degree of support for these hunches in the NHSLS data set, which is by far the best body of data collected on this subject since the Kinsey Report. As would be expected, there are significant variations according to ethnicity and gender.

Euro-American women come closest to the conventional expectations about the effects of a varied early sexual record. Very early entry into vaginal intercourse negatively influences the likelihood of ever being married. Euro-American women who had their first vaginal sexual intercourse at age fourteen or younger reduced their odds of ever being married by 54 percent, when income, class, and the other factors in our logistic models are held constant. On the other hand, delaying first vaginal intercourse until age twenty-two or older increased their odds of ever being married by 88 percent. However, it is only very early entry and very late entry into sex that seem to matter. Models that examined the effect for each succeeding year throughout the teens came up with nothing meaningful.

For Euro-American men, early entry into sex did not lower the odds of ever marrying. To the contrary, the number of their short-term sexual relationships positively enhanced those odds; each one that lasted for a month or more doubled the man's likelihood of ever being married. In spite of the prevailing ideology of gender equality, sowing wild oats not only is still acceptable for men but may even be viewed as a desirable quality for Euro-American males.

The Afro-American experience significantly departs from this majority pattern. None of the variables having to do with sexual history had any significant effect on Afro-American men's odds of ever marrying. Afro-American women were different. While the timing of entry into vaginal sex was not as consequential as it was for Euro-American women, it produced an effect in the same direction. For each year that an Afro-American woman delayed entry into sexual intercourse, her odds of ever being married were improved by 15 percent. Far more important, however, was the strongly negative effect of the number of her sexual relationships that lasted for more than a month. Controlling for other factors such as age, income, and religious behavior, each such relationship reduced her odds of ever marrying by 46 percent.

Let's turn now to the effects of cohabitation. Robert Schoen and Dawn Owens have shown that cohabitation increased dramatically with the generation of Americans born after 1950.[121] Most cohabitations are of short duration. While most first cohabiting unions culminate in marriage, it is also the case that women who cohabit in their first unions are less likely to marry. Schoen and Owens found that Afro-American women tend to cohabit at slightly greater rates than other Americans, their cohabitations last a few months longer, and the probability of their cohabitations ending without marriage is substantially higher than for Latinas or Euro-American women. Furthermore, for Afro-American women, especially those born after the mid-1950s, the probability of ever marrying after cohabiting is about half that for Euro-American women and considerably less than for Mexican-Americans.[122]

I used the NHSLS sample to explore the consequences of the timing of first cohabitation. Although I had surmised that this timing would be at least as important as that of first vaginal intercourse, I found it to be insignificant for Euro-American and Afro-American men. It had roughly similar consequences for Euro- and Afro-American women. For the former, each extra year reduced the odds of ever marrying by 19 percent; for the latter, by 24 percent. A modest, but nontrivial, result. There are two ways to interpret it. It could mean that the younger a woman cohabits, the greater the likelihood of marriage. This is consistent with the established fact that most cohabitations end in marriage, even though a woman's odds of marrying if she cohabits are less than if she doesn't. But it could also mean that an unmarried woman who first enters a cohabitation later in life reduces her odds of ever marrying.

Another kind of premarital behavior that negatively influences the likelihood of marrying is out-of-wedlock childbearing. In 1989 Neil G. Bennett, David Bloom, and Patricia Craig found strong support for their conjecture that "a woman who has an out-of-wedlock birth is less likely ever to marry than one who does not."[123] The reasons for this negative relationship were uncovered in a later and more exhaustive study that drew on several data sources.[124] In 1995 Bennett and his associates found that nonmarital childbearing was not caused by women's low expectation of getting married, as had previously been suggested.[125] Most out-of-wedlock first pregnancies were unintended, and surveys of these mothers strongly indicate that the vast majority wanted to get married. Out-of-wedlock childbearing was the cause, not the consequence, of the reduced expectation and likelihood of first marriages.

Unfortunately, Bennett and his collaborators were unable to identify the main reasons for this effect, although they did rule out or qualify some of the more obvious explanations. Thus, being on welfare reduced further an unmarried mother's chances of getting married. However, this was not due to any reduced incentive to get married as a result of being on welfare but, possibly, to "diminished marriageability of welfare mothers; a relatively low interest in marriage among potential male partners, who themselves may suffer a loss of resources with the cessation of AFDC payments" (at least up until recent reforms in the welfare system); "or a shortage of marriageable men in communities with a high concentration of welfare mothers."[126]

While the presence of children reduced the likelihood of marriage, the authors found no evidence that the amount of time spent on child rearing significantly reduced what they called "marriage market activities," that is, time available for finding a husband. I find this hard to believe. My own ethnographic work among the largely unmarried poor of Kingston, Jamaica, suggests that time availability is important, although it operates in ways too complex to be captured in a regression model. What I found was that conscientious and attractive women who would normally be good prospects for marriage were the ones most likely to take their child-rearing responsibilities seriously and hence were indeed at a disadvantage in the amount of time available to search for a husband. Less responsible mothers, good-timers and other "gal-gal" types who neglected their maternal responsibilities in order to increase the amount of time they had to search for a husband, were the ones least likely to attract one, although they were more likely to find a cohabitant or end up in what Jamaicans call a "friending" relationship. If the same is true of poor urban Afro-Americans, one can easily see how these tendencies cancel each other out in regression models that rely on simple measures of social and labor-market activities.

Another possible explanation of the negative effect of nonmarital childbearing on the likelihood of first marriage, one too hastily dismissed by Bennett and his collaborators, is the role of stigma.[127] The authors found no evidence that out-of-wedlock childbearing turned potential husbands off. This, again, I find hard to believe. The authors themselves qualify their own negative finding by suggesting that stigma may be important during the period before out-of-wedlock mothers reenter the marriage market. My own ethnographic research, again in urban Jamaica, which might or might not be relevant to America, is that there is no such period before reentry into the marriage market. To the contrary, a woman who has an out-of-wedlock baby with an irresponsible father often feels compelled to find a man to help her out as soon as possible. This makes her especially vulnerable to the more predatory men in her community, with the result that she often ends up with yet another unwanted pregnancy and an even lower chance of ever marrying.

It is true that young women themselves, especially the urban poor, feel little or no sense of stigma or shame in having a baby out of wedlock, as was once the case. Up to the end of the 1950s, young women who became pregnant put great, and usually successful, pressure on the fathers of their babies to marry them. This changed with the sexual revolution that came with the sixties. Sara McLanahan and Gary Sandefur think it "likely that the daughters of single mothers were leaders in this respect, since they had a better understanding of how single mothers cope with their situation."[128]

For Afro-American young women, a worst-case scenario may have developed since the sixties. Their own sense of shame and of feeling stigmatized in having a child out of wedlock may have declined at a much faster rate than did the perception of stigma by the men whom they expected to marry. Indeed, these same men, while continuing to devalue women who had children out of wedlock, encouraged these women's "liberated" post-sixties view of out-of-wedlock childbearing by pretending to be themselves more "liberated" than they really were. They knew how to talk the sixties fast-talk. And they exploited it so as to make it easier to seduce and impregnate their willing victims.

Closely related to this is the tendency of some women with out-of-wedlock children to too hastily enter into cohabitations in the hope that they will culminate in marriage. Such cohabitations run the greatest risk of ending without marriage. To make matters worse, a pattern I found among poor urban women of Jamaica who enter cohabitations with what is called on the island "an outside child" seems to occur here also, namely, a tendency to quickly have a baby with the cohabitant. The woman does so for two reasons: in the hope of cementing the new relationship, and with the expectation that making the cohabitant a proud "father" will undo his qualms about supporting and bringing up another man's child.

Unfortunately, these calculations usually have just the opposite effect. Poor men burdened with two or more children, only one of whom is their own, are most at risk of deserting their partners. Again, I have no strong evidence that any of this applies to America, although another finding of Bennett and his associates suggests that it might: among unmarried mothers, cohabitation was found to a certain extent to be a substitute for marriage.[129] Other work tends to confirm this. Thus Ronald Rindfuss and Audrey VandenHeuvel conclude that cohabitation has increasingly become an alternative to being single, rather than a precursor to marriage, in America and further that "the rise of cohabitation implies that individuals will have a greater number of lifetime sexual partners. Further, contrary to earlier expectations, the rise in cohabitation implies an increase in union dissolution rates."[130]

There is evidence, too, that some stigma is still attached to cohabitation, especially among Afro-Americans. James Sweet and Larry Bumpass found: "Groups that are likely to be facing the greatest economic uncertainty (blacks and those with 12 years of education or less) are most likely to approve of cohabitation when there are plans to marry and least likely to approve when there are not." They add that "this is consistent with the view that marriage is the preferred state, but when it is not feasible, cohabitation is acceptable."[131] All this suggests that, at the very least, it is rash to dismiss stigma out of hand as a factor explaining the observed negative effects of premarital childbearing on the likelihood of first marriage.

One other factor derived from my fieldwork experience might also apply to America; indeed, I would be amazed if it did not. It is the simple, stark fact that among the poor, childbearing and single parenting make young women less physically attractive to potential spouses. A young unmarried mother has less time and money to make herself attractive. Among the poor in particular, giving birth is often associated with health complications that sometimes leave women less shapely and attractive to young men when compared with women who do not have children. And the physical act of rearing a young infant or two without the help of a spouse, or regular day care, leaves women very tired and at a disadvantage in competition with childless young women on the marriage market.

Whatever the reasons for the relationship, Bennett and his collaborators have certainly demonstrated with a fair level of confidence that out-of-wedlock childbearing has a crushingly negative effect on the likelihood of ever marrying. These factors operate with special force among Afro-American women, although there is a major class difference, the practice being primarily a lower- and underclass phenomenon.

I examined what the marital consequences of having an out-of-wedlock first child were for the national sample of Americans surveyed by the NHSLS research team. For Afro-American women, there was no significant impact, which is itself substantively very important. But for Afro-American men as well as Euro-American men and women, there were strong and highly significant effects. Among Afro-American men, the odds of ever marrying were increased fivefold by having a first child out of wedlock; for Euro-American women, they were increased three times; and for Euro-American men, nineteen and a half times. This last, extreme effect reveals exactly what is going on. For many Americans, a first child out of wedlock initiates a delayed form of shotgun wedding. Where, in earlier times, a lover's pregnancy prompted hasty wedding plans, in our age couples feel little stigma, waiting until after the baby arrives to get married. However, most couples still feel an obligation to legitimate their childbearing. These results suggest that most American cohabiting couples who have a baby end up marrying each other.

It is really not surprising that Afro-American men share in this pattern of behavior. Recall that, apart from the very youngest age group, Afro-American men have substantially higher marriage rates than Afro-American women in spite of the overall, long-term downward trend in these rates. Afro-Americans have not stopped marrying; rather, they are doing so at declining rates.

It is important to understand the subcultural context within which all this is taking place, especially among the poorer classes. Young men signal their intention to get serious about women by cohabiting with them and getting them pregnant. The big difference with Afro-American men, however, is that the birth of a child does not seal an informal contract to marry the mother. However, it does increase the man's propensity to marry "the right person" when she comes along, preferably one he has not first cohabited with or gotten pregnant. The first pregnancy becomes a rite of passage into manhood and a sort of trial run at fatherhood. Afro-American men are less and less inclined to marry the first woman to bear their children because, among other reasons, (1) there are no economic incentives to do so, as was the case on the sharecropping farms; (2) communal pressures that formerly forced them to honor implicit contracts have collapsed in the ghettoes; and (3) in some cases because the young women themselves do not wish to marry them—partly because of the macho culture of the streets; partly because of not being brought up in homes that instilled the rightness of such actions; and partly because of pressure from their own female kinsmen, especially their mothers, not to marry.

This pattern of behavior has unfortunate consequences for most young Afro-American women who get caught up in it. Some of them do get married. Indeed, we have already seen that in the youngest age cohort more women marry than men. But at a very low overall level. The fact that having a baby out of wedlock has no effect on Afro-American women's likelihood of ever getting married should not be hailed as a signal that such behavior is nondetrimental or even benign. Rather, it should be seen within the broader national context in which having an out-of-wedlock baby in a cohabiting relationship triples the likelihood that the mother will eventually marry, usually to the father of her first child. Seen within this context, the absence of any effect from being an unwed mother is a severe disadvantage for Afro-American women.

These findings fly in the face of a much-cited claim by the economists A. T. Geronimus and S. Korenman that teenage childbearing, as opposed to postponing pregnancy, has no comparative disadvantage for Afro-American and other poor women.[132] This dangerously wrongheaded work, cloaked in the rhetoric of econometrics, has fast become a standard source for misguided Euro-American liberals and Afro-American academics only too eager to defend the self-injuring misjudgments of the urban poor. We begin to grasp the intellectual and moral damage when we read what even so eminent a scholar as Alice S. Rossi has said, on the basis of Geronimus and Korenman's work: "To urge African-American teenage girls to postpone sexual initiation and pregnancies to an older age is shortsighted and neglects the fact that such postponement does not necessarily improve an African-American woman's life chances or even assure greater maternal health."[133] This is liberal nonsense, the most thoughtless statement ever written by this otherwise wise and extremely distinguished scholar. It is also hypocritical, as a moment's self-reflection by these scholars on their own experiences growing up as middle-class women—and on those of young female kinsmen and friends, rich, poor, or mobile—would immediately attest. The young women whose marital and reproductive misjudgments are so misguidedly defended may be Afro-American and poor, but they are Americans too, and however "bounded" the rationalities of their actions, they have a right not to be urged to bound their choices further.

Ontogenic factors clearly play some part in a person's propensity to marry, as well as in the likelihood of marital stability. G. Elder's theory of role transition suggests that a person's inclination to engage in, as well as his or her capacity to adequately perform, roles such as those of husband, wife, and parent depends on the extent to which he or she has rehearsed these roles in the course of growing up. Such rehearsals are obviously based on the person's own parental role models.[134]

However, the ways in which one's experiences growing up influence one's propensity to marry are very complex and vary from one ethnic group to another, not to mention between classes within ethnic groups. In general, it has been found that for those born after the early fifties, being brought up by a single parent increases the likelihood of educational problems and teen childbearing, especially for women, although the effect on early marriage seems contradictory.[135] While this holds true for Euro-Americans, especially middle-class children, McLanahan and Sandefur have found that "the consequences of family disruption are *smaller* for disadvantaged black and Hispanic children than for disadvantaged white children."[136]

My analysis of the NHSLS data only partly supports these earlier findings. The type of family in which Euro-American women grew up, and whether their parents divorce or not, has no effect on their odds of ever being married. For Euro-American men, however, growing up with a single mother reduces the odds of ever marrying by 63 percent, and parental divorce reduces these odds by 70 percent.

The effects differs strikingly for Afro-Americans. I was surprised to find that while single parenting has no significant effect one way or the other on Afro-Americans, growing up with both of one's own natural parents appears to reduce the odds of Afro-American women's ever marrying.

How do we explain this? The answer is partly hidden in my other surprising finding about the relationship between Afro-American women's family of orientation and their odds of ever being married: growing up with two adults, one of whom is a natural parent (usually the mother) and the other a stepparent *increases* these odds sevenfold. I will have far more to say about this in the next part, "Gender Attitudes, Ideology, and Perceptions," because this strange result gets to the heart of what I consider the most fundamental social tragedy of Afro-Americans: the fragility of their gender relations, especially that most important of all such relations, the conjugal. Briefly, the explanation seems to be this. The fragility and tension among Afro-American couples may be resolved in divorce, accounting for the high divorce rate among them. Or the couple may choose to stick it out, "for the sake of the children" or for whatever other reason. The evidence is now quite convincing that the worst possible situation for a child is to be brought up by parents who constantly bicker but insist on staying with each other, especially when the relationship is being maintained for the children. I suspect that this is what explains the negative impact on Afro-American women. The experience of their natural parents' marriage strongly reduces their propensity to marry. Why does this not have the same effect on boys? We'll get to that shortly.

On the other hand, if the parents divorce, the mother has two options. She may remain single. This condition, as we have seen, has no effect one way or the other on the daughter's propensity to marry. However, should the mother remarry, it is likely that the new relationship will be less fraught than that between the natural father and mother. Even if it is not, it is less likely that parental tensions will be translated into conflicts with the daughter. A woman cannot choose the match between her daughter's natural father and the daughter nature deals her, but she can so choose in the case of a stepfather. Afro-American mothers are known to have a very close and empathetic relationship with their daughters, one that would be reinforced by divorce. So there is a strong likelihood that stepfather-stepdaughter compatibility would be an important factor in any remarriage. Hence the sevenfold increase in the marriage odds of Afro-American women brought up by a mother and stepfather.

This explanation and the results it seeks to illuminate are consistent with McLanahan and Sandefur's finding that "living in a stepfamily at age sixteen was more advantageous for blacks than for whites."[137] Their explanation emphasizes the economic and social resources, as well as the "role models and direct supervision," that come with stepparenting. While these may be important in explaining, in general, children's educational outcomes and propensity to marry, they do not explain, in the case of Afro-American female children, the stark differences between stepfamilies and families with two natural parents.

For Afro-American male children it all works differently. As with Afro-American girls, being brought up in a single-female family has no effect on the odds of ever being married. But for the boys, unlike the girls, being brought up in a stepfamily has no effect while being brought up by both natural parents increases the odds 2.8 times. I think the overriding factor here is the presence of the natural father. It is not that parental conflicts have no effects on boys' propensity to marry; rather, the strong effects of a natural paternal presence largely overcome the negative effects of parental conflicts for Afro-American boys.

The reasons for this are not necessarily happy ones. If the main source of the conflict is the father's philandering or abuse of the mother (as is often the case), this is likely to have a more crushing effect on the daughters' propensity to marry than on the sons'. The girl identifies with her mother and is mortified by her father's behavior, taking it as a warning to be wary of marriage. The boy identifies with his father and comes to accept his behavior as the way men and husbands behave. He may even interpret his father's perseverance in the marriage as a strong signal that "real" men not only get married but stay married, even if it means putting the wife in her place from time to time. The result is that the odds of ever being married are increased more than two and three quarters times. But accompanying these odds is an equally increased propensity to replicate the father's marital behavior.

Cultural factors are also critical for any understanding of why people get married. These include broad societal changes in attitudes toward marriage and divorce; changes in sex-role stereotypes and expectations (to be

discussed in the next part); and changing cultural practices such as religious beliefs and behavior.

I have little to add to what has already been written on the subject of
broad cultural changes. Ronald Inglehart has amassed considerable evidence demonstrating that a profound cultural shift has taken place in
America and other industrial societies since the sixties and that a major
component of this change concerns attitudes toward divorce, marriage and
sex-role beliefs.[138] Arland Thornton has attempted to show that these
changing attitudes have had profound consequences for the normative status of marriage and the family in the United States.[139] It has also been argued by some conservative thinkers that the marital and familial behaviors
of Afro-Americans have been negatively, and more than ordinarily, influenced by these changes.[140]

One aspect of cultural behavior that is of special relevance to Afro-
Americans is their religion. In view of the centrality of the church for
Afro-Americans, it is surprising that the relationship between religion and
marriage has not been explored more by social scientists. Afro-Americans
remain among the most ardent churchgoers in the nation. Fifty-one percent of Afro-American men go to church at least once a month, compared
with 37 percent of Euro-American men and 39 percent of Latino men.
Among women, 65 percent of Afro-Americans go to church at least once
per month, compared with 49 percent of Euro-American women and 54
percent of Latinas.

The correlation between churchgoing and marrying is significantly
higher for Afro-Americans than for Euro-Americans. Alas, going to church
once a month is not enough to affect the odds of ever being married, at least
not for Afro-Americans. The NHSLS data indicate that Afro-Americans
need to go to church at least once a week for the Lord to have any influence
on their odds of marrying. Unfortunately, only 31 percent of Afro-
American men keep the faith weekly or more often, compared with 43 percent of Afro-American women. What's more, although still high compared
with those of other men, the numbers are declining as Afro-American men
join the trend toward secularism. In 1992 it was already the case that nearly
half of all Afro-American men (49.4 percent) either never went to church
or did so only a few times yearly. This is very bad sociological news when it
is considered that the Afro-American church has, for so long, stood between
chaos and community, nihilism and hope.

My analyses show that going to church weekly more than doubles Afro-
American women's odds of ever setting married, but in none of the better-

fitting logistic models I tested was Afro-American men's religious behavior remotely significant.[141] It is noteworthy that churchgoing in no way influences Euro-Americans' odds of ever marrying. This is not to say that churchgoing is not important in their lives. Quite apart from the fact that they are more secular than Afro-Americans, marriage is so much more institutionalized, and the propensity to marry so much greater, that the added push of religion is not needed to encourage entry into marriage.

It may be objected that churchgoing is as much a consequence as a cause of ever marrying. This is certainly a possibility, but I think that it is more cause than consequence. Marriage, it is true, almost exactly doubles the likelihood for weekly churchgoing among both sexes of Afro-Americans: from 19 to 38 percent for men, and from 28 to 55 percent for women. But this is almost entirely due to selection factors; people who are religious in the first place are more inclined to marry. The more important point to note about these figures is that the very significant difference in churchgoing behavior between Afro-American men and Afro-American women does not change with marriage.[142] This suggests that marriage has no personal-relational effect on weekly churchgoing behavior. Otherwise, we would see some movement toward a convergence of the percentages of men and women.

Why does religiosity double Afro-American women's likelihood of marrying but have no effect on men? The answer points to interesting gender differences in sex-role expectations that we will examine at greater length below. Whatever their expressed pretensions to a liberated view of sex, when they come to marry, Afro-American men clearly prefer what they consider a "good" woman. Weekly churchgoing by a woman signals all the desired qualities in a bride, including the very high probability that she has not had many or any sexual partners. On the other hand, I suspect that religiosity works in opposing directions in its effects on an Afro-American man's appeal. It signals stability, as well as desirable attitudes toward work, parental responsibility, and so on. But it may also send the wrong message to less intensely Afro-American women: that the man harbors somewhat biblical male chauvinist views, especially the "black Baptist" version, which might be a turnoff for Afro-American women with very independent gender attitudes. Or, worse, weekly churchgoing may signal a lack of the kind of masculinity that Afro-American women prefer. This is especially true for younger, lower-class women who, as we will see below, tend to send mixed sexual messages to young suitors. These two sets of signals cancel each other out. However, the main factor at play may simply be that a large and increasing proportion of Afro-American men are simply not going to church. Hence religion, while remaining an important marital signal for women, is declining or absent as an indicator of marital potential for men.

Nonconforming behavior and a generally oppositional attitude toward societal norms might also influence a person's likelihood of ever marrying. Elijah Anderson claims that the most influential new male role model emerging in the Afro-American inner cities is "at best indifferent to the law and traditional values . . . derides family values and has a 'string' of women."[143] One simple indicator of nonconformism is provided by the NHSLS data: whether or not a person has ever spent a night in jail. It is now well known that a disproportionate number of Afro-American men in their twenties end up under the supervision of the criminal justice system—nearly a third of them in any given day in 1995, according to one report.[144] While the horribly unfair drug-sentencing guidelines of the nation's courts partly account for the high rate of incarceration, not even the most defensive advocate denies that the main reason for it is the tendency to commit more illegal acts.

Below I will have more to say about the oppositional, "cool pose" culture, but for now I merely wish to explore the degree to which a commitment to it influences Afro-American men's propensity to marry. I found that a night ever spent in jail reduces their odds of ever marrying by 76 percent. It is interesting to note that a night ever spent in jail has no effect on the marriage odds of Euro-American or Latino men, or for that matter on those of any group of women. This is not due to the fact that other groups have far less familiarity with a night in jail. While 31 percent of all Afro-American men in 1992 had spent at least a night in jail, 21 percent of all Euro-American men and, more tellingly, 42 percent of all Latino men had done so. The fact that this experience predicts the odds of marriage only for Afro-American men strongly suggests that for them the experience is indicative of a nonconforming, oppositional syndrome that devalues marriage. And it cannot be argued that oppositional behavior is merely a reflection of poverty, age, family form, or father-absence, since my models controlled for all these factors.

Divorce and Separation

Not only are Afro-Americans marrying each other at declining rates, but as we have seen, their marriages are extremely fragile and dissolve at greater rates than those of other groups. Why is this?

Since the sixties, Afro-Americans have experienced the same cultural changes, mentioned earlier, that have eroded the normative pressures against divorce for other Americans. While it would be idle to dispute the reality of these cultural changes, there remains a serious question of causal direction. Thus, Andrew Cherlin has cogently argued that "changes in attitude toward divorce *followed* changes in divorce behavior." He suspects that the initial rise in divorce during the sixties was due to factors other than attitude, chief among them being women's increased labor-force participation, and "that the rise in divorce may have prompted people to begin to reassess their attitudes."[145] Of course, once this reassessment took place, the newly established attitudes then became causal. This argument is well taken for the population at large, but there is a complication in regard to Afro-Americans, among whom women have always participated in the labor market at unusually high rates. Market forces partly account for the high Afro-American divorce rate but cannot explain the *increase* in recent decades.

Social scientists who emphasize the life-cycle approach have identified other predictors of divorce. Early marriage is one of the strongest.[146] Others have found that children from higher-income families—or, at any rate, families with resources to help them as they enter adulthood and marriage—tend to have happier marriages and lower divorce rates.[147] This effect is partly mediated by the greater likelihood that children from such families will marry later and thus have better resources and education themselves, which, in turn, lower the risk of divorce.[148] Several studies have found that parental divorce increases the risk of the parents' offspring divorcing, although less so for Afro-Americans than others.[149] Paul Amato and Alan Booth found that it increases by 76 percent, with the odds greatest when one's parents divorce during one's teenage and early adult years rather than before one reaches the age of twelve. They reasoned that this is because (1) children of divorced parents have less negative attitudes toward divorce and are consequently less committed to the value of marriage as a lifelong relationship; (2) the products of high-tension marriages tend, themselves, to have poor interpersonal skills; and (3) some of these children tend to marry early in order to get away from the parental home. However, they were unable to support the view that parental divorce has anything to do with the quality of the children's marriages.[150]

Amato and Booth also found that children of mothers who work full-time and of parents with "non-traditional" gender attitudes are more likely to see their own marriages end in divorce. The risk, they claimed, is stronger for women because daughters from such homes tend to have far higher expectations of their spouses than do sons. They concluded that "high expectations for marriage, and mixed restrictions on divorce, work together to erode marital satisfaction and elevate divorce to record highs that are unlikely to subside in the future."[151]

My analysis of the NHSLS data offers only partial support for some of these earlier findings and reveals distinct causal patterns for men and women as well as Euro-Americans and Afro-Americans. Being poor substantially reduces the risk of divorce and separation for men and women in both groups. Controlling for other factors, poverty reduces the risk of marital disruption by 77 percent for Euro-American men, by about 60 percent for Euro-American women, and by about 90 percent for Afro-Americans. Since it is well established that divorce results in lower income and hence increases the risk of poverty, especially for women, it may well be that it is the anticipated descent into greater poverty that accounts for the lowered likelihood of the poor disrupting their unions. The legal costs of divorce and the tendency of the poor to avoid having anything to do with the courts are important contributing factors, especially among Afro-Americans.

While the nonpoor face higher risks of divorce, income does not have a simple linear effect on the odds of divorce. People in the highest-income category also divorce less, partly because they have more to lose, but also possibly because they marry later and hence choose their spouses more carefully. Among Euro-American men, upper-middle-class status reduces the risk of divorce to almost exactly the same degree as does poverty.

Another important cause of divorce or separation common to all subgroups is infidelity. First, let's be clear about the state of infidelity in the nation. Americans are, on the whole, surprisingly faithful sexually to their spouses; only 19 percent of Americans who have ever been married claim to have had an extramarital sexual relationship. Overall, the differences among the major ethnic groups are significant[152] but not that great; 13 percent of Latinos, 19 percent of Euro-Americans, and 27 percent of Afro-Americans have been unfaithful.

But important differences emerge when we look at the gender impact of this factor within groups. Women not only are more faithful than men but vary less from each other across subgroups; 15 percent of Euro-American women who have ever been married have been unfaithful, compared with 18 percent of Afro-American women and 7 percent of Latinas. The difference between Afro-American and Euro-American women is, in fact, not important.[153] Among men, however, there are sizable variations:

23 percent of Euro-American, 28 percent of Latino, and 44 percent of Afro-American men have been unfaithful to their wives.

The higher rate of poverty among Afro-Americans does not explain this gap. Among Euro-Americans the poor are more maritally faithful than the nonpoor, but among Afro-Americans the poor and nonpoor are adulterous at exactly the same rate (30 percent for each group). There is a slightly greater tendency for poor than for nonpoor Afro-American and Latino men to be unfaithful, but these differences are unimportant, as are those between the poor and nonpoor among Euro-American and Afro-American women. Only among Euro-American men and Latinas does poverty matter. Nonpoor Euro-American men are twice as likely to be unfaithful as their poorer brothers. And poor Latinas, a faithful lot by any standard (only 14 percent have ever done it), are seven times more likely to be unfaithful than their unusually faithful nonpoor sisters.

It has been suggested that the low sex ratio among most cohorts of Afro-Americans largely explains the greater tendency toward male marital infidelity and disruption.[154] There is some truth to this, especially among middle-class Afro-American men. The large pool of marriageable women—the obverse of the female marriage squeeze—not only is a constant source of temptation for married men but heightens the probability that when discord arises in a marriage, as it inevitably does, men will leave their current wives for other women. The cry for help from a distraught wife, published in the *Essence* advice column of the Afro-American psychologist Dr. Gwen Goldsby Grant, may not be uncommon: "My husband is a successful attorney who is constantly the object of sexual advances from women who find him attractive. I get angry and feel totally out of control. How can I learn to handle my jealousy?"[155]

The tendency toward male marital infidelity is intensified by the fact that so many middle-class Afro-American women not only work full-time but, as we have seen, often earn incomes much closer to the median male Afro-American income than Euro-American women do. Consequently, the economic cost of divorce—traditionally a major disincentive—is likely to be much lower for middle-class Afro-American men than for their Euro-American counterparts. Where, for example, the typical middle-class Euro-American male is likely to lose his home and all its comforts upon divorce, and must start all over again, the middle-class Afro-American divorced male can usually walk straight into the welcoming home of his career-established future wife or cohabitant. Afro-American men between thirty-five and forty-four in fact remain divorced, widowed, or separated at a substantially lower rate than Afro-American women of the same age group—only 21 percent, compared with 37 percent for Afro-American women in 1996.[156]

Nonetheless, it is important not to exaggerate the significance of sex ratios in explaining infidelity or marital mores generally. As Richard Posner eruditely observes, scholars such as Marcia Guttentag and Paul Secord who place excessive explanatory weight on the sex ratio would have to predict similar sexual mores among the ancient Greeks and Jews, both of whom had chronically high sex ratios but hardly similar sexual practices or attitudes.[157] We can make the same point with less exotic data. The NHSLS survey shows that the rate of infidelity and cheating in early relationships and cohabitations is no different among Afro-American men between fifteen and twenty-four years of age, in spite of the much lower sex ratio of that cohort.

With this backdrop, we can now examine the effect of infidelity on the odds of marital disruption. Marital unfaithfulness on the part of Euro-American men increases the risk of breakup by 86 percent, but infidelity by Euro-American women increases it more than fivefold. This is clear evidence that aspects of the old double standard continue among Euro-Americans.

It is also alive and well among Afro-American men, as we will see later, but Afro-American women are obviously far less forgiving than Euro-American women. Infidelity by Afro-American women increases the odds of divorce 3.78 times; but it also increases the odds 3.24 times among Afro-American men. In other words, all other factors held constant, Afro-American women get rid of unfaithful spouses almost as frequently as their menfolk do.

Working for income strongly predicts women's likelihood of divorce, as nearly all previous scholars have attested. It more than triples the odds of divorce for Euro-American women and doubles them for Afro-Americans. Of course, divorce itself is likely to increase a woman's odds of working, so the causal effect goes both ways. However, the historical evidence is incontestable that employment, by making women more financially independent, lowers the cost of leaving an unhappy marriage.

Having a first child out of wedlock has no effect on men's odds of marital disruption. However, it more than halves the odds of divorce for both Euro-American and Afro-American women. One explanation for this is that there is a greater chance of poorer women having children out of wedlock. Hence, a higher proportion of wives with first children born out of wedlock would be poor. This, in turn, would reduce the likelihood of divorce, since, as we have seen, poorer people tend to disrupt their marriages less. Women who have had a first child out of wedlock may also feel that their chances of remarriage are lower. Therefore, they may choose to stick to the known evil in a less-than-happy union. Emotional factors may also be part of the explanation. Women who bear their first child out of wedlock may have more vulnerable, less resilient types of personalities with higher thresholds of tolerance for unsatisfactory relationships.

Education affects women's experience of divorce in contradictory ways. On the one hand, it cultivates more attractive personalities and adds to women's earning power, which makes them not only more desirable as potential spouses but also less likely to be divorced by their husbands in situations of marital conflict. On the other hand, by making women more independent, it increases their propensity to leave unhappy marriages. Among Euro-American women surveyed by the NHSLS team, each level of education between grade school and college increased the odds of divorce by 38 percent. Among Afro-American women, the opposing effects of education cancel themselves out. Highly educated, well-off women and poorly educated, economically poor women both have low odds of divorce or separation from their spouses (that is, when they *do* marry). For women between these two extremes, the female-independence factor cancels out the tendency of Afro-American men not to divorce women with better education and, presumably, better earning capacity.

Cohabitation, as I have already pointed out, has become an important alternative to marriage for some Americans, even as it continues to be a precursor to the institution for many. Whatever the motivations for entering it, Ronald Rindfuss and Audrey VandenHeuvel are probably right in their prediction that "the rise of cohabitation implies an increase in union dissolution rates" and that this "is likely to be the case for cohabiting unions themselves as well as for cohabiting unions that become marriages," with the result that "the rise in cohabitation could have a feedback effect on the institution of marriage, further weakening its central foundation of permanence."[158]

My analysis of the NHSLS data shows that each cohabitation lasting for more than a month that a person has engaged in influences the odds of divorce for Afro-American men and women and Euro-American men, but not for Euro-American women. It has the strongest effect on Afro-American men, for whom each such cohabitation more than doubles the odds (220 percent) of being divorced. Each such cohabitation increases the odds by 44 percent for Afro-American women and by 27 percent for Euro-

American men. The much lower impact on Euro-American men and the absence of any effect on Euro-American women strongly suggest that co-habitation is more a precursor to marriage for Euro-Americans whereas it is mainly an alternative to marriage for Afro-Americans.

In fact, 59 percent of Euro-American men's and 66 percent of Euro-American women's first cohabitations end in marriage, in contrast with only 38 percent of Afro-American men's and 49 percent of Afro-American women's. If cohabitation is a precursor to a marriage that would take place anyway, then it is likely to have only a modest impact, if any, on the like-lihood of marital disruption. However, if a couple is committed to co-habitation as a desirable alternative to marriage, one would expect a greater likelihood of marital disruption if they convert their cohabitation to marriage under parental or general normative pressures, or to legiti-mate the status of an offspring.

In this regard, it is interesting that Afro-American women are the only subgroup for whom each year of delaying their first vaginal intercourse in-creases their odds of divorce. We have already seen that delaying their first intercourse also increases their odds of ever marrying. One interpretation of this is that Afro-American women who delay entry into sex are more inclined, and perhaps better able, to pressure Afro-American men, who would normally prefer cohabitation, to reluctantly enter into marital unions, thereby increasing the likelihood of marriage but, by the same token, the likelihood of being left by husbands unable or unwilling to cope with the demands of marriage.

Family type does not significantly affect children's odds of divorcing. As I have already pointed out, growing up with badly conflicted parents is more damaging than growing up with a stable, loving remarried couple. I have also noted that a parental divorce that occurs early in children's lives has fewer consequences for them emotionally, for the quality of their mar-riages, and for their risks of divorce than one that occurs when they are teenagers or young adults.

Afro-American men are the exception. For them, as indicated by the NHSLS survey, growing up with both natural parents triples the odds of marital disruption. I have already shown that this same factor increases their odds of ever marrying by 278 percent (in striking contrast with Afro-American women's odds of marrying, which it lowers dramatically), and I argued then that this has to do with the presence of the natural father, al-ways a powerful factor for Afro-American men. However, the fact that the natural father's presence so strongly predicts divorce for Afro-American men is strong indirect evidence of the conflictual nature of Afro-American marriages. What seems to be going on here is an intergenerational transmission of poor marital quality, in this case male conjugal behavior, along the lines definitively demonstrated by Amato and Booth in their recent study.[159]

Researchers have come to conflicting conclusions about the influence of parental divorce on offsprings' propensity to divorce. Euro-American women were the only subgroup I examined whose odds of divorce or separation were influenced by whether or not their parents had divorced. Controlling for socioeconomic and other factors, parental divorce increased the odds of Euro-American women's own marriage breaking up by 67 percent. This is reassuringly close to the odds of 76 percent found by Amato and Booth in their study conducted between 1980 and 1995, although they imply that the effect held for both genders.[160]

Similarly, research on the effects of parental educational attainment on offspring's odds of divorce or separation has come up with inconsistent results. One research team found that the daughters of less-educated mothers, especially mothers on welfare, are more prone to divorce.[161] Amato and Booth could not replicate this, but they found some evidence indicating that having a better-educated father lowers the risk of divorce for both sons and daughters.[162] In my examination of the NHSLS data I found no indication that paternal education influences the risk of divorce in any way, but persuasive evidence that maternal education is important, although in opposing directions for different subgroups. For Euro-American men, having a better-educated mother had a modest and questionable positive impact on the odds of divorce, increasing it by about 13 percent. The effect was in the same direction for Afro-American men, only stronger, increasing their odds of marital disruption by 40 percent.

The effects were quite different for women. If their mothers went to college, Afro-American women's odds of divorce increased nearly elevenfold (by 10.79 times), but Euro-American women's odds decreased by almost 50 percent. To complicate matters further, among Afro-American women whose mothers had not gone to college—the vast majority—the odds of divorce were reduced by half with each additional level of education their mothers attained.

How do we explain these results? It could be that the sons of better-educated women come to expect more from their wives than the latter are able to deliver or to put up with. This is consistent with the well established fact that men tend to marry spouses less educated than they are. In other words, men with better-educated mothers who marry women less educated than themselves are asking for marital failure, especially if—as is true of many Afro-American men—they want a wife just like Mama.

The small but growing minority of Afro-American women whose mothers went to college are likely to have been brought up by mothers with extremely progressive gender-role expectations and very egalitarian expectations of spouses. Given the long-established tradition of labor force participation by Afro-American women of all levels of education, we would also expect these mothers to be economically independent. It could be argued that the daughters of such women are likely themselves to be well educated and earning relatively high incomes and that it is these factors that either directly account for the daughters' greater odds of divorce or, at least, mediate the influence of their mothers. However, we have already seen that this is not the case. Education has no effect on the odds of divorce, perhaps because it operates simultaneously in opposite directions, and higher income *reduces* the odds of divorce. Hence, by a process of elimination, we must conclude that it is the mothers' values that are influencing the daughters' greater odds of divorce. These values operate indirectly through their inculcation into the daughters while growing up, and directly in the mothers' support for, or lack of active opposition to, the daughters' decisions to divorce or separate from problematic spouses.

The situation is different with Euro-American women, among whom going to college has been a practice of long standing. Class seems to be the decisive factor here. Euro-American mothers with a college education are likely to rear middle-class daughters who tend to marry later and would be encouraged to do so by their mothers.

Euro-American mothers are also less likely to support a daughter's decision to divorce than are their Afro-American counterparts. In his revealing analysis of the National Survey of Families and Households, conducted between 1987 and 1988, Scott J. South found that as Euro-American women grow older, their expectation that their standard of living will improve from being married rises substantially and surpasses even that of Euro-American men, who likewise grow more optimistic about the material rewards of marriage.[163] This strikingly contrasts with the expectation of Afro-American women, who are the only subgroup of women or men who feel that the economic benefits of marriage will decline with age. Indeed, by about age thirty-three Afro-American women perceive fewer material benefits from marriage than do Afro-American men. Afro-American women are also unique in being the only subgroup who, as they grow older, expect the level and quality of their friendships to decline as a result of being married. In addition, like Euro-American women, they expect their levels of overall happiness, personal freedom, and emotional security to fall the older they get, except that the descent from youthful optimism about marriage is steeper among them.[164]

In other words, of all the subgroups of women studied, Afro-American women begin their adult lives with the highest levels of optimism concerning the emotional, relational, and economic rewards of marriage, but by about their thirtieth birthday they have already become the most pessimistic on every measure of marital benefits, and their pessimism worsens with each passing year. In light of all this, it is easier to understand why having a mother with a college education so powerfully influences their odds of divorce. The level of pessimism about the returns from marriage would be greatest among such mothers at precisely the age in life when their daughters would be turning to them for advice about marital problems. Afro-American mothers with less than a college education have far less influence on their daughters' odds of divorcing, and in the opposite direction. It is likely that, for better-off working-class Afro-American mothers, however much their youthful optimism about marriage may have waned, the material and social benefits of staying married would outweigh other factors. Therefore, they would be likely to urge their daughters to patch things up with their spouses, as they might have done, rather than separate or divorce.

The detailed questioning of respondents about their sexual histories by the NHSLS team allows us to examine the effect of child abuse on the odds of divorce. One of the worst consequences of childhood sexual abuse is its deleterious effects on the quality of intimate relationships for the victims when they grow up. Most victims of child abuse survive their trauma and manage to establish healthy relationships with their partners and children, but a disproportionate number of adults who abuse their own spouses have had a history of being victims of sexual abuse themselves. If it is true that there is an intergenerational transmission of child abuse, one might reasonably expect this to have adverse effects on the victim's marriage, not only as a result of conflicts over the treatment of the couple's children but because of the greater likelihood of abusive marital relationships.[165]

Respondents were asked whether or not they had been sexually touched by someone before puberty. Because responses to this question are highly correlated with those to other questions on childhood sexual abuse, I used it for this part of my analysis. Only for Euro-American women and Afro-American men did childhood sexual abuse influence the odds of marital disruption, although in opposing directions; it reduced the odds by nearly half for the former, but increased them three and a half times for the latter. The experience may make Euro-American women more emotionally needy, more vulnerable and submissive, and more willing to put up with unhappy marriages. If it occurred within a context of interparental abuse, such daughters may grow up with a high threshold for conflictual marriages and hence a low propensity to divorce or leave abusive spouses.

In the case of Afro-American men, the psychosocial dynamics would obviously differ, for both gender and ethnic reasons. Men who are abused as boys tend to be sexually abusive themselves. Childhood abuse, unless treated, is likely to generate cynicism and instability in intimate relations. The presence of a father would no doubt mitigate these negative effects (assuming that the father was not the abuser), but there is no such presence for many Afro-American boys. The result is that they grow up into men who have difficulty with intimate relationships, especially in marriage.

Moving now to the role of religion, it is interesting that Afro-American men in the NHSLS sample are the only subgroup for whom going to church on a weekly basis lowers the odds of divorce. Earlier we saw that this practice, while important in increasing Afro-American women's odds of marrying, has no effect on the marriage rate of Afro-American men. However, for those Afro-American men who do marry and are religious—alas, only a minority—going to church regularly reduces the odds of marital disruption by 84 percent, other factors being constant. Unlike with marriage, we need not concern ourselves here with the problem of causal direction. While it is not unreasonable to argue that being married increases the likelihood of going to church, it makes little sense to claim that a lowered propensity to get divorced will send a man to church.

But why does churchgoing not affect Afro-American women's odds of divorcing? As I argued earlier, piety may make an Afro-American, or for that matter any other, more attractive as a potential spouse. But it is likely to work in opposing directions once she becomes one. The very qualities that attracted her husband at first—her sexual decorum, her conscientiousness, her high moral standards—may become problems a few years into the marriage. They might cause her to become disillusioned should her husband turn out to have a roving eye or fail in other ways to live up to her marital and moral expectations. And these same qualities might also be disillusioning for him if they prevented her from meeting his sexual needs. For many sexually demanding men, piety in a woman increases their initial demand for her as greatly as it subsequently diminishes returns, a contradiction with unhappy consequences for any union. But not all men allow their sexual needs to obscure the virtues of a pious woman, and not all pious women lack passion in bed. So churchiness in Afro-American women is likely to influence their marriage in both directions and hence ends up having no net effect on their odds of marital disruption.

Finally, there is the NHSLS finding that a night in jail, and all that it entails, increases the odds of marital disruption for Euro-American men. This is so for obvious reasons. Such men are likely to be too nonconformist and problematic to submit to the social and interpersonal demands of marriage. It is very likely that the same applies to Afro-American men, but so few of those who have been to jail ever bother to get married that the numbers are not there in our sample to calculate any meaningful odds of disruption.

GENDER ATTITUDES, IDEOLOGIES, AND PERCEPTIONS

THE MAINLY STRUCTURAL FACTORS we have examined so far cannot sufficiently explain the far lower rates of marriage and higher rates of marital discord and dissolution among Afro-Americans. Nor do they sufficiently address the broader problem of gender relations, especially those occurring outside of marriage. To better understand what is going on, we must take a closer look at Afro-Americans' attitudes toward, and the actual distribution of power in, the interpersonal relations of Afro-American couples.

A frequently expressed view is that Afro-American women have among the most liberated attitudes toward gender equality in the nation. Historical racial discrimination, this argument goes, and recent efforts to alleviate the racist past have combined to produce in Afro-American women a strong sense of their own worth and capacities. In an exquisite Rousseauian twist, racism and class oppression have forced Afro-American women to be free.

Paralleling this line of argument is the view that the same forces that have unwittingly liberated Afro-American women have both constrained Afro-American men and generated a compensating male-macho mentality. The civil rights and Afro-American identity struggles have had a major impact on Afro-American men's *ethnic* self-esteem—"black pride" and all that—but have only marginally influenced their personal self-esteem and may have encouraged them to develop negative gender attitudes.[166] Indeed, many Afro-American feminists contend that radical Afro-American men, by equating Euro-American domination with castration and emasculation, have come to identify freedom with manhood and sexual domination. In the process, bell hooks argues, these men have taken over the sexual metaphor of freedom from the very oppressors they claimed to be fighting, forging a bond with them: "They shared the patriarchal belief that revolutionary struggle was really about the erect phallus."[167] And Patricia Hill Collins, drawing on a long line of Afro-American women writers, states flatly: "Some African-American men feel they cannot be men unless they dominate a Black woman." The most militant group of Afro-American men, those belonging to the Nation of Islam, openly acknowledge an extreme sexist view and have persuaded the women who belong to their group that this is in the best interest of the "race," as the incredible diatribe by Shahrazadi Ali, *The Blackman's Guide to Understanding the Blackwoman,* attests.[168]

But the Nation of Islam is a small minority of Afro-American men. And while the literary and autobiographical sources favored by Afro-American feminists are suggestive and valuable in their own right, one must examine how their assertions about Afro-American men stand up to less-subjective and more-representative data.

One of the earliest sociological studies based on national samples—from the seventies—supported many of the assertions of Afro-American feminists about Afro-American men, but found no evidence for the "'already liberated' black female."[169] On political and economic issues, there were few differences between Euro-American and Afro-American women except that more well-to-do Afro-American women tended to hold more traditional gender views than their Euro-American counterparts.

There were major differences between Afro-American men and Euro-American men. While generally supportive of women working, Afro-American men were found to be more traditional than Euro-American men, especially in their views on a woman's place in the home and on the question of "the emotional suitability of women in politics." Ransford and Miller also found that, like middle-class Afro-American women, middle-class Afro-American men were far more traditional in their views than middle-class Euro-Americans, whereas working- and lower-class Afro-American men (or those who so defined themselves) tended to differ far less from their Euro-American class equals. What is more, although growing up with a working mother had a liberalizing effect on Euro-American men, it had no such effect on Afro-American men.

Ransford and Miller concluded that their findings were consistent with the view that Afro-American women had "a stronger tradition of autonomy and independence [than Euro-American women], but that experience did not take them all the way to a feminist outlook," at least not to a radically defined one. Autonomy for Afro-American women meant economic self-sufficiency, reliability, and trust, but might "not carry all the way to a general critique of women's traditional roles."[170]

Ransford and Miller's study is useful as a baseline, but it used a limited number of questions and, as mentioned earlier, was based on data from the seventies. Gender views are more complex than the questions allowed and have undoubtedly changed since then.

It now seems clear that there is no single domain of gender attitudes. I propose to distinguish broadly between five domains of such attitudes: the *public* domain, pertaining to work, politics, and civil society; the *domestic*, having to do with male-female roles and relationships in the home; the *public-domestic interface*, which includes the relationship between work and home life; the *global*, which refers to gender relations in general, the significance of gender in one's life, and one's perceptions and evaluations of the changes that have taken place in these relations; and the *intimate*, concerning sexual and related forms of intergender relations. Studies by others, and my own analyses, suggest that one may be progressive, even radical in one domain, yet be moderate and even conservative in another. And this turns out to be particularly true of Afro-Americans, among whom ethnic issues interact with personal ones to create unexpected patterns of gender attitudes.

Regarding the public domain, Emily Kane has persuasively shown that not only are Afro-American women the most radical gender group in their critique of gender stratification at the workplace and in the public sector generally but there is far greater agreement between Afro-American men and women in this area than is found between their Euro-American counterparts. She concludes:

> Being black is associated with greater criticism of the gendered status quo. Especially among men; this attitude draws them closer to black women. Being a woman is associated with greater criticism, especially among whites; this attitude draws white women farther from white men and leads to greater disagreement among whites. As a result, white men are left as the least critical group, black men and white women occupy the middle of the criticism hierarchy, and black women are generally the most critical.[171]

She found, further, that ethnicity (what she calls "race") is more important than gender in explaining agreement on the need for radical social
policy regarding gender; that ethnicity and gender have about equal explanatory power in accounting for agreement on attitudes toward work;
and that gender is more singularly at play in understanding "home-related
issues." On these "home-related issues"—the main part of what I refer to
as the domestic domain of gender attitudes—it turns out that Afro-
American women are generally more conservative than Euro-American
women. Kane endorses Patricia Hill Collins' view that this "reflects [on
the part of Afro-American women] a more positive and more strength-
oriented image of women's role in reproduction and child-rearing."[172]

My own findings, based on my reanalysis of the HWPK survey, generally support Kane's. Figure 1.19 and Table 1.1 report in greater detail typical responses to a set of questions relating to careers and the workplace.
On almost every question pertaining to gender discrimination in the economic and educational sector, Afro-American women either lead in saying that gender discrimination exists or are statistically tied with
whichever other group is most critical of the status quo. This is true of
their views on getting a college education and getting into graduate
schools, even though, as we have already seen, they are way ahead of Afro-
American men in both enrollment and completed degrees.

Afro-American women's attitudes about gender discrimination sometimes reflect a general ethnic position (i.e., they agree with Afro-American
men); at other times, a gender position (i.e., they disagree with men of all
ethnic groups); and at still other times, an interaction of ethnicity and
gender. On whether or not women face discrimination in obtaining a college education, Afro-American women's view that they do is largely an
ethnic position shared with Afro-American men. There are no intraethnic
gender disagreements on this issue; women and men differ in their views
along strictly ethnic lines, with Euro-Americans least critical of the status
quo, Afro-Americans most critical, and Latinos in between.

Regarding women's access to graduate and professional schools, we find
a nearly similar pattern, except that there is now an intraethnic gender disagreement among Euro-Americans. Euro-American women are still significantly less critical of the status quo than are Afro-American women, but
they also differ with Euro-American men, who are, again, the least critical.

On the question of whether women are discriminated against in obtaining executive jobs, we find Afro-American women taking mainly a gender
position. Indeed, the percentile gap between them and Afro-American men

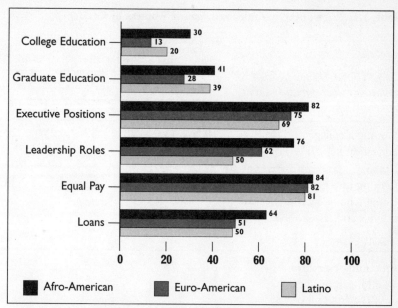

FIGURE 1.19. Percentage of Female Respondents Saying There Is Gender Discrimination in Selected Areas, by Ethnicity, 1997. NOTE: Ethnic differences statistically significant at under .05 levels only for college and graduate education. SOURCE: Author's tabulation from HWPK data.

is virtually the same as the gap that separates Euro-American men and women. The only reason why this gap is not statistically significant is the smaller sample size for Afro-American women. There are no interethnic disagreements on this issue; all three ethnic groups are in general agreement that women face discrimination in getting executive jobs.

Gender is also foremost in explaining the position of Afro-American women on the issue of whether women are discriminated against in being given leadership responsibility over mixed groups of men and women. Afro-American women not only are the most radical critics on this score but differ most with the men of their own ethnic group.

Afro-American women also take a gender position on discrimination against women in the military and on getting equal pay for similar work. In all three ethnic groups, we find important disagreements between men and women on these issues. There is an unusual level of agreement among men across ethnic lines and similarly among women.

The only issue on which Euro-Americans are more critical of the treatment women receive than are Afro-Americans is the matter of obtaining

Table 1.1   Views on Discrimination against Women, by Gender.

QUESTION: *Do you feel that women are discriminated against or not in:*	Euro-Americans % "Yes"		Afro-Americans % "Yes"		Latinos % "Yes"	
	M	W	M	W	M	W
Getting a college education (*E, M, W*)	10.5	13	28	32	25	23
Getting into graduate professional schools such as medical schools and law schools (*E, G, M*)	19 *	28 *	37	43	31	34
Obtaining executive positions in business (*G*)	61 *	75 *	72	85	61	64
Being given leadership responsibility in groups with both men and women (*E, G*)	49 *	62 *	61	75	64.5	67
Obtaining loans and mortgages on their own (*G, M*)	42 *	51 *	18	39	19	22
Obtaining top jobs in the military (*G*)	65 *	82 *	80	79	68	76
Getting equal salaries with men for doing similar work (*G*)	67 *	82 *	69	83	59 *	80 *

NOTES:
*   male-female differences within this ethnic group are significant at under .05 p-level
E   overall inter-ethnic differences are significant at the .05 p-level
M   inter-ethnic differences between men are significant at the .05 p-level
W   inter-ethnic differences between women are significant at the .05 p-level
G   overall gender differences are significant (regardless of ethnicity) at the .05 p-level.
SOURCE: Computed from Harvard/*Washington Post*/Kaiser survey data, 1997.

loans and mortgages. This may seem odd in light of recent public furor over the ethnic biases of the nation's mortgage industry. The results are understandable, however, in view of the much higher rate of home ownership among Euro-Americans and this issue's greater salience in their lives. Presumably Euro-American women make more frequent efforts than minority women to obtain loans, resulting in more experiences of rejection, even if the *rate* of rejection is less for them than for minority women. Ironically, Euro-American men are more than twice as critical of lending practices toward women as are men from minority groups, even though they are significantly less critical than Euro-American women. Presumably Euro-American men get involved with this issue because of their much higher marriage rates and hence more frequent joint ownership of homes. Having their joint mortgage applications, or applications by their wives or cohabiting female partners, rejected because of financial prejudices about the stability of wives' income sources would be a radicalizing experience for them to a far greater degree than it would for minority men and women among whom home ownership is yet to become an economic rite of passage.

Looking now at Table 1.2, we find a similar range of gender and ethnic positions in response to the question why there are very few women in top-level executive and professional jobs. For Afro-Americans, ethnicity trumps gender in the acceptance and rejection of various explanations for the glass ceiling. If we look only at what Afro-Americans give as the major reason for this ceiling, they would seem, again, to be the most liberal group. But a closer look at the full range or responses suggests a more nuanced set of attitudinal differences between ethnic groups and genders. Afro-Americans are less inclined to reject outright some of the more conservative explanations. It is surprising that less than half of Afro-American women reject the view that men are better suited emotionally to be executives and that only 18 percent oppose the statement that women are likely to bring to the workplace personal and family problems that interfere with their job performance. What these responses suggest is that Afro-Americans more radically favor political and educational explanations ("men don't want women to get ahead" or "inadequate training") than do the other two ethnic groups but also are more willing to entertain, at least as a minor factor, naturalistic explanations having to do with gender dispositions.

All things considered, though, we find very little gender disagreement among Afro-Americans on the question of women's role in the workplace.

Table 1.2   Reasons Given for "Glass Ceiling" in the Workplace.

QUESTION: *As you may know, though women have moved into the work force in great numbers, very few top level executive and professional positions in this country are filled by women. Here is a list of some of the possible reasons. For each one, please tell me whether you think it is (A) a major reason, (B) a minor reason, or (C) not a reason.*

		Euro-Americans		Afro-Americans		Latinos	
		M %	W %	M %	W %	M %	W %
"Men don't want women	(A)	40	56	67	70	53	71
to get ahead in the	(B)	39	31	25	22	28	24
workplace" (*E, M*)	(C)	22	12	8	8	19	4
		*	*			(**)	(**)
"Most men are better	(A)	12	13	17	10	25	22
suited emotionally to be	(B)	31	29	44	45	22	27
executives than most	(C)	57	58	39	45	58	51
women are." (*E, W*)							
"Women have inadequate	(A)	11	13	39	28	37.5	33
education and training	(B)	28	33	25	35	22	38
for management leader-	(C)	61	54	36	37	41	29
ship." (*E, M, W*)							
"Women don't want to	(A)	9	8	11	12	18	11
be top executives or	(B)	33	34	25	37	34	43
professionals."	(C)	58	58	64	52	47	45
"Women are likely to	(A)	19.5	22.5	22	22	34	33
bring personal and family	(B)	33	38	53	50	31	47
problems to the work-	(C)	42	39	25	28	34	20
place, and that interferes							
with their job perfor-							
mance." (*E-A*)							

NOTE:
* male-female differences within this ethnic group are significant at under .05 level
** the difference is acceptable only at under .10 level
E overall inter-ethnic differences are significant at under the .05 level
M inter-ethnic differences between men are significant at under the .05 level
W inter-ethnic differences between women are significant under the .05 level
E-A there is an inter-ethnic difference between Euro-Americans and Afro-Americans at under the .05 level, but not for all three ethnic groups taken together
SOURCE: Computed from Harvard/*Washington Post*/Kaiser survey data, 1997.

I should also add that in spite of the ethnic and gender disagreements I have pinpointed, there is a broad overarching consensus among Americans about the economic role of women. Euro-American men are the most conservative, yet over 60 percent of them agree that there is serious discrimination against women. And they reject explanations based on inherent gender qualities to a greater degree than do minority men. We should be careful not to over-"racialize" these results, or for that matter exaggerate disagreements between men and women.

LET US MOVE NOW to a consideration of domestic gender attitudes. Early studies of the subject reported that both male and female Afro-Americans held highly egalitarian attitudes regarding the division of family tasks between husband and wife.[173] Closer examination of these attitudes, however, reveals a more complex pattern, with potential for conflict. In an excellent study of the modes of interaction of Afro-American couples in Los Angeles, Sandra DeJarnett and Bertram H. Raven paid special attention to the degree and *kind* of power sharing that took place.[174] They confirmed previous findings that, overall, Afro-American couples did indeed tend to be egalitarian in their interactions and that, in this regard, there was little difference between lower- and middle-class Afro-Americans. However, they uncovered levels of complexity and conflict not detected by earlier studies.

While there was a balance of authority between couples, this rested on clearly demarcated spheres of authority in which each gender exercised complete control. To put this another way, there was a high level of sex segregation in which power was distributed separately but equally. However, DeJarnett and Raven also found that Afro-American men of both the lower and the middle classes, but especially the latter, continued to hold highly sexist views about male dominance and woman's place in the home and in society at large. Seventy-one percent of middle-class Afro-American men believed that husbands should have the final say in all matters, and 42 percent of them held the highly reactionary view that the idea of "women in authority" is "against human nature." Afro-American women strongly rejected both of these sexist views.

In domestic relations, then, this study suggests that there is a contradiction between Afro-American men's male-dominance ideology and the more egalitarian power relations they are actually obliged to live by with their spouses. Indeed, the contradiction runs even deeper. It was found that the stronger their commitment to a male dominance ideology, the less power middle class men actually had in their relations with their spouses!

DeJarnett and Raven were at a loss to explain this unusual finding. They concluded, rather cautiously: "It does suggest that there is indeed a discrepancy between how partners in black couples influence one another and the ideal way in which they should influence one another." This discrepancy may be one important source of Afro-Americans' high rate of marital and cohabitational disruption. Support for this is found in Shirley J. Hatchett's study, which noted that, in spite of overtly expressed egalitarian attitudes, "marriages were . . . unstable if Afro-American men felt their wives had equal power in the family."[175]

Several questions in the HWPK survey probed domestic gender attitudes. Respondents were asked whether they agreed or disagreed with the statement "For a woman, taking care of the children is the main thing, but for a man, his job is." Surprisingly, half of all Americans agreed. There were no overall ethnic differences; 50 percent of Euro-Americans, 48 percent of Afro-Americans, and 47 percent of Latinos agreed, 41 percent of Latinos agreeing very strongly. The gender differences were even more surprising. In all three ethnic groups, more women agreed with the statement, and agreed more strongly than the men.

It appears that the developmental psychologist Wade C. Mackey is correct in his observation that, "in what can be loosely labeled 'traditional' American society, females, as a class, have been socialized in preparation for the traditional role as primary child caretaker, whereas men, as a class, are socialized in preparation for their traditional role as primary economic provider and protector of hearth and kin."[176] This might be the clue to understanding what agreement with the statement really means. Respondents might have been making not so much a normative statement as a confirmation of the sociological fact that in American society— as in nearly all other societies—this is how men and women have been socialized. "In terms of fathering, not mothering," adds Mackey, "there is no available data base that suggests, much less demonstrates, that American fathers are not doing normal things in normal amounts or normal durations."[177]

In this regard, the fact that Afro-American men are the ones most inclined to dissent from the statement may be interpreted as an indication of a progressive viewpoint on domestic gender issues, but only if it is assumed that rejecting the view that "taking care of the children is the main thing for a woman" implies that her husband should equally share the bringing up of the children. Such an implication does not necessary follow, as the experience of millions of Russian women will attest. There, as is well known, men fully expect women to work full-time jobs but also to assume the major role in childrearing. It might be that there is a similar Russian-type assumption behind the seemingly progressive responses of Afro-American men, but I do not wish to prejudge the issue. Only careful, detailed ethnographic studies can settle the question of whether Afro-American men's disagreement with the statement in this question indicate a genuinely liberated approach to women's domestic role, or what I am calling a Russian-type approach, or the fact that they have simply learned how to say the politically correct thing. And available ethnographic studies speak strongly against a liberated viewpoint.[178]

On another, related, and more clearly normative probe—"A husband's job is more important than a wife's"—there was no disagreement between Afro-Americans and Euro-Americans. Nearly 80 percent of Euro-American men and women, as well as Afro-American women, objected to this statement, once I controlled for socioeconomic status, political views, and whether or not the respondent was a parent. With these controls, Afro-American men had the highest predicted likelihood (28 percent) of agreeing with it. This tends to reinforce my suspicion that women's agreement with the statement that, "for a woman, taking care of the children is the main thing" is more an acknowledgment of an existing reality, with perhaps even a hint of pessimism about men's desire or capacity to do more than they presently do, than an expression of a normative preference.

Two other questions in the HWPK survey addressed the issue of domestic gender attitudes and relations and are of special relevance to Afro-Americans. People were asked: "Generally speaking, are women capable on their own of successfully raising boys into men, or not?" And, similarly: "Are men capable on their own of successfully raising girls into women, or not?" Most Americans, of all ethnic groups, agreed that a woman is able to successfully raise a boy on her own. Over 80 percent of Euro- and Afro-Americans thought so. While Latinos as a group were a bit more skeptical, fully 73 percent of them were in agreement. Men are generally less likely to agree with this statement than women: almost a quarter of them disagreed, compared with only 13 percent of women. This gender difference remains significant within all ethnic groups.

When socioeconomic status and other factors such as age and political views are held constant, Afro-American women's odds of agreeing with this view increase dramatically; they are five times more likely to do so than others. For Euro-American women and Latinas, the odds are increased by 190 and 236 percent, respectively. On the other hand, the likelihood of agreeing is reduced by 34 percent if the respondent is an Afro-American man and by 48 percent if he is a Latino man. The higher a person's income, the greater the likelihood of concurring with this view, while age, political conservatism, and religiosity have the opposite effect.[179]

The most intriguing effects were found when the presence of children of various ages was examined. Having a child of six or younger makes one more likely to agree that a woman can successfully raise a boy. However, it is a different matter with parents of children between six and seventeen years of age; this cuts by half the chances of agreeing. Why the difference? It is a generally accepted fact of developmental psychology, as well as folk wisdom, that boys and girls begin to differ more markedly after age six or so. Most mothers, but especially single ones, will have serious second thoughts about bringing up a boy on their own once the realities of this task set in.

Is there a Murphy Brown effect? I mean, are the divorced and unmarried more likely to insist that a woman has no problem bringing up a son? It would appear so. Being married diminishes the odds of concurring by 43 percent. If a person's spouse earns the same or more than he or she does, the chances are lowered further. However, those who have never been married are 2.75 times more likely to agree, and the divorced and separated 63 percent more likely. Gender and ethnicity intersect in interesting ways when the responses of the divorced and separated are considered. Euro-American divorced men are markedly less likely than Euro-American divorced women to believe that a woman can successfully bring up a boy on her own (75 versus 94 percent). The gender gap is also striking among Afro-Americans, except that it runs in exactly the opposite direction; 83 percent of divorced or separated Afro-American men think that a woman on her own can do just fine bringing up a boy, but only two-thirds of divorced or separated Afro-American women are inclined to think so.

And what do people think about men's capacity to successfully raise a daughter on their own? Although a substantial majority of Americans (71.5 percent) agreed that a man can bring up a daughter, there were more dissenters to this than to the idea that a woman can bring up a son: 28.5 versus 18 percent. On this issue, there were no disagreements between Afro-Americans and other groups. In striking contrast with attitudes toward the capacity of women to raise sons, there were also no over-all gender gaps, nor were there any gender gaps between or within ethnic groups. Americans seem to be in remarkable agreement on this subject, though in somewhat more muted terms than their views on a single woman's capacity to rear sons.

ॐ

TWO SETS OF QUESTIONS in the HWPK survey probed the interface between domestic and public gender attitudes. One concerned attitudes toward the effects of women's greater labor-force participation on their marriages and personal lives. The other examined the extent to which people perceive conflicts between being a good parent and being a successful worker.

With women working, is it easier or harder for parents to raise children? This question is often raised in public debates over "family values." The great majority of Americans (85 percent) think that the phenomenon of women working has made it harder to raise children, and more women than men believe this to be the case (87 versus 81 percent). While three-quarters of Afro-Americans also agree, they nonetheless stand out from Euro-Americans and Latinos in the size of the minority (one in four) who believe that it has become easier to raise kids as a result of women's greater labor-force participation. Of the three groups, Afro-Americans are the only one among whom there is no gender disagreement on this question; there is moderate disagreement among Euro-Americans, and there are rather strong disagreements between Latino men and Latinas.[180] This obviously reflects Afro-American women's longer tradition of working.

How about the effect that women's working has had on marriages? Has it made it harder for marriages to succeed? Again, the majority of Americans (69 percent) think so, with somewhat more women agreeing.[181] Afro-Americans also agree, but to a substantially lower degree than other Americans; 38 percent say marriages have become easier, compared with only a quarter of other Americans.[182] However, unlike the question about parenting, here we find a serious disagreement between Afro-American men and women. Afro-American women do not differ from Euro-American women in thinking that their participation in the workforce has made it more difficult for their marriages to succeed,[183] but Afro-American men take a very different view. They are the only group of men examined among whom a majority (51 percent) believe that it has become easier for marriages to be successful as a result of women's increased labor-force participation.[184]

How do we explain this gender discrepancy? The answer cannot be that Afro-American men are more used to a tradition of women working, since this argument should apply equally to Afro-American women. We also saw earlier that Afro-American women are in no disagreement with Afro-American men about the effects of women's labor-force participation on raising children. One is tempted to say that with their much lower marriage rate, Afro-American men are out of touch with the realities of work and marriage when compared with other, more married groups of men; but again, the same holds for Afro-American women. The answer, I suspect, is the contrasting marriage-market prospects for Afro-American men and women. These are the best of times for any Afro-American man who really wants to get married, and the worst for Afro-American women as long as they choose to remain endogamous, as almost all of them do. This simple fact will explain many of the other discrepancies to be encountered later.

When asked if the increased participation of women in the workforce has made it easier or harder for women to lead satisfying lives, or has made no difference, a slight majority of Americans (55 percent) said that it has made it easier. Slightly more Afro-American women (57 percent) and slightly fewer Euro-American women (54 percent) think so, but the difference is unimportant. This seems to reflect a guardedly optimistic approach on the part of both groups of women, and Euro-American men are of the same opinion, 56 percent of them agreeing. Afro-American men are far less guarded; 69 percent think that work has made it much easier for women to lead satisfying lives. And Latino men seem to be completely out of touch with the views of Latinas. Similarly to Afro-American men, 71 percent think that work has made it easier for women, while Latinas are the only group of women among whom a substantial majority (60 percent) think that more work has made it harder for them to lead satisfying lives.[185]

And what about men's lives? I found the responses curious. Americans are undecided on the issue; virtually the same proportion think that women's increased workforce participation has made it easier for men to lead satisfying lives (46 percent) as believe that it has made it harder (47 percent), the remainder thinking that it has made no difference. Exactly the same percentages of men and women believe that it has made it harder (47 percent), and there are no disagreements between ethnic groups.

There are also no gender disagreements within ethnic groups, even among Latinos.[186]

It is hard to decide which is more puzzling: the unexpected proportion of Americans who believe that it has become more difficult for men to lead satisfying lives because of the increased engagement of women with the workplace, or the unusual level of agreement between all groups and both genders on the issue. It is interesting that Afro-American and Latino men, who largely believe that women have come to lead more satisfying lives as a result of working more, are far less sanguine about the effects of this development on their own lives. Half of all Afro-American men and 45 percent of Latino men think that their own lives have become harder, quite a difference from the majorities thinking that women are leading better lives. At the same time, the women of both these groups feel that the impact of their greater labor-force participation has been about the same on men as on themselves.

What are we to make of all this? Why do nearly half of all men think that it has become harder for them to lead satisfying lives because women are working more? It cannot be because they think it undesirable per se for a woman to work; as we have seen, sizable majorities of Afro-American and Latino men think that working has been good for women. The only answer is that women's absence from their traditional roles as full-time wives is considered a loss for men. And since Afro-American men do not believe that women's working has negatively influenced the capacity of parents to raise children, their responses must mean that it would be easier for them to lead satisfying lives as husbands—as distinct from the satisfactions of fatherhood—if women stayed home more. The fact—or men's belief in the fact—that women are leading more satisfying lives somehow does not enhance women's roles as wives or complement the lives of their husbands. I find this odd.

Whatever misgivings they may have about conflicts between work and marriage, a firm majority of married Americans who work reject all suggestions that they are failing in their roles as parents because of their jobs. Raising children may have become more difficult, but married-and-working Americans are confident that they have risen to the challenge. When it was put to them that having the type of job they do makes it harder for them to do things for their families, 61 percent of Americans disagreed, 40 percent strongly. There were no overall ethnic differences and no intraethnic gender differences on this issue. Euro-American and Afro-American women were about average in their responses, while

Latinas were most emphatic in rejecting this suggestion.[187] The pattern of male responses was similar.[188]

Married-and-working Americans, especially Afro-Americans, were even more insistent in rejecting the suggestion that the demands of their families made it harder for them to devote complete attention to their work. Seventy-two percent of married-and-working Americans rejected it, and there were no ethnic differences. As one would suspect, men tended to oppose this suggestion more than women (76 percent versus 65 percent). However, this was due largely to the third of Euro-American women who admitted that family demands did interfere with their work. Afro-American women were in complete agreement with Afro-American men; 82 percent of each gender said they had no such problem.

Finally, Americans were asked whether "a woman must decide between having a very successful, high-paying career or being a good mother" or whether she can do both. Most (72 percent) thought that a woman can do both, and slightly more women thought so than men.[189] There were ethnic disagreements, but they came mainly from the varying responses of women; men's responses were roughly similar from group to group.[190] While 71 percent of Euro-American women believed that a woman can do both, 86 percent of Latinas and nearly all Afro-American women (93 percent) were of this opinion. So overwhelming was Afro-American women's confidence in their ability to do both that although 73 percent of Afro-American men agreed with them, there was nonetheless an important gender gap in their responses.[191] Income levels and age had little or no effect on how people answered this question, and education and religion hardly any. However, as might be expected, declaring oneself a political conservative did reduce by a third the odds of thinking that a woman can pursue both a brilliant career and be a good mother.

IN THE THREE DOMAINS we have examined so far, Afro-American men and women have emerged as the most progressive group on most aspects of gender relations. It would be going too far to claim, as some have done, that Afro-American women are unusually radical in their views. Instead, on most issues we find them to be fully in tune with the views of the majority: somewhat more liberal on economic issues, slightly more centrist on domestic matters, and more to the left in their insistence on the compatibility of domestic and work roles. Afro-American men also come out as the most progressive group of men on public gender roles and on the interface of the public and domestic roles of women. We have detected elements of conservatism in some of their views on the domestic role of women, but these elements can hardly be said to add up to a chauvinistic outlook. What is more, on most issues discussed so far, we have found a surprising level of agreement in the views of Afro-American men and women. Insofar as there are any severe gender cleavages within ethnic groups, our analysis so far points toward Latinos as the group with a problem, not Afro-Americans.

Let us turn now to what I have called global gender attitudes. Previous scholars have come up with mixed results in their attempts to verify the commonly held view that Afro-American women are unusually liberated in their sex-role expectations and differentiations.[192] In a probing study of upwardly mobile Afro-Americans and Euro-Americans in Houston in the late seventies and early eighties, Jim Millham and Lynette Smith found, overall, a much greater tendency among Afro-Americans to minimize sex-role differentiation.[193] Euro-American men and women differentiated between male- and female-specific gender traits to a considerable degree; that is, both sexes agreed on a large number of traits as being peculiarly masculine or feminine. Remarkably, apart from the tautologous choice of the terms *masculine* and *feminine* as being appropriate to men and women, Afro-American respondents could *together* agree on only two traits as appropriate to a particular sex. It was agreed that being "bold" and being "rugged" are appropriately masculine. Beyond this, Millham and Smith reported, there was no significant agreement between Afro-American men and women concerning what are appropriately male or female traits, whether they be "aggressive," "businesslike," "cries without shame," "independent," "glamorous," or "helpless." All this is good news to those holding progressive gender views. This is a major ethnic difference from Euro-Americans, where the sexes are in much closer agreement about gender-specific traits.

How do these findings hold up when we examine a national sample? First, let us try to get some idea of how firmly gender identities are demarcated. In the HWPK survey, Americans were asked whether "it would be better if men behaved more like women, or if women behaved more like men." A plurality of 46 percent were satisfied with the way men and women presently defined themselves. Few people (11 percent) wanted women to be more like men, but 37 percent felt that it would be better if men were more like women, and another 7 percent thought it would be good if both changed.

On this question, there were no ethnic disagreements overall, but very interesting gender disagreements. As many women (44 percent) wanted to see men become more like women as wished identities to remain as they were, but only 29 percent of men thought such a change was desirable.[194] Men tended to agree with each other across ethnic groups, and women with each other. These gender disagreements were confined to Euro-Americans and Afro-Americans and were especially pronounced in the latter. There was a 14-point gap between Euro-American men and women; 43 percent of the women wanted men to be more like women, compared with 29 percent of the men.[195] The most striking gap, however, was between Afro-American men and women. Although 35 percent of Afro-American men said they would prefer men to be more like women, making them the most flexible group of men on this question, a majority of Afro-American women, 54 percent, wanted men to be more like women, and an additional 5 percent said they wanted both genders to change. Afro-American women were the only subgroup of Americans—male or female—among whom a majority wanted such changes in men.[196]

Afro-American women were also far more confident than any other subgroup that they knew what they were talking about. When Americans were asked if they thought most women understood the problems that men faced, 64 percent of them said that women understood men fairly or very well. Although a majority of men thought so (56 percent), women of all three ethnic groups were far more likely to take this view (71 percent). Afro-Americans were the most inclined to believe that women understood men's problems. Once again, although Afro-American men were more willing to believe this than any other group of men, there was nonetheless a major gap between them and Afro-American women, nearly all of whom (87 percent) were of the opinion that women understood the problems that men faced.[197]

At the same time, it was generally agreed by Americans that men were largely ignorant of the problems that women faced as women. The level of agreement on this question was pretty impressive. Only about a third of Americans were prepared to entertain the idea that men knew anything about women's lives, and of that third, all but 3 percent said men understood only "fairly well." This was true of both genders and of all three ethnic groups.

The implication of these findings is that a plurality of women in general, and a majority of Afro-American women, feel that they understand men quite well and are not altogether happy with what they see. How do they account for the differences they perceive between men and women? An important element of global gender attitudes, explored by the HWPK survey, is whether an individual tends to explain male-female differences in biological terms or to see them as mainly due to the ways in which men and women are brought up. There were unexpected ethnic and gender disagreements in responses to this query.

Half of all Americans thought that male-female differences were due mainly to upbringing, a little over a third attributed them to biological makeup, and 13 percent credited both. A slight majority of all women and a 45-percent plurality of men gave upbringing as their main reason. Afro-Americans, taken together, differed from other groups in their greater emphasis on upbringing.[198] However, their environmental emphasis was entirely due to Afro-American women, who were far more likely to account for gender differences in terms of upbringing than were either Afro-American men or other women. Indeed, this is the issue on which there seems to be the most extreme disagreement between Afro-American men and women. Afro-American men, along with Latino men, are the subgroup most prone to attribute gender differences to nature, in striking contrast with Afro-American women.

More detailed analyses of the HWPK data confirmed the importance of gender in the views of Afro-American women and Latinas, but they also suggest the need for caution in what we say about Afro-American and other men. Even when socioeconomic, political, and other factors (such as having a child in the household) are held constant, the odds of explaining gender differences in genetic terms are reduced by some 80 percent if the person is an Afro-American woman and by about 75 percent if she is a Latina. However, when these factors are considered, being male had little or no effect on the odds of agreeing with the naturalistic or genetic viewpoint, and the same seems to be true of Euro-American women. Thus, while we can definitely say that Afro-American women and Latinas are, by virtue of being women, strongly committed to an environmental view of gender differences, we must be wary of inferring that any of the male subgroups, including Afro-Americans, are pro-genetic simply by virtue of being men or, conversely, that Euro-American women are pro-environmental simply because they are women.

Having a child in one's care heightens the odds of explaining gender differences in genetic terms. This tendency increases as the child grows older. The presence in the household of a child under six increases the odds by about 35 percent; that of a child between six and seventeen, by about 62 percent. Clearly, parents conclude from their own observations that the differences between boys and girls are due mainly to nature. Also, as people grow older, they incline more toward this view. Defining one-self as a political conservative increases the odds of a genetic explanation by some 40 percent, and being religious increases them slightly but significantly. While a high income modestly promotes the tendency to attribute gender differences to nature, having a spouse with a high income promotes it even more; the odds are increased by 29 percent if one's spouse earns more than, or about the same as, oneself. This may explain why gender is not an important factor in explaining the responses of Euro-American women once we control for other factors. Finally, I was surprised to find that one's education has no effect on the odds of taking a naturalistic approach, even though the educational level of one's spouse does negatively influence these odds; each level of educational attainment of one's spouse reduces the likelihood of explaining gender differences naturalistically by about 15 percent.

The expressed wish of a majority of Afro-American women for men to be more like women led me to wonder what they think about the changes that have occurred in women's roles and their relations with men over the past four decades, particularly the cultural and economic changes that came about with the sixties. Given Afro-American women's very liberal, and sometimes even radical, views regarding the role of women in the public domain and their insistence that there is no conflict between their domestic and public lives, I assumed that they would express the desire for more change along the lines of the past few decades.

According to the HWPK data, somewhere over three-quarters of all Americans think that "quite a lot" or "a great deal" of changes have taken place in recent years "in the relationship between men and women in their roles in families, the workplace, and society." There are no disagreements between men and women or between women of different ethnic groups on this matter. However, there are striking ethnic disagreements between men in their assessment of how much change has occurred. At one extreme are Afro-American men, 87 percent of whom think that there have been changes, half of those 87 percent saying "a great deal" of change. At the other extreme are Latino men, who, once again, seem to be at complete odds with the women of their group; only 51 percent acknowledge any changes, in contrast with 89 percent of Latinas, who think the opposite. Between the two extremes are Euro-American men, 79 percent of whom assert that there have been important changes in gender roles and relations. There are some minor regional differences, but only among men. Midwestern and Southern men, especially Euro-Americans, claim to have seen the greatest changes.

What do men and women think of these changes? "Have they been mainly good for the country," Americans were asked, "have they been mainly bad, have they been both good and bad or have they made no difference?" Most people, as might have been guessed, thought the changes had had both good and bad consequences, with women being slightly more inclined than men to say both good and bad. There were hardly any gender or ethnic disagreements.[199] Ask an ambiguous question, you get an ambiguous answer.

Let's try again. People were asked directly: "Considering everything, do you think it would be better or worse for the country if men and women went back to the traditional roles they had in the fifties, or don't you think it would make a difference?" The answers were wholly unexpected. Fully 41 percent of Americans thought that it would be better to go back to the "traditional" gender roles of the fifties, 34 percent thought it would be worse, and a quarter thought that it would make no difference. Women and Southerners, especially Southern women, are slightly more inclined than men and non-Southerners to think it would be better (38 versus 43 percent), but only by a few percentage points. There were no general ethnic disagreements. Indeed, the level of gender and ethnic uniformity in responding to this question was remarkable.

What came as the greatest surprise, however, was the percentage of Afro-American women who said it would be better if gender roles were to return to the fifties. Half of all Afro-American women considered such a return desirable, compared with 42 percent of Euro-American women and 44 percent of Latinas. At the same time, we find Afro-American men at the other extreme of responses. Only 28 percent of them thought such a change would be better, and 41 percent were certain that it would make things worse.[200]

When I analyzed these results further, I found that income and education reduce, to about the same degree, the likelihood of thinking that going back to the traditional roles of the fifties would be better for the country. Being married and being older have the opposite effect, again to about the same degree.

The gap between Afro-American men and women became even more pronounced when married people were asked not whether a return to the traditional roles of the fifties would be good for the country in general but whether it would be good for them personally if they and their spouses were to go back to those roles. Fewer people thought this would be good for *them* than felt it would be good for the country (29 versus 41 percent). This is another one of those many instances in which Americans are more conservative in their views about what is good for the country than they are about their own lives. A plurality of 37 percent thought that if they and their spouses went back to the ways of the fifties, it would make no difference to their own lives, and about the same proportion (34 percent) felt that it would make things worse. On this question, there were no gender differences among Euro-Americans and Latinos. However, we find an even greater interaction of gender and ethnicity among Afro-Americans than when they were asked what would be good for the country in general. As Figure 1.20 shows, Afro-American men were the subgroup most inclined to think that a return to traditional gender roles would make things worse for them and their marriages and least inclined to say that things would get better, while Afro-American women were almost the exact opposite, being the subgroup least inclined to say that their lives would get worse and, along with Latinas, most inclined to think that their lives would get better.

The results of my analysis of the HWPK data indicate that having a higher income, being better educated, and being fully employed all reduce people's probability of believing that a return to traditional values would make things better for their own marriages. As one would expect, being older makes such a belief more likely. However, when we control for these factors, the gulf between Afro-American men and women widens even further. Afro-American men are now 56 percent more likely to say that going back to traditional values would be worse for them and their marriages, while Afro-American women are 68 percent more likely to think that it would make things better. What is more, Afro-Americans are the only group for whom ethnicity matters in holding these views; once we control for the factors mentioned above, being a Euro-American or Latino makes no difference in the way a person feels about a return to the gender values of the fifties.

How do we explain such wholly unexpected results? Why would Afro-American women, who are so liberal on public and domestic gender issues and so confident about the compatibility of their public and domestic lives, want to go back to the gender roles of the fifties in their marriages? And how do we explain such extreme gender disagreement on this score when in so many of the other domains of gender attitudes Afro-American men and women are in close agreement?

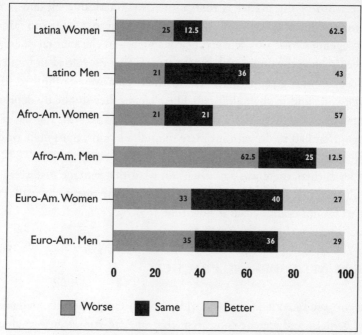

FIGURE 1.20. Percentage of Respondents Thinking a Return to Gender Roles of the Fifties Would be Worse, the Same, or Better for Them, by Ethnicity and Gender, 1997. SOURCE: Author's tabulation from HWPK data.

One possible answer might be that referring back to the fifties has a different meaning for Afro-American women than for other women. This is certainly true of public and domestic gender roles. As we have repeatedly noted, Afro-American women have participated fully in the workplace from the day their ancestors landed in this country. Thus, going back to the fifties would perhaps not mean a return to full-time homemaking and isolation from work as it would for Euro-American women and Latinas.

There are two problems with this explanation. The first is that if this is what returning to the fifties really meant to the Afro-American women answering this question, then we would have expected a much higher probability of their answering that such a return would make no difference, not that it would be a positively good thing. Clearly, they had something else in mind. The second problem is one we have encountered before. Afro-American men are also used to a tradition in which their mothers and other women worked, so they too would have been expected to say that a return to the fifties would not make much difference to their marriages.

The truth of the matter is that both Afro-American men and Afro-American women clearly took the question to mean a return to "traditional" gender roles—as it is explicitly stated—in the marital relations between men and women. What Afro-American women had in mind by "traditional" was a stable marriage in which men were faithful to their marital vows and to their children. The changes they implicitly deplored in their responses were those that they assumed came with the sixties— changes that had to do with intimate marital relations, not public or domestic roles or their interface.

At least, then, there was agreement on what this extreme disagreement was all about. It focused on intimate relations, the one domain that we have so far not examined. It is now time to do so.

SEXUAL ATTITUDES AND PRACTICES

FEW SUBJECTS ARE MORE BURDENED with oversensitivity, defensiveness, denials, and stereotyping than that of Afro-American sexual attitudes and behavior. The horrors of the plantation seem to cast a shadow on every utterance. Lingering racist stereotypes are replaced by liberal hypocrisies; outrage over past atrocities justifies silence over present crises such as the AIDS epidemic that is ravaging the community.

The truth of the matter is that Afro-Americans, informed as they are by their largely fundamentalist Christian tradition, share the same sexual morality as Euro-Americans and Latinos. The NHSLS, which is the most authoritative and up-to-date national survey on the subject of sexuality, reveals that in most matters Afro-Americans' values are identical to those of the other two groups. To cite a few examples taken almost at random: The same proportions of all three groups find the idea of group sex "appealing" (22 percent of Euro-Americans, 20 percent Afro-Americans, 18 percent of Latinos) or "very appealing" (exactly 6 percent of each group). Other practices that attract about the same percentages from each group are homosexual relations (5 percent overall, 3 percent of Afro-American men, 6 percent of Afro-American and Euro-American women, and 7 percent of Latinas); sex with a complete stranger (between 30 and 31 percent of all men and between 7 and 9 percent of all women); and forcing sex on others (2 percent overall). The Marquis de Sade would find few playmates among modern Americans of any ethnic group. Only 2 percent of Euro-Americans and Latinos say they enjoy this kind of stuff, and less than 1 percent of Afro-

Americans do. I could go on, but I think I have made my point. Contrary to what racists think, and also contrary to what Afro-American rap singers and star athletes love to brag about, the Afro-American population is not quite the group of libertines that some would like to imagine.

However, as in other areas, Afro-Americans tend to emphasize certain values more than others. On some sexual issues, they are actually on the conservative side of Euro-Americans; on others, they are found to the left. In a few areas, they are distinctive mainly because of the prevalence and intensity with which they cling to certain sexual attitudes and behaviors that others in the population consider marginal. Their problems tend to be more extreme versions of Euro-American problems, often magnified by and contributing to the greater fragility of their social institutions.

The biggest issue that the NHSLS study raises about the sexuality of Afro-Americans is not so much the ways in which they differ from other ethnic groups as the disparity between Afro-American men and women in their attitudes toward a few important sexual practices and attitudes. This may be due largely to the greater involvement of Afro-American women with the church. Whatever the reason, on important moral and behavioral aspects of sexuality, we often find Afro-American women to the right, and Afro-American men to the left, of their Euro-American counterparts. The resulting gender gap has serious consequences for relations between Afro-American men and women.

Afro-American intimate relations are beset by four basic problems that together seriously impair their premarital and marital intimate relations. These are (1) some fundamental gender disagreements concerning sexual morality; (2) a serious mismatch in regard to preferences for certain kinds of sexual practices; (3) significant gender differences in levels of sexual activity; and (4) problems with sexual infidelity both before and after marriage.

Looking first at sexual morality, here are some of the more important areas of disagreement between the two genders. Asked if teenage sex was wrong, 83 percent of Afro-American women agreed that it was, nearly identical with the 85 percent of Euro-American women and 88 percent of women overall who agreed. Indeed, more Afro-American women than Euro-American women or Latinas said that teenage sex was "always wrong" under all circumstances. On the other hand, only two-thirds of Afro-American men held a similar view. [201] In all three groups, the middle classes were more inclined to agree with this view, mainly because more middle-class men disapproved of teenage sexuality. However, the gender gaps remained; there is a 16-point gap, for example, between middle-class Afro-American men and women on the issue.

Related to this are disagreements over the immorality of premarital sex. Only one in four Afro-American men thinks it is wrong, a ratio similar to that for other American men. While Afro-American women can hardly be called prudes, they disapprove in greater numbers and with greater intensity than Euro-American women; 38 percent of them say premarital sex is wrong (compared with 30 percent of Euro-Americans), and of these, 28 percent say uncompromisingly that it is "always wrong." These disagreements turn out to be even more pronounced when we analyze the results with controls for socioeconomic status and religiosity. If the respondent is an Afro-American woman, the odds of insisting that premarital sex is wrong double; if an Afro-American man, they are reduced by over 50 percent.[202] We find the same pattern of gender disagreements among other ethnic groups, but nothing as extreme. The factor that most accounts for the Afro-American gender gap is the greater religiosity of Afro-American women. Thus, for an Afro-American, going to church on a weekly basis increases the odds of disapproving of premarital sex by 490 percent. True, weekly religion increases the odds of disapproval by 900 percent for a Euro-American, but as we noted much earlier on, there is a far greater gender discrepancy in church attendance among Afro-Americans than Euro-Americans.

This comes out even more clearly when people are asked if religion and religious beliefs guide their sexual behavior. There are no disagreements among American men. Afro-American men fall between Euro-American and Latino men; half of them say their religious beliefs guide their sexual conduct, compared with 45 percent of Euro-American men and 52 percent of Latino men. However, Afro-American women differ importantly with other women, 69 percent claiming religious guidance.[203]

This nearly 20-point gap between Afro-American men and women must surely be a problem for their gender relations. I was left in no doubt when I analyzed their responses further. Holding socioeconomic status factors constant, Afro-American women are 260 percent more likely than others to say that religion guides their sexual conduct, while being an Afro-American man reduces the odds of such a response by 66 percent. Marriage increases the odds of religious guidance to a greater degree (by 290 percent) among Afro-Americans than among other groups. Having one or more children increases the odds among Afro-Americans, but decreases them among Euro-Americans and Latinos. Just the opposite is true if the person is an unwed mother. This experience increases Euro-Americans' and Latinas' likelihood of turning to God for guidance in their subsequent sexual behavior, but substantially decreases that of Afro-Americans.[204] One possible explanation for this is that Euro-Americans and Latinas who have babies out of wedlock tend to get married anyway, either to the father of their out-of-wedlock child or to someone else. They get another chance to start their lives over, so to speak, and perhaps embrace religion more fervently as a result. Unwed Afro-American women who have babies are less likely to be so fortunate and hence do not respond in quite the same way.

Perhaps the issue on which Afro-American men and women are most in disagreement is their attitude toward extramarital affairs. The great majority of Americans, including Afro-Americans as a group, consider extramarital sex wrong. The differences between Afro-Americans and other groups on this matter, however, are not trivial,[205] and they are due almost entirely to the gap between Afro-American men and women. As on so many other subjects, Afro-American women are almost identical in their views with other American women, 92 percent holding extramarital sex to be wrong.

Let's be clear about one thing. It's not as if Afro-American men were abandoning the ramparts; 79 percent of them *do* think that marital infidelity is wrong, which hardly disgraces their religious values. The problem, once again, is that Afro-American women are so much more virtuous. Not only do 92 percent of them hold extramarital sex to be wrong, but fully 84 percent say that it is wrong under all circumstances, no qualifications, no excuses. So, with only 70 percent of Afro-American men saying that it is *always* wrong, we end up with yet another serious gender gap of 14 points, which is over two times the gap that separates Latinos and twice that separating Euro-Americans.[206]

Next, let us look at how Afro-Americans and others view the relationship between sex and love. The NHSLS team asked people how strongly they agreed or disagreed with the statement "I would not have sex with someone unless I was in love with them." Two-thirds of Americans agreed with it, and there were no ethnic differences overall. Women, however, were far more inclined to agree (77 percent versus 53 percent of men), and there were important interactions between gender and ethnicity. There were no differences among women[207] but important variations among men. Afro-American men were the only subgroup among whom a majority rejected the statement, only 43 percent agreeing with it, compared with 53 percent of Euro-American men and 61 percent of Latino men. The result, once again, was a pronounced gender gap of 33 percentage points between Afro-American men and women, with far less severe gender gaps in the other two ethnic groups.[208]

Among all groups, being upper middle class increases the odds of agreeing that there should be no sex without love, although more so for Euro-Americans. Religiosity and marriage strongly increase the likelihood of agreeing, most powerfully for Latinos, while education reduces the odds slightly. Being divorced has different effects for the three groups. It moderately increases Euro-Americans' odds of agreeing (by 40 percent) and more than doubles Latinos' odds. However, divorce has the opposite effect on Afro-Americans, reducing their odds of agreeing with the statement by 28 percent.

I wondered what effect the experience of having been sexually molested as a child would have on views about sex and love. Sadly, and for all groups, it powerfully decreases the likelihood of agreeing that love has anything to do with sex, most so for Latinos, least so for Afro-Americans.[209]

Considering the marked differences in sexual values between Afro-American men and women, one is led to wonder what goes on between them when they actually get together. So far my analysis has focused on individual views of sexual morality, but sex is quintessentially about couples; which brings us to the second area of intimate relations: sexual practices. Because simple percentages tell us only a part of the story of what happens when two individuals meet, I will follow the lead of Edward O. Laumann and his associates by assuming a mating model in which sexual pairs are randomly sorted.[210] In the NHSLS study, people were asked whether they liked or disliked various sexual practices. As regards any given practice, by using the percentages of Afro-American males and females who claimed to like it as indicators of their respective probabilities of preferring that practice, we can calculate the likely matches and mismatches among random pairs.

Take, for example, the practice of cunnilingus. When a heterosexual couple gets together, only three possibilities are likely, one of which constitutes a match and the other two a mismatch. They may both prefer cunnilingus, in which case there is a happy match between them. Or one of them may like it and the other not, and the one not liking it may be either the man or the woman. This is the first possible kind of mismatch. It is also possible that neither may like cunnilingus, and this constitutes the second kind of mismatch.

It may be protested that the second kind of mismatch is really a match. After all, a mutual dislike for something does constitute a kind of agreement that may draw two people together. We all know of couples who share a common distaste for certain things and, indeed, seem to share only that. But this is always a precarious basis for a relationship, especially a sexual one. People need to like things together if they are to bond physically and emotionally. If a couple starts off only disliking things together, it will not be long—indeed, it may take less than a first fumbling night—before they come to the realization that one of the things they most despise together is each other.

Under the random mating model, the probabilities of matches and of the two kinds of mismatches are easily calculated.[211] Figure 1.21 gives the results of these calculations for six sexual practices among Afro-Americans. For each practice, the first two bars give the raw percentages for men and women, respectively, who report liking the practice. The third, fourth, and fifth bars represent, respectively, the probabilities of a match, or of only one person liking the practice, or of both disliking it.

The chart immediately demonstrates how the individual percentages easily underestimate the degree of potential conflict. In the case of cunnilingus, the raw percentage responses show that 47 percent of Afro-American men and 48 percent of Afro-American women like it, and nearly identical percentages dislike it. One would be tempted to believe that there is only harmony here, but nothing could be further from the truth. Our model shows that such a distribution of preferences spells trouble in bed, the reason being that there will be a 50 percent probability of disagreement between any randomly selected pair of Afro-Americans over whether they are going to make cunnilingus a part of their sex or not.[212]

Fellatio presents even more problems for Afro-American couples and has been the ruin of many an otherwise promising relationship. Afro-American men like it somewhat more than other men, although not all that much more; 63 percent of them do, compared with 56 percent of Euro-American men. However, it has long been a matter of common knowledge within the Afro-American community that Afro-American women have a particularly strong distaste for fellatio, anecdotal evidence that has the full support of the few professional studies that have been done on the subject. What one of her informants told the sociologist Claire Sterk-Elifson during her study of sexuality among Afro-American women in Atlanta is typical: "Oral sex should make people vomit. It is sex

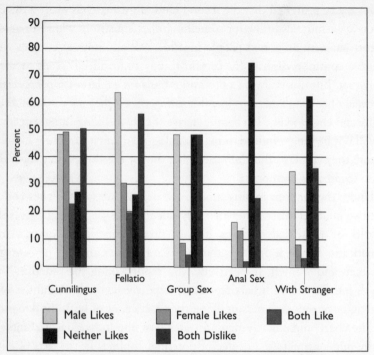

FIGURE 1.21. Match/Mismatch on Selected Sexual Practices Between Random Afro-American Gender Dyads, 1992. SOURCE: Author's tabulation from NHSLS data.

invented by whites."[213] Professor Sterk-Elifson claimed that two-thirds of her respondents would concur with this view, which is only about 3 percent less than the 70 percent of Afro-American women who expressed a similar dislike for the practice in the NHSLS national sample.

Any form of sex involving more than two persons is likely to be equally problematic. Anal sex presents fewer problems, mainly because there is a high level of distaste found in both genders, but there is still a one-in-four likelihood of serious disagreement.

I would like to draw particular attention to the last set of bars in Figure 1.21, representing preferences for sex with a stranger. This seemingly innocuous cluster of bars may well hold the key to explaining the number of sensational allegations of sexual harassment brought by Afro-American women against prominent Afro-American men, which have rocked the Afro-American community. Thirty-four percent of Afro-American men claim to like sex with a stranger (again, not all that out of line with the preferences of Euro-American men), but the vast majority of Afro-American women (92 percent) consider it an abomination. The result is a 36-percent likelihood that any randomly selected pair of Afro-Americans will be headed for serious sexual misunderstanding, for that is the probability of an unwanted sexual advance. Of course, one may choose to emphasize the positive side of this chart and point out that there is a 61-percent likelihood that a couple of Afro-Americans meeting for the first time will disapprove of such behavior. But in the high-powered world where Afro-American middle-class men and women now find themselves, a 36-percent probability of such an occurrence is a horrendous state of affairs. There was a time when Afro-American women did not report the unpleasant experiences that are clearly implied by our model, but those times are over. We can expect many more Clarence-and-Anita scandals in the years to come.

Before concluding this discussion of the mismatch in regard to sexual practices, let's be clear once again that Afro-Americans are not the only group facing these misunderstandings. I have addressed their problems because that is the focus of this book, but just to get things straight, I have calculated the probabilities of disagreement for Euro-Americans and compared them with those for Afro-Americans. It turns out that Euro-American men and women are a little more likely to have serious sexual disagreements over group sex and sex with strangers and are substantially more likely to encounter disagreements over anal sex than is the case with Afro-Americans.

The third area of intimate relations I want to discuss focuses on actual sexual behavior as distinct from sexual values and preferred kinds of sexual practices. The sexual behavior of Afro-Americans is not, on average, that much different from that of Euro-Americans and Latinos. However, there are important differences when gender, class, and age factors are taken into account. In what follows I will concentrate on two important indicators of sexual behavior from the NHSLS: the first experience of vaginal sex, and the number of sexual partners a subject had since the age of eighteen and in the twelve months before the interview in 1992.

Americans, on average, have their first experience of vaginal intercourse at the median age of seventeen, men at seventeen and women at eighteen. The median is the same for Latinos, except that men begin at sixteen and women at seventeen. For Afro-Americans, as was mentioned earlier, the median age is sixteen, men beginning at fifteen and women at seventeen.

These figures immediately reveal what is most striking about the sexual behavior of contemporary Americans: the fact that there is a considerable degree of uniformity in the sexual behavior of American women regardless of ethnic differences. Nearly all the ethnic variation in sexual behavior comes from male class differences, from gender differences between men and women within ethnic groups, and from differences between men across ethnic lines.

To some extent we have already come across this female uniformity in our discussion of the other domains of gender, but it is most evident in the sexual behavior of American women. In light of the considerable public attention paid to the issue of teenage and out-of-wedlock pregnancy among Afro-Americans, this might seem to be a questionable assertion. However, it is important not to confuse the question of pregnancy with sexuality. A suburban Euro-American teenager who routinely uses contraceptives can be a sexual libertine and never get pregnant while her far less sexually active fellow American in the ghetto who is careless about contraceptives, or has to contend with boyfriends who have primitive views about condoms, ends up with two kids before she is twenty. This should be obvious to all, but the imputation of sexual promiscuity to women who have children out of wedlock is a medieval misconception that dies hard in America, especially among conservative pundits.

This pattern of female uniformity and male variation holds when we take class into consideration. For all Americans who are poor, the median age of first vaginal intercourse is, again, seventeen, but men now begin at sixteen and women still at seventeen. Poor women of all three ethnic groups under consideration experience their first intercourse at the median age of seventeen. Poor Afro-American men, however, have the earliest median age of first intercourse of all subgroups, at age fifteen, in contrast with poor Euro-American men, who begin at sixteen, and Latinos, who start at seventeen.

Among the nonpoor working class, as well as the middle and upper classes, the median age of first intercourse is seventeen for Afro-American men and eighteen for Euro-American women. Afro-Americans of these classes begin at the same ages as their poor counterparts: seventeen for women and fifteen for men. This absence of class variation among Afro-Americans may be due to the fact that those of the higher classes are upwardly mobile and are likely to have been brought up poor, or it may mean that the adolescent sexual practices of lower-class youth influence those who are better off. At any rate, the two-year gender gap in age at first intercourse remains true for all classes of Afro-Americans.

I pointed out earlier that there are a larger number of men in the Afro-American teenage cohort, a number magnified by the sexual precocity of younger men as well as the demands of older ones. It may well be wondered who the women are who meet the needs of these men, in light of the fact that Afro-American women and Latinas have their first intercourse at the median age of seventeen. The answer is a minority of more sexually precocious and active teenage women. When we examine the age distribution of first sexual activity more closely, we find that 13 percent of Afro-American girls and 15 percent of Latinas have already had sex by age fourteen, and a quarter of both groups of girls by age fifteen. The proportions are considerably higher among lower-class Latinas, though only a percentage point higher among Afro-American girls who are poor.[214] However, they are unusually high among Afro-American young men of all classes, especially those who are poor. A third of all Afro-American young men have engaged in vaginal sex by age fourteen and over a half by age fifteen.[215] So we are still to explain where the sexual demands of the men are met. The answer is partly to be found in the considerably higher intensity of sexual activity among those Afro-American teenager girls who are sexually active, with consequently higher risks of pregnancy, as we earlier noted. But another explanation, to be discussed below, is the much greater tendency of Afro-American men to mate exogamously when compared with the women of their group.

The NHSLS figures we have just discussed come mainly from respondents reporting on their sexual behavior during their own youth. Since the average age of the Afro-American and Euro-American interviewees was thirty-six and the interviews were conducted in 1992, what we have just discussed, then, refers to the behavior of teenagers during the early seventies. Has there been much change in recent years? We can get at this by confining our examination to people who were themselves teenagers or in their early twenties at the time of the interviews. Looking at these subjects, our results show that Americans of all classes and ethnic groups are having their first sexual experience at much earlier ages. A third of Euro-American young men and a little over a quarter of Euro-American young women had already had their first sexual experience by age fifteen. By that age, 53 percent of Afro-American young men and 39 percent of their female counterparts had done so; indeed, over a third of the Afro-American men and one in five of the Afro-American women had already experienced vaginal sex by age fourteen.[216] The teenage pregnancy and birth rates are going down, then, not because teenagers are having sex less often, as some people like to imagine, but because they are using contraceptives more often and more carefully.

The first sexual experience is an emotionally formative one for many people, especially young women. It can influence their view of members of the other gender for life. We have already seen how being sexually molested as a child strongly influences how people view the relationship between love and sex. An exploitative and unloving first experience can often have the same effect. It is important to know, then, just what motivated young Afro-Americans and their fellow Americans to engage in sex for the first time.

The reasons given were categorized under eight heads.[217] They differed significantly for men and women, both between and within ethnic groups. The most common reason given by men was that they were curious or ready for sex (51 percent), while for women affection for their partner was the main reason (43 percent). Only 24 percent of men gave affection as their main reason, and only 24 percent of women said they did it because they were curious or ready. One in five women were virgins when they got married, this being the occasion for their first sexual experience, but only 7 percent of men were. Surprisingly few of these young Americans listed peer pressure as a reason for first intercourse: 4 percent of men and 3 percent of women. And with the exception of poor Latinas, almost none gave the desire for a baby as their main reason for first engaging in sex.

Afro-Americans differed from other ethnic groups in only two respects: more of them engaged in sex for the first time because they were curious or felt themselves ready for it (43 percent), and fewer of them did it the first time because it was their wedding night.[218] This was true for both genders.

The really striking differences were those between men and women in each of the ethnic groups. The greatest number of gender differences were found among Latinos, the least among Euro-Americans. Afro-Americans stood between. Just a little under half of all Afro-American women said they made love for the first time because of their affection for their partner (48.5 percent), but only 18 percent of men gave this reason. On the other hand, 60 percent of men said that they did it because they were curious or felt that they were ready for it, while 35 percent of women felt this way. Afro-American men cited affection less often than any of the other subgroups.[219] Class had surprisingly little effect on these patterns of gender differences, especially among Afro-Americans.[220]

Moving now to the role of sexual history, the NHSLS collected information on people's lifetime number of sexual partners, as well as their number of sexual partners during the previous twelve months. The latter is clearly more reliable, especially if people have had a lot of partners; this should be borne in mind in the following discussion. It is also important to keep in mind the average ages of the different subgroups. The mean ages of Euro-Americans and Afro-Americans in this survey were 36.8 and 36.2 years, respectively. On average, Euro-American men were 36.2; Afro-American men, 35.9; Euro-American women, 37.2; and Afro-American women, 36.4.

Afro-American women had led sexual lives very similar to those of their Euro-American sisters; both had had a median of three partners since their eighteenth birthday. In all ethnic groups, men had had twice as many partners in their lifetimes as women, but Afro-American men had had more varied experiences, and the gap between their experiences and those of Afro-American women was greater than those separating the genders of the other groups. There were no class differences among Afro-American women and Latinas. It is significant that of the men, lower-class Euro-Americans and Latinos had had the fewest partners during their lives, whereas lower-class Afro-Americans reported the most. I should point out that a small minority of lower-class Afro-American men admitted to an enormous number of sexual partners.

Regression analyses indicate that, among Afro-Americans, poverty is positively related to the number of partners in one's lifetime, increasing them by over eleven persons, whereas among Euro-Americans and Latinos it is negatively associated, reducing the number by two. Having spent a night in jail, and all that that indicates, has a powerful positive effect on the lifetime number of sexual partners among Afro-Americans and Euro-Americans; it is associated with an increase of 37 partners among the former and with 13 among the latter, but it appears to have no relation to the sexual history of Latinos.

Other than being female, the factors that are most powerfully associated with a reduction in the lifetime number of partners among Afro-Americans are regular, weekly church attendance; marriage; and a commitment to the belief that extramarital sex is wrong. The age at which an Afro-American first engages in sex is also negatively, though modestly, related to the lifetime number of sexual partners. These factors are also important for Euro-Americans and Latinos, but to a lesser degree. Once again, we see that marriage and religion have far stronger effects on the lives of Afro-Americans—where they are allowed to operate—than on those of other groups.

More accurate, because more recent, are the respondents' sexual experiences over the twelve months prior to the interviews in 1992. On this measure, the median number of partners for Americans of all subgroups was only one person, but as Figure 1.22 shows, there was quite a bit of variation around this central tendency. We see, first, that Afro-American women were the subgroup with the highest percentage of persons who had had no sex partners the previous year. In spite of their low marriage rate, they were similar to other women in that the great majority of them (83 percent) had had either no or one sexual partner the previous year.

Abstinence is obviously one way in which Afro-American women deal with the problem of the low propensity of the men of their group to marry or cohabit. For many, this results in periodic loss of interest in sex. When Americans were asked if they had experienced any lack of interest in sex over the previous twelve months, 31 percent of Euro-American women, 32 percent of Latinas, and 43 percent of Afro-American women answered in the affirmative. And while there were important differences between the poor and the middle classes among Euro-American women and Latinas, this was hardly the case among Afro-Americans.[221]

At the other extreme of the distribution shown by Figure 1.22 are Afro-American men, whose behavior resulted in an extremely lopsided gender pattern for Afro-Americans. Almost one in six of the women in the group had abstained over the previous year, while over one in five of the men had had multiple partners. This was possible partly because of the 5.5 percent of Afro-American women with three to four partners the previous year, but mainly because Afro-American men have sexual networks that extend beyond the boundaries of the ethnic group, while Afro-American women remain the most endogamous gender group in the nation. Among sexually active Afro-American men, 23 percent had had Euro-American partners, compared with only 6 percent of Afro-American women.

Class strongly influences the number of sexual partners of Euro-Americans, especially women, but not Afro-Americans and Latinos. There are twice as many Euro-American women with multiple partners among the poor than the middle classes, but the difference between middle-class and poor Afro-American women is not significant. What is noticeable is the fact that the highest income bracket of Afro-American men has the same proportion of persons with multiple partners (40 percent) as does the the lowest.[222]

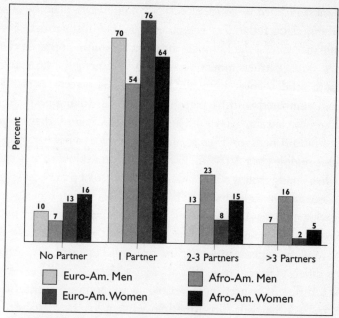

FIGURE 1.22. Number of Sexual Partners in Previous Year, by Gender and Ethnicity, 1992. NOTE: Gender differences are significant for both ethnic groups at under .05 level. SOURCE: Author's tabulation from NHSLS data.

Having looked at the other three basic problems that impair the intimate relations of Afro-American men and women, I come finally to the issue that is perhaps the most divisive of all, and the one that is undoubtedly the major source of instability in their unions. This is the problem of infidelity. We saw earlier that there was a huge gap between the proportions of Afro-American men and women who approved of extramarital relations. Several questions in the NHSLS probed the extent to which Afro-Americans and other Americans actually engaged in unfaithful relationships both before and after marriage. I will focus on two of them.

First, people were asked if they had had sexual relations with another partner while they were involved with their first sexual partner, before settling down to marriage or cohabitation. A surprising number of all Americans cheated on their first sexual partners (41 percent). Presumably young people feel that they are under no commitment and are free to explore their sexual options. There is some reason in this, but as someone who grew up in the fifties I cannot help wondering what happened to romance.

Be that as it may, there are significant gender, ethnic, and class variations in the likelihood of cheating on one's first sexual partner. Afro-Americans are the most inclined to do so, especially young men, a majority of whom (56 percent) claimed that they had cheated on their first partner.[223] It is remarkable that among the Euro-American poor, women appear to cheat on their first sexual partners more than men do.[224] Among the Afro-American poor, both genders cheat at equally high rates, 64 percent of men saying they had, compared with 61 percent of women. Among nonpoor Afro-Americans, by contrast, gender differences are important, as they are among nonpoor Euro-Americans. Even so, one does detect a somewhat greater tendency for middle-class Afro-American women to explore their sexual options when young than is found among the women of other ethnic groups; 47 percent of them said that they had had relations with others while involved with their first sexual partner. They can hardly be blamed for doing so, given that the majority of young men in their group do this.[225] This is one of the few respects in which the sexual behavior of Afro-American women differs markedly from that of other women.

It is a different matter, however, when we come to marital unions. Once they get married, Afro-American women live by their own strong commitment to the norm of marital fidelity and are here no different from Euro-American women: when asked if they had ever been unfaithful to their spouse, 83 percent of them said that they had not, compared with 85 percent of Euro-American women. The gulf here with Afro-American men is vast: 43 percent of them admitted to marital infidelity, a 26-point gap. This gap is widest among the poor (45 percentage points) and lowest among the working nonpoor and middle class (12 points). Among the most prosperous group of Afro-Americans, it widens again to lower class levels (40 points). Affluent Afro-American women are, along with well-to-do Latinas, the most conjugally faithful group of women in the country, while well-off Afro-American men are among the most unfaithful. There is no other way of putting it: this is a deplorable situation—for the women betrayed, for the marriages disrupted, and for the children disturbed by this chronic pattern of male infidelity, which, as I argued earlier, is without a doubt a major reason for the high divorce rate among Afro-Americans.

How does all of this influence the actual physical experience of sex for Afro-American women? From their own accounts, when they do engage intimately they have a healthy level of sexual functioning. When asked about their last sexual experience, only 18 percent of Afro-American women claimed that they had not had an orgasm, compared with 23 percent of Euro-American women and 31 percent of Latinas. Indeed, almost one in four (23 percent) said that they had experienced two orgasms, compared with 11 percent of Euro-American women and 14 percent of Latinas.[226]

However, being able to function sexually is hardly the same as enjoying sex physically and emotionally. In light of the normalcy of their sexual functioning, their responses to questions about how physically and emotionally satisfying they found their sexual experiences are especially poignant. There was no gender gap in the expression of physical satisfaction among poor Americans of any ethnic group. However, middle-class Afro-American women were the subgroup least likely to say that they found sex with their primary partner physically satisfying—74 percent said it was—and the gap between what they reported and what their middle-class male counterparts claimed is extremely revealing: 94 percent of men declared themselves very or extremely satisfied.[227] The responses to the question about emotional satisfaction were similar. Afro-American middle-class women were among those least inclined to say they were very or extremely satisfied emotionally with their sex lives (74 percent), and the gap between them and middle class Afro-American men was also the widest in any class or ethnic group.

One wonders how Afro-American men reconcile their own attitudes and behaviors with those of the women of their ethnic group, or how they reconcile their relatively progressive public and domestic gender attitudes with the deceitfulness and double standards of their intimate norms and practices. The study by Jim Millham and Lynette Smith mentioned earlier provides one clue as to how men come to live with these contradictions. Among Euro-Americans, Millham and Smith note, men and women, both together and separately, tended to view socially undesirable behaviors as more offensive when found in a man than in a woman. Afro-American women also saw things this way. It was, however, quite different with Afro-American men. They held firmly to the belief that undesirable behaviors were to be judged less harshly when practiced by men. The authors' comment on this double standard is so forcefully on the mark that it is worth quoting:

> Thus within the present sample of black Americans, men set lower standards of behavior for themselves than they set for women, *and lower standards than women set for men.* If these results are shown subsequently to have a broad generalizability across black American culture, they indicate potential con-

flict for [the] black [man] between behavior and performance influenced by [his] value standards, and . . . the standards set for [him] by black women and by the majority white society. . . . To the extent that other black men ratify his perception of the [lack of] seriousness of his behavioral transgression, he may develop . . . *a view of women as inappropriately harsh or negative in their evaluation of him.* In a like manner, to the extent that many of these negative characteristics (e.g., cynical, forgetful, obstinate, over-confident, rebellious, suspicious, tactless, secretive) are focused upon in the economic and vocational sphere, the black man may find himself angry about what he views as inappropriate and unduly harsh censure for negative behavior.[228] (Emphasis added)

I think my findings, based on two national samples, demonstrate that this acute observation can be generalized to Afro-American men at large. Afro-American women, we have seen, hold values, beliefs, and norms that are nearly identical to those of women in the broader American society, especially Euro-American women. The discrepancy between their attitudes and behavior and those of the men of their group amounts to a discrepancy between Afro-American male attitudes and behaviors and those of the broader society. This is the fundamental problem.

But where did it come from? How do we explain such an unusual gender gap in attitudes and behavior? Why do Afro-American men treat such deserving women the way they do? Why do they abandon their marriages when the material rewards of marriage should be so obvious to them? Why do they abandon their children in the unheard of numbers and proportions that they do?

Two sets of factors explain these conundrums. One we have already explored: the holocaust of slavery and the neo-dulotic sharecropping system. The other, to which we now turn, is their immediate socio-cultural environment, especially their families of orientation.

THE SOCIAL SOURCES OF THE CRISIS WITH SPECIAL REFERENCE TO CLASS

PARENTS' ECONOMIC RESOURCES and their degree of support or alienation from friends, relatives, and other networks in the communities where they live all influence the ways in which they bring up their children. How parents influence their children is also linked to subcultural norms, beliefs, and practices about child-rearing.[229] It is these factors that structure the intergenerational process that we call socialization. The process varies according to class. In what follows I will focus on the poor and underclasses, then turn briefly to a consideration of the stable working and middle classes.

In spite of the high proportion of single-parent families among lower-class Afro-Americans, their economic hardships, the social stresses of their environment, and the often tense state of their adult gender relationships, most of them grow up to be psychologically healthy people leading productive and enriching lives. Nonetheless, low income Afro-American mothers are not superwomen. They have faults, like everyone else. They are the products of a peculiar tradition that, as we have seen, grossly short-changed them in the parental practices they inherited. And they are vulnerable to social and economic injuries from the high-risk neighborhoods in which they live. Inevitably, these forces take their toll in dysfunctional child-rearing patterns and in the disproportionately high rate of child neglect and other forms of maltreatment of children.

"Decades of research," writes Joan I. Vondra, "support the link between low socioeconomic status and styles of childrearing that emphasize authoritarian control, encouragement of conformity, and punitive disciplinary techniques, all of which increase the probability of child maltreatment." Also, the very American tradition of parental privacy encourages poor parents to believe that their children are their property, which "opens the way for child victimization."[230]

In a study based on over six years of close participant observations, Carl H. Nightingale takes issue with the current conventional wisdom among sociologists and social psychologists that minimizes the importance of family background in explaining the violence of young men in the ghetto. Nightingale agrees that there has been an overemphasis on household type as an explanatory factor. This variable indeed explains little, he correctly notes, and to emphasize it is to miss the main point: that the parenting of boys and girls by the Afro-American lower classes has become increasingly abusive. "Almost without exception," he writes, "parents [see] severe punishments—like prolonged isolation from friends, beatings, and other uses of force—as the best means to educate kids in values of social responsibility and respect for parents."[231] This tendency, he points out, is reinforced and legitimized by the traditional fundamentalist reluctance to spare the rod and spoil the child, by law enforcement agencies, by the courts and the prison system, and by primitive mainstream law-and-order rhetoric, resulting in "parental behavior that leaves children with hurtful and even traumatic memories."[232] Almost every study of child rearing and child maltreatment supports these observations.[233]

I pointed out earlier that Afro-American men and women both agree that boys and girls should be brought up in the same manner. Some scholars, such as E. J. Smith,[234] have found that Afro-Americans not only believe but practice this. I have no doubt that Afro-American lower-class parents mean it when they say that they do not think boys and girls should be raised differently. But what parents mean or intend is usually the least part of what actually determines different gender outcomes for boys and girls. Whatever a single mother intends, rearing children without a father will have different consequences for daughters and sons. Whatever parents intend, a father's abusive behavior toward the mother, or his abandonment of his home and children, will be interpreted differently by girls and boys. However a mother may try not to show it, her bitterness and sense of betrayal at being abandoned by the man that she gave her love to and that she allowed to father her children will be sensed by boys and girls and will be psychologically processed in different ways by each gender. Whatever parents intend, rearing children in communities infested with adolescent male gangs will have different consequences for boys and girls. And whatever a mother intends, the fact that her daughter is of the same gender as she will have consequences for their relationship that will inevitably make it different from the one she has with her son.

One of those consequences is that mothers can more easily establish physical and emotional empathy with their daughters. Because single mothers often have no intimate and stable partners in their households or their lives, it is only human that they turn to their daughters for companionship and emotional support, treating them as friends and helpmates and projecting onto them many of their unrealized ambitions. "The girl's instrumental role within the household," wrote Lee Rainwater in his classic *Behind Ghetto Walls*, "is an important part of her growing sense of identity as a woman-to-be. As her ability to function effectively increases, the recognition her mother gives her in this identity becomes more and more important to her. . . . Mothers generally seem to prefer their girls, in the sense that they have closer and more taken-for-granted relationships with them." Boys, on the other hand, "live in a more anxious and ambiguous situation. . . . Their sense of solidarity with their mothers is not strong, and they do not acquire the girls' feeling that a recognized and valued identity is coming into being."[235]

I am not sure that this is always in the best interest of poor and working-class Afro-American girls. Too many responsibilities are thrust on them too early. Not only do they become privy to intimate aspects of their mother's lives that are hard for a child to process, but they are often made into virtual mother surrogates for their younger siblings. The result is that they often grow up too fast and seem amazingly mature for their years. But this maturity is deceptive. In Jamaica, where the same thing happens, this is called being "force-ripe." Not only are daughters robbed of their childhood, but their seeming maturity invites the devastating attention of older men and precocious age-mates. In the city of Chicago, where Afro-Americans are a minority, of the 13,090 cases of sexual abuse recorded by the police between 1990 and 1997, between 66 and 72 percent were Afro-American children.[236]

Most lower-class Afro-American girls are spared this trauma, although most are aware of someone who experienced it. However, force-ripe socialization is the fate of nearly all, and this, combined with what they observe of the treatment of their mothers by the latter's boyfriends or their own fathers, makes them extremely distrustful of men.

If girls are socialized too quickly into adulthood, boys are often either overdisciplined or else neglected, especially when they grow too big to be beaten into obedience by their overstressed, overworked, and emotionally exhausted mothers. In Afro-American lower-class families, boys, especially very young ones, are at as great a risk of abuse as girls are, often at the hands of their mothers' boyfriends, who attempt to discipline them. Afro-American boys from one to four years old are murdered at the rate of 8.7 per 100,000, which is 28 percent higher than the homicide rate for Euro-American boys of the same age and more than 4 times the rate at which Afro-American infant girls are murdered. Between age five and fourteen, Afro-American boys are murdered at the rate of 5 per 100,000, over 2.27 times that for Euro-American boys and 3.8 times that for Afro-American girls. Nearly all the murderers of Afro-American boys are either the parents, mothers' boyfriends, or close relatives of the victims.[237] As bad as these figures are, it is likely that they are greatly underestimated. In 1993 the National Research Council of the National Academy of Sciences estimated that as many as 85 percent of fatal child abuse cases are systematically misidentified.[238]

Although the murder rate of Afro-American boys is relatively high, it affects only a tiny fraction of children. Far more common are the neglect and physical abuse that most boys, and many girls, experience under their parents' mistaken view that they are disciplining them. A national study in 1985—which probably understated the problem, since it was based on parents' reports of their own violent behavior toward their children— found that 15 percent of children in poor families were either severely or very severely abused, compared with 10 percent of children living in households above the poverty line.[239] The figure for Afro-American children is likely to be much higher than this. The most recent report by the U.S. Department of Health and Human Services found that "African American and Native American children were abused and neglected at a rate almost twice their proportion in the national child population."[240]

The commonest form of maltreatment of children in Afro-American families is physical neglect (about 46 percent), followed by physical abuse (about 29 percent) and sexual abuse (approximately 7 percent).[241] The reasons for child abuse vary somewhat across ethnic lines. What Jessica Daniel and her associates found to be true of Afro-American families studied in 1983 still holds: "The contexts of child abuse appear to be those of severe economic adversity, no one to turn to for help, a death in the family, a history of having suffered serious personal violence, and a child who may be delayed in social and cognitive development."[242] Other factors shown to be of special relevance to poor Afro-Americans are alcohol and other drug use and poor child-rearing skills.[243] For single mothers of whatever ethnic group, however, loneliness, stress, and social isolation from supportive networks are especially important in explaining why they neglect or abuse their children.[244]

A terrible price is paid for this maltreatment and neglect in the wasted lives of the disproportionately large number of violent and sexually abusive young adults that so many abused and neglected Afro-American children grow into. The murderous aggressiveness and self-destructive violence of a disproportionate number of under- and lower-class Afro-American men,[245] their posturing and braggadocio, their misogynistic abuse of women, and their identification of manliness with the impregnation and abandonment of mothers[246] are the direct result of their abandonment by their fathers and of the way they are brought up. But as I have already argued, their parents' or parent-surrogates' way of bringing them up is itself the product of the abuse these adults suffered during the course of their own upbringing by parents who were themselves abused, all leading back to that most heinous form of abusive socialization: the slave plantation, which, let it not be forgotten, is less than three generations away. Many of the grandparents who brought up the parents of today's underclass children were themselves brought up by ex-slaves. There is no gainsaying the fact that the cool-pose culture of the ghettos is simply the modernized version of a brutal behavior complex going back to the Afro-American holocaust.[247]

This behavior complex is of course exacerbated by the horribly depressed conditions of the ghetto. What is more, it is a pattern that darkly mirrors, and is legitimized by, the mainstream culture, not simply, as Paul E. Peterson thinks, because of declining mainstream support for familial, communal, and religious values[248] but, more paradoxically, as Nightingale shows, precisely because of the mass media's glorification of the very mainstream values of violence (cowboys), sexuality (Madonna), and cutthroat greed (Wall Street).[249] However, this behavior complex is not new, even if in certain of the larger, more media-saturated urban ghettoes it is getting worse. Tragically, it is an intergenerational pattern. Like all behaviors transmitted from one generation to the next, it is reproduced through the process of socialization, the "parent-child system (the crucible of child maltreatment)" that, as Jay Belsky argued in 1980 in his seminal paper on the subject, "is nested within the spousal relationship," or more properly the gender relations, whether spousal or not, of the child's adult caretakers.[250] "What happens between husbands and wives," Belsky elaborated, "has implications for what happens between parents and their children."

The street culture and the home mutually reinforce and reproduce each other. As David H. Schulz observed thirty years ago, "a woman's experience of being exploited by men influences her attitude toward her son."[251] As a result, "in the ghetto the sexes are pitted against each other from an early age," and "mistrust is built into the socialization process very early in a child's life."[252] Carol Stack found that "many women tend to debase men and especially young boys, regarding them as inherently 'bad,' more susceptible to sin, drinking, [and] going around with women."[253] This view is shared by the Afro-American educationalist Charles Willie, who finds a fear of trust in the lower-class family, where there is "fierce loyalty" between mothers and offspring but "little love."[254] Not only are Afro-American boys given conflicting messages about women, but, as G. I. Joseph and other researchers have pointed out, so too are Afro-American girls about men.[255]

One revealing finding from recent studies of young Afro-American street-gang members is that they are attracted to gangs because gang leaders become parent-substitutes, providing them with the security, and sometimes care, that they feel their mothers have failed to give them. This is forcefully demonstrated by the case of Terence, the second child of LaJoe, the mother of the Chicago ghetto family so movingly portrayed by Alex Kotlowitz in *There Are No Children Here*. Terence dearly loved his mother when he was young and felt deeply betrayed, and abandoned, when she went on to have six more children. This was no ordinary case of sibling rivalry, for Terence saw clearly the implications of his mother's childbearing: that she would have less time and energy to love him. When, at the age of ten, he left home to become a gang member and his mother confronted the gang leader, demanding her son back, the gang leader informed her in no uncertain terms that he was now Terence's parent.

"I want my son," she told him.
"Terence is my son. He belongs to me," Charles replied.

Also poignant was the case of Bird Leg, who, "his mother suspect[ed], sought protection from the gang in the same way he sought love from his dogs."[256]

What is true of Chicago holds equally for Milwaukee. When Tony, a member of the Four Corner Hustlers gang, was asked by sociologist John M. Hagedorn, "What does being in a gang mean to you?" he replied: "Being in a gang to me means if I didn't have no family I'll think that's where I'd be. To me it's like community help without all the community. They'll understand better than my mother and father."[257]

The research on the role of gangs in the socialization of Afro-American males dovetails with an intriguing finding reported by Bruce R. Hare. In his study of self-esteem among boys and girls, he found that, unlike Euro-American youths, "black boys scored significantly lower than their female counterparts in mathematics ability and achievement orientation and displayed a trend toward lower school self-esteem." The one area in which Afro-American boys scored higher than girls, indeed on a par with Euro-American boys, was on "non-school social abilities and higher peer self-esteem."[258] In other words, young Afro-American males felt good about themselves, in spite of their poor performance in school, not only because school meant little to them but because they had much greater concern with developing their social abilities, and their really important significant others were not their mothers or teachers but their peer gang members.

The Body Stolen

Captives being sent into
bondage—witnessed by
Henry Stanley, ca. 1860s
(Courtesy of The
Library of Congress)

The Body Inspected

Inspection and sale
of a captive on the
West African coast,
ca. 1850
(Courtesy of The
Library of Congress)

The Body in Passage

The Body as Cargo

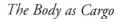

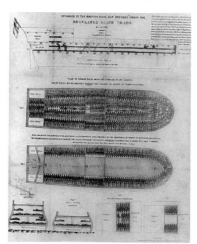

Stowage of the British slave ship
Brookes under the regulated
slave trade act of 1788
(Courtesy of The Library of Congress)

The Africans on deck of the slave
bark *Wildfire* brought into
Key West on April 30, 1860
(Courtesy of The Library of Congress)

TO BE SOLD on board the
Ship *Bance-Iſland*, on tueſday the 6th
of *May* next, at *Aſhley-Ferry* ; a choice
cargo of about 250 fine healthy
NEGROES,
juſt arrived from the
Windward & Rice Coaſt.
—The utmoſt care has
already been taken, and
ſhall be continued, to keep them free from
the leaſt danger of being infected with the
SMALL-POX, no boat having been on
board, and all other communication with
people from *Charles-Town* prevented.
Auſtin, Laurens, & Appleby.

N. B. Full one Half of the above Negroes have had the
SMALL-POX in their own Country.

Notice of sale of Africans on board
the ship *Bance Island,* ca. 1780
(Courtesy of The Library of Congress)

Shop on Whitehall
Street, Atlanta, Ga.
photographed in 1864
(Courtesy of The Library of Congress)

A slave auction in the South from an original sketch by Theodore R. Davis, 1861
(Courtesy of The Library of Congress)

The Faces of Social Death

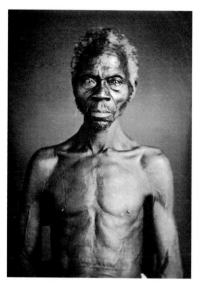

Renty, a Congo slave on
plantation of B. F. Taylor,
Columbia, S.C., 1850
(Daguerreotype courtesy of The Peabody
Museum, Harvard University)

Fasseena, Mandingo slave on the
plantation of Col. Wade Hampton,
near Colombia, S.C., 1850
(Daguerreotype courtesy of The Peabody
Museum, Harvard University)

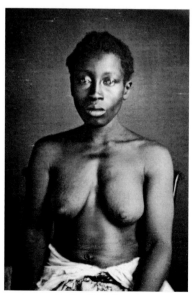

Delia, U.S. born
daughter of Renty, 1850
(Daguerreotype courtesy of The Peabody
Museum, Harvard University)

Slave boy in schoolboy-style uniform
on South Carolina plantation, 1850
(Daguerreotype courtesy of The Peabody
Museum, Harvard University)

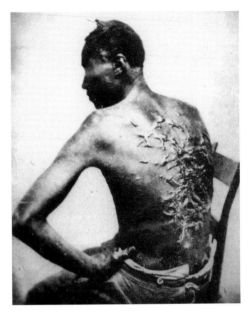

Peter, tortured slave
from Louisiana, 1863
(Courtesy of the
U.S. National Archives)

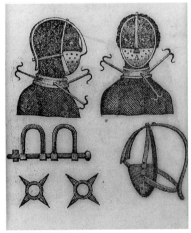

Iron mask, leg shackles, and spurs
used as instruments of torture, 1807
(Courtesy of The Library of Congress)

Wilson Chinn, a branded
slave from Louisiana exhibiting
instruments of torture used
to punish slaves, ca. 1863
(Courtesy of The Library of Congress)

Slave Reproduction Unit, a.k.a., "the Stable Family"

Five generations on Smith's plantation,
Beaufort, South Carolina, 1862
(Courtesy of The Library of Congress)

The American Gulag, a.k.a., "the Slave Community"

Large group of slaves standing in front of buildings on Smith's
plantation in Beaufort, South Carolina, 1862
(Courtesy of The Library of Congress)

The Body in Revolt

Death of Capt. Ferrer, the Captain of the Amistad, July, 1839.

Don Jose Ruiz and Don Pedro Montez, of the Island of Cuba, having purchased fifty-three slaves at Havana, recently imported from Africa, put them on board the Amistad, Capt. Ferrer, in order to transport them to Principe, another port on the Island of Cuba. After being out from Havana about four days, the African captives on board, in order to obtain their freedom, and return to Africa, armed themselves with cane knives, and rose upon the Captain and crew of the vessel. Capt. Ferrer and the cook of the vessel were killed; two of the crew escaped; Ruiz and Montez were made prisoners.

Amistad Revolt, 1839
(Courtesy of The Library of Congress)

Print depicting scenes from Nat Turner's revolt, 1831
(Courtesy of The Library of Congress)

Reproduction of a broadside from 1861, Ripley Country, Missouri
(Courtesy of The Library of Congress)

Fugitive slaves being ambushed by armed bounty hunters in cornfield
(Courtesy of The Library of Congress)

Resurrection of Henry Box Brown at Philadelphia, who escaped from Richmond, Va. in a box 3 ft. long, 2 1/2 ft. deep, and 2 ft. wide
(Courtesy of The Library of Congress)

Fighting for Freedom

Contrabands at
Camp Brightwood,
Washington, D.C.,
ca. 1863
(Courtesy of The
Library of Congress)

Christian Fleethood of the
4th U.S. Colored Infantry,
who received the
Congressional Medal of
Honor for action in battle
near Richmond, Va., 1864
(Courtesy of The
Library of Congress)

The Taste of Freedom

1st South Carolina Volunteers, hearing
Emancipation Proclamation, January 1, 1863
(Courtesy of The Library of Congress)

Victorious soldiers return home to
Little Rock, Arkansas, April 20, 1865
(Courtesy of The Library of Congress)

Exit Slavery, Enter Jim Crow: The Body Appropriated

The Original Jim Crow:
T. Rice in full regalia
(Courtesy of The
Harvard Theatre Collection)

The Body Hunted

An ordinary
lynching: young
Southern gentle-
men pose with
their kill
(Courtesy of The
Carpenter Center
for the Visual Arts,
Harvard University)

The Body Caricatured

(Courtesy of The Harvard Theatre Collection)

The Body Sacrificed

Double crucifixion: Abram South, 19, and Thomas Shipp, 18,
sacrificed in Marion, Indiana, August 9, 1930
(UPI/Corbis Bettman)

The Body As Gladiator:
The Dancing Ring

William Henry Lane
("Juba") imitating
himself at the Vauxhall,
New York, 1841
(Courtesy of The Harvard
Theatre Collection)

The Body As Gladiator: The Boxing Ring

Jack Johnson vs. James Jeffries at
World Championship battle, Reno, Nevada, July 4, 1910
(Courtesy of The Library of Congress)

The Body As Collectibles

"Aunt Jemina and
Uncle Mose":
salt and pepper shakers,
ca. 1940–50
(Courtesy of Professor
Kenneth W. Goings)

Cream of Wheat
advertisement, 1921
(Courtesy of Professor
Kenneth W. Goings)

Celluloid alligator letter opener holding a pencil in the shape of an
Afro-American man in his mouth
(Courtesy of Professor Kenneth W. Goings)

The Body As Demon

Convicted murderer and rapist
William Horton Jr., used by
Vice President George Bush in his
1988 campaign ads to
portray Governor Michael Dukakis
as a liberal soft on crime
(A/P *Lawrence Eagle Tribune*)

The Body As Victim

Attorney Steven Lerman holds a large photo of Rodney
King, victim of a videotaped police beating, 1991
(Reuters/Corbis-Bettmann)

The Demigod As Demon

Los Angeles newsstand, June 20, 1994. The O. J. Simpson
murder case was front cover on three magazines,
including *Time,* which deliberately
darkened Simpson's face, stirring controversy.
(Reuters/Corbis-Bettmann)

Rites of Reversal: Blackface and Drag

Middle class Euro-American ca. 1950
"Black is to white as female is to . . ." Got it?
(Courtesy of The Carpenter Center for the Visual Arts, Harvard University)

Rites of Reversal: Whiteface and Drag

Michael Jackson as Afro-American
he-boy, June 1976
(UPI/Corbis-Bettmann)

Michael Jackson as Euro-American
she-man, May 1998
(Agence France/Corbis-Bettmann)

The Body As Sexual Outlaw

Raquel Welsh resists forced romantic attention of Jim Brown, but moments later willingly submits, in the film *100 Rifles*
(UPI/Corbis-Bettmann)

The Body As Demigod

Chicago Bulls' guard Michael Jordan in action during NBA finals, Chicago, June 13, 1993
(Reuters/Corbis-Bettmann)

Rites of Reversal: An Afro-American Marriage

A bond too fragile for smiles
(Courtesy of The Carpenter Center for the Visual Arts, Harvard University)

Rites of Reversal: Dionysus and Maenads in Gotham

Chicago Bulls' forward Dennis Rodman, dressed as a bride, poses at a New York bookstore, August 21, 1996, while promoting his book, *Bad As I Wanna Be*
(AP Photo/Mark Lennihan)

Afro-American underclass and marginal working class girls, on the other hand, developed such enormous self-confidence from their socialization that they both performed better and realistically rated their school self-esteem higher than Afro-American boys. What is more, their self-esteem, both in social abilities and in school related activities, was higher than the Euro-American girls', even though the latter were, in fact, performing far better than them in school. Hare could only explain this difference in terms of the boost to their self-confidence that came to lower-class Afro-American girls from so persistently outperforming their male counterparts. He further attributed this striking discrepancy not simply to the input of the school environment but to the "consequences of differentiated sex socialization within black families."[259]

Another important difference is the obvious, but infrequently recognized, fact that during the tumultuous period of adolescence, girls' delinquent behavior is eventually rewarded by a closer, even more intimate bonding with their mother and other female relatives, not to mention the financial support of welfare payments with its symbolic confirmation of adult status,[260] whereas boys' delinquent behaviors result, all too often, in parental rejection and a jail term. We should not let our sympathy for the plight of the teenage mother, and especially of her infant, blind us to the fact that teenage childbearing is a delinquent act, *and is so considered by lower-class Afro-American adults.* Its long-term negative consequences are far greater than those from the typical cool-pose delinquencies of Afro-American boys. It is usually catastrophic for the life-chances not only of the teenage mother but of (1) her own mother, who is further burdened just when she begins to look forward to relief from the trials of child rearing under poverty; (2) her younger siblings, who receive even less attention as their already burdened mother now takes on the role of grandmother;[261] and above all (3) the unfortunate child she brings into the world. Recent research demonstrates that children of adolescent mothers are far more likely than other children to have lower intelligence and poorer academic performance, to drop out of school, and to suffer from "social impairment (e.g., poor control of anger, feelings of inferiority, fearfulness, etc.) and mild behavior disorders." Further, the sons of teenage mothers are more likely to be violent, to abuse drugs, and to engage in early sexual activity. Worst of all, the daughters are far more likely to become adolescent mothers themselves, thus perpetuating the pattern of poverty and destructive gender and parenting behavior.[262] Teenage childbearing is both the consequence and one of the major causes of chronic poverty among Afro-Americans.[263]

We should also take account of two kinds of double messages, reported by sociologists and psychologists, that Afro-American young men receive from women in their roles as mothers and mates. Phyllis Harrison-Ross and Barbara Wyden argue that lower-class Afro-American women have an understandable ambivalence toward sex and men that leads them to abusively overreact to normal displays of "healthy aggression" by their sons. At the same time, these mothers urge their sons, from too early an age, to regard themselves as the "man of the house," in this way pushing them to a premature sense of manliness. "One part of [the double message] is: 'You hurry and grow up and take care of me the way your father never did. Be the man of the house.' And the other part is: 'You better grow up gentle and obedient and do everything I tell you.'" This kind of behavior may sometimes be part of a broader maternal syndrome that some clinicians have called role reversal and is summed up by Belsky as follows: "Parents [when their spouses fail to meet their emotional needs] turn to their offspring for the love and caring denied them as children. . . . Maltreatment then occurs as parents become frustrated and angered by their children's inability to take care of them satisfactorily."[264] Whatever its deeper psychological origins, this double message generates enormous tension in lower-class Afro-American boys and results in feelings of both dependency and aggression, as well as excessive attraction toward, and repulsion from, women.[265]

In the street culture, young men confront another double message from women. Thomas Kochman found that "rapping to a woman is a colorful way of 'asking for some pussy.'" The "mack man" who is good at "pimp talk" is a "person of considerable status in the street hierarchy."[266] Two other students of the street culture, Majors and Billson, also report that, while Afro-American lower-class women may declare that they dislike the cool style, they persistently send a "double message" to Afro-American men by rewarding coolness: "Black females are sometimes turned on by or attracted to Black males who act and look cool. Those males who do not act cool may suffer a heavy penalty of rejection. Some women are attracted to the urbane, emotionless, smooth, fearless, aloof, apparently masculine qualities of cool pose."[267] The result is a marked absence of intimacy in gender relations:

> For black women who wish to develop intimate relationships
> with black men who act and look cool, it is the cool pose that

attracts them. Ultimately, these cool behaviors may prevent couples from establishing strong, committed, and authentic relationships. The games and masks, the highly stylized expression of self that makes the cool male attractive, are the very same artifices that inhibit intimacy and genuine companionship.[268]

Carl Nightingale also informs us that, while predatory sexuality is "distinctly gender specific" and is not required by young women for their feminine identity, they nonetheless "often take pride in their 'attitude.'" "Round-the-way" and other kinds of "nasty" girls not only fight rivals and goad men into violence but "pride themselves in sexual adventure and their ability to manipulate men."[269]

The childhood experiences of lower-class men, their chronic ambivalence and predatory attitudes toward women, and the pattern of mutual cynicism and distrust between the sexes find full expression in the popular culture of Afro-Americans, which is itself largely the creation of the lower class, especially in the "verbal art" of signifying.[270] It is not accidental that one of the most commonly used terms in this culture, both in and out of ritual insult situations, is *motherfucker*. Now, while I fully agree with Henry Louis Gates that past interpreters have given undue attention to insult rituals, which constitute merely one form subsumed under the more general cultural style of signifying,[271] the fact remains that this particular ritual form is perhaps the most frequently enacted in the urban ghettos today and the most distinctively Afro-American. I know of no other cultural tradition outside the Afro-American lower class where the trope *motherfucker* is so inscribed, not even the closely related Afro-Caribbean lower-class cultures, which have many similar insult rituals directed at the mother.[272] Further, we have it on Gates's authority that "your Mama" jokes "abound in [Afro-American] discourse, all the way from the field and the street to Langston Hughes."[273] The misogyny evident in the sexual style of contemporary ghetto youth and in rap music has deep roots in the traditional culture, as Lawrence Levine has shown.[274]

Consider the following from the St. Louis ghetto of the late sixties:

> I was walking in the jungle
> With my dick in my hand
> I was the baddest motherfucker
> In the jungle land.
> I looked up in the tree

And what did I see?
Your little black mamma
Trying to piss on me.
I picked up a rock
And hit her in the cock
And knocked that bitch
A half a block.[275]

One could write a whole volume of interpretation on this single verse. What, for example, is the significance of the fact that in this, as in many other "joaning" and "dozens" rhymes, the mother has a "cock"? It is now de rigueur to deny that the antimaternal verbal content of the "dozens" and other Afro-American tropes is in any way connected to problems in the actual mother-son relationship. I find this politically correct denial simply preposterous.[276] Recognizing the cultural assumptions of Freudian theory (as Freud, incidentally, did) does not commit one to the aridity of relativism. As Peter Blos has pointed out, Freud's real insight concerning the mother-son relationship lay in his emphasis on the problem of attachment and the need to overcome it; ironically, what makes Freud important here is less the Oedipal complex (which may well be a largely Euro-American bourgeois phenomenon) than his recognition of "the need of the growing [male] child to distance himself from the central female careperson."[277] In every culture boys must find ways of resisting the pull of maternal dependency, and lower-class Afro-American youth are no exception, any more, for example, than privileged Japanese youth who have reacted to the commuting father's vanishing role, and the resulting excessive dependence on and "psychological presence" of the mother, by taking to a pattern of juvenile delinquency with a pathological focus on mother beating and even matricide.[278]

What all the sociological and psychological research makes clear is that there is no provision within the lower-class pattern of child rearing for the separation of the son from the mother. Those who deny that there is a serious problem here often make reference to extended networks of kinsmen and male friends who help to raise Afro-American boys. There are two problems with this argument. One, to which I will return later, is that the common claim of an extended network of ties is an exaggeration. The second, as we noted earlier in the essay, is that if we closely examine whatever kinship ties do exist, we find that when men, including natural fathers, attempt to help, they tend to do so through their own mothers, sisters, and other female relatives. It is the father's female kin who activate and assert paternal rights, if and when these rights are claimed: "Mothers expect little from the father; they just hope that he will help out. But they do expect something from his kin, especially his mother and sisters."[279] The prevailing dogma that effective father-substitutes exist in the network of support mobilized by poor Afro-American women to raise their male children is pure Afrocentric myth, as is the twin dogma that father-absence doesn't matter anyway. Even among the stable working class studied by John H. Scanzoni, he was unable to find consistent father-substitutes in the small minority of female-headed families in his sample: "If a father substitute was used by the child, he participated only minimally in the child's socialization."[280]

The lower-class male child of a single woman, then, has no assistance, no ally within the family, in his struggle to separate from his mother. The neglected clinical literature has documented the serious psychological consequences of this failure to separate, especially when the mother is neglectful or abusive. The case of Virgil, a troubled, anxious five-year-old, analyzed by Dale R. Meers, illustrates the problem:

> He turns his aggression back on himself in a range of accidents and provoked punishments. . . . Virgil's masculinity has a profound sadistic base, and his compensating defenses have led to regressive, passive, effeminate accommodation. Virgil's dominant fears *are of his painful, emerging fantasies and dreams of being a girl.* Such passivity and effeminate inclinations, however, outrage his self-esteem, and his acting out appears as a chronic need to reestablish his sense of masculinity.[281] (Emphasis added)

It is thus easy to see the powerful attraction of the street gang and cool-pose culture for under- and lower-class youth. The mother abuse and promiscuous sexual and physical violence of the street culture act as a belated, but savagely effective, means of breaking with the mother. The androgynous figure in the "dozens" represents the mother with the "cock" who also fathers, who claims to love the son yet debases the man he will become, who nurtures and brutally disciplines. At the same time, in its antimaternal misogyny, the street culture clobbers into deep repression the painful transsexual fantasies generated by this mother who is at once loved and feared, and whose psychological presence is overwhelming. The result is the "b-boy" (*b* for "baad") masculinity that brooks no "dissing," that "links gender identity with predatory violence" against women, and that seeks respect through murder and suicide.[282] The murder of fellow Afro-American males, it should be further noted, is a pathologically gratifying way of gaining the approval of the internalized mother, who reviles "rotten, no-good, motherfucking' men." And suicide is the ultimate high, especially in its "macho" guise, for in one fell swoop it wins the respect of peers, since the victim appears to have gone down gunning; it satisfies the internal impulse to be punished, as the inner mother dictates; it compels the attention and love of the outer mother, who recognizes at last what she has lost, even as it punishes her through the grief it is bound to cause; and not least, it expresses the frustration, the self-loathing, the sense of meaninglessness and worthlessness, and the utter nihilism of growing up desperately poor, Afro-American, brutalized, and neglected in late-twentieth-century America.

The disastrous, and rapid, social consequences of this psychocultural pattern are reflected daily in the newspapers, where we read the fate of all the little Virgils of the ghettos. Consider the case of Robert Sandifer, alias "Yummy," an underweight eleven-year-old boy from the South Side of Chicago, whose story could still shock a nearly jaded nation in the mid-nineties. He had been so severely beaten and burned with cigarette butts by his drug-addicted mother, who had had the first of seven children at the age of fifteen, that he had been taken from her by the Illinois Department of Children and Family Services and placed in the custody of his maternal grandmother, who, however, with several minor children of her own, had simply neglected him. He began accumulating a police record from the age of six. By the time he was ten, he was already a hardened criminal and gang member. In mid-August 1994, Yummy, who once told a psychologist that life was like "serving time," emotionally exploded. He gave away his hoard of stolen teddy bears to his siblings, got himself a gun, and two weeks later went on a shooting spree that resulted in the death of a fifteen-year-old girl and the wounding of two other teenagers. Several days later he was found dead, shot in the head by his fellow gang-members who feared that, if caught, he would squeal on them.

Yummy's case is not an isolated one. Within days of his execution, another eleven-year-old Chicagoan was charged with the brutal murder of an old woman the previous year, when he was only ten. Between 1990 and 1994, thirty-four children under fourteen, six of them between eleven and twelve years of age, had been charged with homicide in Chicago alone. But one detail in the police profile sent out on Yummy during their manhunt for him is as poignant as it is revealing. On the frail arm of this paternally abandoned and maternally abused child were tattooed the words "I love Mommy."

I have focused on the mother-child relationship in this analysis only because, for most lower- and underclass Afro-Americans, the mother is the only significant parent. Nothing I have said implies that mothers are more to be blamed than natural fathers in accounting for this social disaster. Indeed, if one must assign blame, the major part must surely be placed on the men who so wantonly impregnate these mothers, then abandon them and their children. It is hard to imagine a more execrable form of immorality and irresponsible behavior than that. The worst part of all is that the fathers' immorality and irresponsibility are reproduced in their own sons. The economic deprivation, loneliness, social isolation, stress, and emotional and physical exhaustion of mothers that account for the mother-child syndrome I have just analyzed are all, in the first place, either largely caused or else critically exacerbated by the natural fathers' betrayal and abandonment. When these factors are added to a tradition of weak child-rearing skills inherited from a traumatized past, the resulting disastrous offspring is well nigh inevitable.

IT MUST BE EMPHASIZED that the situation I have just described refers primarily to the bottom 30 percent or so of underclass and lower-class Afro-Americans, though obviously not to everyone belonging to these groups.[283] I suspect that it also applies, to some extent, to marginal working-class people and, as such, embraces perhaps some 35 percent or so of the Afro-American population. The vast majority of middle-class, and stable working-class, Afro-Americans themselves come from secure middle-class, or working-class, homes.[284]

Studies of the more prosperous segments of the Afro-American population suggest that families function well in socializing children and indeed make extraordinary sacrifices to ensure their success in the wider society. Scanzoni, like Andrew Billingsley[285] before him, found no evidence of "female dominance" in these families. Nor did he find the slightest trace of a distinctively Afro-American "ethnic family form." The middle- and stable working-class Afro-American family functions, in most respects, very much like its Euro-American counterpart, except that it is under greater financial strain and must socialize its offspring to cope with the social and psychological cancer of racism.[286] McAdoo's study of middle- and lower-middle-class parenting styles among Afro-Americans in the Baltimore-Washington area, for example, found that relations between mothers and children were "warm . . . loving and devoid of conflict" and that the children had high self-esteem.[287]

And in a major comparative study of family dynamics in Afro-American and Euro-American middle-class and secure working-class families in the Chicago area, Walter Allen found few really sharp differences between the ethnic groups. Afro-American mothers tended to occupy a more central position in their families. Their sons tended to identify strongly with them, even though the sons considered the mothers to be somewhat less approving of them when compared with the attitude of Euro-American sons toward their mothers. However, this seems to have been good for Afro-American sons because they generally "sensed themselves to be in greater control of their lives" than did Euro-American sons.[288] Middle- and working-class Afro-American fathers also seem to be no less effective than their Euro-American counterparts in the socialization of their children. One study even suggests that Afro-American fathers behave in a manner that tends to make their daughters very independent,[289] although, as we will see later, the reasons are rather complex.

But the research also suggests that adult gender relations, including marriage, are far more complex and problematic than the parent-child relationship. Most middle- and working-class Afro-Americans seem to view the relations between men and women as fragile or worse. Behind the bourgeois and neat working-class curtains are serious problems. In the first place, the Afro-American middle and working classes are unusual not only in their low rates of marriage, upon which we have already commented, but in the fact that they marry less than their lower-class counterparts. Income levels and the rate of marriage are negatively related among Afro-Americans, whereas they are positively related among other groups, and this is true of both genders. Only 43 percent of Afro-American working-class men and women are currently married. By contrast, in the Euro-American working class, 59 percent of men and 61 percent of women are married; among the Latino working class, 51 percent of men and 70 percent of women. Even more unusual is the fact that upper-middle-class and more prosperous Afro-Americans have lower rates of marriage than the poor.

Intimate gender relations are problematic both before and during marriage. The middle-class Afro-American women interviewed by Claire

Sterk-Elifson were as disillusioned with their relationships as their lower-class counterparts. Only three of the thirty-three women she interviewed considered their current relationship ideal. Four of the single middle-class women said they often felt used in their sexual relationships and resented it deeply, one of them, a divorced company executive, complaining, "I am not going to be pushed around at my job nor in my bed."[290]

When Afro-Americans do get married, there is evidence of an unusual degree of marital dissatisfaction, especially on the part of wives. One major study reported that the majority of residents in a solidly middle-class Afro-American neighborhood in Atlanta described their marriages as "weak."[291] Of the women Sterk-Elifson interviewed, two-thirds of those who were married or in long-term relationships were uncertain whether their relationships would last, even though all of her interviewees "expressed the feeling that 'deep inside' they longed for a steady, male life companion."[292] The sad truth is that relationships do not last. Middle-class Afro-Americans are unusual in their extremely high rates of divorce.

The high level of unhappiness that middle-class Afro-Americans feel about their relationships is surprising since there is now a near consensus among students of marriage that people with higher incomes and educational levels tend to enjoy better marital relations.[293] These unhappy marital relationships partly account for the high divorce rate, which is unusual not only in its overall magnitude but in the fact that the higher the income category, the higher it gets. Cherlin estimated that between 1965 and 1979, 47 percent of Afro-American married women saw their marriages collapse within a decade, a rate of disruption that was two-thirds greater than for Latinas and 80 percent greater than for Euro-Americans.

One reason for this is the problem of infidelity. We have already discussed this, but the point I wish to draw attention to here is that, in contrast with the pattern in other ethnic groups, infidelity is highest among the most prosperous class of Afro-American men.

Another factor is the mismatch in the educational and occupational statuses of Afro-American middle-class couples. Figure 1.23 shows the extent to which the prestige rankings of NHSLS respondents' levels of educational and occupational attainment are correlated with those of their sexual partners.[294] The correlations found in Euro-American couples are typical of those found in most other groups in the nation: nowhere near perfect, reflecting some restraint or flexibility in the tendency toward assortative mating, but substantial for both genders, especially in regard to educational matching. Afro-Americans depart considerably from these

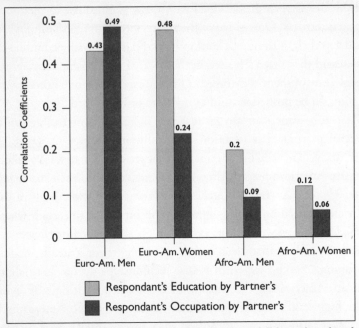

FIGURE 1.23. Correlation between Respondents' Educational and Occupational Levels and Those of Their Sexual Partners, by Ethnicity, 1992. SOURCE: Author's tabulation from NHSLS data.

patterns. There is almost no correlation between the prestige rankings of occupations among couples, and the educational correlations are extremely low. When we look more closely at educational matching, we find, for example, that 45 percent of female Afro-Americans with a college degree had a current sexual partner whose education amounted to a high school diploma or less, and the same was true of 43 percent of Afro-American men with college degrees. By way of contrast, this was the case for only 19 and 27 percent of Euro-American females and males respectively. And in the case of Asian Americans, only 14 percent of male college graduates had sexual partners with only a high school diploma or less, and not a single female Asian American college graduate in the NHSLS sample had a sexual partner who had not had some college education.

These discrepancies were already to be found in the old days of segregation when educational and occupational opportunities were limited for all but a few. However, the mismatches were far less severe at that time, for the simple reason that very few Afro-Americans had any higher education. Today they are much wider and often include couples in which one person has an advanced degree from a major university while another is a bus driver or professional boxer with a high school certificate. This new development more adversely affects women than men. As is well known, men have fewer problems with partners who are not their educational or occupational equals than women do. And with the growing discrepancy in the educational performance of Afro-American men and women, this problem is likely to get worse.

The low level of assortative mating among Afro-Americans may be related to another problem found in Afro-American working-class families. I observed earlier that these families do a decent job of bringing up their children. But all is not well even here, and there is one problem between fathers and their children that suggests this class is not immune from the ravages to the father role among the poor. Given their recency as members of the middle class and the fact that a large proportion of them are upwardly mobile, we would be surprised to find no problems among them.

The sociologist John Scanzoni, in his meticulous study of the family among middle- and stable working-class Afro-Americans in Indianapolis, discovered several troubling aspects of the relationship between fathers and their children. First, he found that only a minority of men (36 percent) and women (29 percent) from stable two-parent families positively identified with their father. Almost the same proportion of men (36 percent) and women (37 percent) negatively identified with him. He was rejected as their ideal, becoming a countermodel, the kind of person they emphatically did not want to be like. Scanzoni concurs with those social psychologists who argue that there is nothing necessarily problematic in this, that indeed, in some cases, such negative identification might even be healthy. I am very skeptical about such arguments. As the father of two daughters myself, I would consider my fathering a failure were I to be told by a psychologist that my children rejected me as a model to be identified with or emulated.

However, what is even more puzzling about the middle-class Afro-Americans studied by Scanzoni—and in this respect they are unique among American ethnic groups—is his related finding: that there was a positive relationship between rejection of the father and socioeconomic success! The relationship was very strong, and held even when Scanzoni controlled for class background of parents, family composition, education, and, most puzzling of all, parental resources and support. That is, all other factors held constant, middle-class Afro-Americans were more likely to succeed if, when going through adolescence, they rejected their father than if they identified with him, even under circumstances in which he provided the most generous support that he could afford.[295]

It should be emphasized that this does not mean that women or men who identified with their father, or were indifferent to him, necessarily failed. What it does mean is that the most successful women and men tended to be those who had rejected their father as adolescents.

I suggested earlier that this problem might be related to the educational and occupational mismatch among couples. Apparently Afro-American women have been mating down as one way of solving their marriage-squeeze problem. But this is a solution fraught with sociological and psychological dangers for them and their children. The differences in values and behaviors between spouses of very different educational and occupational attainments would almost certainly result in chronic marital conflicts, which would, in turn, adversely influence the relationship between a father and his children, especially his daughters, who clearly dis-identify with him because of the problems they see their mother having with him.

THE ISOLATION OF THE AFRO-AMERICAN:
Marriage and Impoverished Networks

IN THE INTRODUCTION I noted that Afro-Americans are the most isolated ethnic group in America. Their isolation, it was further argued, is both external and internal: they are isolated from other ethnic groups in the society and they are isolated from each other. These two forms of isolation have grievous social and economic consequences, for they mean that Afro-Americans are unconnected to networks that are vital for success or even moderate functioning in the society. Low marriage rates are at the heart of both forms of isolation: the extremely low rate of intermarriage with persons who are not Afro-Americans account for their external separation, and the low rate of marriage among themselves explain their internal unconnectedness.

In this section I will first draw on the *General Social Survey*'s data to demonstrate the network implications of the low marriage rate and high rate of divorce and separation among Afro-Americans, in the process challenging what I have called the myth of the 'hood. Second, I will briefly discuss the isolation of Afro-Americans from other Americans due to their high levels of endogamy and spatial segregation. But first, let me say something about the work of sociologists who specialize in the study of social networks.

The fundamental insight of network sociologists is that characteristics of a person's network of ties to others structure the flow of information that both socialize people as they grow up and provide social resources critical for competent functioning in the society. Economic behavior in particular, as noted by Mark Granovetter, is "heavily embedded in other social processees that closely constrain and determine its course and results.[296] Without denying the importance of individual attributes in accounting for success, network sociologists nevertheless consider past and present structures of network ties and their attendant information flows to be of at least equal importance in explaining a person's achievements. Networks, for example, explain why a Euro-American construction worker with no more than a high-school degree may earn more than the typical male Afro-American college graduate. "Blacks are at a disadvantage in using channels of job information," wrote Granovetter in his seminal work, *Getting a Job*, "not because they have failed to 'develop an informal structure' suitable to the need, but because they are presently under-represented in the structure of employment itself. If those presently employed in a given industry or firm have no black friends, no blacks will enter those settings through personal contacts."[297]

There are three things to note about networks. First, their size, the total number of other persons that an individual can reach out to if and when she needs help of any kind. Second, their density, by which is meant the extent to which individuals in the effective group of contacts that a person has also know each other. If every person in someone's network knows everyone else in it we say that she has a very dense network. This might be good for emotional support and partying, but it is a disadvantage for most purposes, such as getting a job. If everyone I know well knows the same set of people well, the chances are that the job information they have I already know, or at any rate I can get it all by talking to just one member of my network. It is much better for individuals to have networks possessing the third important feature of networks: range. A person's network has wide range if a high proportion of the people he knows are merely acquaintances who themselves do not share his own dense network ties but have their own such networks. In this case a close friend of my friend is not necessarily my close friend, too, or may even not be known to me. The advantage of this is that the person will have access to a much wider range of information about matters such as getting a job, locating a rental apartment, or even finding a suitable spouse. Thus if one is searching for a potential spouse, it is pointless asking a close friend in a dense network for help since the persons of the opposite sex he or she knows one is already likely to know. On the other hand, a mere acquaintance—what Granovetter calls a "weak tie"—is likely to know such a person in his or her own dense cluster of ties.

To simplify somewhat, the basic sociological recipe for success in modern America is this: a person should have as large a network as possible with a fair number of dense ties consisting of close friends and kinsmen, but with the greater proportion of all ties being casual or weak contacts that will ensure access to a wide range of information, persons, situations, and experiences.

Internal Isolation and the Myth of the 'Hood

In 1985—the last time that network data were collected in a national survey that oversampled the Afro-American population—Americans were asked the following question by the research team of the General Social Survey: "From time to time, most people discuss important matters with other people. Looking back over the last six months, who are the people with whom you discussed matters important to you?" If the respondents mentioned less than five persons the fact was noted but they were then probed to mention other persons—weaker ties—they may have overlooked precisely because they were weak. In this way, information was obtained on both the density and range of ties. The idea behind the question is that the people first mentioned—referred to as "alters"—would in all likelihood be the respondent's core network of contacts.[298]

Here, briefly, is what my analysis of these results uncovered:

- Afro-Americans have the smallest number of persons in their core discussion networks. Euro-Americans, on average, mentioned 3 persons and others who were not Afro-Americans mentioned 2.8. The mean size of Afro-American core networks was 2.2 persons.
- Afro-Americans' networks had the highest density of all American groups.[299]
- Although denser than others, the networks of Afro-Americans were striking for the low proportion of ties that were kinsmen. Kinsmen made up 19.8 percent of network members mentioned, compared

with 31.8 percent of Euro-Americans' and 24 percent of other Americans'. This was extremely surprising in view of claims made by Afro-Americans and urban ethnographers who have erroneously generalized from small scale case studies about the important role of kinsmen in Afro-American social relations. Indeed, more detailed analysis revealed that almost half of all Afro-Americans—47 percent—had no kinsmen in their networks. This was true of only 24 percent of Euro-Americans. On the other hand, only 11 percent of Afro-Americans had networks in which kinsmen made up more than a half, in contrast with Euro-Americans, among whom this was true for a quarter of all persons.

◆ Among Americans in general, the higher the educational attainment of respondents, the lower was the density of their networks. This is consistent with the prediction of network analysts that successful persons have a higher proportion of weak ties than the less successful, thereby expanding their network range. Among Euro-Americans in particular, there was a strong inverse relationship between level of educational attainment and density of network ties.[300] Among Afro-Americans, however, there was no relationship whatsoever between network density and levels of educational attainment.[301] As dry as it may seem, this was a truly startling finding. It meant that Afro-Americans were gaining little in terms of enlarged range of ties from their educational experiences.

◆ The same disturbing patterns held in regard to employment. Among employed Euro-Americans and those unemployed but seeking work I found a near identical pattern: over 60 percent fell in the category of persons with the lowest density of ties (and conversely, the widest range) in striking contrast with retired persons, the majority of whom had networks with very high or above average densities. There was no such relationship among Afro-Americans. Although retired persons had a significantly higher percentage of persons with high network densities, there was no meaningful difference between retired and employed persons as regard to the possession of low density networks. In other words, retired persons had about as wide a range of contacts as those still in the labor market.[302]

◆ Among Americans as a whole, upper-class persons had the lowest densities, lower-class persons the highest. Afro-Americans were, once again, exceptional in the absence of any relationship between class and network density. If anything, working-class Afro-Americans had lower network densities than those of the middle class, but the difference was not statistically significant.

♦ There was, however, one distinctive class dimension of Afro-American networks. Lower-class Afro-Americans were more cut off from ties to kinsmen than any other group of Americans. While middle- and working-class Afro-Americans had significantly lower proportions of kinsmen in their networks than Euro-Americans, the patterns were roughly similar. Lower-class Afro-Americans, however, stood out from all other groups: fully 91 percent claimed that they had no kinsmen in their closest circle of contacts. This contrasts with 44 and 23 percent, respectively, of lower- and middle-class Euro-Americans, and with 44 and 37 percent, respectively, of working- and middle-class Afro-Americans who also reported no kinsmen in their core networks.

♦ The major source of these ethnic and class differences is marriage. Among Americans generally, and Euro-Americans in particular, marriage was strongly related to the proportion of a person's core network that was made up of kinsmen. Euro-Americans who were not currently married, or had never been married, were twice as likely to report no kinsmen among their core networks. Marriage, however, bore little or no relationship to the network composition of Afro-Americans. The class differences within the Afro-American group in this regard must be explained by other factors. No doubt higher income permits middle-class Afro-Americans to compensate somewhat for the negative effect of their low marriage rates on the kinship composition of their own networks.

With the above in mind, I can now state one-half of the fundamental sociological dilemma of the Afro-American condition. Afro-Americans are in the worst possible situation in regard to the composition of their social ties. Their networks are smaller than those of nearly all other groups, and they are denser and hence their range of contacts narrower than those of other Americans. What is more, they do not enjoy the main benefits that usually come with dense networks—the security and support of kinsmen. For, contrary to conventional wisdom and ideology, their networks have the smallest proportion of kinsmen of all native-born Americans.

External Isolation:
The Consequences of Ethnic Endogamy

As discouraging as the above analysis is, it only tells half of the story. As I stated earlier, Afro-Americans are even more isolated from other ethnic groups than they are from each other. And, as with their internal isolation, low rates of marriage are the root of the problem.

Welcomed to the neighborhoods, clubs, and churches of existing groups, Euro-American newcomers have quickly been able to develop the dense ties that were essential for their transition to the new country. Complementing this process, however, was the high rate of intermarriage between the different ethnic groups which contributed to immigrants' success both by extending their range of ties and by involving them in new dense networks of affinal (in-law) ties. Intermarriage enhances bargaining skills in two ways: it encourages creative thinking about the networking process itself (imagine an Irish or Jewish American groom's first Sunday dinner with his Italian or WASP fiancee's family). And it teaches traditions of network bargaining peculiar to the spouse's ethnic group.

But there is a broader, more powerful way in which intermarriage has influenced both the successful integration of Euro-American and other immigrants and the vitality of American civilization. When we marry, we engage in an exchange of social and cultural dowries potentially far more valuable than gold-rimmed china. The cultural capital exchanged in ethnic intermarriage is considerably greater than that within ethnic groups. We may think of America as an environment remarkably rich in cultural resources, of which the most important are the different child-rearing practices of all the many ethnic groups and the tacit regional and ethnic subcultures of business. Intermarriage not only promotes the interests of the individuals involved but encourages cultural and business innovation. The explosive growth of artistic, scientific, technical, and entrepreneurial innovations in the United States is intimately linked to the high rate of intermarriage of individuals from different ethnic groups.

Afro-Americans, however, have been almost completely isolated from this national process. As is well known, they are residentially segregated. The main intent and effect of segregation has been to deny Afro-Americans access to the nation's rich marital market, propinquity being one of the most important factors explaining choice of spouse.

There are, to be sure, some positive signs in recent years regarding the high rate of residential segregation. As I noted in *The Ordeal of*

Integration, there has been a surprising level of contact and reported friendships between Afro-Americans and Euro-Americans originating mainly at work. And American attitudes toward "interracial" marriage have changed substantially, especially among the young. Nonetheless, it is astonishing that after living over three centuries in this country Afro-Americans have remained so spatially isolated. A major cause and consequence of this spatial isolation is their ethnic endogamy, an exclusion that was for centuries legally and violently imposed by Euro-Americans, but is now, sadly in my view, voluntarily pursued by Afro-Americans themselves out of a sense of ethnic hurt and pride.

Most people are unaware of the extent of Afro-American marital isolation from the rest of the society, largely because the wrong indices of intermarriage have been used when talking about the subject. Scholars and laymen alike often express the extent of intermarriage in terms of the proportion of all marriages that are "interracial." On this score, America's "interracial" marriage rate is hardly worth speaking of. Only two and a half percent of all marriages in 1995 were "interracial," and only a fraction of these involved marriages between Afro-Americans and Euro-Americans. According to the most recent census data, only a little over a half of one percent of all marriages involve Afro- and Euro-Americans. This way of looking at the rates, however, is hopelessly inadequate. It fails to take account of the relative sizes of the different groups. Since Afro-Americans are only 13 percent of the population, even if all of them married Euro-Americans the vast majority of all marriages would still be endogamous. This compositional factor, as sociologists call it, also bedevils other more refined attempts to measure the extent of inter-ethnic (including "interracial") marriages. Thus, counting only the proportion of women from a given ethnic group who marry men from other ethnic groups does not get around the problem.

A much better approach, that taken by Stanley Lieberson and Mary Waters in their book *From Many Strands,*[303] is to measure intermarriage by first estimating the rate that would be expected if spouses were chosen randomly by women from the population, without any regard to the ethnic origin of their spouses, then compare those results with the observed proportion of out-marriages among women. Using this random model we, in effect, control for the varying sizes of the different ethnic groups.

I used this approach in constructing Table 1.3. Column 1 of the table shows that Afro-American women have by far the highest in-marriage rate of all ethnic groups. Nonetheless, this figure grossly underestimates the true level of marital isolation by not taking account of the small relative

Table 1.3   Intermarriage Rates for Women Born in the United States or
Puerto Rico, 1990

	Women in-Married	All Husbands	In-Out Ratio Group	Others	Odds Ratio
English	60.7%	11.5%	1,544	0.097	15.91
German	68.0	22.5	2.125	0.219	9.70
Irish	53.1	10.1	1.132	0.092	12.185
French	41.2	2.6	0.700	0.025	28
Italian	54.5	4.6	1.197	0.041	29.19
Polish	49.8	2.8	0.992	0.024	41.33
Swedish	40.5	1.4	0.680	0.014	48.5
Afro-American	98.8	5.1	82.333	0.003	27,444
Mexican	83.1	1.8	4.917	0.005	983.4
Puerto Rican	84.7	.4	5.535	0.002	2,767.5
Total	63.7% of women marry men of same first choice ancestry				

SOURCE: Tabulated from 1990 U.S. Census, 5% PUMS

size of the Afro-American population, and hence the large number of potential mates from whose marital market Afro-American women are excluded. Column 2, the proportion of husbands of each ethnic group in
the population as a whole, is the proportion of such husbands we would
expect to find in each ethnic group under conditions of random, non-
ethnic marital choice. The percentage of Afro-American husbands in the
population as a whole, 5.1, is what the in-marriage rate of Afro-American
women would be if marital choices were random. Column 3 shows the
ratio of in- to out-marriages. For Afro-American women it is 82.3, and
here we begin to see the true extent of Afro-American marital isolation.
But this is not yet the complete picture. Column 4 tells us what the ratio
of Afro-American husbands is to non-Afro-American husbands for all
women who are not Afro-Americans. Column 5, finally, gives us the true
extent of Afro-American marital isolation.[304]

It tells us that the odds that an Afro-American woman will marry an
Afro-American man are 27,444 times greater than that a non-Afro-
American woman will marry an Afro-American man. This is the true
measure of Afro-American marital, and hence familial, isolation from the
rest of the American population. This is what three and a half centuries

of slavery, Jim Crow, lynching, racist caricature, minstrelsy, public dishonor, anti-miscegenation laws and sentiments, economic discrimination, and residential segregation have achieved.

It's dispiriting. But it is not hopeless. For the truth is that today attitudes toward marriage between Afro-Americans and Euro-Americans have radically changed. As I pointed out in *The Ordeal of Integration,* for most young Americans inter-ethnic dating is viewed as "no big deal" by the typical youth, and Euro-American parents, especially in the North and West of the country, are surprisingly unbothered by the practice. While a large number of Euro-Americans are still not prepared to marry across the color line, that line is rapidly being blurred by the recent wave of immigrants from countries whose populations are neither of African nor European ancestry and who refuse to play by the old American either/or, binary rules of "racial" conception and interaction. The truth of the matter is that, today, the pressure toward endogamy is as strong among Afro-Americans as it is among Euro-Americans, indeed may even be stronger. In purely demographic terms, when we take account of the fifth or so of all Euro-Americans who would seriously consider marrying across the color line, it can be said that, in theory, America could solve its "racial" problem overnight by this means, if Afro-Americans chose to make a point of marrying out. However, I see little prospect of that happening now or in the near future, given the present mood of Afro-American intellectual, political, and cultural leadership and the understandable distrust of ordinary Afro-Americans who, while willing to forgive, still find it much too hard to do the kind of forgetting required of an "interracial" marriage.

CONCLUSION

A GROUP'S BEHAVIOR in any given area of life is always the product of their responses to the proximate exigencies and challenges of their social environment at given periods of time, and of the inherited cultural resources they deploy in meeting these challenges. These resources, in turn, are nothing more than the practices, values, and beliefs that were found to work in previous periods and that, over time, became routinized and normative. The advantage of these cultural patterns is that they are tried strategies that save people time and social energy in meeting the demands of daily life. The problem with them is that what worked under one set of circumstances in a previous period may not work in another and may even be counterproductive. This is especially true when environments go through frequent and extreme changes, as was the case with Afro-Americans.

In this essay I have sought to understand the familial and gender relations of Afro-Americans. I have, for the most part, focused on contemporary socioeconomic factors in explaining them. But we have seen that these factors, while a necessary and important part of any explanation, can never be sufficient. This is so for two compelling comparative reasons that add up to a logical imperative. The first is that groups facing similar or even more extreme socioeconomic circumstances than Afro-Americans have not responded with the same set of familial and gender problems. I have noted that other groups, including some in the United States, have experienced rural and urban poverty, ethnic persecution, and economic discrimination, yet do not exhibit the same high rates of marital dissolution and paternal abandonment that Afro-Americans do.

The second reason is that Afro-Americans share precisely these problematic gender and familial patterns with groups throughout the Western Hemisphere from which they differ radically. Afro-Americans are an integral part of the wealthiest, most powerful, and most advanced country in the world today. The poorest Afro-American is ten to twenty times wealthier, even in constant (purchasing parity) dollars, than the average Haitian, Afro-Brazilian, or Afro–West Indian. In the West Indies, we find independent states where over 90 percent of the populations are of African ancestry and the leadership are all from this majority group, in marked contrast to the minority status of Afro-Americans. Yet all these African-ancestry, New World societies, in common with Afro-Americans, exhibit nearly identical patterns of gender conflicts, pre- and nonmarital births, high rates of disruption of common-law and marital unions, and massive abandonment of children by their fathers.[305] The only possible reasons why this peculiar set of familial and gender problems would exist in groups living in environments so different from each other and from Afro-Americans' are the other two things that Afro-Americans share with all of them: (1) their West African regional and cultural provenance; and (2) the experience of plantation slavery over several centuries under slaveholders of European ancestry who culturally justified their depredations with the ideology of racism. In all of these New World slave systems, we find similarly vicious assaults on the roles of father and husband. In all of them, we find the most violent sexual abuse of slave girls and women and the utter insecurity of slave men about the biological parentage of their children or, to use the vivid Afro-Jamaican creole expression, about whether they had been "jacketed." In all of them we find extremely hostile conditions for pregnant women, childbirth, infancy, and child rearing—conditions that engendered distinctive reproductive strategies by slave men and women. In all of them, ex-slaves emerged after emancipation with chronic gender and familial problems.[306]

We are therefore led to the logical conclusion that however important and necessary we may find proximate, socioeconomic factors to be in explaining modern Afro-American gender and familial relations, a sufficient explanation requires some consideration of the role of slavery and the West African cultural past. We have seen that this inference from the logic of comparative New World history has strong empirical support. Samuel H. Preston and his colleagues can hardly be accused of being soft culturalists or of neglecting hard proximate socioeconomic data. Yet they could write of Afro-American gender and familial problems:

> Large historical differences underscore the importance of long-term factors. Among these are race relations that have produced socioeconomic disadvantages for African-Americans for centuries. Although the mechanisms through which discrimination manifests itself have changed (from slavery to Jim Crow to residential segregation), African-Americans remain a large and visible group with unequal access to economic opportunities. . . . Whatever the factors that produced the contemporary differences between black and white marital patterns, our results suggest that these differences contain more historical continuity than seemingly straightforward tabulations in census volumes would imply. [307]

I began this essay by observing that Afro-American men and women are, today, moving on very different socioeconomic trajectories. Afro-American women do considerably better than men on all the vital demographic indicators of health and physical survival. Further, they are fast closing the income gap between the genders and are already significantly ahead of Afro-American men in the acquisition of educational and occupational skills and positions. The problem here is not that women are catching up or forging ahead but that in many areas, such as the educational, men are falling behind in both absolute and relative terms.

Next, we saw that Afro-Americans now have extremely low levels of marriage and cohabitation, far lower than those that prevailed for most of the present century; extremely high rates of marital dissolution; and very fragile relations among those couples who do remain married or otherwise partnered. Associated with, and partly explaining, these problems are gender attitudes on the part of Afro-American men and women that, while progressive and in general agreement with each other in the domain of public issues, are extremely discordant in the domain of familial and intimate relations. In general, Afro-American women hold gender attitudes and values that are very similar to those of other women in the nation, especially Euro-American women, except for Afro-American women's somewhat more liberal views on public issues and their unusually strong valorization of motherhood, while Afro-American men subscribe to views that are at the extreme, male dominance end of the nation's spectrum of gender values. Finally, we looked at some serious differences in the sexual beliefs and practices of Afro-American men and women, the most important being Afro-American women's strong commitment to the ideal and practice of sexual fidelity, in contrast with the permissiveness and infidelity of unusually large numbers of Afro-American men.

The net results of these gender problems are that most young Afro-Americans are now growing up fatherless, many with impoverished single mothers who are economically and emotionally stressed; that most Afro-American women, whether or not they get married, are destined to spend most of their adult lives as single women; and that most Afro-American men under forty will go through life experiencing long periods of either being single or in short-lived relationships.

The consequences, in turn, of this resulting crisis are enormous. Its economic effects are well known, and I have discussed them at length in my previous work: married Afro-American families have almost closed the income gap with Euro-American two-parent families, earning 87 percent of what they do; conversely, families headed by unmarried Afro-American women are at the highest risk of poverty in the nation, with 45 percent of them below the poverty line; and poor Afro-American children are six times more likely to be in female-headed families.[308] But the noneconomic costs are equally severe.

As a result of their gender and familial problems, Afro-Americans are isolated not only from other Americans but from each other. Ironically, just the opposite stereotype about themselves prevails among Afro-Americans, in what I have called the myth of the "hood": the popular misconception that Afro-Americans compensate for their unmarried state by a higher involvement with their kinsmen and their communities. This may have been so in the rural South, but as we have seen the best available evidence indicates that it is simply no longer the case for Afro-Americans at large. Community is celebrated, especially by urban community leaders and activists, but the truth is that Afro-Americans lead the nation in their unconnectedness to community support groups.

The isolation of adult Afro-Americans from each other generates, in turn, numerous psychological, physical, and social problems. People who live alone are far more prone to stress, especially men. There can be no doubt that the high incidence of hypertension among Afro-American men is due partly to their isolation from stable relationships, which compounds the stresses induced by economic insecurity and racial discrimination. Loneliness and isolation are also expressed in the unexpectedly high and growing rates of suicide among Afro-American men of all classes. And living on one's own makes one more prone to high-risk behavior that would be restrained in the presence of a caring and knowing partner. Married or otherwise stably partnered men commit far fewer crimes than single ones, and the far greater crime rate among Afro-American men must in great part be explained by their unmarried and largely unpartnered existence.

Although women are more tied to available community resources such as the church, and to kinsmen, isolation and loneliness also take their toll among them. The most tragic result is the high and escalating rate of child abuse and neglect in Afro-American households headed by overstressed and depressed single women (and even more so in the small number of households headed by single men). Students of child abuse have found isolation from kinsmen, friends, and community support groups to be the major cause of the abuse of Afro-American children by their mothers. Sadly, much of this abuse turns out to be unintended or due to ignorance. Lacking friends and kinsmen who normally monitor the behavior of those they are close to, isolated single mothers frequently abuse their children in the belief that they are disciplining them or grossly neglect them thinking that their behavior is normal.

And there can be no doubt that the relatively high rate of drug addiction, especially to crack, among Afro-American women is directly attributable to the loneliness and frustration that come from living without a partner. Many, perhaps most, female Afro-American drug addicts begin their descent into addiction by taking crack and other drugs as a treatment for depression.

We have seen, also, that as a result of the near complete endogamy that was historically imposed upon them, but that is now also voluntary, Afro-Americans remain cut off from intimate familial ties with other Americans. The consequences of this are twofold. They have been, and remain, isolated from the priceless social capital of the majority's interlocking social networks. And they have been shut out of the nation's most important cultural process—that dynamic exchange of cultural dowries that are at the heart of the civilization's dazzling intellectual, artistic, technological, and entrepreneurial achievements.

WHAT CAN BE DONE about this complex set of problems? The answers would require another volume. What follows are some of the major implications of my analysis.

First, let us be clear about what are not presently the causes of the problem: low income or joblessness among Afro-American men. If my analysis has demonstrated anything, it is the fact that *current* economic factors are no longer at the root of the problem. Prosperous Afro-American men have rates of marriage that are as low as poor ones; their sexual practices and gender attitudes are hardly any different; and their rates of marital disruption are likely to be just as high, if not higher. To be sure, low income and economic discrimination and exclusion from the better paying jobs in the economy were historically among the principal factors explaining how the problem came about, since these were the main means by which the manhood of Afro-American men, already shattered during the centuries of slavery, was further assaulted and their demoralization sustained. The cultural damage already done, today these factors make no difference.

My analysis also does not lend much support to the popular view that demographic shortages of men during the crucial younger adult years is the main reason for the low rate of marriage. This shortfall is partly due to the relatively high incarceration rates of young Afro-American men, and we have shown that incarceration is associated with lowered odds of marriage. However, the high incarceration rate is both the effect and the cause of involvement with illicit activities, especially drug dealing and the oppositional street culture. There can be no doubt that the ethnically unfair drug sentencing laws partly explain these rates. A change of policy away from the present system toward one that equalizes drug sentencing laws and emphasizes drug-prevention and rehabilitation programs for nonviolent youth will be more effective and far less costly. Whether it would have much of an impact on the marriage prospects for Afro-American women is open to question. To repeat, the basic problem is Afro-American men's low propensity to marry, whatever their socioeconomic status or prospects.

Educational differences are an important source of the marital crisis. Something must be done about the present gender disparity in the educational performance of Afro-Americans. Young men, especially those from poor families, have got to find ways not only to stay in school but to become engaged with their educational pursuits. The problem is obviously motivational and social rather than economic, given the remarkable differences in the performance of girls and boys. My analysis suggests that fatherlessness and disrupted families more adversely affect boys than girls. So we are led back to the need for stable co-parenting as the major solution to this problem.

Stable co-parenting, however, will not be possible under the present sexual code and behavior of Afro-American men. My analysis has made it clear that this problem originates largely among men. True, it takes two to be unfaithful, and single Afro-American women who have affairs with married or cohabiting men, especially those with children, should do better. But the marriage market is so bleak for Afro-American women that their behavior in this regard is understandable, if not to be countenanced. The problem and the solution are overwhelmingly in the hands of Afro-American men. They must radically alter their ways. They must change their gender attitudes, their sexual morality, their low opinion of marriage and their chronic infidelity in marriages and cohabiting unions. This is not a moral plea. It is a sociological imperative if Afro-Americans hope to have the remotest chance of ever catching up socioeconomically with other Americans.

There is another way in which the educational system could make a difference. It is time that educators include in the curriculum of the nation's schools courses in child-rearing. It really is absurd that the most important skill of all—raising a child—has been left to the vagaries of chance and informal learning. For children in middle-class and stable working-class families this may not be a great problem. But for children growing up in single families where many mothers themselves were still children when they became mothers, or in traditions such as those of lower-class Afro-Americans where child-rearing practices were devastated historically by oppressive external forces, it is imperative that schools teach the basics of child-rearing.

Government must pursue more family-friendly policies that take account of the special problems of poor, especially Afro-American women. Focusing on tax relief or tax credits, as conservatives are wont to do, is a travesty, since such policies help precisely those families least in need of assistance. Instead, government policy should focus on two areas if reality is to replace "family values" rhetoric.

There should be a considerable expansion of day-care and early intervention programs specially geared to the needs of children from problem families. These programs, reinforced by others such as year-round classes on a full-time basis, regular home visits, subsidized summer schools, professional and volunteer mentoring and counseling, the provision of after-school facilities, and the upgrading of existing informal child-caring facilities, have been shown by numerous studies to work and to have striking long-term consequences. They are the program most likely to have an impact, in the long run, on the marriage market in that they improve the educational performance of both boys and girls, significantly increase the graduation rates of both genders, and at the same time substantially reduce rates of juvenile deliquency and crime.

The carrot of these programs should be complemented by the heavy stick of rigorously enforced laws against deadbeat fathers. All fathers, whether married to the mothers of their children or not, should be held accountable for the support of their children. A lien should be placed on the income of all absent fathers and their property subject to seizure. This will not only offer some compensation to taxpayers burdened with the support of their progeny, but would also have the effect of encouraging more responsible parenting. The important point is to make the costs of irresponsible paternity as painfully high as possible, lasting until children are no longer supported by the state. There has been a great deal of rhetoric on this subject in recent years, but still too little action.

I urge Afro-Americans, especially Afro-American women, to engage more in out-marriage. This would immediately help to solve the marriage squeeze of Afro-American women. And with the sexual and marital competition of men from other ethnic groups Afro-American men may well be prompted to alter their own attitudes and behavior. Afro-American women should realize that they do not have to wait for *all* other Americans to cease being "racially" endogamous for them to greatly increase their marital options. Given that Afro-Americans are only thirteen percent of the population, even if only one in five men who are not Afro-Americans are interested in inter-marrying with them this would immediately double the market of available spouses for them. I strongly suspect that the proportion of non-Afro-Americans so willing is indeed greater than one-fifth. Hence, Afro-American women should immediately consider doing what one very attractive sister who has just recovered from her second failed marriage to Afro-American men told me recently: that she is now strongly believes in extending the equal opportunity principle to the marriage market.

What is more, not only would out-marriage immediately improve the marital prospects of Afro-American women, but it would lead to the all-important exchange of cultural dowries that other Americans now take for granted.

We need to change our urban policy from an emphasis on improving the ghettos—through community development programs, enterprise zones, housing schemes, or whatever—to policies aimed at their removal. Ghettos were racist in their origins and are racist in their perpetuation, whatever short-term benefits that may accrue to Afro-American community leaders and politicians. Enormous social and economic costs are incurred growing up in a neighborhood with a concentration of poor persons nearly all of whom share the same set of chronic socioeconomic, educational, sexual, marital, and familial problems. A simple solution is to for Afro-Americans to be scattered among the rest of the population, and government policy should shift to such a focus.

This would almost certainly have a positive effect on the marital and familial experience of Afro-Americans. Propinquity, as I have repeatedly pointed out, is a major factor in marital choice. In this regard, ghettoization has been, in part, a highly successful reproductive strategy by the dominant group to keep Afro-Americans out of their marriage market. This must stop. And Afro-Americans should stop undermining their own best interests by misguidedly favoring policies that preserve their ghetto neighborhoods, especially in light of the fact that the 'hood itself is not what it has been made out to be.

My analysis, it should be clear by now, offers no comfort to conservatives and reactionaries. Before jubilantly pointing to my conclusion that *current* socioeconomic conditions are no longer the proximate causes of Afro-American marital and familial problems, they must explain the centuries of unrelieved oppression and economic discrimination that have resulted in the cultural patterns that now obviate the need for them. The nation as a whole, and Afro-Americans in particular, are still paying the ethnocidal price of slavery and the neo-dulotic Jim Crow system.

American conservatives, after all, are the people who never tire of reminding us that we must take history and culture seriously.

Nonetheless, it cannot be overstated that, in the final analysis, the problems analyzed in this essay can only be solved by Afro-Americans themselves, especially Afro-American men, through a radical recommitment to stable gender, marital, and parental attitudes and behavior. What the novelist and social critic Toni Cade Bambara wrote over a quarter of a century ago is still powerfully relevant today: "Revolution begins with the self, in the self. The individual, the basic revolutionary unit, must be purged of poison and lies that assault the ego and threaten the heart, that hazard the next larger unit—the couple or pair—that jeopardize the still larger unit—the family or cell—that put the entire movement at peril."[309]

Afro-American men and women of all classes have a terribly troubled relationship. Slavery and the system of racial oppression engendered it, and poverty, economic insecurity, and lingering racism sustain it. But blaming these injustices alone will get them nowhere. Not only because it is Afro-Americans themselves, especially men, who now inflict these wounds upon themselves—through the ways they betray those who love them and bear their progeny, through the ways they bring up or abandon their children, through the ways they relate, or fail to relate, to each other, through the values and attitudes they cherish and the ones they choose to spurn, through their comforting ethnic myths about their neighborhoods, through their self-indulgences, denials, and deceits—but because only they as individual men and women can find the antidote to heal themselves.

Two

FEAST
OF BLOOD

"Race," Religion, and Human Sacrifice in the Postbellum South

$$\mathfrak{Z}$$

For the life of the flesh is in the blood: and I have given it to you upon the altar to make atonement for your souls: for it is the blood that maketh an atonement for the soul. Leviticus 17:11

Almost all Maryville [Missouri]—3,000 strong, it is reported—turned out for the feast of blood. A strong wind was blowing, and the little schoolhouse, with the Negro bound on the ridge-pole, and plentifully soaked with gasoline, made a spectacular blaze. Literary Digest, January 31, 1931.

JASPER, TEXAS, COULD EASILY BE a postcard model for a modern Southern small town. Surrounded by verdant meadows rolling into a cool, friendly forest, it is home to an ethnically mixed population who interact at school, at work, and in public spaces with an unforced cordiality that would put the "racial" avoidance rituals of Northern cities to shame. On the night of June 7, 1998, however, Jasper had a horrible reminder of its inglorious past. James Byrd, an Afro-American part-time musician, became America's most recent lynch victim. On the picturesque country road running through the forest, he was chained by his feet to the back of a pick-up truck by three Euro-American men and dragged along the road until his spray-painted head tore away from his grated, mutilated body, rolling into a ditch.

The nation's writers, especially its pundits on "race," were quick to draw the facile and predictable conclusion that this proves that not much has really changed in American "race" relations. Whatever the public displays of interethnic civility, ran the argument that rang from the nation's editorial pages, America is still a chronically racist place, and the "races" remain as far apart as ever. That Euro- and Afro-Americans still keep largely separate in their intimate relations and private social interactions is indeed true, and this is the best measure of how much remains to be done before America can declare itself a truly integrated society. But it is equally true that enormous progress has been made in the all-important spheres of work, politics, security, and the sharing of public spaces, spectacles, and culture. Most important of all has been the sea change in Euro-American attitudes toward Afro-Americans, now seen as fellow citizens, fully and equally participating in the civic life of their communities.

And there was no better proof of this than the political composition of Jasper and the reaction of its citizens to the lynchlike murder of James Byrd. Although 55 percent of Jasper's population is Euro-American, its mayor, its hospital administrator, the president of its chamber of commerce, the executive director of the East Texas Council of Government, and the past president of its school board are all Afro-Americans. There was genuine outrage and disgust on the part of nearly all citizens at what had happened, and the Euro-American sheriff, Billy Rowles, had the full support and gratitude of both ethnic groups for his investigation and quick arrest of the culprits. The co-owner of one of the town's main restaurants spoke for most Euro-American citizens of Jasper when she told the *Dallas Morning News* that, upon hearing the news of the lynching, she gathered her Afro-American employees in her office and prayed with them. "I asked God's forgiveness that this happened, that it came from my race. And I asked God's mercy and I asked God to bless them and their families. They cried; we all cried."[1] And the parents of James Byrd reflected the mood of most Afro-American residents—if not of the race leaders who showed up smarting for a "racial" fight—when they publicly expressed Christian forgiveness to the lynchers and their families, praised the town's record of ethnic relations, and appealed for peace.

To describe Jasper as merely "a town divided but civil," as the journalists of the *Dallas Morning News* did, is sociologically correct insofar as it refers to the still nearly complete segregation of private life along ethnic lines. But it unfairly downplays the ethnic changes that this town, like the nation at large, has gone through over the past half century, changes that—in light of the sheer horror of the nation's "racial" past—can only be described as extraordinary. In this essay I will explore the vilest aspect of that monstrous past—the terrorization of Afro-Americans by lynch mobs and their ritualized killing in communal acts of human sacrifice. I explore it not only because it is one of those collective traumas that, like the Nazi Holocaust, our humanity demands we never forget but because nothing better demonstrates just how far this nation has come in its unfinished journey toward becoming the first genuinely multiethnic society among the great powers of the world. Jasper, we will see, is important as a historical and symbolic point of reference precisely because it lies in eastern Texas, which was the center of Ku Klux Klan killings during the heyday of lynching. Indeed, Vidor, only fifty miles to the south, is still a haven for what remains of the Klan. The three men who killed James Byrd that June night were banal human brutes, and no more. Their behavior was in no way sanctioned by their communities. To the contrary, it elicited the fullest expression of shame, abhorrence, and condemnation, as well as the swift arm of the law. And that's the critical point. During the era of lynching, the ritualized murder of Afro-Americans had the full tacit or active support of all classes of Euro-Americans. Indeed, lynchings were communal events. One genre of them, on which I will concentrate, had all the trappings of a sacred ritual and was often presided over by a clergyman. What is more, the people who participated in these orgies of violence were not deviants and outlaws. As W. E. B. Du Bois, who lived through this horror, clearly saw, it was "its nucleus of ordinary men that continually [gave] the mob its initial and awful impetus" to maim, defile, kill, and burn innocent Afro-Americans.[2]

It will no doubt come as a shock to nearly all Americans to learn that Euro-Americans were the last Western people to practice the grim ancient ritual and that these rituals of human sacrifice continued until as late as the early thirties of this century. I refer here to hundreds of the more than five thousand lynchings of Afro-American people in America between the end of the Civil War and 1968. There is abundant evidence that a significant minority of these thousands of killings were sacrificial murders, possessing all the ritual, communal, and, in many cases, religious characteristics of classic human sacrifice. This essay will provide both evidence and theoretical grounds for this claim.

Ralph Ellison is among the few Americans to have recognized the stark fact that lynching was human sacrifice, laden with religious and political significance for his culture. He found it "instructive that Hemingway, born into a culture characterized by violence," should have used the Spanish bullfight as his prototype of ritualized violence when "he might have studied that ritual of violence closer to home, that ritual in which the sacrifice is that of a human scapegoat, the lynching bee."[3] To be sure, many other writers, especially novelists, have commented, and drawn, sometimes directly, on the obviously ritualistic nature of lynching. Richard Wright's "Big Boy Leaves Home," James Baldwin's *Going to Meet the Man*, Faulkner's *Light in August*, and Lillian Smith's *Killers of the Dream* spring to mind. As Trudier Harris has argued, lynching was a "peculiarly American ritual" which no novelist worthy of the name could fail to take account of in any literary treatment of "black-white" relations.

However, Harris, like the writers she discusses, places too heavy an interpretive burden on what she calls the "emotional cause of lynching," especially neo-Freudian explanations.[4] There can be no doubt, as Nancy MacLean and Leon Litwack, among others, have demonstrated, that a major factor in lynching was the desire by Euro-American men to keep Afro-American men from any intimate contact with Euro-American women and to keep both in their places; the former as powerless members of an inferior "race"; the latter, of an inferior gender, mere icons of a male chivalric code.[5] Obvious, too, are the elements of sexual fear and competition. The castration of many of the Afro-American victims was indeed a kind of communal rape, as Harris suggests. It may well have been indicative of sexual jealousy and castration anxieties on the part of the Euro-American oppressors and their need to deny any hint of manhood and independence to Afro-American males.

Even agreeing that sexuality was important, however, many would question whether the real issue was Euro-American men's castration complex. The historian Forrest Wood suggests that it was just the opposite—their indulgence of their own all-too-potent sexuality, and their need to control Euro-American women: "For generations, southern white men had successfully dehumanized their women in order to perpetuate their own privileged position and rationalize their own sexual excesses. If white women took it upon themselves to express their sexuality fully, the presence of high-powered animalistic Negroes would allow them to destroy completely the socio-sexual culture that had evolved over the decades. The Civil War abolished slavery, it did not abolish the southern way of life."[6]

Quite apart from the uncertainty of interpretation, some caution is strongly suggested by the simple fact that, of the reasons given by those who took part in lynchings, rape or attempted rape was mentioned in only a quarter of the cases occurring between 1882 and 1968 (see Table 2.1). Not that such statistical evidence is decisive. Most Euro-American Southerners were of the opinion that rape and attempted rape were the main reasons for lynching, and it is this racist tradition that, ironically, in-

TABLE 2.1. Alleged Reasons for Lynching, 1882–1968

Year	Homicide	Assault	Rape	Attempted Rape	Robbery & Theft	Insult to Whites	Other Reasons
1882–89	537	4	259	9	58	5	331
1890–99	606	37	317	75	87	10	408
1900–09	372	56	155	99	13	11	160
1910–19	278	51	88	56	38	31	81
1920–29	100	40	70	22	6	17	60
1930–39	39	14	22	21	6	8	20
1940–49	5	2	0	6	4	2	14
1950–59	0	1	1	0	0	1	5
1960–68	0	0	0	0	0	0	5
Total	1937	205	912	288	212	85	1084
% of Total	40.8	4.3	19.3	6.0	4.9	1.8	22.8

SOURCE. Data from Daniel T. Williams, "The Lynching Records at Tuskegee Institute," in *Eight Negro Bibliographies,* compiled by Daniel T. Williams (New York: Kraus Reprint, 1970).

forms the neo-Freudian interpretation. Nonetheless, it might be important, in itself, that most Euro-American Southerners insisted on contradicting the evidence of what the lynchers and their communities themselves said. Indeed, as W. Fitzhugh Brundage has pointed out, the Southern male conception of sexual threat was broad enough to embrace most crimes, especially when allegedly committed by Afro-Americans. One Methodist minister went so far as to state, in all seriousness, that "danger to women is inherent in every offense against white men."[7]

My main problem with this approach is that the structural and cultural dimension of lynching is seriously neglected by too great an emphasis on the psychological. Beyond satisfying psychological needs and the will to power, the sacrificial ritual, as we will see, performed vital social and cultural functions for Southern postbellum communities. As Mary Douglas and other anthropologists have demonstrated, sacrifice enacts and symbolically recreates a disrupted or threatened social world, and it resolves, through the shedding of blood, a specific crisis of transition.[8] It is a brutal rite of passage enacted not primarily for the individual but for the community. Because it is, above all, a communal act, to focus on its psychological processes runs the risk of misplaced emphasis.

THE HISTORY AND SOCIOLOGY OF U.S. LYNCHINGS

IN THE UNITED STATES lynching began in the mid-eighteenth century as a way for citizens to protect themselves against lawless individuals whom the authorities were unable to control.[9] Before 1830 it was largely confined to the frontier regions, and the victims were almost all Euro-Americans. After 1830 it became increasingly a Southern phenomenon, especially with the growth of the antislavery movement. Most of the victims, however, were still Euro-Americans, alleged criminals, although a growing number were freedmen and slaves suspected of subversion.[10]

After the Civil War the situation changed dramatically, especially after the end of Reconstruction (see Figure 2.1). Of persons lynched between 1882 and 1968, 72 percent were Afro-Americans.[11] It was in the South that the vast majority—80 percent—of lynchings occurred (see Figure 2.2). Mississippi had the greatest number of lynchings during this period, followed by Georgia, Texas, Louisiana, Alabama, and Arkansas. As one would expect, a very high proportion of those lynched in the Deep South were Afro-Americans. Thus, 90 percent of persons lynched between 1882 and 1968 in the Deep South states of Alabama, Georgia, Louisiana, Mississippi, and South Carolina were Afro-Americans, compared with 78 percent of those lynched in the border states of Arkansas, Florida, Kentucky, North Carolina, and Texas. And in the western states with a well-developed tradition of lynching—Colorado, California, Montana, Nebraska, and Wyoming—only 5 percent of victims were Afro-Americans.

Not all lynchings were interethnic. Indeed, as one would expect, nearly all Euro-American victims were lynched by other Euro-Americans. But there are rare cases on record of Afro-Americans lynching Euro-Americans and getting away with it. For example, when three Afro-American men lynched a Euro-American man for raping a thirteen-year-old Afro-American girl in South Carolina, the governor pardoned the three after receiving over three thousand petitions. Ironically, as many Euro-Americans approvingly observed, this action only reinforced the culture of lynching in the state.[12] Tragically, the lynching of Afro-Americans by fellow Afro-Americans further reinforced the custom. Two researchers found that 6 percent of Afro-American victims of lynchings between 1882 and 1930 in the ten Southern states they studied were killed by fellow Afro-Americans.[13] Like intraethnic killings among Euro-Americans, these Afro-American lynchings were most pronounced during the 1880s and peaked during the

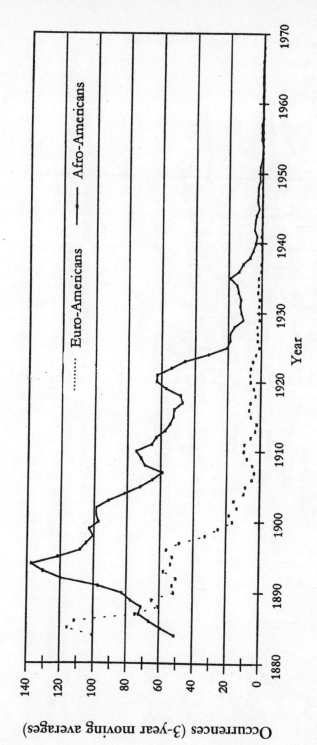

Figure 2.1. **Afro-American and Euro-American Lynch Victims, 1882–1968.** SOURCE: Based on data from Daniel T. Williams, "The Lynching Records at Tuskagee Institute," in *Eight Negro Bibliographies*, compiled by Daniel T. Williams (New York: Kraus Reprint, 1970).

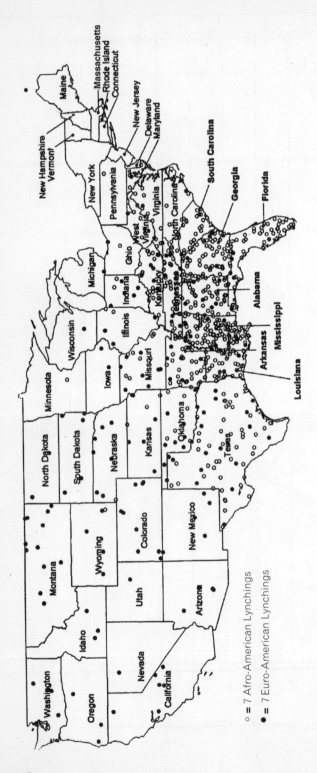

Figure 2.2. **Distribution of Lynchings of Euro-Americans and Afro-Americans, 1882–1968.** SOURCE: Map created for author by Harvard Map Services, based on data from Daniel T. Williams, "The Lynching Records at Tuskegee Institute," in *Eight Negro Bibliographies*, compiled by Daniel T. Williams (New York: Kraus Reprint, 1970).

○ = 7 Afro-American Lynchings

● = 7 Euro-American Lynchings

1890s. The majority were in the newly settled states of Mississippi, Arkansas, and Louisiana and may have been a form of punishment for serious crimes "in the absence of an efficient, formal law enforcement authority."[14]

Only a minority of lynchings qualify as ritual or sacrificial murder. Some indication of the proportion of killings that had a genuinely ritualistic aspect is given by Walter White, who found that of 416 blacks slaughtered between 1918 and 1927, 62 "were done to death with abnormal savagery." Of these, 43 were burned alive, and in 15 cases the bodies were burned after death. Torture, mass attendance, and burning are the three main indicators of ritual killings that acquired a sacrificial nature.

W. Fitzhugh Brundage has classified lynchers into four types: (1) small-time terrorists; (2) private gangs involved in moral and antigovernmental crusades and the settlement of private grievances; (3) large-scale semilegal posses; and (4) mass mobs numbering between fifty and several thousands, which had the full support of the community for their extralegal and illegal activities. Only the last—the mass mob—he argues, demonstrated the "highly ritualized choreography" of the chase, the careful selection of the sacrificial site, the sadistic torture and burning (often alive) of the victim, the collection of mementos from the victim's body and the site of his sacrifice, and the postsacrificial ritual of the kangaroo "coroner's jury" verdict. Brundage estimates that 34 percent of all lynchings in Georgia and 40 percent of those in Virginia were of this type.[15] This seems a fair estimate of the proportion of lynching that may be considered sacrificial.

The main reasons given for the lynching of Afro-Americans were murder and rape or attempted rape (see Table 2.1). During the period between 1882 and 1968, of the 4,743 cases on record of which some alleged reason is known, 1,937 were allegedly for homicide, 912 for rape, 288 for attempted rape, 232 for robbery and theft, 205 for felonious assault, 85 for insult to whites, and 1,084 attributed to a variety of "other causes."[16] None of these were proven charges. In keeping with the tribal nature of the killings, victims frequently were randomly selected from the kinsmen of the accused when he could not be found.

While the vast majority of those lynched were males, it should be noted that females were sometimes killed. Of the 2,701 persons lynched in ten Southern states between 1882 and 1930, 74 were Afro-American women and five Euro-American women.[17] Few, if any, of the women lynched, however, were sacrificially murdered, although one of the most heinous acts of savagery ever recorded involved the lynching of an Afro-American woman, Martha Turner, after she threatened to take legal action against the killers who had just lynched her husband. Eight months pregnant, she was hung by her ankles from a tree by the leaders of a mob of several hundred men and women. Her dress was doused with gasoline and burned from her body and her belly ripped open with a hog knife while she was still alive. When her baby fell to the ground and uttered its first cry, its head was crushed to pulp by the stomping feet of the frenzied men and women.[18]

There have been numerous attempts to explain lynchings in socio-economic terms, but as two scholars admitted in 1992, "We still know little about the underlying causes of mob violence during this period."[19] An early work suggested an association between the proportion of the population who were fundamentalist Christians (Methodists and Baptists) and the total number of people lynched, though no attempt was made to demonstrate a causal link.[20] Others have argued that lynching was a form of "repressive justice" used to resolve the crisis of communal solidarity caused by the Populist rupture of the "solid South." The attempt by the Populists to bridge "racial" division through class and political coalition created an enormous breach in the solidarity of Southern society. When the movement collapsed, Afro-Americans were scapegoated in the "ritual punishments" of lynching, which both expressed and enhanced the process of reunification.[21] One group of sociologists has analyzed lynchings as "contingent historical unfoldings," an interpretation that, I regret to say, I have tried, but failed, to understand.[22] Another sociologist has characterized them as a form of social control that "defines and responds to conduct as deviant" depending on the social and cultural distance "between the parties."[23]

Demographic and political factors have long been proposed as major causes. The greater the relative size of the Afro-American population, it has been argued, the greater the "racial" threat felt by Euro-Americans, and hence the greater the tendency to lynch Afro-Americans.[24] However, the empirical and methodological grounds for these claims have been sharply questioned in the past decade.[25]

A long tradition of scholarship has emphasized economic factors. Some in this tradition have focused on economic competition between poor Euro-Americans and Afro-Americans, a competition exacerbated by immigration, Euro-American unionization, and urbanization.[26] Others have isolated macroeconomic factors as the major culprit, attempting to show that the rate of lynching rose and fell according to the interaction between the price of cotton and the level of production.[27]

Of these economic explanations, by far the most nuanced and persuasive has been offered by E. M. Beck and Stewart Tolnay,[28] who argue, with new and better data than earlier scholars, that different classes of Euro-Americans supported lynching for somewhat different economic reasons. Lower-class Euro-Americans were threatened by competition from cheap Afro-American labor, while the elite planters who desired such labor were threatened by any condition that promoted the solidarity of Afro-American and Euro-American labor. During periods of economic depression in the cotton industry, there was a lethal convergence of Euro-American hostility toward Afro-Americans, with the poor resenting and scapegoating Afro-American labor, and the elite finding inter-"racial" violence the best safeguard against the Afro-American and Euro-American poor uniting against them. These relationships, Beck and Tolnay further argue, held mainly during the last quarter of the nineteenth century. Afterwards, the link between lynching and market forces weakened. The changing character of the Southern economy in the early twentieth century; the outmigration of both Euro-Americans and Afro-Americans from the Deep South; and the political and legal disenfranchisement of Afro-Americans—these factors obviated the need for ritualized mob violence as a means of controlling Afro-Americans.

These essentially structuralist accounts of lynching provide a useful framework for the discussion of the cultural aspects of the phenomenon. None of them, however, tells us anything about the meaning and cultural import of lynchings, although some strongly hint at the kinds of cultural explanations we must invoke in any attempt to understand this horrible phenomenon of American history. While some of them clearly acknowledge the ritualistic nature of these killings, they completely miss the most remarkable attribute of these rituals—their sacrificial nature. It is to an understanding of how and why such a thing as human sacrifice was possible in what was already emerging as one of the most advanced areas of the Western world that we now turn.

HUMAN AND NONHUMAN SACRIFICE THROUGH THE AGES

THE RITUAL KILLING OF human beings is, of course, the ultimate form of blood-sacrifice. The practice has existed, at some time, among nearly all peoples. Contrary to common belief, it was not confined to the most primitive peoples but tended to be found more among highly advanced premodern peoples. It was evident in all the advanced ancient Near Eastern civilizations, including that of the ancient Hebrews—as the tradition of the Aqedah, or Binding, (i.e., Abraham's binding and offering of his only son, Isaac, as a human sacrifice on Mount Moriah) attests—and throughout pre-Christian Europe.[29] As I have shown elsewhere, human sacrifice is closely related to slaveholding. Indeed, among many peoples, ranging from the Northwest Coast Indians of America to the Aztecs, Ashantis, and Carthaginians, human sacrifice was one of the main reasons for the holding of slaves and the taking of prisoners of war.[30]

What is sacrifice, and why is it that its most brutal form—the slaughter of fellow human beings—tends to be among mankind's most sacred rituals? Among most peoples, the primitive belief persists that blood "constitutes an animating principle of a living organism" and, as such, "its outpouring establishes a vital alliance between those united in a blood-bond. Consequently [blood] was a potent agent in consolidating tribal relationships and effecting intercommunion between the human and the sacred."[31] The sacrifice is often, although not always, a gift to a god. It propitiates and it atones, but it also performs vital social and psychological functions for the participants. Two forms of blood-sacrifice are particularly horrifying to the modern mind: cannibalism and human sacrifice, the two often going together. The sacrifice of nonhuman creatures was often a substitute for human sacrifice and, I should now add, for cannibalism, where it was associated with human sacrifice.[32] Another kind of substitute for human sacrifice was the giving of a piece of the flesh of living persons. The classic case of this was circumcision, but closely related to this were other practices such as bloodletting and finger sacrifice.[33]

Sacrifice has received considerable attention from anthropologists before and since Henri Hubert and Marcel Mauss wrote at the end of the last century, but Hubert and Mauss's work is still the most penetrating statement on the subject.[34] First, they showed that sacrifice was always a highly ritualized act. Like all ritual, it involved drama, celebration, and play. An essential feature of the sacrificial drama, Hubert and Mauss noted, was its "perfect continuity. From the beginning to the end it must continue without interruption and in the ritual order."[35] The climax of the drama was the killing of the victim, at which point there was usually absolute quiet, often in stark contrast to the mirth and singing, even rowdiness, of preceding and later stages.

Second, the sacrifice was usually performed either in a permanently sacred place or in a place that had been consecrated beforehand or was consecrated by the sacrifice itself. The most common way of consecrating a place for sacrifice was to build a fire.

Third, the fire was important in itself, for it invariably symbolized the deity. As the victim was consumed by the flames, he was symbolically devoured by the god.

The fourth important element of the sacrifice was the stake to which the victim was tied. Often special trees were required, and the victim had to be tied in a special way. The region around the stake also became a magical circle.

Fifth, there were always certain sets of ideas about the victim. He could be symbolic of good or evil, and sometimes both, depending on the objective of the sacrificial ritual and the character of the deity or cause to which he was being sacrificed. The victim mediated between the sacred and the profane. Killing the victim involved not just the gift of a valued object but the liberation of his life-spirit and the creation of a compact between the sacrificers and God or some transcending entity. For this reason, there was usually some form of physical contact made with the victim, although this was sometimes mediated by official sacrificers.

Finally, what remained of the victim after he had been killed and burnt might be allotted completely to the sacred world, or it might be allotted completely to the secular world, in which case it was eaten, or parts might be given to the gods and parts kept by the sacrificers. If not literally eaten, the sacrificed victim was often symbolically eaten, in that he was carved up and pieces of his body taken as sacred ritual mementos. Often there was a common meal at the end of the sacrifice, which in many cases acted as a substitute for the actual consumption of the sacrificed object. Such commensality was sometimes ritually important, but as Meyer Fortes has noted, "it could also be for the actors no more than . . . festal addition to the specifically efficacious ritual act."[36]

The sacrificial ritual created not only a compact between the sacrificers and their god but a compact of fellowship among the sacrificers themselves. It had other sociological functions as well. As Durkheim and his followers emphasized, the sacrifice maintained the links between the society and its god or gods, in this way strengthening the power of the community. The sacrifice reinforced the most strongly held values of the group. Among the primitive Tupinamba of South America, it was critically related to their extremely martial and honorific view of the world.

The same was true, however, of far more advanced militaristic cultures such as those of the Dahomeans, Ashantis, and Carthaginians.

Nietzsche emphasized this moral aspect of sacrifice in his remarkable discussion of the subject. For him, it was one of the tragedies of humanity that "blood and cruelty is the foundation of all 'good things.'" In order to stamp on the mind "a few primal postulates of social intercourse" that the group considers vital to its way of life, the cruelty of sacrifice becomes necessary: "When man thinks it necessary to make for himself a memory, he never accomplishes it without blood, tortures and sacrifice; the most dreadful sacrifice and forfeitures (among them sacrifice of the first-born), the most loathsome mutilation (for instance castration), and the most cruel rites of all the religious cults (for all religions are really at bottom systems of cruelty)—all these things originate from that instinct which found in pain its most potent mnemonic."[37] One need not concur with Nietzsche's general condemnation of religions to accept the truth of this insight.[38]

There is another feature of sacrifice that Nietzsche could have mentioned in support of his argument, namely, that the most cruel of sacrifices were usually also forms of recreation. As Edward Norbeck observed, not only is play a biological imperative for all human life, but for "most of man's history, religion has been the primary vehicle for man's form of play." Norbeck notes that as with religion, "the keynote of play is transcendence, a departure from ordinary states of being to another realm of perception of existence."[39] In addition, play is pleasure. It is make-believe, it is art, and it is ritual. And nowhere is play more congruent with religious behavior than in the ritual of blood-sacrifice. Sacrifice is recreation in its two senses; it is recreation in the sense of play and drama, and it is re-creation, by means of play and drama.

Sometimes the need to create is necessitated by the threat of chaos and violence. René Girard has proposed that sacrifice is a way of dealing with violence in the absence of legal institutions; the victim diverts and displaces the violence that threatens to tear both the self and the community apart.[40] It is an attractive idea, especially if one thinks of frontier-type communities similar to the more primitive societies Girard had in mind.

The absence of control is central to one of the most important functions of sacrifice: its role as a rite of passage. Passages are, of course, of many kinds. For individuals, there are life passages such as those from childhood to adulthood, classically analyzed by Van Gennep, in which sacrifice plays a vital role in warding off danger during the liminal, or dangerously exposed, transition period between one stage of life and another. Individuals also undergo passages between crucial social statuses—for example, between freedom and enslavement, or between lay and priestly status. For societies, there are passages between unusual events, such as war or famine, and normalcy. Godfrey Ashby glosses Edmund Leach in pointing out "that the change of status of a person or of a society involves passing into a 'holy state,' in a sense outside the normal time sequence and outside that society, before achieving the new status. At the danger point of separation from a status A and aggregation into status B, rites are required, purification is needed—a separating off of pure from impure."[41]

Societal transitions, moments when the entire community or nation is at risk, are, of course, the most serious, demanding the greatest sacrifices. There is a veritable convergence of liminal, or dangerous, transitional states: that of each and every individual whose life is at risk; that of the entire community, whose whole way of life is in peril; and that of time and history itself, which has been halted in the chaos of meaning as people try to come to terms with what has happened to them, to their community, to their culture, and to their history. It is during such moments of extreme, total transition that the most extreme form of sacrifice—human sacrifice—is called for.

Precisely such a period of acute liminal transition was faced by the Old South after the collapse of its system of slavery and during its forced transition to a new form of society, a transition that took some fifty years. That period, especially after the end of Reconstruction, was perhaps the worst episode in the history of Afro-Americans, for as we will see, it was they who paid the expiatory and propitiatory price of the South's transition, in increasingly savage rituals of human sacrifice.

Human Sacrifice: A Primitive Example

Before examining the Southern case, let me illustrate all that I've said so far with an example taken from a completely different society that practiced human sacrifice in its most extreme form: the cannibalistic feasting on the victim's body. The pre-Columbian Tupinamba were a hunter-gathering tribe who lived on the coastal strip of Brazil south of what is now Sao Paulo.[42] They were one of the most primitive groups on record, far removed from the advanced capitalistic economy of the Old South. Nonetheless, they shared two social features with the Old South. First, they were an extremely militaristic and honorific group. Warfare and the exhibition and defense of honor were central values in this totally male-dominated culture. Second, slavery was of enormous cultural importance to the Tupinamba. Unlike in the South, slavery had no economic significance, and there were only a few slaves at any given time. These few slaves, however, played a vital role in the religious and secular life of the Tupinamba, for their sacrifice marked the high point of the tribe's religious, political, and recreational practices.

Up to the moment of his sacrifice, the slave was generally treated well, as long as he remained under the protective power of his master. However, if he attempted to run away, his action incited the wrath of the entire community. Upon being caught and returned by the equivalent of what were called "patrollers" in the Old South, the runaway was abused by an angry mob. According to one eyewitness: "The old women go to meet him shouting to those who bring him back: 'He is ours, give him to us, we want to eat him.'"[43] This reflected the strong belief that once the slave broke away from the protective power of his master, he endangered the entire community and, as such, belonged to the group.

The sacrificial murder of the slave was undertaken with what Florestan Fernandez had identifyed as six distinct types of ritual.[44] Because the slave had been earlier incorporated by the rites of enslavement as a part of the community—as one who was in it, though never a member of it—it was necessary before his sacrifice to exclude him once again. Between exclusion and the actual sacrifice the slave was a masterless, uncontrolled person in their midst. In this state of intense liminality, he was a mortal danger to the community and greatly feared. The *rites of segregation* were quickly followed by *rites of inculpation,* in which the slave and his tribe of origin were accused and reviled. Next came, in this order, *rites of preparation* for the sacrifice, usually the day before the execution; *rites of symbolic escape and recapture,* in which the slave was deliberately allowed to escape, then was retaken with much abuse; *rites of vengeance;* and *rites of slaughter.* This complex of rites was followed by the cannibalistic feast, which also had its own elaborate rules and taboos, especially for the slaveholder who had done the killing. After this came, finally, rites of purification.

A. Metraux, basing his account on the numerous eyewitness reports from the sixteenth century, summarizes the sacrificial ceremony as follows:

> The rope was taken from his neck, passed around his waist,
> and held at both ends by two or more men. Again he was al-

lowed to give vent to his feelings by throwing fruits or pot-
sherds at his enemies. He was surrounded by women who vied
in their insults. Old women, painted black and red, with
necklaces of human teeth, darted out of their huts carrying
newly painted vases to receive the victim's blood and entrails.
A fire was lit and the ceremonial club was shown to the captive. Every man present handled the club for a while, thus ac-
quiring the power to catch a prisoner in the future. Then the
executioner appeared in full array, painted and covered with a
long feather cloak. He was followed by relatives who sang and
beat drums. Their bodies, like that of the executioner, were
smeared with white ashes. The club was handed to the executioner by a famous old warrior, who performed a few ritual
gestures with it. The executioner derided the prisoner for his
imminent death, while the latter foretold the vengeance that
his relatives would take and boasted of his past deeds. . . . The
execution itself was a cruel game. Enough liberty was allowed
the prisoner to dodge the blows, and sometimes a club was put
in his hands so that he could parry with them without being
able to strike. When at last he fell down, his skull shattered,
everybody shouted and whistled. The position of the body was
interpreted as an omen for the executioner. The prisoner's wife
shed a few tears over his body and then joined in the cannibalistic banquet. Old women rushed to drink the warm blood,
and children were invited to dip their hands in it. Mothers
would smear their nipples with blood so that even babies
could taste of it. The body, cut into quarters, was roasted on a
barbecue and the old women, who were the most eager for
human flesh, licked the grease running along the sticks. Some
portions, reputed to be delicacies or sacred, such as the fingers
or the grease around the liver or heart, were allotted to distinguished guests.[45]

The sacrifice of the slave among the Tupinamba exhibited most of the
attributes and functions of human sacrifice found in other parts of the
world, especially among honorific and militaristic cultures, where a slave
or prisoner of war was the typical victim. The sacrifice of the slave, the ultimate domestic enemy, made possible not just the pursuit of vengeance
but the propitiation of, and giving of thanks to, the local gods, as well as

the imbibing of the enemy's power in the very process of expelling and destroying him. Further, the sacrificial ritual brought together the entire community in their common feasting on the enemy's body. In the process, it united them with their own supernatural beings, who were also believed to partake in the ceremony. By identifying and consuming the domestic enemy, the Tupinamba recreated joyously, re-created their cultural life, and redefined themselves.

Human Sacrifice and Ritual Cannibalism in the Postbellum South

Many Americans, especially in the Northeast, expressed horror at the escalating rate of lynching in the nation toward the end of the nineteenth century, although few were prepared to do much about it beyond bemoan what seemed like a regression to primitivism. From time to time, attention was drawn to one aspect of lynching that seems to have left observers bewildered. An editorial that appeared in a Massachusetts weekly in April 1899, commenting on an unusually sadistic lynching, was typical:

> The nation and the whole civilized world must stand aghast at the revelation. A civilized community numbering thousands, at the drop of a hat, throws off the restraints and effects of many centuries of progress and stands forth in the naked savagery of the primitive man. Men and women cheer and express feelings of triumph and joy as the victim is hurried on to the stake *to make a Sunday holiday in one of the most orthodox religious communities in the United States.* They cut off his ears, his fingers and other members of his body, and strip him and pour oil upon him while the spectators crowd desperately for positions of advantage in the great work of torture and death. [46]

What horrified the editorialist almost as much as the sadism of the mob was the fact that these monstrosities were taking place in what was the most fervently Christian part of the United States. For most Americans who thought about the matter, the implications were usually too disturbing to contemplate seriously. Most Northerners tended to attribute the association of lynching with Christianity to what one Boston preacher called the "Philistinish provincialism" of the South. At least one Northern Methodist bishop, though, disturbed by the refusal of his fellow Southern

Methodists to condemn lynching or to contemplate desegregating their churches, came closer to the truth when he wondered aloud whether "it [was] high time for those who believe[d] in practical Christianity to ask if the Master [was] being crucified afresh."[47]

For the isolated and courageous Southern liberal churchman Lewis Harvie Blair, it was simply impossible to dismiss lynching as mere Southern provincialism. He was close enough to the scene of these rituals to know that something deeper, and far more disturbing, was going on. With cutting irony, he called lynching "a fine art" that was a "distinguishing feature of American Evangelical civilization." Of a recent lynching—in which a young Afro-American, William Black, had been tied to a tree by a Euro-American, David Ready, who then knelt and prayed for the salvation of the victim's soul, said, "Amen," got up, and shot him in cold blood—Blair wrote:

> The scene is highly Druidistic and therefore dramatic; twilight; gloomy forest; long sepulchral moss swaying solemnly to the evening breeze; a youth returning home, carolling perhaps a song of deliverance [Black had just been released from prison for stealing from Ready]; David Ready as envious Fate, surrounded by approving neighbors, in solemn enclave; the joyous and unsuspecting youth suddenly seized by David Ready as Fate, and bound to a tree; David Ready as priest wrestling in prayer for deliverance of the youth; the fatal shot and death of innocent youth.[48]

While he expressed his views in sarcastic terms, it is a mistake to believe that Blair did not literally mean what he said. Few Americans were as horrified and mortified by these rituals as Blair was, and the lynching of a young man who had already served his sentence for stealing some articles of clothing is not something he would have joked about. Blair, it is clear, used the language of irony only as a way of relieving the chilling horror of the insight he had brought to bear on the subject of lynching. It is precisely that insight which I propose to explore here.

The South, Eugene Genovese has observed, "became the regime of lynching par excellence during antebellum times,"[49] although then, as we have seen, most victims were Euro-Americans. As with the Tupinamba, in the antebellum South violence and warfare were integral parts of life and of the conception of dignity and manhood. John Hope Franklin, Bertram Wyatt-Brown, and many others have ably analyzed the central role of violence and honor in Southern culture as well as their relation to slavery and frontier life.[50] The chase, the gun, the horse, and warfare were all glorified, along with a fighting spirit that informed all social relations. The result was chronic violence in day-to-day relations, to the point where homicide came to be accepted as a regular part of life, as long as certain rules of etiquette had not been breached. The fighting spirit—sometimes formalized in duels and gunplays, but more often expressed in violent rowdiness—pervaded all ethnicities, became a code of honor, and was proudly displayed and celebrated.

So ingrained and completely institutionalized was the culture of honor and violence in the Old South that it persists right down to the present. A 1996 study by a research team led by one of the nation's leading social psychologists, Richard E. Nisbett, summarized its findings as follows:

> With archival methods using census and crime reports, we have collected evidence showing that the homicide rate of the South, especially the rural South, remains high relative to the rest of the country. Using survey techniques, we have collected evidence indicating that the values of southerners favor violence for purposes of protection of property, for retaliation for an insult, and for the socialization of children. Employing experimental methods, we have collected evidence showing that southerners respond to insults in ways that are cognitively, emotionally, physiologically, and behaviorally quite different from the pattern shown by northerners. In field experiments, we have shown that southern institutions are more accepting of individuals who have committed violent crimes in defense of their honor. And with archival methods, we have collected evidence indicating that many of the social institutions and contemporary public policies of the South have their roots in the culture of honor—including the acceptance of violence to protect property and personal and national honor.[51]

Nisbett and his associate D. V. Cohen do not dispute the commonly held view that slavery was a major source of the culture of honor and violence in the South. But they argue strongly that slavery cannot *entirely* account for it. A complete explanation, they contend, must attribute this culture partly to the honorific traditions brought over by Scotch-Irish immigrants who arrived in the South between the late seventeenth and early nineteenth centuries and partly to the frontier environment of the South.[52]

I would put it this way: what both the transmitted Celtic herding culture of honor and the frontier environment initiated, the institution of slavery and the secular religion of racism institutionalized. In a celebrated section of his *Notes on Virginia,* Jefferson spoke from personal experience of the disastrous effects slavery had on the mind of the growing male Euro-American child. No one, however, has more incisively described these psychological effects than W. E. B. Du Bois:

> The Southern planter suffered, not simply for his economic mistakes—the psychological effects of slavery upon him were fatal. The mere fact that a man could be, under the law, the actual master of the mind and body of human beings had to have disastrous effects. It tended to inflate the ego of most planters beyond all reason; they became arrogant, strutting, quarrelsome kinglets; they issued commands; they made laws; they shouted their orders; they expected deference and self-abasement; they were choleric and easily insulted. Their 'honor' became a vast and awful thing, requiring wide and insistent deference. Such of them as were inherently weak and inefficient were all the more easily angered, jealous and resentful; while the few who were superior, physically or mentally, conceived no bounds to their power and personal prestige. As the world had long learned, nothing is so calculated to ruin human nature as absolute power over human beings.[53]

Even before the South's defeat in war and its Reconstruction, the Afro-American had acquired a special role in its honorific culture of violence, as the "domestic enemy" who should be feared and watched, a view well expressed by a South Carolinian who wrote in 1822 that Afro-Americans "should be watched with an eye of steady and unremitting observation. . . . Let it never be forgotten, that our Negroes are freely the JACOBINS of the country; that they are the ANARCHISTS and the DOMESTIC ENEMY: the COMMON ENEMY OF CIVILIZED SOCIETY, and the BARBARIANS WHO WOULD, IF THEY COULD, BECOME THE DESTROYERS OF OUR RACE" (uppercase in original).[54]

As with the Tupinamba, violence against the domestic enemy became more than a simple matter of control. As Ira Berlin observes: "Southerners incorporated the right of whites to discipline any 'uppity' Negro into their code of chivalry. After a Memphis mob lynched a fugitive slave who had killed a city official in attempting to escape, the city's largest newspaper admitted the act had been distasteful, but that those 'who could have been here yesterday, and not felt as *all* here felt would have been *more* or *less* than a MAN'" (newspaper's uppercase and italics).[55]

And, as with the Tupinamba, lynching was in many cases an act of sacrifice. It is not without significance that in the Memphis example it was a runaway slave who was lynched. We have already seen the reaction of the Tupinamba populace to the slave who left the protective control of the master: "He is ours, give him to us, we want to eat him." In both cultures, the rapacious savagery of the mob sprang from their deep hatred and fear of the domestic enemy let loose in their midst; in both cultures, the masterless slave was not just a legal menace but a threat to everything they held dear, to the whole basis of their civilization, and an insult to the gods.

We can now understand why the lynching of Afro-Americans escalated immediately after the end of Reconstruction. Few today would deny that, for the Afro-American, the main achievement of the Civil War was the *legal* abolition of slavery. The economic, cultural, and political status of the ex-slaves, far from improving, actually worsened after the Civil War and Reconstruction, for now Euro-American Southerners were faced with a vast mass of domestic enemies, an army of masterless slaves in their midst. Add to this the bitterness of defeat in war by a people obsessed with their sense of martial superiority. Add further the fact that the reason for this collective loss of honor was the very army of masterless slaves among them. Add also the economic insecurities of the times, the frenzy of violence that the Civil War had unleashed, and finally, the fundamentalist religious fanaticism of the region, and one finds in the masterless slaves of the postbellum South the perfect scapegoats, the ultimate sacrificial victims. Throughout the South, among all classes the preoccupation with the ex-slaves became obsessive. The hatred, fear, loathing, and horror of Afro-Americans attained levels of emotional, political, and religious intensity that are hard to imagine. Forrest G. Wood, in his study of the Southern response to emancipation, cites a prominent Republican writer's new "first commandment": "Thou shalt hate the Nigger with all thy heart, and with all thy soul, and with all thy mind and with all thy strength." Wood goes on to show how the old pro-slavery argument that slavery was a blessing for Afro-Americans in that it provided the schooling that elevated them from savagery to civilization was abandoned in favor of the view that Afro-Americans were unchangeable savages who, if left masterless, would undermine everything worthwhile and "civilized" in Southern life.[56]

THREE CASES OF LYNCHING typified this form of sacrificial murder as it was practiced in the South. First was the slaughter of an insane ex-slave, Henry Smith, who had allegedly killed the young daughter of a brutal Texas policeman after the policeman had assaulted him.[57] Although the child had not been sexually molested, a local clergyman, Bishop Haygood, fueled the growing hysteria with lurid tales of how the child had been "taken by her heels and torn asunder in the mad wantonness of gorilla ferocity." The suspect was captured in Arkansas. After he "confessed," he was brought back by train to Paris, Texas. The newspapers announced his capture and the details of his return, and thousands of onlookers thronged the stations where the train carrying Smith stopped. At one station, speeches were made by the leaders of the Paris citizenry.

Then, from one eyewitness account:

> Arriving here (Paris, Texas) at 12 o'clock the train was met by a surging mass of humanity 10,000 strong. The Negro was placed upon a carnival float in mockery of a king upon his throne, and, followed by an immense crowd, was escorted through the city so that all might see the most inhuman monster known in current history. . . . His clothes were torn off piecemeal and scattered in the crowd, people catching the shreds and putting them away as mementos. The child's father, her brother, and two uncles then gathered about the Negro as he lay fastened to the torture platform and thrust hot irons into his quivering flesh. It was horrible—the man dying by slow torture in the midst of smoke from his own burning flesh. Every groan from the fiend, every contortion of his body was cheered by the thickly packed crowd of 10,000 persons, the mass of beings 600 yards in diameter, the scaffold being the center. After burning the feet and legs, the hot irons—plenty of fresh ones being at hand—were rolled up and down Smith's stomach, back and arms. Then the eyes were burned out and irons were thrust down his throat.
>
> The men of the [child's] family having wreaked vengeance, the crowd piled all kinds of combustible stuff around the scaf-

fold, poured oil on it and set it afire. The Negro rolled and
tossed out of the mass, only to be pushed back by the people
nearest him. He tossed out again and was roped and pulled
back.[58]

According to another eyewitness, there were many small children present,
some perched on their fathers' shoulders to get a better view. He suggested
that the children should be sent away. "'No, no' shouted a hundred mad-
dened voices, 'let them learn a lesson.'" This same eyewitness adds another significant detail. The crowd worked itself up to a frenzy as the
victim writhed under the flames. Then, at the point of death, "for an in-
stant a hush spread over the people."[59]

This awed hush, in the face and smell of death, exactly conforms to
Hubert and Mauss's model of sacrifice. An essential part of the sacrificial
rite is that some profound change occurs in the sacrificed object, and
there is awe in actually witnessing the transition from a state of life to a
state of death. It is remarkable how often eyewitnesses were impressed
with this hush of transition. Thus, when John Pennington was burned
alive in Birmingham, Alabama, on August 7, 1901, he writhed in agony,
and finally, "as the flames leaped up and encircled his neck an unearthly
shriek was heard. . . . Nothing could be seen excepting a wriggling motion in the center of the circle of fire. A deathly silence followed."[60]
Something similar occurred in 1923, when a group of students at the
University of Missouri helped a mob lynch an Afro-American janitor
charged with attempted assault on the daughter of the head of the
German department. Upon the noisy mob's throwing the victim over a
railroad bridge with a noose around his neck, an eyewitness reports, "his
neck snapped audibly. [His] body swayed in mid-air for nearly a minute
as the mob mutely watched it."[61]

The second typifying case comes from a newspaper account of a sacrifice in Georgia the same year (1899). An Afro-American farm laborer,
Sam Holt, had been charged with killing his Euro-American employer
during a quarrel over wages.

In the presence of nearly 2000 people, who sent aloft yells of
defiance and shouts of joy, Sam Holt was burned at the stake
in a public road. Before the torch was applied to the pyre, the
Negro was deprived of his ears, fingers, and other portions of
his body with surprising fortitude. Before the body was cool,

it was cut to pieces, the bones were crushed into small bits and even the tree upon which the wretch met his fate was torn up and disposed of as souvenirs.

The Negro's heart was cut in small pieces, as was also his liver. Those unable to obtain the ghastly relics directly, paid more fortunate possessors extravagant sums for them. Small pieces of bone went for 25 cents and a bit of liver, crisply cooked, for 10 cents.[62]

In all human sacrifices, relics are taken by the participants, sometimes after a wild scramble and fighting for them. In the United States, this almost invariably occurred, sometimes in ghoulish ways. Thus, after Richard Coleman, a twenty-year-old, was burned alive in Maysville, Kentucky, in 1899, "relic-hunters visited the scene and carried away pieces of flesh and the negro's teeth. Others got pieces of fingers and toes and proudly exhibit the ghastly souvenirs."[63]

The third case not only makes the cannibalistic aspect of the sacrifice explicit but illustrates the importance of continuity in the ritual. It concerns the sacrifice on May 25, 1912, of Dan Davis, an Afro-American man charged with the attempted rape of a Euro-American woman:

There was some disappointment in the crowd and criticism of those who had bossed the arrangements, because the fire was so slow in reaching the Negro. It was really only ten minutes after the fire started that the smoking shoe soles and twitching of the Negro's feet indicated that his lower extremities were burning, but the time seemed much longer. The spectators had wanted so long to see him tortured that they begrudged the ten minutes before his suffering really began.

The Negro had uttered but few words. When he was led to where he was to be burned he said quite calmly, "I wish some of you gentlemen would be Christian enough to cut my throat," but nobody responded. When the fire started, he screamed "Lord, have mercy on my soul," and that was the last word he spoke, though he was conscious for fully twenty minutes after that. His exhibition of nerve aroused the admiration even of his torturers.

A slight hitch in the proceeding occurred when the Negro was about half burned. His clothing had been stripped off and burned to ashes by the flames and his black body hung nude in the gray dawn light. The flesh had been burned from his legs as high as the knees when it was seen that the wood supply was running short. None of the men or boys were willing to miss an incident of the torture. All feared something of more than usual interest might happen, and it would be embarrassing to admit later on of not having seen it on account of being absent after more wood.

Something had to be done, however, and a few men by the edge of the crowd, ran after more dry-goods boxes, and by reason of this "public-service" gained standing room in the inner circle after having delivered the fuel. Meanwhile the crowd jeered the dying man *and uttered shocking comments suggestive of a cannibalistic spirit.* Some danced and sang to testify to their enjoyment of the occasion. (Emphasis added)[64]

Like this one, all the sacrificial lynchings were highly ritualistic.[65] They were also full of drama and play culminating in the sacrifice of the victim. Because the sacrifices did not take place in already consecrated places such as churches, the use of fire as a consecrating agent became necessary, in this way serving the multiple functions of consecration, torture, and the divine devouring of the victim's soul. The stakes to which the victims were tied were obviously consecrated in the process also, since they became relics to be treasured. Further, we find that the site of the sacrifice became something of a shrine afterwards, as Hubert and Mauss's analysis predicts. Eyewitnesses who visited these sites long after testify to their special status. Thus, Walter White, a Caucasian-looking NAACP official, explains:

[In Florida one morning,] I walked along the road which led from [a] beautiful little town to the spot where five Negroes had been burned [a few years before]. Three shining-eyed, healthy, cleanly children, headed for school, approached me. As I neared them, the eldest, a ruddy-cheeked girl of nine or ten, asked if I was going to the place where "the niggers" had been killed. I told her I might stop and see the spot. Animatedly, almost as joyously as though the memory were of Christmas morning or the circus, she told me—of "the fun we had burning the niggers."[66]

The incredible brutality with which the victims were killed was also typical of human sacrifices. Unusually reminiscent of the Tupinamba, and of all scapegoat rituals involving either humans or animals, were the carnival atmosphere of these sacrificial lynchings, the occasional dressing up of the victim, and the alternate admiration and abuse of the victim. There are even many accounts of the Afro-American victim, like his Tupinamba counterpart, not only defiantly facing his torturers but cursing them to the very end to the alternate delight and outrage of the sacrificers. This was true, for example, of the victim Jim McIlherron, a proud, moderately prosperous Afro-American man who was sacrificed in Tennessee after shooting two Euro-American youths who had insulted him. In an uncanny replay of a Tupinamba sacrifice we are told:

> Bars of iron were heated and the mob amused itself by putting them close to the victim, at first without touching him. One bar he grasped and as it was jerked from his grasp all the inside of his hand came with it. Then the real torturing began, lasting for twenty minutes. During that time, while his flesh was slowly roasting, the Negro never lost his nerve. He cursed those who tortured him and almost to the last breath derided the attempts of the mob to break his spirit.[67]

FROM THE CASES we have cited, and from all other accounts of sacrificial lynching, it is no exaggeration to describe these particular cases, and a significant number of all the others, as forms of ritual cannibalism, which, as with the Tupinamba and the Aztecs, often accompanies human sacrifice. Most forms of cannibalism, it should be noted, were ritualistic, with participants merely tasting or smelling small morsels of the victim's flesh. The Southern sacrificers, as one of our cases indicates, shouted statements that were openly cannibalistic.

Sometimes we find outright cannibalism, of the kind referred to by anthropologists as autocannibalism, the victim being forced to eat his own flesh. This was the case in one of the most famous lynchings of all time, one that attracted the attention of the nation and the world even before it happened, since the AP wire service broadcast the lynchers' intention while they were still holding the victim before sacrificing him. Claude Neal was sacrificed in Jackson County, Florida, on October 27, 1934, in a "bacchanalian" ceremony of over two thousand persons organized by what appears to have been a largely middle-class group of politically connected Euro-Americans. Formal invitations had been issued for the sacrifice and announced in the local newspapers. This is how one of the sacrificers later described what had happened, as quoted by James McGovern in *Anatomy of a Lynching*:

> "After taking the nigger to the woods about four miles from Greenwood, they cut off his penis. He was made to eat it. Then they cut off his testicles and made him eat them and say he liked it" (I gathered that this barbarous act consumed considerable time and that other means of torture were used from time to time on Neal). "Then they sliced his sides and stomach with knives and every now and then somebody would cut off a finger or toe. Red hot irons were used on the nigger to burn him from top to bottom." From time to time during the torture a rope would be tied around Neal's neck and he was pulled up over a limb and held there until he almost choked to death when he would be let down and the torture began all over again.[68]

Neal's skinned and mutilated body was photographed, and copies were sold briskly for fifty cents each. Body parts were also prized mementos: "One store owner," writes McGovern, "recalled the pride with which a man came into his store that morning" and showed off one of Neal's fingers.[69]

If the victim was sometimes forced to cannibalize his own body, it was always the case that the Euro-American lynchers cannibalized that of the victim. To appreciate how and why the sacrificial burning of Afro-Americans went beyond ritual cannibalism into the real thing, we must briefly summarize modern scientific findings on the sense of smell. The common observation that our sense of taste is strongly related to our sense of smell, and that tasting is in large part actually smelling, has now been scientifically proven. In particular, the psychophysicist Claire Murphy has demonstrated that "a near perfect additivity" exists between odorants and tastants and that "there is no true sensory inhibition between olfaction and taste." In layman's language, this means that taste and smell stimulants add up to the same sensation and that their effects are not perceived differently by the brain.[70] The experience, then, of being suffused with the odor of the lynch victim's roasting body amounted literally to the cannibalistic devouring of his body.

Two features of Southern culture would have made it impossible for the participants to deny the gastronomic and religious nature of the event. The first is that, in the South and the Southwest, one of the most popular forms of food was the barbecued steak. Eating barbecued cow's steak while savoring the smell from a piece of barbecued human flesh that one has carried away as a memento clearly crosses the line between ritual and actual cannibalism. The lynchers themselves explicitly referred to the roasted Afro-Americans as barbecued meat. Thus, when two Afro-American brothers, Irving and Herman Arthur, were lynched and burned in Paris, Texas, in August 1920, their roasted bodies were chained to the back of an automobile and dragged through the streets, the celebrants shouting jubilantly as they drove through the Afro-American neighborhood: "Here come the barbecued niggers."[71]

The second point to note is that Southern lynchers did not have to await the modern scientific study of olfaction to realize that they were actually eating the Afro-American sacrificial victim as they consumed the fumes from his burning body and went around savoring little pieces of his barbecued flesh. This scientific finding had long been anticipated by the Bible. Every fundamentalist Southerner, thoroughly versed in the Old Testament language of sacrifice, would be aware of the classic biblical descriptions, especially in Leviticus, of how God consumed the sacrificial burnt offering—by smelling the "soothing odor" and consuming the "sweet savor" of the animal's burning flesh. Very early in the Bible, the Christian learns that the Old Testament God is keenly sensitive to smell. Moses is ordered to make a special perfume from sweet spices for the exclusive use of the Lord; "whosoever shall make like unto that, to smell thereto, shall ever be cut off from his people."[72] In one passage of Leviticus, God is conceived as the fire consuming the burnt offering on the altar, "which when all the people saw, they shouted, and fell on their faces."[73] However, the typical description of the various burnt offerings suggests that God consumes the sacrificed animal by savoring its burning fragrance. After each law on burnt meat offerings is pronounced, there is the closing litany "It is a burnt sacrifice, an offering made by fire, of a sweet savor unto the Lord." Indeed, one passage emphasizes that the fire is not the Lord but the means whereby he is fed the savored burnt offering: "and Moses burnt the whole ram upon the altar: it *was* a burnt sacrifice for a sweet savor, *and* an offering made by fire unto the Lord; as the Lord commanded Moses" (emphasis in King James Version).[74]

There are two other distinctive features of the sense of smell that powerfully align it with ritual events and with sacrifices involving burnt offerings in particular. One is the fact that for animals the sense of smell is the most powerful, and sometimes the only, means of identifying oneself, and of determining "how much like oneself another individual may be."[75] Among humans smell is used not only by infants to identify their mothers but by adults as a socially reconstructed means of distinguishing between classes, kinsmen, castes, and ethnic groups.[76] In France and England up to the early part of this century, the ruling and middle classes were obsessed with the odor of the lower classes, which was obviously a way of defining the poor as dirty and of demarcating class lines. In the South, this obsession was redirected from the Euro-American lower class to Afro-Americans. Like very poor, working people everywhere, both the Euro-American and the Afro-American lower classes would have smelled, but the "racial" caste system selectively emphasized the odor from the sweat of the Afro-American poor only—as a way of defining all Euro-Americans as one's own kin, as "white" self versus the Negro non-self.

With the sacrificed, burnt body of the Negro, however, the attitude toward smelling him changed radically. And here we have a remarkable example of Levi-Strauss's celebrated distinction between the raw and the cooked in the symbolism of food.[77] Levi-Strauss has shown that this distinction is a metaphor for the distinction between nature and culture. Uncooked meat is nature in the raw, nature to be shunned, whereas cooked meat is nature transformed by culture, nature civilized. Cooked meat is not only good to eat but, as Levi-Strauss famously observed, "good to think." Judith Goode summarizes the findings of modern symbolic anthropology thus: "The unique, incorporative nature of eating (assimilating) makes food an important sacred and social symbol. Relationships between a group and its gods, as well as between members of the community, are manifested in events of food sharing and exchange."[78] Applying all this to the social and sacrificial treatment of Afro-Americans in the postbellum South, it is easy to see how the live Negro, in the Southern sacrificial and food symbolism, is uncooked nature in the raw—a beast, a savage, whose odor is to be avoided at all cost. On the other hand, the cooked Negro, properly roasted, has been tamed and culturally transformed and can now be eaten, communally, in imitation of the Euro-Americans' own God savoring his burnt offering.

There is a second distinctive feature of the neurobiology and sociology of smell that bears directly on the sacrificial burning of Negroes and the food practices of the South. The psychophysicist Trygg Engen, in his urbane treatise on the psychophysics of odor, observes that the "special and perhaps unique role of the sense of smell is to reinstate the past experience with odors, whether involving nutrition, odors of other people, or pollution."[79] Odor differs from the other senses in being "impervious to time." We rapidly forget a tune, or the shape or sight of an object, but rarely forget a smell. And this is socially valuable: "Odor memory serves the primitive protection function of making sure that significant events, involving food, people, or places are not forgotten."[80] Odor, finally, not only encodes memories but it does so contextually: "Odor perception is situational, contextual, and ecological. Odors are not stored in memory as unique entities. Rather, they are always interrelated with other sensory perceptions—gustatory, cutaneous, visual, auditory, and thermal—that happen to coincide with them. Unlike sensations of sounds and colors, odors can hardly be isolated and identified by their own names."[81]

It takes little imagination to understand, now, how the powerful—and for the children who were forced to watch, no doubt traumatic—experience of watching the torture, mutilation, and burning alive of the Afro-American victim would have become encoded forever, through the overwhelming odor of his roasting body, on the memories of all who participated. The shrieking frenzy as men and women pushed their way from the outer to the inner ring of the circle around the victim; the swelling and contracting of his neck and face with the tightening and untightening of the noose; the tearing away of his clothes and the sudden exposure of his dark, naked body; the popping of gunshot; the screaming of the victim as his penis, his testicles, and other pieces of his body were chopped and carved from his trunk; the kicking, tearing, spitting, spiking, scratching at the body by the stronger men and women at the center; the disappointed cries of anguish from the older men and women forced to watch from the outer circle; the hissing sound and first singeing odor as hot irons were rolled down his body, peeling off the outer skin of face, neck, chest, belly, blooded groin, thighs, calves, and toes; the distinctive sizzle and smell of burning blood fusing with the odor of singed flesh; the piling up of wood and pine faggots; the sudden burst of flame from the kerosene-soaked pyre beneath the hanging body; the involuntary twitching and pitching of the victim's body as it was burned alive; the sudden, jubilant cry of sacred joy as the fat of the fired body fed the flame and issued forth billows of barbecue-smelling smoke. The sudden silence as the crowd, in religious awe, savored the burning body.

All of this would have been forever encoded by the odor memory of the sacrificed Negro. Because that odor memory was so closely related to the odor of barbecued cow's meat, one of the meats most commonly consumed by the sacrificers, and because "a salient characteristic of the sense of smell is its ability to remember" and to "recall experiences" fully in context,[82] the sacrifice would have been relived each time the sacrificers sat at their family table to consume their favorite dish of barbecued meat. Indeed, the recollection and reliving of the sacrifice often began almost immediately after the ritual was over. It is significant that after a lynching many spectators felt voraciously hungry and went immediately to eat and drink. Thus a reporter for the *Memphis News-Scimitar* concluded his account of a sacrifice in Mississippi as follows: "The mob walked away. In the vanguard of the mob I noticed a woman. She seemed to be rather young, yet it is hard to tell about women of her type; strong and healthy, apparently a woman of the country. She walked with a firm even stride. She was beautiful in a way. . . . 'I'm hungry,' someone complained, 'Let's get something to eat.'"[83]

ALTHOUGH RARELY MADE EXPLICIT, there is no denying the profound religious significance that these sacrificial murders had for Southerners. As I have noted, fundamentalist preachers not only condoned the sacrifices but actively incited many of them. They were at the vanguard of such organizations as the Ku Klux Klan. Wyn C. Wade estimates that some 40,000 fundamentalist ministers joined the Klan: "Many of them became the first Exalted Cyclopes of their local communities. In Pennsylvania, Texas, North Dakota, and Colorado they became Grand Dragons of their entire states. Others preached pro-Klan sermons from their pulpits, turned churches over to Klan meetings, spoke at Klan rallies, or became national lecturers for Imperial Headquarters (of thirty-nine Klokards or national lecturers employed by the Klan, 26 of them were fundamentalist ministers)."[84] Without these ministers and the fundamentalist revival of the twenties, Wade concludes, "the KKK could never have enrolled the fantastic numbers nor have gained the remarkable power it wielded between 1922 and 1925."[85]

It is no accident that in one of the last, and most thoroughly documented, of all sacrificial lynchings, that of Mack Charles Parker in Poplarville, Mississippi, in 1959, one of the co-organizers was the Baptist preacher James Floren Lee, descended from a long line of such preachers.

As Howard Smead writes in his exhaustive study of the lynching: "If Walker [the other coleader of the sacrifice] made the mob a cohesive unit with himself at the center, Lee gave it inspiration with his Biblical invective, chapter-and-verse references to the black man's innate inferiority, and wrathful tirades against Parker." He adds: "The presence of a preacher in the conspiracy was not at all unusual. . . . They were men given to extreme violence who invoked the Bible to justify black subordination."[86]

It would be a mistake, however, to conclude that only semiliterate "holy rollers" such as Lee were involved in lynchings. Highly educated preachers from the more respectable denominations were just as implicated, as the sacrifice of George White in Wilmington, Delaware, on the night of June 22, 1903, demonstrates. White was being held as a suspect in the rape and murder of one Helen Bishop, and a lynch mob had gathered, determined to sacrifice him rather than allow a trial to take place. The father of the murder victim was a clergyman of the more genteel tradition. He wrote a letter addressed to the mob, pleading for the law to take its course. The letter concludes:

> In the meantime the culprit is shut up with his guilty conscience, a hell of itself, and knows he must meet the demands of law and justice with his life. Any other course of procedure *would bring a glory for those of his class*, would intensify the suffering of the afflicted family, *possibly endanger the life of a delicate woman*, and certainly would dishonor the laws of our commonwealth. Let us not try to atone for one crime, no matter how hellish, by committing another. (Emphasis added)[87]

That was the civilized voice of the border-state South, the best that Afro-Americans could hope for: the certainty of being hung. But it was not enough for the negrophobic mob, which, in spite of the clergyman's letter, was whipped into a frenzy of vengeance by a sermon preached by another respected middle-class minister, the Reverend Robert Elwood, pastor of the Olivet Presbyterian Church. Taking as his text Corinthians 5:13—"Therefore put away from among ourselves that wicked person"—the pastor disingenuously appealed to the clause in the Constitution requiring a "speedy and public trial." He urged the courts not to wait a day longer:

> O, honorable judges, call the court, establish a precedent, and
> the girls of this state, the wives of our homes and the mothers

of our fireside and our beloved sisters will not be sorry and neither will you. And honorable judges, if you do not hear and heed these appeals, and that prisoner should be taken out and lynched, then let me say to you with full realization of the responsibility of my words, even as Nathan said to King David of old, after his soldiers had killed Uriah, "Thou art the man," so I would say to you. The responsibility for lynching would be yours for delaying the execution of the law. If the judges insist that the trial of the murderer of Miss Bishop be delayed until September, then should he be lynched? I say, Yes.[88]

Following the sermon, a mob of several thousand persons stormed the jail, overpowered the guards, dragged the prisoner "to a previously selected site at Price's Corner," and there burned him alive. (Another clergyman later examined the evidence and "expressed grave doubts of White's guilt.")[89]

Given the intense fundamentalist religiosity of both the sacrificers and their victims, it was hard to avoid explicit, as well as covert, religious references in these sacrifices. Thus, many of the victims died praying or singing hymns. George White "prayed fervently to God" in his last moments; another victim cried, "Oh, my God! Oh, Jesus."[90] Yet another, Richard Coleman, cried out like Jesus on the cross as he was roasted alive in Maysville, Kentucky, in December 1899: "Oh! Give me water!" And John Henry Williams, sentenced to death by a court in Moultrie, Georgia, was handed over by the twenty armed officers of the court to a sacrificial mob led by the Ku Klux Klan, too hungry for the smell of his burning body to permit a lawful execution. He was tied to a tree and tortured for nearly an hour in a Christlike way as the sacrificers "poked him in the ribs, cursed him, spit upon him and called him vile names." Finally, he was set afire. "For a time the winds carried the flames and smoke directly in his face so that he could not speak. Later the winds shifted and members of the mob, unaffected, recognized the hymn he sang as, 'Nearer My God to Thee.'"[91]

Sunday was a favorite day for lynching. Zachariah Walker, whose sacrifice is the subject of a full-length study, was dragged from his hospital room and burned alive on "the Sabbath."[92] Although not the most popular sites, churchyards were often used for lynching, and it was not uncommon to burn Afro-American churches before and after sacrificial lynchings. The religious symbolism of the sacrifice was made explicit by a sacrificial mob in Nowata, Oklahoma, in 1916 when, on passing a Methodist church with a large tree, one man shouted: "Let's lynch the nigger on holy ground." The victim was half dead before the minister rushed out from his study and pleaded with them to finish the killing somewhere else.[93] Although the Methodist clergy largely condoned, and sometimes participated in, lynchings, doing so on church ground made the religious symbolism too uncomfortably explicit, especially in light of Northern Methodism's condemnation of the practice.

The selection of the lynch site was a decision loaded with religio-political symbolism. All accounts make clear that the site was very carefully chosen, sometimes days and weeks in advance, long before the victim was apprehended. Most favored was a tree near the center of the community. Trees are powerfully symbolic objects, universally associated with both sacred and profane myths and rituals. In some cultures they have actually been worshipped (for example, in ancient Minoan religion), but more often they are regarded as the abodes of spirits and gods or the sites of critical communal rituals. Osiris, the Egyptian god of the underworld, was reborn from an oak tree. In ancient Greek religion, the oak was associated with Zeus; the olive tree, with Athena and, of course, with Olympia. And in Rome the fig tree of Romulus (*ficus Ruminalis*) was the most sacred symbol of the city.

But it was in Christianity, above all other universal creeds, that the tree acquired major mythic and ritual significance. The two most critical events in Christian cosmology are associated with the tree. The fall of Adam, and with him mankind, came with eating the fruit from the tree of knowledge; and Jesus' death on the cross, which is usually symbolically conflated with a tree in Christian thought and ritual, symbolizes the return to salvation and grace (Jesus, the second Adam, was nailed back to the tree from which the first Adam had fallen). The religion scholar Alan W. Watts has this to say:

> The symbolism of the Tree [in Christianity] is quite clearly that the Tree is the world—Life itself—having its stem rooted in the unknown. Its branches, leaves, flowers, and fruit form the multiplicity of creatures—"I am the vine; ye are the branches"—which blossom from the ever-fertile source of life. The *wood* of the Tree is matter, *prima materia*, out of which all things are made, so that it is not unfitting that, in his earthly incarnation, the Son of God should be also the son of the car-

penter—Joseph. . . . To this Tree, image of the finite world, the Son of God is nailed by his hands and feet, and a spear is thrust in his side.[94]

In light of all this, the frequency with which Afro-Americans were sacrificed from trees and the care with which the trees were chosen by these fundamentalist ritualists, who knew their Bible well and took its every word literally, are highly significant. After Richard Coleman was burned alive in 1899, for example, a newspaper account stated: "The place of execution had been selected weeks ago, in accordance with all the other arranged details of the programme mapped out by the leaders of the mob. The prisoner was dragged to the sapling and strapped against the tree, facing the husband of the victim."[95] And in 1914 in Louisiana, even before the ritual slaughter of Watkins Lewis, the hushed sense of the sacred overcame the mob as they approached the carefully preselected site: "Not a word was spoken as the little cavalcade formed, and with the Negro in the center marched to a giant tree near the Texas line. Lewis was bound to the trunk. Fallen trees and branches were heaped about him."[96] Oak trees were especially favored. In a sacrifice in Princess Anne, Maryland in 1933, described by a *New York Times* reporter as "the wildest lynching orgy the state has ever witnessed," a mob of three thousand men, women, and children seized the victim from the authorities and led him off to the sacrifice:

> The march to the scene of the lynching of Armwood was wild in the extreme. The mob members seemed crazed, continually leaping on the Negro, even after he fell to the ground and was unable to rise. One boy, apparently about 18 years old, slashed the Negro's ear almost off with a knife. Under the oak tree, despite the presence of women and children, all the victim's clothes were torn from his body and he hung there for some minutes nude. After they had burned the body, the mob members disbanded.[97]

Another popular sacrificial lynch site was a bridge, which, as all students of symbolism and mythology know, is a universal symbol of transition, of crossing from one state, period, or form to another, and hence a site for the most sacred and powerful rituals. It is striking that, even when the ritual required the burning of the victim's body, he was often first hanged from a bridge, as happened in the sacrifice of George Ward in Terre Haute, Indiana, in 1901. Ward's body was "tumbled off the bridge" then burned on the banks of the Wabash.[98] Even when the victim was hanged and burned in the public square—which was usually a more convenient site—it was understood that a bridge would have been more symbolically suitable. The mob of five hundred that lynched James T. Scott in Columbia, Missouri, in 1923 "dragged Scott through the streets to the Missouri, Kansas and Texas Railroad bridge that spans a deep ravine just outside the university [of Missouri] section."[99] The bridge had special political, as well as religious, symbolism in the mythology of the South, as we will see shortly.

So symbolically powerful were trees and bridges that sacrificial mobs were sometimes undecided as to which to choose as the site. In Waco, Texas, in 1916 the ideal solution was reached by a mob that used both in the lynching of eighteen-year-old Jesse Washington. According to the *New York World:* "The first suggestion was to hang him from the suspension bridge, and a chain was tied around his neck and he was dragged, yelling, in that direction. 'Burn him!' roared hundreds of voices all raised at once, and the idea pleased the mob. So the Negro was dragged by the chain to the City Hall square. There the ringleaders stood him under a tree and threw the chain over a limb. Boxes and sticks of wood were piled around him and then he was hoisted over the pile."[100]

Other favored sites also emphasized universal symbols of transition: crossroads, railroad crossings, the border between two states, and rivers and ponds. The leaders of the mob that sacrificed Henry Lowry of Nodena, Arkansas, exhibited an instinctive flair for the symbolism of place. According to the *Memphis Press:* "The setting was a natural amphitheater between two bluffs, with the Mississippi River on one side and a huge lake, created by backwater, on the other."[101] This site, it need hardly be added, was also ideal for evangelical baptisms.

The Southern theologian James Sellers has persuasively argued that Euro-American supremacy and commitment to segregation constituted for the South "a religion, a theology. It is, in fact, the unrepentant Southern kingdom of God." Further: "Segregation is a system of belief that would protect its devotees from all that looms on their horizon as 'the powers of death and destruction.' It is a way of handling the menace to salvation of one's own impulses and the perils of the world as well. It therefore becomes a holy path, complete with commandments, priests, theologians, and a plan of salvation."[102] In this religion, slaves, ex-slaves, and their descendants came to play the same critical role that slaves played in the religion of the Tupinamba. Segregating the Afro-American man became "the way of life"; integrating him, "a way of death." In an interpretation highly reminiscent of Nietzsche's theory of sacrifice, Sellers argues that the conception of Afro-Americans as beasts and criminal savages to be brutally ill-used had a critical moral function: "The idea is to terrify Southerners about their very lives, or symbolically, about the very life of the white race, so they can be offered the way of salvation: continued segregation."[103]

I am in general agreement with Sellers's probing analysis, except for his interpretation of the meaning of Christ in Southerners' religious worldview. Sellers observes, rightly, that Southerners rejected Jesus' social ethic, especially his gospel of brotherhood. I cannot, however, agree with his conclusion that Christ had "little place in defining the nature of God for the segregationist." This may be true of Sellers's version of Christ, but certainly not of the version practiced by Southerners during this period, which consciously fused Christian and "racial"-supremacist civic religion so that each powerfully supported the other.

Christianity is not simply a profoundly sacrificial religion. As Godfrey Ashby, the Anglican bishop and historian of religion, has observed, "It is salutary to remember that Christianity is founded upon an event that can hardly be described as anything but a human sacrifice!"[104] Once we understand this, the religious significance of the sacrificial murder of slaves and ex-slaves for Southern fundamentalists becomes more readily understandable. While progressive Protestantism underplays, is indeed embarrassed by, this conception of Christ, fundamentalism emphasizes Christ as the suffering victim who sacrificed his life for the salvation of sinners.[105]

AFTER THE SOUTH'S DEFEAT in the Civil War, a complex "religion of the Lost Cause" emerged. As Charles R. Wilson cogently argues, the secular and the sacred fused to create a Southern civil religion wherein political symbols and rituals had religious meaning and Christian symbols and rituals had politico-cultural meaning. Southern culture, society, and landscape became a sacred space, the home of a "chosen people." "The Southern civil religion emerged because the experience of defeat in the Civil War had created a spiritual and psychological need for Southerners to reaffirm their identity, an identity which came to have outright religious dimensions. Each Lost Cause ritual and organization was tangible evidence that Southerners had made a religion out of their history."[106]

This fusion of the sacred and secular in postbellum Southern culture explains why the mere absence of explicit Christian references cannot be taken as an indication that a ritual of that time lacked religious content. The major role of preachers in lynching rituals has already been noted. Their extremely prominent role in the KKK is further evidence of this vital link between the secular, the religious, and the ideology of "race" supremacy. As is well known, the KKK fused, in their negrophobic gospel, Confederate and social Darwinian notions of Afro-American degeneracy—already "deeply rooted traditions of Southern thought," as George Fredrickson shows[107]—with Christian and Celtic mystical symbolism and ritual. In "the fundamentalist world view," Nancy MacLean explains in her well-documented study of the Klan movement, "Klan leaders found the spiritual anchor for their ideology. . . . In the Klan's hands, Protestantism was thus very much a political creed: it provided answers to the basic questions about who should wield power over whom, and how and why."[108] Furthermore, she adds: "By mystifying relations of power and promoting uncritical awe of 'higher authority,'" fundamentalism performed a vital service for the Klan. Klan leaders consciously employed the power of 'ritual and formalism,' in the conviction that 'the people want and need faith and symbolism.'"[109] Another study concluded: "Kloran, Klan oaths and other ceremonies were essentially religious rites, complete with prayers and hymns."[110] However, the support was mutual. Fundamentalist and other Protestant clergymen soon discovered that their increased Klan activity resulted in bigger congregations and generous donations from the Klan. In addition, the Klan, during what has been called "the bigoted twenties," turned out to be a unifying force for the different Protestant sects of the South.[111]

Once we understand this conflation of the sacred and the secular, the latent meaning of certain features of the sacrificial slaughter of Afro-Americans becomes clearer. To take one example, I noted earlier the preference for bridges as sites for sacrifice. The overt reason given by the lynchers was that the sight of the victim's body, which was usually left hanging for several days if he was not burned, would further terrorize all Afro-Americans who passed over the bridge. But this hardly made sense, for nearly all Afro-Americans kept away from lynch sites for days or weeks afterwards, long after the body had been removed or eaten by scavenging animals. Beyond their universal symbolism in rites of transition, bridges over rivers had special meaning for Southerners. In the postbellum civil religion, they were the major symbol of the fusion of the historical, the political, and the religious. One of the greatest heroes in the pantheon of this religion was Stonewall Jackson, who became a virtual saint. His sanctification was formalized by the Southern Methodist church when it officially adopted the popular hymn that began, "Let us pass over the river/ And rest under the shade of the tree." These very words were the last spoken by the dying Jackson.[112] Thus the popular choice of the bridge as the place from which to hang the sacrificed Afro-American victim symbolically addressed both the crisis of transition from slavery to an as-yet-undefined postslavery regime and the fusion of the sacred and the political in the postbellum civil religion that was taking shape.

The sacrificed Afro-American victim performed three powerful functions in the symbolic universe of postbellum Southern culture and religion: the first spiritual and internal, the second related to the outer sacralized sociopolitical space, and the third addressing the crisis of history and collective transition in the half century after slavery.

As regards the first function, the slave and ex-slave had always been the major symbol of sin in Christian theology. Christianity from its beginnings had identified the state of sin as one of enslavement to the flesh.[113] David Brion Davis has brilliantly explored precisely this aspect of Christianity. As he cogently puts it: "For some two thousand years men thought of sin as a kind of slavery. One day they would come to think of slavery as sin."[114] Not all men, however. The South never made this moral transition. Throughout the Civil War, even when they faced certain defeat, nearly all the ministers of religion in the South insisted that their cause was righteous and that God was on their side. By 1861 churchmen in the Upper South, initially skeptical of secession, had closed ranks with their colleagues in the Lower South, presenting a unified theology of defense for the Confederate cause. "In the period of warfare, as in the secession crisis," writes H. Shelton Smith, "clergymen were second to no other professional class in buttressing the struggle for Southern independence."[115] Even after Appomattox, Clement Eaton has pointed out, Southerners "seldom attributed the defeat of their cause to the sin of slavery, for as a whole they did not believe the ownership of slaves to be a sin."[116] Instead, the Southern Protestants simply maintained and reinvigorated the original Pauline notion of sin as a kind of spiritual slavery from which the Christian had been redeemed (Latin: *redemptio*, "to purchase a slave out of slavery into freedom").

In this, the Afro-American slave or ex-slave was the perfect symbol of sin in two critical senses. First, in his slaveness he represented enslavement to the flesh and to sin. But to the social meaning of his slave status the Afro-American victim added the body symbolism of his "blackness," which brings us to the second symbolic function of the Afro-American in postbellum Southern culture. As Winthrop D. Jordan has shown, traditional color symbolism, which identified whiteness with goodness, purity, and beauty, and blackness with ugliness and evil, was fused with "racial" and religious symbolism. "Blackness was eminently functional in a slave society where white men were masters. It served as an easily grasped symbol of the Negro's baseness and wickedness."[117] It proved that he was a descendant of Ham; it confirmed the concept of degeneration from pristine whiteness. Thus: "The cruelties of slavery inevitably produced a sense of *dissociation*. To the horrified witness of a scene of torture, the victim becomes a 'poor devil,' a 'mangled creature.' He is no longer a man. He can no longer be human because to credit him with one's own human attributes would be too horrible" (emphasis added).[118]

It is just this dissociation that made the ex-slave the most exquisitely appropriate representational object. Victor Turner, in his analysis of Ndembu rituals, draws on William James's "law of dissociation" in explaining the dual nature of symbolic objects—their tendency to be both man and beast or both man and monster:

> When *a* and *b* occurred together as parts of the same total object, without being discriminated, the recurrence of one of these, *a*, in a new combination *a* [plus] *x*, favors the discrimination of *a*, *b*, and *x* from one another. As James himself put it, "What is associated now with one thing and now with another, tends to become dissociated from either, and grow into an object of abstract contemplation by the mind. One might call this the law of dissociation by varying concomitants."[119]

The association of "blackness" first with humans, then with beasts, leads to the dissociation of "blackness" from both, thereby becoming an object of intense contemplation. This not only thoroughly alienated "blackness," but the exclusive humanness of "whiteness." To the Greeks, the slave had been "two-footed stock"; to the Romans, "a vocal instrument"; and to the Southerners, a black beast, the archetypal *bête noire*, a Sambo devoid of manhood. Then, with the horror of the slave's legal emancipation and employment as a soldier during the Civil War, several incongruous associations took place: black = beast = free; black = beast =

man; black = beast = white status (soldier). It was enough to drive all good Southerners into a frenzy not only of outrage but of fear. A veteran of the Confederate army, when he wrote to his mother in December 1865, spoke with the heartfelt grief all Southerners must have felt:

> And then when to their animal nature, ready for anything like riot or robbery, is applied the teachings and drilling, which those Negro troops that have infested our country have been so eager to inculcate, when from the ignorant he rises into the bloodthirsty and revengeful brute, eager to possess all he sees, unable to look beyond the present but merely acting under the direction of blind and maddened impulse, of animal desires and passions. Mother, I shuddered yesterday, when I was having some hogs killed, to see the fiendish eagerness of some of them to stab and kill, the delight in the suffering of others![120]

The ritual of sacrifice violently emphasized and dissociated the incongruity, in the process first isolating and then reconstructing the only acceptable association of qualities: freedom = manhood = white status. We need hardly dwell on the irony that the last sentence of the letter cited above is a near perfect description of a Southern Euro-American lynch mob. Psychologically, the "fiendish eagerness" with which Afro-Americans were stabbed and killed, and the "delight in the suffering" they went through, not only vented all the rage of the Euro-American Southern male over the loss of his beloved dulotic way of life but projected all his chronic violence upon the Afro-American. Spiritually, the degenerate, masterless slave who dared to assert his manhood or freedom became the ideal sacrificial victim. As ex-slave, he symbolized the human wickedness and sin that haunted the fundamentalist souls of his executioners. And as "black beast," he could be horribly sacrificed, without any sense of guilt, to a wrathful, vengeful God as a prime offering of blood and human flesh and as the soul of his enemy, Satan.

Mention of Satan brings us to the third important symbolic function of the sacrifice of Afro-Americans. For it was through the association of Satan with "the Negro" that Southerners were able to resolve what was the single most crushing problem of the postbellum period: how to explain their defeat—a God-fearing, chosen people with a proud martial tradition—by a bunch of sinful, effete, "nigger-loving" Yankees.

"Like a massive earthquake," writes Eric Foner, "the Civil War and the devastation of slavery permanently altered the landscape of Southern life, exposing and widening fault lines that had lain barely visible just beneath the surface. White society was transformed no less fully than black, as traditional animosities grew more acute, longstanding conflicts acquired altered meanings, and new groups emerged into political consciousness."[121] Not only had the Southern plantocracy been devastated as a class "physically, economically and psychologically," but nearly everyone suffered from the massive loss of life—over one-fifth of the entire Southern adult male population had perished in the war—and the ruin of the economy.[122]

When men and women face such massive insecurities and painful exposure to the contradictions of their social order, it is always to religion that they turn for solace, explanation, reconsistency, and moral and social reconstruction. At Appomattox the Southerners' God had abandoned them, which is the religious way of saying that everything had fallen apart. "I have no country, no flag, no emblems, no public spirit," wrote a member of the fallen Southern gentry in his diary after the surrender. "I live now simply to live, and for my family."[123] It was, in the words of a South Carolina planter, "perpetual trouble that belongs to a time of social change."[124] During the years after the defeat, Southern theologians and ordinary preachers worked hard to come up with a satisfactory explanation for it. The hand of Providence was one; another was that the wrathful God in whom they believed had punished them for not living sufficiently righteously.[125] Neither explanation was fully satisfactory, especially in light of the way of life of the Yankee victors.

More sophisticated and comforting were the explanations of the more moderate wing of the Lost Cause ideologists. They argued that the South's defeat had been a test and sacrifice, a kind of disciplining by God of his chosen people, in preparation for an even greater future in which they would be vindicated. In these explanations, great emphasis was placed on the creative role of sacrifice and suffering, and there was considerable identification with the cross and the blood of Jesus. Many Confederate war heroes, such as Sam Davis, were identified as Christ figures. Moreover, all Southerners came to see themselves as a chosen people under trial by an inscrutable God. The Aqedah (Abraham's offering to sacrifice his son) became a favored theme of sermons. Job's cry of loyalty to God was frequently uttered: "Though he slay me, yet will I trust him."[126]

For the despised Afro-American ex-slaves, this theological mood was dangerous enough. But, at least, many of the clergymen who held these views belonged to the more genteel tradition of the South, which, while fully accepting the inferiority and segregation of Afro-Americans, nonetheless took a patronizing approach to them. It was a position that could even embrace the idea that while slavery was right, perhaps not enough had been done for the soul of the Afro-American man by his Euro-American master, another possible source of God's wrath.[127] All waxed nostalgic about the qualities of the "old Negro," mentally retarded but uncomplaining, faithful, humble, chidlike, religious, and endearing.[128] Many were convinced that Afro-Americans, unable to survive as free men and women, would face extermination. Du Bois sarcastically quotes "the Provisional Governor of Florida [who] became almost tearful over the impending fate of the Negroes and the guilt of the North."[129]

Nostalgia for the "Old Negro," however, was in direct proportion to the hatred and loathing of what Southern Euro-Americans came to call the "New Negro." "The compelling need to immortalize the 'old Negro,'" writes Litwack,

> reinforced fears of the "New Negro." . . . If the image of the New Negro brought pride to many blacks as a sign of race re-generation, that same image frightened whites into thoughts of racial degeneration, suggesting a Negro who had cast off those endearing and comforting qualities associated with the old Negro. Worst of all, the New Negro violated white expectations of black people, confounded their feelings of superiority, and violated white stereotypes long assimilated into the white psyche.[130]

It was to meet this threat that the radical, negrophobic wing of the new civil religion emerged. These were the Euro-American supremacists for whom "race" was central to the theology of the Lost Cause, the people who eventually founded the KKK and who led the sacrificial lynch mobs. Negrophobia tended to go along with a different theological explanation of the tragedy of Southern defeat, one that blamed Satan and "satanic influences" as the cause of the great evil.

The belief in, and theological use of, Satan is underplayed, and even viewed with some embarrassment, in high Protestantism (in much the same way, and for many of the same reasons, that the death of Jesus as a human sacrifice is shunned by sophisticated Christian theology). The opposite is true in the hell-and-brimstone theology of popular Southern fundamentalism. The fundamentalist emphasis on satanic influences was a symbolic disaster for Afro-Americans, for it was all too easy to identify the hated ex-slaves with the satanic presence. Afro-Americans became to the body politic what Satan was to the individual and collective soul of the South. For both, the same metaphor of a "black" malignancy to be excised was employed. As is well known, Satan, like sin, is always portrayed as black. Satan destroys from within in much the same way that "the domestic enemy" was consuming and threatening the body politic from within the community. Almost exactly the same language used to describe the Afro-American presence was used of the satanic presence. Thus Afro-Americans were seen not only as the domestic enemy but as "an eating cancer." The famous Ku Klux Klan intellectual Thomas Dixon, whose 1905 novel *The Clansman* was the basis for the notorious negrophobic film *Birth of a Nation,* called them "a possible beast to be feared and guarded." Paralleling the image of the Afro-American male as a sexual monster, always on the alert to consume Euro-American women (symbolically identified with Euro-American chivalric culture), was that of the Afro-American woman as a symbol of Southern doom who, without the control of slavery, would, in the words of one Southerner, "breed the future incubus of your descendants."[131]

Meyer Fortes has pointed out that all acts of sacrifice are "rituals of defense" against external vulnerability to "war and social upheaval" and internal vulnerability to weakness of the flesh and mind.[132] In the civilizations of the ancient Near East, human sacrifices to the gods took place especially during times of crisis, the victims substituting for the king, who was required to give his life to avert evil consequences to the state.[133] After the trauma of Appomattox, the Southern community had to be restored in the most extreme compact of blood, and its God propitiated in the most extreme form of sacrifice known to man. Incredibly, irresponsibly, the Northern victors, having created the problem, then presented the solution by soon abandoning the domestic enemy, whom they had simply made masterless and vulnerable, to their humiliated exmasters. It takes little imagination, and almost no feeling for the workings of the religious mind, to understand how, as the flames devoured the flesh and soul of each Afro-American victim, every participant in these heinous rituals of human sacrifice must have felt the deepest and most gratifying sense of expiation and atonement. When a Southern educator summarized what he called "a creed of a people—a part of their morality and religion," he listed the first two of fifteen principles of the faith as "Blood will tell" and "The white race must dominate"; the last two, as "Let the lowest white man count for more than the highest Negro" and "The above statements indicate the leadings of Providence."[134]

The lynchings may also have served another, purely superstitious defensive function in the popular fundamentalist religion of the region. Keith Thomas has pointed out that Protestantism, especially in its more zealously Puritan forms, created a crisis for believers when, on the one hand, it reinvigorated the notion of an ever-present Satan who, even in all-Caucasian Europe, had been "customarily personified in the crude form of a black man or a strange animal" while, on the other hand, it ridiculed and rejected the Catholic Church's well-tried means of exorcizing satanic mischief, especially aspects of devilry such as witchcraft.[135] In England the onus of checking witchcraft fell, as a result of the impasse, on the courts; hence the judicially sanctioned great periods of witch-hunting and burning in England and elsewhere during the late sixteenth and seventeenth centuries. In theocratic Massachusetts of the late seventeenth century, church and state together resolved the impasse, after which the whole notion of witchcraft itself was brought into disrepute following the antiwitchcraft orgy in Salem.

In the fundamentalist South not only was the impasse never settled, by either church or state, but it was made worse by the extremity of belief in, and sermonic tirades against, Satan's workings and the fire and brimstone that awaited all those who succumbed to him. In other words, even in the absence of slavery and defeat in the Civil War, evangelical Christianity of the type practiced by the masses of the South would by itself have induced strong tendencies toward scapegoating and witch-hunting. The vulnerable and despised Afro-Americans were easy substitutes for the poor and despised women of seventeenth-century England accused of "necromancy and nigromancy."[136]

The crude symbolic identification of the lynched Afro-American with Satan was, however, a simplified version of a far more complex symbolic narrative. It no doubt worked well enough for the mass of semiliterate participants who easily conflated rituals of purification and expulsion without any awareness of the profound theological inconsistencies involved. Furthermore, if it crossed the minds of any in the lynch mob that there were odd and disturbing parallels between their ritualized crucifixion of Negroes and the legalized lynching of the Christ they worshipped, none left any record of being troubled by them.

For Southerners more knowledgeable about the nature and meaning of Christian sacrifice, however, the parallels must have been all too obvious.

Religiously sophisticated enough to detect, and be bothered by, the parallels, they no doubt possessed the theological means to resolve whatever dilemma they created. But there may have been no dilemma; far from being troubled by it, it seems that they deliberately embraced the association of the crucified Christ with the Negro. Why?

The answer is found in that most powerful symbol of the bourgeois Euro-American supremacist: the burning cross. Here there is no room for doubt. The cross—Christianity's central symbol of Christ's sacrificial death—became identified with the crucifixion of the Negro, the dominant symbol of the Southern Euro-American supremacist's civil religion. According to tradition, during the fourteenth century the highland clans of Scotland burned crosses as a signal. Thomas Dixon in his *The Clansman* first suggested the idea as a Klan rite. Its first recorded use in America was by a Ku Klux Klan lynch mob in Georgia, the Knights of Mary Phagan, on top of Stone Mountain on October 16, 1915.[137]

The ritual of the burning cross had exactly the effect intended by Klan intellectuals and theologians; it terrified Afro-Americans and awed Euro-Americans. Here is Wyn C. Wade's account:

> Though similar to the pagan fire festivals of central Europe during the middle ages, the Klan's cross burnings in the 1920s were invariably constrained by a strict Christian ritual. The ceremony opened with a prayer by the Kludd or Klavern minister. The multitude then sang "Onward Christian Soldiers!" After the hymn, the cross was lit and the explosion of kerosene and the rush of flames over the timbers were thrilling, to say the least. (In the mining districts of Pennsylvania, Klansmen augmented the effect by simultaneously detonating charges of dynamite). Children sometimes wet their pants. . . . Bathed in warmth, left arm outstretched toward the blazing icon and voices raised in "The Old Rugged Cross," Klansmen felt as one body. These were moments they would always remember. To outside foes who witnessed them, cross burnings were something they would never forget. They were grotesque rituals to be enacted on American soil. They were spectacles no one had ever seen before. And their likes wouldn't be seen again until Berlin of the 1930s.[138]

What lies behind this association? Why would the highly educated Southern clergymen and intellectuals who formed the core of the KKK leadership choose as the master symbol of their movement an act that seems to besmirch their God by associating him with the despised Negro and, as if that were not bad enough, to court blasphemy in the image of the burning cross? We should not let our horror and contempt for this most gruesome iconic act of American culture obscure our understanding of its symbolic power, ingenuity, and alas yes, cultural and religious sophistication. It is as important for all Americans to understand the burning cross as symbol as for all modern Germans—Gentiles and Jews—to understand the meaning and power of the iron cross. Of that other civil religious symbol of evil and destruction with deep roots in the Christian and European heritage, J. Pelican wisely observes: "To trace the historical variations and permutations of the kinship of Jesus in its interaction with other political themes and symbols is to understand a large part of what is noble and a large part of what is demonic in the political history of the West: even the Nazi swastika was used as an obscene parody of the cross of Christ."[139]

THE CHRISTIAN BI-FOCAL NARRATIVE OF SACRIFICE AND THE "RACIAL" THEOLOGY OF THE NEW SOUTH

To UNDERSTAND THE POWER of the burning cross and why so evil an icon could draw so much of its symbolic energy from Christianity and could appeal to so wide a cross-section of the Southern population, one must first note an important distinction that holds for all sacrifical symbols. When a soul, body, or community is polluted by some alien agency—be it Satan, a lower-caste Indian, an ex-slave, or a witch—two forms of atonement are called for: (1) the polluting agent must be expelled through what have been called sacrificial rituals of aversion; and (2) the polluted body must then be purified through sacrificial rituals of purification and propitiation. In most religions the two sets of rituals are distinct. Christianity is unusual in its attempt—not entirely successful—to incorporate both into the single sacrificial act of Christ's crucifixion and the surrogative rituals pertaining to it, most notably the Eucharist.

This tension, however, has created great confusion in Christianity and has been the source of endless theological disputation. For the simple truth of the matter is, as Frances Young bluntly puts it: "There is a fundamental inconsistency between thinking of Christ's sacrifice as an act performed by God to avert the devil and thinking of it as an offering made to God to appease his wrath."[140] The theological solution to this dilemma has been the construction of two closely linked sacrificial narratives in the Christian tradition. As the historian and theologian S.W. Sykes explains:

> the Christian *account* of God is in two stories, not one: a story of power, transcendence and judgment—and a story of weakness, immanence and forgiveness. The sacrifice, which is the death of Christ, is at once a powerful condemnation of sin, and a victory over the forces of evil, and also a supreme act of humble self-identification with the powerless. From this bi-focal view springs the enormous resilience of Christian faith and its capacity for adaptation to vastly different circumstances; from it similarly springs the ambivalence in its attitude to worldly power, whether that of its own hierarchy or that of the state.[141]

In what follows, I depart in important ways from Sykes, while maintaining his basic insight of a bi-focal narrative.[142] The two narratives originated in the Christologies that the primitive church developed to explain the degradation of the cross and the absurdity, to their fellow Jews, of a Messiah being hung from the stake with common criminals, especially in light of Deuteronomy's unambiguous declaration that one who is hung from a tree is cursed.[143] Those Christologies, in turn, focused on the two sacrificial goats associated with the Day of Atonement.[144]

One of these goats, Leviticus directs, is to be sacrificed on the altar as a sin offering "for the Lord" and "for the people." It is essentially an expiatory and propitiatory sacrifice, making "an atonement for the holy place, because of the [Israelites'] uncleanliness . . . and transgressions in all their sins." The second goat is the prototype of the scapegoat, and I follow Frances Young in considering this the classic sacrifice of aversion.[145]

The biblical scholar John Dominic Crossan has recently argued that the early Christians' choice of the Day of Atonement as their means of explaining the crucifixion was not "a very happy one," since one or the other of the goats was bound to be redundant. This is certainly true. Indeed, even singly, the two symbols are not very tidy, since the Hebraic scapegoat was set free in the wilderness. Anyone who knows anything about goats will know that they can survive anywhere, whereas Jesus did not escape.[146] The symbolic untidiness aside, it is the dual narrative tradition that rescues the more serious symbolic inconsistency of conflating aversion with purification.

Over the Christian centuries, one narrative—that of Christ Triumphant—focused on the goat sacrificed at the altar. What emerged in later versions of the story was a vision of Christ's sacrifice as a victory over the forces of darkness, sin, chaos, and ignorance.[147] Two symbolic tropes introduced into this triumphant narrative during the era of the church fathers are of special relevance to developments in the postbellum South. First, Young has pointed out that the early martyrs of the church were the first surrogates for Christ's sacrifice; indeed, it "is highly probable that the tradition that a martyr's death could expiate sin was in fact the earliest positive means of understanding the death of Christ."[148] So began a tradition in Christianity that has continued down to modern times.

A second development in the triumphant narrative was the shifting of the story's beginning back to the Aqedah,[149] the origin of all sacrifice in the Hebraic tradition. Indeed, Abraham's attempted human sacrifice may well have furnished the paradigm for the Eucharist. This shift in the story emphasized an understanding not only of Jesus' death as a human sacrifice but of its propitiatory and expiatory meanings as interpreted by the triumphant conception of atonement and the idea of a compact between Israel and God. The goat of Leviticus was now conflated with the lamb that redeemed Isaac, which in turn was symbolically surrogated in Jesus, who became the lamb that triumphs over sin and death and redeems mankind. The principle of substitution easily extended this idea to later martyrs, whose deaths redeem, expiate, and renew the compact.

Although the triumphant narrative of sacrifice was the dominant one throughout the history of the church down to the nineteenth century, it always ran concurrently with the second narrative—that of the humbled Christ evincing the power of the powerless, the despised scapegoat cast out of the community and taking the sins of the world with him. It is in the late-first-century *Epistle of Barnabas* that we find the first clear statement of this sacrificial tradition: "The other [goat] is accursed. Notice how the type of Jesus is manifested. And do ye all spit on it, and goad it, and bind the scarlet wool about its head, and so let it be cast into the desert."[150]

The temptation to read these two narratives of Christ's sacrifice in direct sociopolitical terms—the narrative of triumph appealing to the ruling classes and conservatives, that of aversion appealing to the oppressed masses—is irresistible, and I intend to succumb to it; but it should be treated with caution. Both narratives have been used by rulers and ruled, conservatives and radicals, insiders and outcasts. Herein lies the extraordinary resilience of Christianity.

Nonetheless, throughout the periods of late antiquity and the Middle Ages, conquerors and rulers adapted both narratives to their needs in politically and spiritually subjugating the serf population. And what was learned in the pacification of the European pagans during the Middle Ages was carried over to Latin America, where it was applied with even greater effect in the subjection of the native Indian populations. Here, as Georges Casalis and others have shown, a popular Christology of domination emerged that projected two distinct images of Christ. One was for the subjected masses, of a "suffering Christ who had been thoroughly defeated and humiliated,"[151] celebrated in images of the helpless infant of Mary and in the bleeding victim of Holy Thursday and Good Friday, but not in the triumphant risen Jesus of Easter. This "Creole Christ," as John McKay called it, is a patronized deity "who was born and died but who never lived," or rose again.[152] At the same time, there was the "royal-theocratic image of Christ which made the trip to the New World with the conquistadors." It depicts Jesus "as a celestial monarch who reigns after death as the leader in an imperial, military kingdom," the central ritual of celebration here being the resurrection on Easter Sunday.[153]

Something equally crude and manipulative was attempted in the North American planters' early effort to impose their version of the penitent Christ on the Afro-American slaves, but the effort failed miserably, as Afro-Americans quickly saw through the deception and speedily moved to reconstruct Christianity in their own terms. We will return to this briefly in the last part of this essay.

The narrative of Christ triumphant, on the other hand, fitted perfectly the spiritual and sociopolitical needs of the Euro-American Southerners, especially after the disaster of the Civil War. It now became a story of a chosen people whom a righteous God had tested and disciplined by suffering and defeat. That same God was delivering them from their agony through atoning Christ-figures, such as Lee, Jackson, and Davis, who had given their lives for the cause of the South, a cause that would eventually be vindicated. Charles R. Wilson writes that Sam Davis, the Tennessean hung as a spy by the Union army, "was a Christ figure to Southerners. The focus of his story was on his execution, which was filled with analogies to Christ's crucifixion. For example, Davis' scaffold was 'the Calvary whereon were exhibited the highest characteristics which belong to the Southern character.'"[154] These soteriological expectations were, of course, fulfilled in the triumph of the Compromise of 1877. It is no accident that the quintessential Christian term *Redemption* was used to describe that overthrow of Reconstruction and that the leaders who achieved this were called Redeemers.[155]

While the Redeemers who returned the South to "home rule" "conducted their campaign in the name of white supremacy," negrophobia and "racial" revolution were not, as C. Vann Woodward has shown, the defining elements of their ideology and program, which is reflected in the fact that the triumphant leaders did not make any immediate radical changes in the Reconstruction "racial" system.[156] There was, as I indicated earlier, a place for "the Negro" in the conservative civil religion of the Redeemers, a very inferior one, to be sure, but one that, if acknowledged by Afro-Americans, would have been protected, and even defended, with patriarchal warmth.[157]

But, as Afro-Americans and the North were to learn, even this limited vision of their status was to crumble, along with that other even more ill-fated alternative—radical Populism—in the wholesale capitulation to negrophobia and Jim Crow. Whatever the reasons for the capitulation, its impact on the status and security of Afro-Americans was immediate, brutal, and tragic. Jim Crow rose to power on, was suffused with, and had as the very center of its doctrine not just the permanent segregation and subjugation of Afro-Americans but their demonization, terrorization, and humiliation. The central ritual of this version of the Southern civil religion, we have seen, was the human sacrifice of the lynch mob.

With the removal of what Woodward identifies as the "restraining forces" of Reconstruction—"Northern liberalism, Southern conservatism, and Southern radicalism"—there came to the fore all "the elements of fear, jealousy, proscription, hatred and fanaticism [that] had long been present." And in the Southern civil religion that matured after Reconstruction, all of these elements were focused on the irresistible symbolic figure of the despised "Negro." The brutally sacrificed Negro was the ultimate Christ-figure of the narrative of aversion—Christ the scapegoat—spat upon, mocked, spiked, tortured, and accursed. In expelling "the Negro," all that was most evil and sinful and black and iniquitous and transgressing would be sent away: for "the goat shall bear upon him all their iniquities unto a land not inhabited" (Leviticus 16:21).

However, something extraordinary happened when the despised, scapegoated, dishonored, humbled, crucified Negro became fused with the despised, scapegoated, dishonored, humbled, crucified Christ. Not only was the Negro symbolically discarded, but in one fell swoop so was the image of the crucified, humbled Christ himself! The burning cross can now be better understood. Unlike the Latin American poor, who had been spiritually co-opted and subjected, the Afro-American had refused to go under spiritually, had resisted nobly in the face of inordinate cultural pressure. Because political resistance would have been suicidal, Afro-Americans rationally, heroically, and successfully resisted the dominant group in its own cultural domain that they had usurped, subverted, and mastered: religion. Hence, there was no place any longer for the image of a penitent, humbled Christ. This was a contradiction and an embarrassment for Euro-Americans, a people who considered themselves—all of them, including the lowliest—a triumphant, superior race destined to create a master civilization built in the militaristic, honorific image of a chivalric, conquering "white" Christ.

The Euro-American Southerners' association of the penitent, humbled Christ with the crucified Negro is a perfect case of William James's law of dissociation by varying concomitants, as adapted to the symbolic universe by Victor Turner. The humbled Christ was dissociated from the triumphant Christ by virtue of being associated with the humbled, crucified Negro. Both were then discarded, leaving for contemplation only the triumphant Christ, the only god-figure befitting a chosen, superior "race." With malevolent perfection, the burning cross distilled it all: sacrificed Negro joined by the torch with sacrificed Christ, burnt together and discarded, both *signans* and *signatum* consumed in the triumphant flame of the victorious, militaristic Christ rising above the flowing white robes and galloping white horses in a cloud of Euro-American supremacist glory. "The Klan, which is awakened Protestantism," wrote a Protestant minister and Klansman in the *Kourier,* the magazine of the movement, "realizes the church must be both militant and spiritual, or it will fail." Another clergyman wrote in the same magazine: "As a Protestant minister of the Gospel, I joined the Knights of the Ku Klux Klan because I believed in Jesus Christ and His church; I believed in a militant Christianity; I believed in the Cross—a symbol of service and sacrifice for the right. If there is not enough in that to challenge a real red-blooded, virile minister to a sense of duty, he has lost his vision."[158]

It need hardly be added that this ingenious symbolic perfidy was not only the lowest point in American political culture but one of the most horrible manifestations of the Christology of domination. As Leslie Dunbar observed some thirty years ago: "The greatest of all sinning was not that white men killed and raped and cheated Negroes, nor even that white men induced Negroes to kill and rape and cheat themselves. The mortal sin was that white men united to defend this right, as a way of life, and did so in the name of their God."159

THE AFRO-AMERICAN RESPONSE

BUT WHAT OF THE AFRO-AMERICANS in all this? What were their feelings and reactions? And most problematic of all, how could Afro-Americans reconcile their own Christian faith with this holocaust in which they were literally and figuratively consumed in the name of the faith, and with the very same sacrificial rituals, that they had themselves embraced? Answering these questions properly requires another essay—indeed, a whole volume. Here, by way of conclusion, I will offer only the briefest sketch of Afro-Americans' responses.

As with all oppressed groups, reaction could take one of three forms: rebellion, accommodation, or withdrawal. And it could occur in either the outer political or the inner spiritual realm of being, or in both. With Afro-Americans hopelessly outnumbered, outgunned, and out-fanaticized, it is obvious that any kind of rebellion in the postbellum South, especially after the Northern betrayal, would have been suicidal. Yet some Afro-Americans with enormous courage and dignity chose just this path. The best evidence of this comes from the data on lynchings, especially from the reasons given by the lynchers. We noted at the beginning of this essay an odd paradox in the reports of these causes. From what the lynchers themselves alleged, it is clear that the single most important reason for lynching was murder and assault by Afro-Americans against Euro-American men. In the vast majority of cases, these assaults were noncriminal and protopolitical; Afro-Americans were defending either themselves or the honor of their wives and members of their families, or they had simply had enough of the outrages against them and had exploded in psychologically healthy rage against their torturers and persecutors.

For these offenses, they were lynched. This seems so obvious that one has to ask why the lynchings have not been interpreted in this way. There are two answers. One is the strong tendency of liberal interpreters to claim that all the Afro-Americans lynched were innocent. In the great majority of alleged sexual cases, Afro-Americans may have been legally innocent, but my reading of the lynching data strongly suggests that in the cases of murder and attempted murder most of them were heroically guilty, notwithstanding the fact that many mistakes were made by the lynch mobs in sacrificing the wrong person.

The second answer is equally telling. We have seen that Euro-American Southern interpreters wanted desperately to believe that the vast majority of the lynchings were imposed for alleged sexual crimes against Euro-American women, and persisted in this belief even when confronted with the contradictory evidence of the lynchers themselves. Freudian interpreters, I have argued, were only too willing to accept the Southern distortion, since it dovetailed neatly with their own theories. However, there may have been a much simpler explanation for the Southerners' distortion of their own evidence. The idea of Afro-American men resisting and fighting against the outrages heaped upon them was as much an anathema as was the fantasy of Afro-American men lusting after Euro-American women. Thus the distorting emphasis on the charge of rape and attempted rape accomplished two goals of "racial" oppression in one fell swoop. It promoted the image of the Afro-American male as a sexual fiend, and at the same time it denied all manhood to him. Afro-Americans were damned if they resisted and equally damned if they did not.

The contradiction comes out clearly in another paradox revealed by the causes given for lynchings. In the vast majority of cases, as we have seen, Afro-Americans were lynched and sacrificed as an evil presence to be expelled, and many of the lynchers, who saw them as competitors in the labor market, desired just that. But here the Euro-American gentry parted company with the Euro-American working and lower classes. However much they may have loathed the idea of a dignified Afro-American presence, the gentry badly needed Afro-American labor to farm their lands. Hence the seeming paradox that Afro-Americans were sometimes lynched for advocating withdrawal to Africa. The most blatant case occurred near Jackson, Georgia, in May 1912, when a recruiter for the colonization movement was murdered. As the *Savannah Tribune* of May 4 noted, because of his "apparent success the white farmers in the community, who were depending on these Negroes to gather their crops, became angered and decided to nip the movement in the bud by lynching the leader and holding on to their laborers whose services they were getting for little or nothing." Afro-Americans, then, were damned if they stayed and damned if they tried to leave. The Afro-American poet Sterling A. Brown expressed it best: "They burn us when we dogs/They burn us when we men."[160]

African-Americans' sense of outrage was sometimes expressed in religious terms. An extreme case was the response of the Reverend Montrose

W. Thornton, pastor of the African Methodist Episcopal church in Wilmington, Delaware, to the lynching of George White, mentioned above:

> The white man, in face of his boasted civilization, stands before my eyes tonight the demon of the world's races, a monster incarnate, and in so far as the Negro race is concerned seems to give no quarter. The white is a heathen, a fiend, a monstrosity before God, and is equal to any act in the calendar of crime. I sooner trust myself in a den of hyena as in his arms.
>
> With a court, law, and officers of law in his hands the despised Negro can expect no mercy, justice, nor protection. The Negro is unsafe anywhere in this country. He is the open prey at all times of barbarians who know no restraint and will not be restrained. There is but one part left for the persecuted Negro when charged with crime and when innocent. Be a law unto yourself. You are taught by this lesson of outrage to save yourself from torture at the hands of the blood-seeking public. Save your race from insult and shame. Be your own sheriff, court, and jury, as was the outlaw Tracy. Die in your tracks, perhaps drinking the blood of your pursuers. Booker T. Washington's charity, humanity, advice of forgiveness, love, industry, and so on will never be reciprocated by the white man.[161]

Such language, however, was not typical, even if it may have expressed the feelings of many Afro-Americans about these outrages. Besides, it never addressed the fundamental contradiction that the Euro-American monsters Thornton lambasted were fellow Christians. A disturbing aspect of his language was that it was almost identical to the kind of talk heard from negrophobic Euro-Americans in their verbal assaults against Afro-Americans.

The feeling of shame, touched on by Thornton, mixed with bitterness and muted rage, as well as humiliation at their incapacity to do much about it, characterized the responses of many Afro-Americans, especially those of the middle classes. Typical of this agonized reaction was that of the hero of James Weldon Johnson's *Autobiography*, who describes his feelings on witnessing a lynching from behind the safety of his light-colored skin:

> I walked a short distance away and sat down in order to clear my dazed mind. A great wave of humiliation and shame swept

over me. Shame that I belonged to a race that could be so dealt with; and shame for my country, that it, the great example of democracy to the world, should be the only civilized, if not the only state on earth, where a human being would be burned alive. My heart turned bitter within me. I could understand why Negroes are led to sympathize with even their worst criminals and to protect them when possible. By all the impulses of normal human nature they can and should do nothing less.[162]

For most of the small minority of educated Afro-Americans, and no doubt many noneducated radicals, the contradictions of Christianity were too great for them to keep their faith. As the renowned scholar of Afro-American religion Benjamin Mays pointed out long ago, many of the Afro-American writers of the early part of this century, especially those of the Harlem Renaissance, either considered God impotent or irrelevant or simply abandoned the idea of God altogether.[163] In his poem "Wishing He I Served Were Black," Countee Cullen wonders with weary irony whether an Afro-American God might not have been more responsive. Lynching is his main reason for loss of faith:

> A man was lynched last night;
> God, if He was, kept to His skies,
> And left us to our enemies.[164]

Du Bois in "Dark Water" implores prophetically:

> Keep not Thou Silent, O God!
> Sit not longer blind, Lord God, deaf to our prayer
> And dumb to our dumb suffering. Surely Thou,
> Too, are not white, O Lord, a pale, bloodless,
> Heartless thing.[165]

After embracing communism, Langston Hughes bid Christianity a rude adieu in "Good-bye Christ," and it is typical of Hughes that he draws attention to Christianity's triumphant narrative:

> Listen Christ
> You did all right in your day I reckon

> But that day's gone now.
> They ghosted you up a swell story, too,
> Called it Bible—
> But it's dead now.[166]

However important the writers cited, though, they constituted a distinct minority of Afro-Americans, the overwhelming majority of whom remained firmly committed to their Christian faith. As I noted earlier, many of the sacrificed victims went to their fiery deaths singing hymns or praying.

Many Afro-Americans who remained committed to the sacrificial narratives of Christianity felt they had little choice but to follow the accommodating path of Booker T. Washington, who hoped that Euro-American Christians would "speak out against these burnings in a manner that shall arouse a public sentiment that will compel the mob to cease insulting the courts, our Governors and our legal authority; to cease bringing shame and ridicule upon our Christian civilization."[167]

Others chose the path of religious withdrawal. They expressed their withdrawal in many ways, some of which should clearly be regarded as forms of cultural protest, even radicalism, as G. S. Wilmore argues.[168] Organizationally, they expressed it in the voluntary pullout of Afro-American churches from their Euro-American parent organizations beginning in the early decades of the nineteenth century, a process hastened by forced segregation. Creedally, while fully accepting the basic beliefs of Christianity, they developed a distinctively Afro-American style of worship—based partly on the Baptist-Methodist system, partly on the camp meetings tradition, and partly on vestigial African patterns of worship—which became evident in the early part of the nineteenth century.[169] Mays found that in much of what he called the "mass" literature of the Afro-Americans, religious ideas "adhere[d] strictly to traditional, compensatory patterns," with "primary emphasis upon the magical, spectacular, partial, revengeful, and anthropomorphic nature of God."[170]

Afro-American religious radicalism apparently died in 1915 with Henry M. Turner, the fiery A.M.E. bishop and editor who demanded reparations for the centuries of slavery, advocated a mass return to Africa, and preached a liberation theology focused on a black God.[171] The sad truth is that, thereafter, up to the 1950s, most of the Afro-American churches, especially those led by the large number of semiliterate preachers, preached a gospel of spiritual withdrawal and sociopolitical passivity.

The focus was on the sinfulness of the world, the transgressions of the individual, and the need to accept and be washed clean by the saving, cleansing blood of Christ. Adam Fairclough summarizes the generally accepted view that during this period, Afro-American churchmen "always functioned as leaders and spokesmen, but they . . . usually accommodated to the racial mores of the time; indeed, generations of black activists and intellectuals . . . excoriated the church for its conservatism and lack of social and political awareness." He adds that by the 1930s, when lynchings were still rampant—indeed, were going through a resurgence—"preachers [had] reached the nadir of their prestige."[172]

But there was a third path. Earlier we discussed the bi-focal sacrificial narrative of Christianity. Both focuses, it now seems, placed Afro-Americans in the deplorable situation of choosing between accommodation and withdrawal, however much spiritual consolation one or the other may have offered. The bi-focal narrative of sacrifice, however, must now be understood as something nested within a broader dualism at the heart of Christianity. There are really two religions lurking in the bosom of the Christian church. One is the largely neglected religion that Jesus himself preached. It is, by all accounts, a radical gospel, both spiritually and socially. Spiritually, its program is a loving reengagement with a living God, a call to spiritual watchfulness, and an existential experience of the divine through fellowship with and love of other human beings. Socially and ethically, its message, as Crossan recently reminded us, "taught and acted, theorized and performed against social oppression, cultural materialism, and imperial domination in the first and second centuries."[173] Above all, this religion is all about Jesus' life and the art of living socially and spiritually.

This religion, though, was largely discarded in one of the greatest distortions and misappropriations in the history of the world. In the Christologies that emerged after Jesus' execution, the focus of the young religion shifted completely from his life and message to his death and its sacrificial meaning. Absolutely nothing in the authentic sayings of Jesus suggested anything about his death as a sacrifice. This was all an invention after his death, an invention attributable, above all, to Paul, who became a virtual second founder and who, in his many writings, not only contemptuously neglected the actual sayings of Christ but even hinted that he himself was Christ reincarnated. It is the religion of Paul, then, that we have been discussing for most of this essay.

What became of Jesus' religion and his movement? The story can be simply told: throughout the two thousand years of Christianity, there have been many attempts to revive the religion of Jesus, but all but one have failed. The many peasant revolts of the Middle Ages, led usually by renegade priests appalled by the betrayal of the gospel, were all savagely dealt with. The Reformation, and the modern world, began with another such heroic attempt by the peasants of Germany in 1525, who thought that what Luther was about was the construction of what they called a "religion of the common man." As the world knows, they were horribly mistaken and brutally put down, with Luther leading the forces against them.[174]

We find yet another near miss in England during the middle decades of the seventeenth century, when the world was "turned upside down" and a host of radical Jesus movements were spawned—groups such as the Ranters, the Diggers, and the early, radical Quakers—led by working-class theologians such as Winstanley, in whose vision of brotherhood Jesus stood as the principal equalizer, the "Head Leveller."[175] They, too, were viciously put down. Modern Quakerism survived only through migration to America and a drastic shift to pietism, although not before its earlier, dying radicalism had initiated one of the greatest social and moral movements of the modern world: abolitionism. The Social Gospel movement of the nineteenth century was another attempt at reviving the betrayed cause of the Jewish peasant, but after what seemed a promising start in America, that, too, fell by the wayside, largely the victim of racism.

Then, in the middle of the twentieth century a religion emerged that, for the first time since the death of Jesus, actually succeeded in creating a faith and a community of believers that came fairly close to the gospel of love, fellowship, commitment, and radical engagement that he preached. This was the revitalized Afro-American Christianity that took shape in the church-directed protest movements culminating in the Southern Christian Leadership Conference led by Martin Luther King Jr. The political revolution that this movement stimulated and largely led, in both the Afro-American communities and the nation at large, is now an established fact of history and cause for national celebration.[176] As Leslie Dunbar acutely observed at a time when the process was still unfolding, the successful struggle against segregation and racism demonstrated how it was possible "to shake off the despotism of insitutional rigidity" in America and, as such, served as "the spawning ground [for a] new vitality"—alas, now spent—"in American politics," paving the way for a host of other movements.[177]

What is less celebrated, although within the broad span of Western civilization it will eventually be seen to have been of greater significance, is the extraordinary fact that, after two thousand years, it finally realized, for the first time, the radical gospel preached by Jesus. The gospel of the Afro-American is candidly and unapologetically social, true to the ethic of the Sermon on the Mount. But, as with the religion of Jesus, it is also a gospel that is spiritually radical, responding to his call—nay, his command—to love in a spiritual community wherein service, fellowship, worship, forgiveness, and atonement are intimately linked.

And while it focuses on Jesus' life, his being-in-the-world, and his demonstrative preaching, it does not neglect the sacrificial meaning of his death. Rather, the Afro-American church has simply refused to participate in the two-thousand-year Pauline betrayal of Christ's life, reflected in the outrageous Christological dogma that the whole point of Jesus' life, the only important thing about it, was that it ended on the cross. Frances Young has wisely written that "a good deal of evil is the result of human failure to create community" and that "when we see the sacrifice of Christ in the context of the worshipping community, we have a new perspective." It is precisely this new perspective that the Afro-American church, in its rejection, first, of the reactionary gospel of the plantation and then, later, of the supremacist and segregationist betrayal of Christ, brought back to Christianity, and in the process, the Afro-American church brought Christianity back to its Palestinian roots.

In the Southern religion of the Lost Cause, in the fundamentalist lynch mob's sacrificial feasting on Afro-American blood, and in the negrophobic and supremacist iconoclasm of the burning cross, we find Christianity at its most destructive, its most socially cannibalistic, and its most demonic, on a par with the malevolent distortions of the Crusades, the Thirty Years' War, and the Nazi terror. In the social and spiritual gospel and practice of the Afro-American church, we find Christianity in its most pristine, most liberating, and most authentic form, returning, at last, to the religion not *about* Jesus, but of Jesus, the divine Jewish peasant-rebel from the sticks of Palestine.

I wish it were possible for me to end on this note, but I can't. Alas, the revival of the religion of Jesus in the Southern Christian Leadership Conference ended with the assassination of Martin Luther King. Soon after that tragedy, Afro-Americans rejected his vision of America as "the beloved community" and turned inward upon itself spiritually and culturally, proclaiming an identity movement that denigrates the moral imperatives of the brotherhood and sisterhood of humankind and the politics of coalition that sustained the civil rights movement.

Today, once again, Sunday morning at eleven is America's most segregated hour. Only in moments of crisis and shame such as the horror of the lynching at Jaspers do Euro-Americans and Afro-Americans find it possible to kneel together and pray. Incredibly, there are even religious institutions in America where Afro-American and Euro-American congregations worship separately at the very same Christian church. Sadly, Afro-American ministers and congregations are now among the most ardent defenders of this perfidious religious segregation. And Euro-American Fundamentalists have declared "humanism" and the "Social Gospel" the dirtiest of words. As a devout believer in the social and spiritual message of Jesus the divine carpenter who commanded us to love, but one who has long abandoned Christianity, I can only hope that someday, somewhere, somehow, during the next millennium, the religion of Jesus and his Palestinian movement will finally prevail over the hegemonic religious minstrelsy that is the religion of Paul.

Three

AMERICAN
DIONYSUS

Images of Afro-American Men at the Dawn of the
Twenty-First Century

ONE SUNDAY MORNING IN MARCH 1995, I turned on my television to watch the *CNN World News*. According to this global news organization, three events dominated the news of the world that day. They were presented with unwitting Hegelian flair.

For its thesis, the newscast opened with the full-screen image of a large, burly dark-skinned man staring dementedly at the camera. The fact that he was dressed in suit and tie merely reinforced the frightening gaze of his glazed, protruding eyes and flaring nostrils. The image was that of Colin Ferguson, Euro-America's ultimate nightmare: a psychotic Afro-American man from the New York ghetto who had boarded a commuter train and randomly shot to death six Euro-American suburbanites as the train entered their own green and safely segregated turf.

Ferguson had provided hundreds of hours of newscast time, not to mention endless newspaper columns, in the two years since the massacre. He had already been tried and found guilty. Every aspect of the case had been explored ad nauseam, especially the Euro-American horror at Afro-American ghetto violence breaking out of its segregated boundaries and intruding on the suburbs. One would have thought there was little more to say.

Not so. The fact that eighteen survivors and relatives demanded to make a statement before Ferguson was sentenced was, according to Atlanta, the world's top story. Interestingly, although the story was ostensibly about the grief of the victims' relatives and their need to express their grief, we saw very little of them. Instead, the camera focused relentlessly on America's most fearsome image: the homicidal, maniacal Afro-American man, who was also an immigrant, obligingly gaping with glassy fearsomeness at the camera.

Then, with barely a pause, the antithetical image—that of America's greatest living hero of the day—appeared on the screen. He was tall; he was the very apotheosis of the male human figure in all its perfection, magical in the pure, flowing symmetry of his glowing limbs, godlike in the serenity of his countenance. An awesome radiance seemed to reflect from the lens of the camera as it focused mistily on him. And he was dark—mahogany dark. It was America's only living man-god at his second coming. It was Michael Jordan.

The previous day Jordan had finally put an end to what can only be described as a secular Parousia by confirming that he would be ending his retirement from basketball and returning to play again with his old team, the Chicago Bulls. The frenzy of speculation, of expressions of disbelief and joy, during the previous week and a half was increasingly expressed in terms normally reserved for divinities, and the sportswriters repeatedly made explicit reference to Jordan's divine status. George Papajohn's front-page story in the *Chicago Tribune* that same Sunday morning was typical: "Michael Jordan may be too tall for baseball, too competitive to stay at home and too confident in his fairway wagering, but he is still a basketball god. On Saturday, he answered more than a few prayers by unretiring."[1]

The comments of ordinary Chicagoans, however, made no such qualifications. Without the slightest trace of irony or humor, Jordan was repeatedly called a god—not simply a basketball god—by one and all. It was generally agreed by people of all classes, ethnicities, genders, and sexual orientations that Jordan's return was the very best thing that could happen to the city; nay, to the nation; indeed, to the world. And to make the point, the *Tribune* ran another front-page story on the reaction in Beijing to Jordan's return. There, Chicagoans were proudly told, the news had been greeted with cheers when it was announced before the Beijing vs. Xinan Army basketball game. This was the response of Beijing's star player, Huang Gang, on having heard of the return of "Qiao Dan," as the Great One is known in China: "We adore him. I mean, he's not a normal human being. He is magic. He is a phantom. No ordinary human being can jump like that."[2]

So frequently had Jordan been called a god that, around the time of his retirement, he had, in all seriousness, found it necessary to deny his divinity and affirm the fact that he was merely human: witness his mortal desire to spend more time with his family and be more of a father to his son. However, the near universal tendency of newswriters and ordinary folks alike to call Jordan a god, upon contemplating his return, had began to irk the Great One. If he was not a god, then this was surely blasphemy. If he was indeed a god in human form, then he stood in danger of having his divine secret revealed. As we know from the history of religions, the god who visits the human world must always shroud his divinity in mystery. "Men say that I am . . ." and all that. At any rate, this is how Melissa Isaacson opened the *Chicago Tribune*'s lead story on his first game after his return, under the banner headline, "The Air Up There": "He called the last week embarrassing, this nonsense of being treated as a god. But finally there was Michael Jordan on Sunday, as if a vision had appeared."[3]

After the CNN version of the Jordan story, the broadcast moved in Hegelian synthesis to the third most important event in the world news that day. Again, the camera focused on a large, handsome male figure, the central character in what was, arguably, the most sensational crime story in the history of the nation—indeed, from the intense interest shown around the globe, in the history of the world. Again, the image upon which the camera focused was that of an Afro-American man. It was the face of O. J. Simpson, accused of the murder of his former wife, Nicole Brown Simpson, and a friend, Ronald Goldman, some ten months earlier. The story this time was about the many ordinary people who had become celebrities through their association with the case. Even the dreary-looking, middle-aged detective Philip Vannatter, we were told, had become a star by virtue of being the arresting officer. The O. J. Simpson case had become, according to CNN, "one big celebrity game." This surely was an understatement. The nation's obsessive interest in this case was truly amazing and defied all understanding. A total of 1,159 journalists had been credentialed to cover the case, and one tabloid, the *National Enquirer*, had 20 journalists at a time working on it. The *Enquirer*'s editor, Steve Coz, told the staff of the *Los Angeles Times*: "It's America, it's Hollywood, a big celebrity, a double murder, sex, children, indications of drugs. It's got it all."[4]

Nothing seemed capable of upstaging it for too long, certainly no other murder case, not even one of comparable horror. To take a striking example, the vicious, cold-blooded murder of her two children by Susan Smith, who then proceeded to deceive the entire nation with a trumped-up story of how her boys had been kidnapped by an Afro-American man—yes, him again!—would seem, by any objective standard of comparative evil, to be a story of far greater interest and sensationalism than that of a one-time football star's sleazy murder of his ex-wife and her friend. In a nation obsessed with the decline of "family values" and the changing status of women, what could have been more fixatingly horrible than a mother cold-bloodedly drowning her two cherubic, blue-eyed, blond sons?

But it was not to be. Even during the height of the Susan Smith story in October 1994, the nation's TV studios seemed incapable of staying away from the O. J. case. One got the distinct impression of impatience in the coverage of the Smith case. It was as if the networks felt under an obligation to give coverage to something they and their audience knew in their guts they had had enough of. Indeed, before Smith made her bombshell confession, the nation's TV news had already relegated her to second place, returning relentlessly to O. J. And barely two days after her incredible admission, she was quietly demoted from top billing, never to return to the top of the news, certainly never again to upstage O. J., even during her tearful appearances in court.

By the Sunday morning in March when I watched the *World News,* all memory of Susan Smith had vanished. The O. J. Simpson trial, even on an off-day, the court being closed, was still among the three most important stories in the news of the world.

WHY? WHY, IN THE WEALTHIEST, most powerful, most industrially advanced country on the face of the earth; the nation with the greatest number of Nobel laureates, the most sophisticated system of science, the greatest universities, the most celebrated museums, the finest writers in the English language, the best orchestras; the nation to which the world, including Europe, looks for leadership in politics, for military intervention in times of war, for aid in development—why is it that this nation's most technically powerful and journalistically savvy news organization chose to place at the top of its world news those three stories?

It would be much too easy to dismiss CNN as descending to a vulgar form of tabloid television. In the first place, CNN was doing nothing different from the other television networks and stations around the nation. In the second place, as a network driven by profits, that is to say, by the market, it was presenting the news that people wanted to see and hear. To condemn CNN is to shoot the messenger. Precisely because we know there is one thing CNN is good at—its grasp of what interests its audience most—we are confident in concluding that the triad at the top of the *World News* that Sunday morning was there because the American nation wanted it there. So, again, why? What's going on in the collective psyche of this great nation? Why the obsession with these "black" images?

The answer, perhaps, is hinted at by an exquisite editorial dialectic. In six minutes we stared, first, at America's most terrifying nightmare: the Afro-American male as demon. Then, from the depths of our horror, we were made to soar antithetically to America's fulfillment of that greatest and most elusive of ancient Greek ideals, *arete,* the "notion of ephemeral excellence and of transient triumph," as the classicist Stephen Miller interprets it, imbuing the athlete "with an aura of the quest of man for perfection"[5]—and, we may add, following the journalists of Chicago, for godlike status. And, finally, as if to emphasize the transience of our triumph in the deified Michael, we were reduced to the sordid realities of our existence when we viewed the synthetic image of O. J., the godlike hero-athlete as maniacal killer and demon. With Sunday morning news like this, who needed to go to church?

The question for us, however, is why was it that the central figure in each of these three powerful stories dominating the *CNN World News* that day was an Afro-American man?

AMERICA'S TAR BABY

IN THE MIDST OF THIS NATION of 265 million varied souls, there live some 34 million Afro-Americans, a mere 13 percent. And between them and the 208 million who are Euro-American, there is a strange dialectic, one that has its roots deep in the nation's past, one that—for all its historic savagery and prolonged perversities of repression and rape and lynchings and economic exploitation and social rejection and abandonment, sometimes because of all that—links the two inextricably, obsessively, and, however paradoxical it may seem, transcendently in a civilizational struggle that engenders the best in both groups, even as it brings out the worst in them, that creates even as it destroys, that ennobles even as it degrades.

The Afro-American lies at the heart of Euro-America's conception of itself as a "race," as a culture, as a people, and as a nation. "Blackness" is the canvas against which "whiteness" paints itself, the mirror in which the collective eye sees itself, the catalyst in which this great mass culture explosively creates itself. It has been so from the beginning. I follow Ralph Ellison in viewing "the whole of American life as a drama acted out upon the body of a Negro giant, who, lying trussed up like Gulliver, forms the state and the scene upon which and within which the action unfolds."[6] Virginia, the Western world's first mass democracy since the fall of ancient Athens, was able to recreate this political miracle only in the context of the large contra-distinctive presence of slaves, who gave meaning to freedom by their own lack of freedom, and made unity among Euro-Americans possible by their very "blackness."[7]

Nor was the Afro-American contradistinction confined to the political or the passive use of the slave presence. As the Israeli historian Mechal Sobel demonstrates in her exquisitely detailed account of early Virginia, "Both blacks and whites were crucially influenced by the traditions of the 'other.'" [8] The influence was often direct, from the slave nanny who suckled, to the slave preacher who buried; from the Christian values that the Africans came to cherish, to the English language and musical instruments they syncretized with the remnants of their African heritage. But sometimes the influence came, just as powerfully, in counteridentifying revulsions from each other, as in the elite Southerners' obsession with the secular literature of classical antiquity, which was compelled by the need to distance themselves from the omnipresence of Afro-American orality and preliterate spirituality. Try as each group might, there was no escaping the violent embrace of Africa and Europe that was the crucible of American culture in the Old South. "In perceptions of time, in esthetics, in approaches to ecstatic religious experience and to understanding of the Holy Spirit, in ideas of the afterworld and of the proper ways to honor the spirits of the dead, African influence was deep and far-reaching," says Sobel, as deep and pervasive as was the influence of Euro-Americans on Afro-Americans.[9] Nor did the influence end there. If the way we speak, the accent permanently etched upon our consciousness at our mother's breasts, is one of the things that most defines us, then the Euro-American Southerner is indelibly Afro-American, since his distinctive mode of speech, as J. L. Dillard, one of the nation's leading sociolinguists, has pointed out, can only be explained in terms of the "overwhelming influence of the Negro on Southern whites."[10]

Even so, we should be very careful never to confuse interaction with mutuality. Each group may have influenced the other, but the terms of trade were brutally asymmetric and amounted in most respects to outright social, economic, and cultural parasitism.[11] Or, to draw on Ellison again, the Afro-American came to be "recognized as the human factor placed outside the democratic master plan, a human 'natural' resource who, so that white men could become more human, was elected to undergo a process of institutional dehumanization."[12]

Central to this deeply fraught cultural interaction was a complex interplay of stereotypes and images of the "Other." For Euro-Americans, the three central images have been precisely those beamed from Atlanta that Sunday morning: the age-old image of the Afro-American man as demon; the twentieth-century image of him as athletic demigod; and the more recent and rapidly growing fin de siècle image of him as the American epiphany of Dionysus.

The Afro-American man as demon is the easiest part of the triad to understand, largely because it has been the most thoroughly explored. A long line of historians and cultural analysts have examined and explained how slavery and racism compelled the construction of the Negro as either a childish buffoon, in his place, or a brutish sexual maniac, when out of control.[13] Stanley Elkins's description of the stereotype of the Afro-American man as the quintessential Sambo was excellent historical ethnography. I agree with Elkins that there must have been a behavioral response that was in some way influenced by the stereotype, given the totality of the master's power. We part company in our conception of what that response might have been. Elkins takes the Freudian view that the slaves were eventually infantilized; I see the childish deference as dissemblance. Further, as I have shown elsewhere, Elkins unnecessarily undermined his own argument in his demonstrably false claim that the Sambo stereotype was uniquely American; some version of Sambo can be found wherever slavery existed, from the Roman's stereotype of his Greek slave as a voluble, cowardly Graeculus to the British slaveholder's stereotype of the Afro-Jamaican as Quashee,[14] the lazy, incorrigible man-child.

In all these stereotypes, we find the idea of the slave as a dishonorable brute whose maniacal desires must be kept in check by the master's discipline, and whose word can be accepted only under torture. Like the tick calling the dog a parasite, the stereotype performs an obvious psychological role. Seeing the victim as the aggressor and as the "white man's burden" is a classic instance of projection: at once a denial of one's own moral perversity and violence and a perfect excuse for them. The demonization of the Afro-American male in American society is still very much with us, as the notorious "Willie Horton" political ads used by George Bush in his campaign against Michael Dukakis demonstrate. Only, now it is not the violence of the individual master against his slave that is being denied, but the chronic violence of American society and the dominant group's implication in it.

America has always been a violent place. And quite apart from their involvement with slavery, Euro-Americans have always exhibited a perverse fascination with violence. The violence of Euro-American men against other Euro-American men, and against Euro-American women, needs no documentation. The law of the jungle, of an eye for an eye, has played, and continues to play, a central role in the culture. As noted in the previous essay, lynching was originally developed as a violent means of controlling not Afro-Americans but other violent Euro-American men. Nowhere is the self-contradiction of Euro-Americans more evident than in the powerful hold that the National Rifle Association's utterly irrational opposition to gun control exerts on the American Congress. Euro-American men exhibit a higher rate of homicide and other forms of violence than do the men of any other advanced industrial society; America incarcerates a higher proportion of its Caucasian men than does any other majority-Caucasian society; and America is the only advanced industrial society that practices capital punishment, the majority of those executed being Euro-American men. The experience, and fear of, violence among Euro-Americans is hardly new, even though many analysts erroneously infer, from opinion polls placing fear of crime as the leading concern of Americans today, that this is a modern crisis. In fact, in the cities and frontier towns of nineteenth-century America, the probability of being mugged, beaten, or killed was much greater than in urban America today.[15]

Mention of the frontier immediately suggests the other side of Euro-Americans' experience of violence: their celebration of it. The quintessential American myth is that of the cowboy and the frontier ranch and town. Central to that myth are the role of violence and the reverence for the gun. The counterpart to the Western shoot-out was the urban duel, which epitomized masculine culture in the old South and West. Thus violence is not only shunned and dreaded in American culture; it is also embraced and romanticized.[16]

The Afro-American's role in this extraordinary love-hate relationship with violence is now better understood. The Afro-American man as demon represents the evil side of violence, the violence we dread, the violence that Euro-American males do not dare to admit is a core part of their psychic being. This kind of violence we associate with rapists, with "blackness," with sin. And, as we have seen, to expiate it, the ritual of lynching Afro-Americans was the perfect symbolic tool. Today we no longer lynch in public rituals supervised by local clergymen. Instead, the state hires the hangman to do it. Nonetheless, the Afro-American as demon continues to play the role of parceling out that part of violence which we dread to admit. One day we call it Willie Horton; another, it goes by the name of Colin Ferguson.

The truly egregious aspect of Bush's use of the fearsome-looking Horton as his symbol of crime was not that it called attention to the disproportionate rate of crime among Afro-Americans but that it was simply a modern version of an age-old cultural practice of projecting Euro-American evil onto the demonic Afro-American male. Afro-American crime is a horrible blight on the Afro-American communities of America, and it is a substantial part of America's overall crime problem. But it is not the *major* part of it. The typical Afro-American man is not a criminal. To the contrary, he is inclined to be more God-fearing and conservatively tough on criminals than the rest of the population. Furthermore, the typical criminal is not an Afro-American man but a Euro-American one. And if one includes white-collar crimes in one's count, as well as the unreported violence of alcoholic Euro-American males against their defenseless wives and children—as one should—then it continues to be true that Euro-American males commit not only the majority of crimes of violence in this country but the disproportionate number.[17]

None of this, let me repeat, is to explain or in any way excuse the horror and shame of modern Afro-American crime, over 90 percent of whose victims are fellow Afro-Americans. Rather, it is to explain why it was that, on Sunday morning, March 19, 1995, America's leading electronic voice, the world's only global television network, opened the *World News* with the fearsome image of a demonic "black" man.

THE AFRO-AMERICAN MAN AS DEMIGOD?

BUT WHAT ABOUT THE DEIFIED MICHAEL? Where does he fit in? How could he possibly be reconciled with such a cultural story? Here we must plunge even deeper into the strange, Afro-European splendor that is American symbolic culture. If it is true that the Afro-American male lies at the symbolic core of all that is dark and evil and violent—defining, contra-distinctively, all that is "white" and good and gentlemanly—it is symbolically understandable, indeed necessary, that he must stand at the center of any transcendence of that perverse, yet creative, demonology. The essence of America's greatness as a culture, the undeniable source of its claim to be the originator and propagator of any emerging global culture, is its astonishing capacity not simply to remake itself but to transcend its own limitations—in the process, converting flaws to assets, incorporating the once demonized, making insiders of outsiders, transforming evil into good—and often to do so against the will of its most powerful members.

To understand how the demonized Afro-American male can become the deified hero, one must understand, first, something about the nature of heroes in a mass democracy and, second, the fact that America is the most Christian nation on earth. It is hard, especially hard, in a mass democracy such as America, to worship those whom we take most seriously, to whom we feel the closest kinship, and whom we expect to lead us. Our leader is expected to be one of us. For such a person, reverence becomes a dangerous thing. The hero in America enjoys a most precarious status, and if he is not to join the nation's vast graveyard of toppled idols, must fast heed Emerson's unromantic conception of his achievement: that he is "no braver than an ordinary man, but is braver five minutes longer." Unlike in Europe, where mass democracies exist within the context of old, hierarchical cultures with lingering notions of aristocratic leadership, the leader in America is forced to be one with the people, an ordinary man, whatever his actual class background. Indeed, as the case of George Bush demonstrates, the more pedigreed the class background, the more accentuated the image of an ordinary, regular guy, right down to the affected garbling of the English language by a man with a first-rate undergraduate record at Yale. It should come as no surprise that the perfect leader of this great democracy was a former actor. For, ultimately, only a professional actor can play the role of leader while acting as if he is not; can claim to be not of Washington, when as president he is the ultimate insider; can claim to be a churchman while hardly ever going to church; and can persuade the world that he is the embodiment of "family values," when in reality he is divorced and is the failed patriarch of an unusually dysfunctional family. Ronald Reagan was the supremely popular democratic leader of America precisely because no one revered him. To the American everyman, he was charmingly, embracingly, comfortably one of us. The same set of attitudes explains the paradoxical escalation of President Clinton's approval ratings with the Monica Lewinsky affair.

In a mass democracy such as ours, then, only two types of men can be revered: those who are safely dead and those who least belong. What these two have in common is, of course, their utter otherness: the physical otherness of death and the social otherness of "blackness," or prewar Jewishness, or nineteenth-century Irishness, or whatever the contradistinctive identity of the "Other" group might be. For the average Euro-American aspirant, "the main thing about [becoming] a hero," as Will Rogers observed with his classic American wit, "is to know when to die."

The Christian religiosity of America reinforces all this. For it is in Christianity that we find the classic expression of this dual path to the status of hero. Jesus Christ was a Jew and, as such, belonged to what was, until the imposition of this civilizational role upon Afro-Americans, the most despised group of Others in Christendom. Indeed, the institutionalization of Christianity went hand in hand with increased persecution and exclusion of the Jews, who, in the ancient world, had been no more despised and excluded than any of the numerous other foreign peoples thrown together in the Roman Empire. Precisely because they were God-givers, they had to be despised as God-killers. Christianity's embrace of a Jewish God and of the very Jewish view of the world he preached was only possible because of the active exclusion and demonization of the people and culture that had produced him. We find an exactly similar principle at work in the civilization of America, which eagerly embraces Afro-American heroes and cultural productions even as it segregates and demonizes the people that have produced them.

The timing of Jordan's athletic apotheosis is also striking. It parallels the sequence of events in the passage from mortal to god that Joseph Campbell found in the mythologies of all peoples. First, the hero, while still a mere mortal, mysteriously separates himself from his normal world. Then, in his exilic journeys he encounters enormous trials and struggles with the forces of darkness over which he eventually triumphs. Finally, renewed, he returns home, and in the process of reintegration with the society he reenergizes it, enhancing its sense of community and its most treasured values.[18]

Now, it may be only a coincidence, but the journeys of Michael Jordan between 1993 and 1995 bear a remarkable parallel to these rites of passage. First, while at the height of his powers and earning capacity, he announced to an astonished world that he would retire from basketball. Then came the period of trials. There was the grief of coming to terms with his father's brutal murder shortly before Jordan retired. The mythological potency of this event cannot be exaggerated. As Campbell has shown, atonement with the father is perhaps the most universally attested aspect of the making of a hero into a god.

> The problem of the hero going to meet the father is to open
> his soul beyond terror to such a degree that he will be ripe to
> understand how the sickening and insane tragedies of this vast
> and ruthless cosmos are completely validated in the majesty of
> Being. The hero transcends life with its peculiar blind spot
> and for a moment rises to a glimpse of the source. He beholds
> the face of the father, understands—and the two are atoned.[19]

Jordan's extraordinary composure in confronting the horrible death of his father was almost Job-like in its dignity. By means of his Buddhist faith, his atonement came through the reconciliation of the senseless death of his father, at the hands of a fellow Afro-American and a Euro-American youth, with the transcendent presence of a God who needs no justification.

His heroic patience and dignity were reflected in the other trials during his period of exile: the bitterness of putting up with a suddenly hostile press probing into his gambling habit and constantly questioning his hard-won integrity, and the sometimes humiliating struggle to prove his athletic prowess in the utterly alien world of baseball. While our hero never made it out of the minor league, his honor was spared by the baseball strike—the intervention of the gods?—and he retreated, assuring the world that he had achieved his objective and found peace of mind. The trials and battles of this second phase, the world was to learn, were as much internal as external. What the hero learned from his exile, and taught his pining fans in the many little books of his sayings, was the courage to be humble; the simple wisdom that defining and achieving one's goals, even in so modest and tedious an arena as baseball, could be as gratifying as soaring for the slam dunk; the deep inner peace that comes from close intimacy with one's family in time of grief; and the simple joy of getting to know and play with one's children.

All of this was to change with the return of the hero, which in its amazing publicity and excitement met all the requirements of Campbell's third stage in the hero's rites of passage: the apotheosis in which the hero "comes back as one reborn, made great and filled with creative power." The return and reintegration, as Campbell documents, can often be as trying as the quest in exile. Jordan unwittingly got to the heart of the matter when, a year after his return to basketball, he discussed his reactions with *Chicago Tribune* staff writer Terry Armour. The return was, he noted, a "trial" that he had to "put . . . to rest," and there were "stages" of transition: "There were some preliminary stages I had to go through just to make sure it was the right decision for me and for the rest of the team. But everyone seemed to take it to extreme and I wasn't expecting that. That surprised me. I took a step back and felt like, 'All I want to do is play the game of basketball.' But it was like I was starting a cult or something like that. It was very embarrassing."[20]

Jordan's renewed "creative power" and inspiration were felt most dramatically by his team and its players. "I know Michael more as a person now," teammate Steve Kerr told Armour. "A year ago, he was just kind of this legend who appeared on the scene. It was a dream, almost; it didn't seem real." In the year after his return, Jordan scored more than 2,700 points, playing in over a hundred games, the most sensational highlights of which were no doubt his 55 points against the New York Knicks on March 28, 1995; his astonishing 19 points during the last six minutes of the game against the Vancouver Grizzlies in which he single-handedly snatched victory from the jaws of an impending humiliating defeat; and his 53 points against the Detroit Pistons on March 7, 1996.

Not only did Jordan resume his former glory as a player, breaking record after astonishing record, but the personal transformation he went through during his exilic trials all redounded to his team and his community. "The full round," Campbell tells us, "the norm of the monomyth, requires that the hero shall now begin the labor of bringing the runes of wisdom . . . back into the kingdom of humanity, where the boon may redound to the renewing of the community."[21] No one in the great city of Chicago was in any doubt about the enormous boon brought back by the returning hero, if we are to believe the remarks of the mayor, the leaders of the chamber of commerce, and the city's numerous other community leaders. In this raw hinterland of capitalism, it was inevitable that the return would be acknowledged as the best thing to have happened to the city's vibrant business life.

And it should come as no surprise that after his apotheosis, Jordan, already an advertising icon, began to speak in the language of business. Soon his suppliant fans were to learn that on the rare occasion when the Bulls lost a game, the team had not simply "fucked up" or gotten beaten by the other team, but rather, in the postexilic language of the eternal one of the dream, the Bulls had "not been productive." And a victory, in the new understated corporate rhetoric of the Great One, was "very productive" and "on target." In the interview with Armour, Jordan, without a trace of irony, spoke of his father as "an important support system," without which the renewal of his "career" had been made doubly difficult. Of the game against the Philadelphia '76ers in which he returned to full form, Jordan said: "I had a vision in terms of how I wanted that game to come out and went and executed it." Within a year of his return, numerous little books, all intentionally produced to look like the devotional tracts carried around by devout Christians, began to appear in the bookstores of Chicago, the most successful of which summarized the wise sayings of Michael, sayings that, of course, were phrased in the language of both the new entrepreneurship and Republican family values.

In Jordan, finally, religion, athletic heroism, and the capitalist ethos were all exquisitely distilled. The reporter Cory Johnson tells us that one night in early 1996 a young man suddenly began jumping and hollering in religious fervor in front of Philadelphia's Four Seasons' Hotel: "Joey, I touched God! I touched God!" he exclaimed. "With this hand! I touched him! I touched GOD!" The god to whom he referred was Michael Jordan.[22]

It turns out, too, that not only Jordan but also his head coach, Phil Jackson—the son of a Pentecostal minister from Montana—was a committed Zen Buddhist who brought a "powerful spiritual presence" to the game. Jackson wrote a book in 1995 entitled *Sacred Hoops,* in which he largely attributed the Bulls' success to their spiritual practices and beliefs. Apparently, when the team had one of its losing streaks during the hero's odyssey, they met in a room with incense burning and performed a ceremony to "exorcise the evil spirits that [had] possessed the team." Later Jackson said of his deified guard: "Michael has attained a quality of mind few Zen students ever achieve. His ability to stay calm and intensely focused in the midst of utter chaos is unsurpassed." In *Sacred Hoops* Jackson wrote mystically: "If you meet the Buddha in the lane, feed him the ball."[23] He did not tell Cory Johnson whether Michael had met the

Buddha during his odyssey away from the team, but it is a fair guess that Jackson firmly believed such a meeting occurred.

CROSSING, BLURRING, AND DISSOLVING "RACIAL" BOUNDARIES

ONCE WE UNDERSTAND HOW Americans can both demonize and deify the image of the Afro-American man, it is easier to grasp the extraordinary priorities of the CNN news editors that Sunday morning in March 1995. I suggested earlier that part of the fascination with O. J. Simpson was that he conflated the two extremes of "Otherness" projected on the Afro-American male: that of the superhuman athlete and that of the demonized killer. But while this works well enough in explaining CNN's selection process that Sunday morning—a nice synthesis of the tidy little antithesis the news programmers had set up—it is far too facile an explanation of the prolonged nationwide obsession with this man and his trials.

To understand this obsession, we must turn to what Nietzsche in his first great, if flawed, work called the Dionysian principle,[24] and Charles Segal more recently identified as "the principle that destroys differences."[25] Dionysus, it will be recalled, was the Greek god of wine; of masks, dissemblance, and theatrical performances; of the female votaries, or maenads; and of the underworld.[26] Ambiguity is his essence. This most Greek of gods, nonetheless, is the god from elsewhere. He is twice-born and is both man and god, the son of a woman and a god. He sometimes appears as the most masculine of men, with the beard of a mature older man, but he as often appears as a youth—classically, in Euripides' Bacchae—so effeminate that he questions the distinction between male and female. His followers are the female votaries, yet as the god of wine he occupies a specially male symbolic space. Capable of inspiring the greatest joy and revelry, he is also the source of the most horrible pain and evil. He adopts "a fluid and changeable identity based on disguise, on transformation, and on the simultaneous presence of opposite characteristics."[27]

Dionysus, as Martha Nussbaum reemphasized in her introduction to C. K. Williams's splendid 1990 translation of The Bacchae, not only crosses boundaries but dissolves them.[28] For me, this distinction is critical. In the god's prototypical Greek context, the distinction seems, vaguely, to correlate with the two sets of epiphanies associated with the bearded, mature man and the effeminate youth, with the former more of a liminal crosser of boundaries and the latter both a crosser and a destroyer of boundaries. But there is only a hint of this; I wouldn't push it. In the modern expression of the Dionysian, however, I find a sharp distinction between these two roles.

In *The Bacchae,* Euripides taught us that the urge to follow the call of the Dionysian is deep and irrepressible. However, our failure to control the urge to surrender completely will inevitably lead to catastrophe. In every soul, in every polity, in every culture, there are two cities: the ordered, rational city of Pentheus and the impassioned, frenzied city of Dion. *The Bacchae* is a morality play about the tragic terror of neglecting or overemphasizing either. We are damned if we too worshipfully embrace Dion, as Agave horribly discovers, but we are damned if we don't, which is the fate of Pentheus, the son she unwittingly decapitates, with hints of cannibalism.

Nietzsche generalized this doctrine in terms of the need for balance between the Apollonian and the Dionysian principles in every culture. In this he was correct, but he was not so much wrong as limited in his diagnosis of what Germany needed. What the subsequent history of Germany shows is that it is not enough simply to advocate the Dionysian as a counter to a too-Apollonian discipline. A blend is not necessarily a balance. The monstrous tragedy of modern Germany was precisely its incapacity to forge a balance between these two principles. For, instead of balancing the two, it did the worst possible thing: it conflated both in their extremity, leading to an orgy of criminality and nationalistic passion within the disciplined terror of the Nazi state.

It is the great good fortune of our times that America, the only remaining world power and the one emerging world culture, has, in its rough-and-ready way, achieved just such a balance. How did it do it? Once again, as in the cultural construction of its democracy, it turned to that bountiful symbolic resource in its midst: its great domestic enemy, the people from "elsewhere" who have been here from the beginning, that familiar, cultivated stranger who is embodied in the image of the Afro-American male. What I am suggesting is that, in American civilization, the Afro-American male image not only has functioned as the ultimate symbol of Otherness at its two polar extremes—the Other as chthonic demon and the Other as Olympian demigod—but, coinciding with the postwar rise of America to world supremacy, has emerged as the ultimate Dionysian symbol in both its liminal aspects: the crosser of boundaries and the dissolver of these very boundaries.

Between the Puritanism and "ordered liberty" of the North, the Quaker asceticism and Germanic pietism of the Mid-Atlantic states, and the hierarchical and dulotic authoritarianism of the militaristic South with its tradition of primal honor, early America had no shortage of the Apollonian impulse. Up to the middle of the present century, however, Afro-Americans were simply not available symbolically as a direct Dionysian counterweight. They were too thoroughly the Other, and their images and cultural productions, if used, could be represented only in surrogate forms such as minstrelsy, as we will see shortly.

Here I wish to disagree completely with modern analysts of the Dionysian principle who attempt to identify Dionysus with the Other. Dionysus, even though from elsewhere, was never the Other in the Greek symbolic imagination. Rather, he was, quintessentially, the crosser of boundaries. It was precisely his combination of strangeness and familiarity that made his liminality possible. The Greeks, let it not be forgotten, were in no symbolic shortage of Otherness. Greece was the world's first large-scale slave society, and like America, it used slaves, freedmen, and metics as its embodiment of Otherness. The Other was the barbarian, fit only to be a slave. Dionysus, however, was no barbarian. His strangeness was a mystery, masked by his familiarity. The interesting thing about him was his repeated insistence that he was a god, a Greek god, son of Zeus even if mysteriously from elsewhere. *The Bacchae*, indeed, opens with the god proclaiming with an irritated air of defiance that he is a Greek god, son of Zeus. On the simplest level, the play is about the nasty surprises that await those who diss Dionysus's divinity and, by extension, his Greek identity.

As LONG AS THE Afro-American male symbolically embodied the quintessential Other, then, he could not function *directly* as a symbol of Dionysian liminality and the repressed pleasure principle. But his image could be used *indirectly*, provided that it was camouflaged and enacted through the bodies of "white" men. This is what the obsession of nineteenth-century popular culture with minstrelsy was all about. For nearly a century, between 1830 and 1920, the minstrel show was, in the words of Eric Lott, "ubiquitous, cultural common coin . . . so central to the lives of North Americans that we are hardly aware of its extraordinary influence."[29] Emerging out of the blackface song-and-dance acts performed in the urban centers of the North during the first decades of the nineteenth century, first by Afro-American slaves and ex-slaves, then by Euro-American imitators, minstrelsy consolidated in the early 1840s into America's predominant popular genre. A three-act show, it called for four or five male Euro-American entertainers, made up with burnt cork or greasepaint and garbed in extravagant "Negro" costumes. In part, it was a genuine appropriation of Afro-American music, humor, and dance.[30]

On another level, minstrelsy was simple racist caricature. It not only served as the main form of entertainment for the nation's Euro-American urban masses but, as Alexander Saxon and David Roediger have both argued, performed the latent sociological functions of constructing whiteness, of neutralizing working-class resentment by displacing it from the classes above to the "race" below, and of incorporating the disparate European immigrants into a racially unified "white republic."[31]

Ralph Ellison saw clearly the Dionysian nature of minstrelsy, especially in the centrality of the mask. Agreeing with others that minstrelsy "constituted a ritual of exorcism," he went on to argue that slavery, "the moral heart of the American social drama," had made Afro-Americans "too real for easy fantasy, too serious to be dealt with in anything less than a national art. " It was no accident that the mask and the colors of the national flag, along with bowdlerized versions of the Negro male's body, custom, and costumes, were integral parts of this "national iconography." According to Ellison: "The racial identity of the performer was unimportant, the mask was the thing (the 'thing' in more ways than one) and its function was to veil the humanity of Negroes thus reduced to a sign, and to repress the white audience's awareness of its moral identification with its own acts and with the human ambiguities pushed behind the mask."[32]

There was one critical flaw in Ellison's otherwise brilliant analysis, his assertion that the performer's racial identity was unimportant. More recent and detailed cultural work has focused precisely on this aspect of Dionysian masking in minstrelsy. W. T. Lhamon correctly observes that in the critical transition from early blackface at Catherine's Market in New York to minstrelsy, "what has come inside is blackness, for the most part, not black people."[33] Performers always made sure to "flash white skin beneath a layer of burnt cork." Even so, he argues, they could never completely negate the Afro-American bodies and images they caricatured: "When the white minstrel's engagement with black charisma seemed to be contained, even turned inside out to derogate that charisma, the identification was still there in fact, but encoded. Apparently controlled and debased, it had a momentum of its own. Apparently deflected and defused, blackface was nevertheless raising Cain autonomously."[34] I think this is an important insight even if it runs the risk of reifying cultural forms. Beneath the overt debasement of the Afro-American image, that image was being indelibly inscribed upon the American popular consciousness in these performances, and Afro-American artists would later exploit this inscription.

But Lhamon goes too far in his attempt to underplay the overtly supremacist intent and function that minstrelsy had for its nineteenth-century working-class audiences.[35] Minstrelsy, to use the language of the symbolic anthropologist Victor Turner, became a master symbol of nineteenth-century American culture. Like all such symbols, it was protean and multivocal,[36] capable of isolating the Afro-American man's body even as it incorporated his image, of "enacting miscegenation" and cultural amalgamation even as it violently put down any hint of his manhood or his association with Euro-American women. Most of all, it could shamelessly appropriate and steal Afro-American cultural productions while "scientifically" insisting that Negroes never created anything of value.

And, in what was perhaps its most Dionysian enactment, minstrelsy could pursue and vicariously satisfy the Euro-American male's obsession with the bodies of Afro-American males. This is the fascinating thesis argued by Eric Lott in his remarkable study of the subject. Minstrelsy was "cultural robbery" in which "racial" and sexual desire simmered barely beneath the surface of overt debasement: "This simultaneous production and subjection of black maleness may have been more than a formal consequence of wearing blackface; it may have been the minstrel show's main achievement, articulating precisely a certain structure of racial feeling. The very real instability of white men's investment in black men, however, seems often to have exceeded this happy ambiguity, giving rise to a good deal of trouble."[37]

The trouble, as Lott brilliantly demonstrates, was not only the thinly veiled homoerotic desire for Afro-American bodies but the fact that, for all the minstrel show's ridiculing and buffoonery of the cultural acts it had stolen, aspects of the real thing survived in it.[38] We know that the best of the minstrel performers, such as T. D. Rice—the creator of the popular Jim Crow act—and George Washington Dixon, keenly observed actual Afro-American acts, which they imitated for their own shows. In the end, they were too clever by half, as the English would say. And as Charles Dickens witnessed one night when he saw a rare appearance of an actual

Afro-American male, William Henry Lane, acting in a minstrel show, Afro-American men could imitate Euro-American men imitating Afro-American men.[39] When this happened, the Dionysian mask fell away, and the potentially subversive nature of minstrelsy was revealed. Apparently dropping of the mask often happened, even during ordinary minstrel shows when "white" bodies wore the mask of "black" bodies. At times, the deeply disturbing realization would creep upon the participants that "blackness" was real and somehow there, that in fact, through their seeming debasement of the stolen images of Afro-American maleness and culture, they were unwittingly engaged in the blackening of their own bodies, culture, and consciousness. "The primary purpose of the mask," Lott writes, ". . . may have been as much to maintain control over a potentially subversive act as to ridicule, though the double bind was that blackface performers' attempts at regulation were also capable of producing an aura of 'blackness.' The incident [Dickens's witnessing an Afro-American male imitating Euro-Americans imitating Afro-American males] suggests the danger of simple public display of black practices, the offering of them for Euro-American enjoyment. The moments at which the intended counterfeit broke down and failed to 'seem,' when the fakery evaporated, could result in acts of unsettling authenticity, even if a white man were inside."[40]

This vicarious involvement and subversive pleasure in the Afro-American male body would overlap with, and be partly replaced by, the more directly brutal ritual of the communal lynch ceremony, as we have seen. Indeed, as Lott points out, the castration threat to Euro-American men implicit both in minstrelsy's masking in Afro-American skin and the obsession of its humor with the Afro-American penis was violently and literally reversed in the tendency of lynch ritualists to castrate Afro-American bodies.[41] When both minstrelsy and the lynching cult subsided during the 1920s, a long transitional period emerged—between the mid-twenties and the end of the fifties—during which Afro-American entertainers slowly began to reclaim their images and productions through performances beyond Afro-American communities. Even so, it was never possible for Afro-Americans to directly enter the Dionysian role during this period. All attempts to do so, as with the Euro-American "cult of the Negro" in relation to the Harlem Renaissance and some midcentury responses to jazz, quickly failed.[42]

Other groups were better candidates for this role. In general, any Euro-American immigrant would do, although certain immigrant groups tended to be emphasized. It was especially the Irishman whose image was symbolically exploited for this purpose. Because of all the immigrant groups only the Irish seemed at once so close yet so different, the Irishman became the perfect symbol of Dionysian liminality. He came from a country next to the motherland, England, yet he was a papist and behaved like a drunken savage. He looked "white," but up to the end of the nineteenth century few took his "whiteness" seriously; indeed, even his humanness was questioned in repeated references to his simian nature and appearance.[43] To be liminal, one has to be different, but not the Other; different enough to commit the outrage of crossing, but close enough not to overturn the moral order by so doing. For over half a century, the Irish immigrant fitted this role perfectly. When the Irish were finally accepted as "white" in the early part of this century, what Freud called the "narcissism of small differences" was directed mainly at the Jews and Italians. By the end of the Second World War, however, both these groups were also allowed to enter the American chalk circle.[44] There followed, during the fifties, a Dionysian vacuum in American popular culture, which, to speculate extravagantly, may partly explain the inhibitions, McCarthyism, and martial style of that era.

With the rise and political and cultural success of the civil rights movement, the Afro-American male finally became accessible for this cultural role. Not only did Afro-Americans hasten the process of reclaiming control over their own ethnic cultural productions—a process still underway—but their athletes and entertainers came to play an increasingly prominent role in the nation's popular culture. The nation's protean "racial" symbology is now in full transition. The image of the Afro-American man as the ultimate outsider lingers—as demon and demigod, as we have seen—but is rapidly being replaced by another, an image more like those of the Irish and the Jew in the late nineteenth and early twentieth centuries. Afro-Americans are still different enough to cross and threaten boundaries, but no longer so different, so much the Other, that their liminality threatens disorder. It is no longer necessary for the image of the Afro-American male body to be used indirectly by Euro-American performers masking themselves in it. The Afro-American male body—as superathlete, as irresistible entertainer, as fashionable countercultural activist, as sexual outlaw, as gangster, as "cool pose" rapper, as homeboy fashion icon—is now directly accessible as the nation's Dionysian representation, the man-child of Zeus, playing himself, wearing the ultimate mask, which is the likeness of himself.

Pentheus: And so thine eyes/Saw this God plain; what guise
had he?
Dionysus: What guise/It liked him. 'Twas not I ordained his
shape.[45]

Here, the distinction between boundary-crossing and boundary-dissolution is important. What we find in American popular culture since the political and cultural enfranchisement of the Afro-American man are two kinds of Dionysian figures. One, the more common, is the liminal boundary-crosser. Examples abound: the androgynous Little Richard; the Artist Formerly Known as Prince; and what is no doubt the best example of the type, Michael Jackson.

The other kind of liminal figure is far more rare and dangerous. This is the figure that does not simply cross boundaries but blurs and even threatens to destroy them. O. J. Simpson, I contend, is the perfect example of this second Dionysian type. Others are Dennis Rodman, the basketball star; the "extraterrestrial" Sun Ra with his "Intergalactic Jet-Set Arkestra," who likes to ask his audience, "Have you heard the latest news from Neptune?"; and the kaleidoscopic George Clinton, leader of the crossover P-Funk All Stars, who already knows that "fantasy is reality in the world today" and seems set to inherit the bereaved band of maenadic Deadheads after the return of the body of Jerry Garcia to the Ganges.[46] In order both to understand the nature of Simpson's Dionysian crossings and betrayals and to better place him within the broader context of this latest transfiguration of the Afro-American male image in American culture, let us look more closely at two of the figures I have just mentioned as representing the two types of trespassers: Michael Jackson and Dennis Rodman.

The distinguished classicist Michael Jameson could easily have been speaking of Jackson when, in concluding a discussion of the asexuality of Dionysus, he pointed to the epicene style of the male pop star, for whom there "is a fascination but also a certain horror . . . who cannot be placed and straddles or crosses boundaries."[47] Jackson embodies all the dualities of the Dionysian boundary-crosser, limning the boundaries of age, sexual orientation, gender, and above all "race." A man in his late thirties, he shamelessly plays with toys and teddy bears. A rock star who grabs his crotch and titillates his audience with the cool-pose masculinity of bad, "dangerous" ghetto sexuality, he is nonetheless a timid, effeminate youth who likes to sleep with little boys. Above all else, however, Jackson has exploited the liminal symbolic space made possible by the civil rights revolution: that of crosser of the "racial" boundary. Jackson has been permitted to steal the teeny-bopping hearts of little Euro-American girls—a trespass previously totally forbidden to Afro-American rock stars, who in the early decades of the rock-and-roll revolution saw their music appropriated by "white" male bodies such as Fabian, Elvis, and the improbable Pat Boone "singin' tha blues"—mainly because of his spectacular, extremely public attempt to physically transform himself from a "black" boy into a "white" youth. It is important to understand that Jackson is not passing. Passing was a pre-civil-rights phenomenon requiring the absolute Otherness of the invention known as "the Negro." Because passing was, by definition, secret, it had little symbolic significance; one cannot participate in, or symbolically engage with, a play one cannot see.

In Jackson, the Euro-American world sees enacted before its collective eyes, in the full glare of a prurient mass media, a Dionysian transition from "black" to "white." Why, it may be asked, is it tolerated? Why has middle America, still very uneasy about what enters the heads and sleepover dens of its little curly-locks, allowed Michael Jackson in? The answer goes to the heart of the difference between the boundary-crosser and the boundary-destroyer. The truth that Jackson's spectacular crossing confirms is the immutability of the boundary between "black" and "white" and, just as important, the value of not being "black." For here we have the spectacle of a fine-looking, talented young Afro-American man spending a good part of his fortune on plastic surgeons and submitting himself to considerable physical pain, not to mention public ridicule and contempt, and all for what? To achieve something the meanest, filthiest Euro-American bum on the streets has: being "white." This kind of trespassing, then, is culturally very conservative. The very danger and difficulty of Jackson's transition serves only to emphasize the immutability and value of established "racial" boundaries.

It is quite the opposite with the performances of the multimasked, androgynous Dennis Rodman of the Chicago Bulls, possibly the most authentic epiphany of Dionysus since the fall of ancient culture. Rodman, like his ancient counterpart, is "twice-born," first to a single Afro-American woman in the ghettos of Dallas where he grew up (from whom he is now partly estranged), then, miraculously, to the conservative Euro-American farm couple who adopted him in his late teens in the heart of all-Euro-American Durant, Oklahoma (one is reminded of that other "baad" Dionysian figure, Mike Tyson, also with an adoptive Euro-American mother).[48] The couple's teenage son had brought young Dennis home to the farm like a stray dog after taking a sudden, mysterious liking to him. Rodman is also twice-born in the sense that one night, upon his contemplating suicide, it came to him that he would, instead, kill "the person on the outside," which he had come to hate, and be reborn as "the person on the inside," the liberated, "bad as I wanna be" free spirit he had repressed.[49]

A paragon of ambiguity, he absolutely delights in crossing and blurring every border he confronts. A supermale athletic star who relishes cross-dressing in sequined halter tops, tights and skirts, makeup, and cobalt-blue fingernails; a macho heterosexual who frequents gay bars, admits to being "mentally bi-sexual," rides a pink Harley-Davidson, and fantasizes about sex with other men; above all, a tall, very "black" man who returns to the ghetto secretly to keep contact with his roots, who nonetheless openly admits that he feels and acts "white" and often wants to be "white," who dyes his hair, and who keeps only Euro-American friends and lovers, Rodman exhibits a powerful instinct for the Dionysian in everything he does.

"The Dennis Rodman you see now," he writes in his 1996 autobiography, "is a prototype." Heavens! Is he right! As if he has read Euripides, he repeatedly describes himself as "straight out of nowhere." Unwittingly echoing the sports-to-reality vanishing act of O. J. Simpson, he tells us: "I came out of nowhere, like I do when I fly for a rebound. Nobody made me. I made myself."[50] In spite of the very physical nature of his "black-ness," we believe him, even as we are astonished, when he writes: "I'm color neutral. I'm black, but MY FRIENDS JOKE ABOUT ME BEING A 'WHITE' BLACK MAN" (bold and uppercase in original).[51] As with his ancient prototype, Rodman's whole life has become a performance, one drawing attention to itself—"I'm too different, too weird"—as a means of dissolving not only the color and gender lines he so flagrantly crosses but the very boundary between the performative and the real, the bizarre and the normal.

And he succeeds, wonderfully. As Amanda Cruz, a curator at the Museum of Contemporary Art in Chicago, told Mike Royko:

> I am not a sports fan, but I am completely fascinated by
> Dennis Rodman because he is a performance artist. *He is art.*
> He uses his body and his hair as a canvas, the piercings and
> the tattoos and the different hair colors. He has this anti-
> authoritarian stance on the court—the way he theatrically

tests calls by the refs, the way he poses on the covers of magazines. He is pushing the boundaries of what's acceptable.
Artists suggest alternatives to our mundane existence and
thinking in new and different ways. He is the only sports figure I know who merges theatricality with incredible athletic
ability. (Emphasis added)

Added Tom Mapp, professor of painting at the University of Chicago:
"He is art living on two wheels. He's a fascinating person. He should take
Howard Stern on a date. I think he changes some of the formal expectations we have of athletes and males. By doing that transformation, *he is
art*" (emphasis added).[52]

But it is not only the literati who have embraced Rodman. What began
as a voyeuristic, mocking interest in his idiosyncrasies—the endless calls
to radio shows speculating on his next hair color, his sexuality, his nail
polish—has now become, to the dismay of the conservative talk-show
hosts and sports commentators, a genuine love and affection for the man.
Rodman is now easily one of the most famous living stars in the popular
firmament of sports, at times soaring even beyond the popularity of his
fellow Bull Michael Jordan. For weeks, his autobiography topped the *New
York Times* best-seller list. A front-page story on him in the *Chicago
Tribune* on Sunday, May 5, 1996, began: "This is Dennis Rodman's
world, and we're just living in it."

Indeed. And he is adulated precisely because of his desecration of once-
sacred boundaries. The plain, awkward kid who was rejected by the Afro-
American women in the projects has now become one of the great lovers of
our times, adored by women—Afro-American and Euro-American—precisely because of his ethnic and sexual ambiguity. Indeed, the twenty-first
century of American popular culture can be said to have begun in 1994, on
that wonderful night in Miami when Dennis first bedded down with
Madonna, the ultimate Euro-American sex goddess. Not since Dionysus
laid Ariadne on the island of Naxos has there been a coupling quite like
that, although, to tell the truth, it was most ungentlemanly of Rodman—
but so cryptic and Dionysian—to have refused the repeated pleas of the
Euro-American goddess for a little cunnilingus. And America—all America,
Euro-America and Afro-America—loved it. For better or for worse, that's
how far we have come in American "race" relations.

LET US RETURN NOW to the O. J. phenomenon that so riveted America for the better part of a year. O. J. Simpson's most important cultural achievement was to have made himself the first man in America's tortuous ethnic history to successfully dissolve, rather than simply cross, the centuries-old "racial" barrier. Consider his extraordinary career.

Born and raised in the Potrero Hills section of San Francisco, he had a typical ghetto upbringing. He was abandoned by his father from an early age and brought up by a single mother. He had a classic disease of poverty, rickets, which almost deformed him. He did poorly in school, joined a gang, stole from the local liquor stores, and had his brushes with the law. Yet he was able to overcome his physical disabilities and blossomed as a superior athlete, which became his ticket out of the ghetto. His football career at the University of Southern California was legendary. He is still considered by many to have been the greatest football player in the history of college sports, winning every national trophy and breaking almost every record on the books.

"Visibility," one of his biographers tells us, "was the key to O. J.'s success. He parlayed an impressive college football career . . . into phenomenal pro football careers with the Buffalo Bills and later the 49ers. After that, each of his goals off the playing field fell like dominoes—the endorsements, the broadcasting contract, the movies, television."[53] Even though playing on a losing team, Simpson quickly won the hearts of sports fans and the broader public. Later, with his extremely effective Hertz ads, he became one of the nation's most visible celebrities and, more remarkably, one of its most beloved. Repeated polls placed him at the top of the list of people that Euro-Americans admired. Euro-American grade-schoolers in a 1976 poll ranked him above Neil Armstrong, John Wayne, Robert Redford, and other notable Euro-Americans as their favorite hero.[54]

Simpson's unique style of playing football already gives us a clue to his pathbreaking later cultural role. Where other great running backs fought their way through the opposing team's defenses, O. J. seemed somehow to make the barriers set up against him disappear. Miraculously, he seemed simply to run through them as if they were not there. "Now You See Him, Now You Don't," was the revealing title of a *Sports Illustrated* appreciation of his art. Or, as an opponent, "Mean" Joe Green, more tellingly put it: "He'd appear in front on you—he'd look you in the eyes, and then he was gone."[55] This sounds for all the world like the boy-god Dionysus simply walking through the prison doors of Pentheus. Right down to the famous look. Throughout O. J.'s criminal trial, Americans

stared back at that strange, evasive smile on his face—the same smile before the vanishing act that tantalized Mean Joe Green. That same "frontal
face and irritating smile" that, as Albert Hendrichs reminds us, "are visual
hallmarks of Dionysus' self-revelation in art and literature."[56]

An important aspect of O. J.'s triumphant image as a star was his famous moniker, "the Juice." It is a powerfully multivalent term. Most obviously, it came from the coincidence of his initials with that of the
popular term for orange juice. According to people who knew him when
he was young, Simpson got the nickname "O. J." because of the large
amounts of orange juice he had to drink to relieve his vitamin deficiency,
an unflattering account he denies. Whatever the origins of the tag "O. J.,"
this happy accident was the source of one of his earliest lucrative endorsements, for it was not long before the orange juice industry began
using him to sell its products. The association with orange juice, that
most wholesome of American drinks, further enhanced his reputation
among middle Americans. A male counterpart to the Euro-American girl
in the Dove soap commercial, O. J. became a household symbol of the
healthy, clean, vigorous, handsome all-American boy.

But there was clearly more to it than that. During his great days with
the Trojans at USC, the name was shortened simply to "the Juice." Fans
would scream for "the Juice" when he did not have the ball, or urge him
on with "Go, Juice, Go!" when he finally got it and went sailing through
the defensive wall. The term *juice* positively explodes with meaning. It
suggests energy and speed—Simpson's favored explanation of the nickname—as in the use of the term for electricity. *Juice* is also a popular syn-
onym for money, and indeed, another explanation of the origin of the
name is the vast fortune Simpson made from his endorsements. But juice
is also, of course, a highly sexual image, as in bodily juices, especially the
male juice that is the embodiment of potency. Distilled in this moniker,
then, was a union of opposites that was every woman's dream date, every
red-blooded male American's fantasy of who he would like to be: the
wholesome, clean-living boy, the Horatio Alger who was also the sexual
lion. It came as no surprise when, in 1976, Simpson was voted by the two
thousand female members of the worldwide organization Man Watchers,
Inc., as the most "watchable" man alive.

All of these images were used to powerful effect by the Hertz
Corporation in their highly successful commercial featuring O. J., dressed
in business attire, dashing through the airport to his waiting rental car.
This was the ad that not only made Simpson a household name but, in

its subtext, had him dissolving the "racial" barrier. For the Simpson that emerged after years of exposure was, to Euro-American audiences, no longer a "black" man but a "white" man—culturally, verbally, sartorially, and even in his body language—masquerading as an Afro-American athlete. Simpson had more than crossed over "racially." Euro-Americans ceased to see him as Afro-American. The Juice was one of them. They had drunk of his charisma. He had married into the tribe, taken one of its golden princesses, and they loved him for it, swallowed every bit of gossip about the golden couple served up by the tabloids. And, miraculously, he had done it, unlike the pathetic Michael Jackson, without the aid of a surgeon's knife. How? It is impossible to say, and anyway, who cared? All the Euro-American world knew, all it needed to know, was that the Afro-American frog from the Potrero Hills ghetto with the rickety bandy-legs and suspect Afro had become the handsome prince married to the willowy blond beauty. Simpson himself repeatedly commented on this "racial" transformation. Occasionally he would describe himself as being the perfect "racial" crossover baby. But more frequently he was prone to describe what had happened with a far more accurate term: he would say that he had become "colorless."

Exactly. *Colorless.* The boundaries had not simply been crossed, their permanence pronounced by the danger of the crossing. The "racial" boundary had been dissolved, as totally and miraculously as had the boundary of the mystified defensive wall in O. J.'s old football days.

This, then, was the great American success story that came crashing down when the legend was arrested and charged with the double murder of his former wife and her friend. Even by the standards of Los Angeles, the murder was extraordinary in its brutality. Ronald Goldman's throat and lungs had been slashed. Nicole Brown Simpson had apparently been first knocked senseless; then her head had been pulled back by her silken blond hair and her bare "white" neck slashed from ear to ear, so deeply that it had severed her spinal cord. This was a murder worthy of Dionysus in his most savage epiphany. Indeed, one of the grand jurors who examined the police photographs of the crime described the murder as "something out of antiquity."[57]

The incredible week after the murder has been correctly described by the staff of the *Los Angeles Times* as a week of "startling images." To the historical sociologist of culture, it was perhaps the modern world's most amazing week of images of reversal. Not since the decline of the indigenous Native American cultures of the Northwest Coast, with their magnificent annual festivals of reversals, had the continent witnessed such a sustained series of symbolic reversals. Here is how the bewildered staff of the *Los Angeles Times* summarized it:

> O. J. Simpson handcuffed and hauled to police headquarters. The running back so astoundingly agile, shackled? O. J. Simpson, sedated, mourning at his ex-wife's funeral. The actor so winningly glib, silent? Crime-scene tape blocking O. J. Simpson's Brentwood home. The estate, so symbolic of triumph, bloodied? It all seemed so impossible. And then came an event so unthinkable that the other images faded in comparison. Then came, "The Chase."[58]

In the early decades of this century, the great media phenomenon Rudolph Valentino had remarked during his tragic final days that the American media was a great monster that made idols for the sheer pleasure of destroying and consuming them. But the fade-out of Valentino was trivial compared to what the audience of 95 million viewers witnessed the evening of June 17, 1994.

The slow-speed chase by the Los Angeles police of Simpson's white Bronco, sadly evocative of his heroic exploits as the crafty horse of his Trojan team, the superstar holding a revolver to his own head, threatening suicide, his childhood friend Al Cowlings trying to talk him out of it; these sights will almost certainly go down in popular memory as among the most unforgettable images of fin de siècle America. Here, in prime time, and slow motion, was a man made by the media disintegrating before the entire nation on the medium that had made him. The timing could not have been more perfect. Simpson's vehicle had been identified just before 6:30 P.M., giving the TV reporters just enough time to cover the chase for the evening news. The couple who spotted Simpson had been struck by the famous look, as powerfully as Mean Joe Green had been on the defensive football line. Only now it was a look of death. "He stared us down, like he was death," shuddered the young man who had called the police. Then, the *Los Angeles Times* reported, "hundreds of onlookers jammed onto overpasses and stopped on the freeway, cheering and waving at the passing Bronco. For nearly two hours, the chase utterly dominated. It disrupted the telecast of a championship basketball game. (How appropriate!) It stopped conversations in mid-sentence. It froze shoppers in front of the nearest T.V."[59]

The "trial of the century" was, in essence, the dramatic public exposure and recognition of what traditional America was loath to admit: that many of its most treasured boundaries and certitudes had been successfully assaulted. In Marcia Clark, millions of transfixed viewers saw daily a paragon of modern womanhood—resolute yet feminine, highly professional yet impassioned, divorced yet independent—meticulously practicing her craft and holding her own against a phalanx of high-priced male lawyers. And she did it dressed not in the symbolic badges of the traditional female boundary-crosser—the dowdy attire and surrogate blue-stockings—but in sexy short skirts and hairstyles that dramatically changed through the course of the trial from mulatto curls to Caucasian dead-straight. In Christopher Darden, they saw a tall, imposing Afro-American man with a shorn head and permanent stubble—the quintessential "Euro-American" image of a "bad nigger" during the era of the color line—fiercely prosecuting a crossover Afro-American hero for the murder of his Euro-American wife, and breaking into tears at the injustice of O. J.'s acquittal. In Judge Lance Ito, they saw a Japanese-American—whose ancestors less than a generation earlier had been barred as the "yellow peril" threatening the nation's borders and herded into concentration camps—married to a tall, blond police captain, occupying the classic Euro-American male authority role. It was a reversal of fortune and images that so traumatized the reactionary Senator Alphonse D'Amato that he made a racist spectacle of himself in his vain attempt to mock it. In Johnnie Cochran—"Mr. Johnnie" to the Latina witness—and his inter-"ethnic" "dream team," they witnessed a cool, commanding Afro-American man at the height of his powers, wholly at ease with his Rolls Royce and upper-class status.

It is significant that, for weeks after Simpson's arrest, his Euro-American fans refused to believe that he had committed the crime. Indeed, all those who hung around the entry to his estate demonstrating their support were young Euro-American men. There was not a single Afro-American in sight. Few events could have been more symbolic of how far American "race" relations had come than the sight of these loyal Euro-American supporters. For this was the same America in which, less than fifty years earlier, Afro-American men were being lynched and burned alive at the mere suspicion of having violated or attempted to violate Euro-American women. These very same young men were typical of the vigilantes, "patrollers," and protectors of Euro-American women's honor who had made up the lynch mob. And here they were, day in and day out, pleading the innocence of their beloved "Juice."

We can now understand the reaction of Euro-Americans to the dramatic shift in defense strategy when Simpson and his lawyers decided to "play the race card." The trial of the century had started off as a "raceless" event appropriate for a defendant who had succeeded in being colorless. Simpson and his lawyers had repeatedly promised not to drag "race" into the trial. The crossover hero seemed to be remaining true to form. His Euro-American fans remained loyal. Around the dining tables and cocktail bars of Euro-America the trial began as a largely Euro-American gender thing, a case for the advocates of the victims of domestic violence. Afro-American folks could care less, for they had long accepted O. J. as he had presented himself: as an Afro-American man who had crossed over to "whiteness," who had long ago lost touch with his roots.

The sudden turn to "race," then, was experienced as a terrible symbolic and "racial" betrayal, especially by the millions of young Euro-American men still bellowing their belief in Simpson's innocence over beer during Monday night football. The adopted son had disadopted himself. What Euro-America had come to believe in, from those ubiquitous Hertz ads and the endless tabloid portraits of the beautiful couple, was a "black" man who had turned "white." Now he unmasked himself as a "black" man who had all along been only masquerading as one of them. This was too much. Euro-America could perhaps accept a blurring of the "racial" boundaries, but it was simply not ready for so blatant a manipulation of them. This was like a perverse ballplayer shifting the boundaries of the field to make sure his ball stayed in. Better no boundaries than that. Then, when the misguided Afro-American community answered Simpson's Dionysian call by collectively springing to his defense like an army of bemused maenads, the "racial" die was cast. The "racial" clock had suddenly been turned back. Old grievances were unburied, old scores were once more up for settlement, old sores unscabbed.

If Simpson dissolved boundaries, it is also true that he recreated them. That he should have done so when it suited him, that he should have betrayed his Euro-American fans as he had earlier abandoned his Afro-American heritage and fans and then returned to his fellow Afro-Americans when he needed them, were all highly consistent with the Dionysian tendencies in him. Remember Agave: disloyalty is the hallmark of this god of transitions.

LAYERS OF TRUTH IN THE CULTURAL DRAMA

IN THIS ESSAY I HAVE FOCUSED on the various images of Afro-American men in the broader national culture. I have explored the symbolic uses and meanings, for Euro-Americans, of the Afro-American male body and Afro-American cultural productions, but one final question remains. What consequences did this use and misuse of their images and creations have for Afro-Americans themselves? It is tempting to interpret America's cultural history as a "war of images," a contest between "hegemonic" and exploitative Euro-Americans and protesting Afro-Americans, who struggled mightily both to undo the violations done by Euro-American appropriation and caricature and to gain control over their own images and culture. This is how Jannette Dates and William Barlow, editors of a fine book on Afro-Americans in the mass media, and their collaborators see it: "The dominant trend in African American portraiture has been created and nurtured by succeeding generations of white image makers, beginning as far back as the colonial era. Its opposite has been created and maintained by Afro-American image makers in response to the omissions and distortions of the former. This war of images casts light on the historical trajectory of the race issue in American society from both sides of the controversy. Thus, the definition and control of Afro-American images in the mass media have been contested from the outset along racial lines, and with white cultural domination provoking African American cultural resistance."[60]

There is a great deal of truth in this observation, as in the other very insightful contributions to Dates and Barlow's important volume. But there are far more layers of truth to the American cultural "drama acted out upon the body of a Negro giant." And the elegant sociological simplicities of the Italian Marxist theorist Antonio Gramsci, upon whom these authors rely, are hopelessly inappropriate for the task of understanding anything so complex and un-European as the violent and contradictory, yet explosively generative, synthesis of Europe, Africa, and the genocidal frontier that became the capitalist civilization of America.

For one thing, as we have already seen, there was a tar-baby contamination for Euro-Americans in their wholesale cultural theft, misrepresentations, and disfiguring caricatures. They became trapped by the images they appropriated and denigrated. These images were everywhere, especially in salt-and-pepper shakers and cookie jars depicting "Aunt Jemima" and "Uncle Mose," mechanical cast-iron "jolly niggers," the Gold Dust Twins on washing-powder boxes, Cream of Wheat's "Giddap Uncle," ceramic hot-pot holders with caricatures of Afro-American children, postcards of "little pickaninnies," sheet-music covers with "little laughing redheads" and "phrenologist coons," and postcards from the many "Coon Chicken Inns" around the country, to list only a few of the Negro collectibles that, as Kenneth W. Goings has shown, were common household wares.[61] Not only were these images undoubtedly racist, but as Goings points out, by using them "in an everyday, familiar manner . . . the user consciously and unconsciously accepted the stereotypes they presented."[62] But it could not have stopped there. To the wisdom of the old German proverb "we are what we eat" may be added that of the sociology of everyday life: our identities are fashioned by the ordinary implements that are part and parcel of our daily lives, which, by their very familiarity, constitute our most abiding conceptions of self and place. Indeed, both symbolic functions are illustrated by these collectibles, for it should not go unnoticed that a disproportionate number of them—and the only ones to survive today—are associated with eating: Uncle Ben's rice, Aunt Jemima's pancakes, McCoy cookie jars modeled after Hattie McDaniel, watermelon "pickaninnies."

Significantly, the one explicitly brutal figure pictured in Goings's book about these objects is a celluloid letter opener and pencil in the shape of an alligator holding the head of an Afro-American male in its mouth. It is the most horribly accurate distillation of American "racial" symbology I have ever seen. Note, first, that this is a pencil, the instrument of writing and intellection, as well as a letter opener, letters being the most potent symbol of office and of engagement with the broader public life of the state. Second, it is an Afro-American male that is being consumed. Third, it is his head, the seat of his intellect and will, that is being devoured. And finally, while this image, like those of the other collectibles, associates the Negro with a familiar object and with eating, now it is explicitly not a Euro-American body that is eating the Negro and thus symbolically becoming part Negro, as is true with Aunt Jemima's pancakes or the docile Uncle Ben's rice. Instead, the eater is a loathed reptile. In the familiar, homey, self-nourishing association between the friendly, essential, everyday tool and the food that Euro-American bodies are made from, there is no place for the severed head of the Afro-American man.

But this image is the exception that proves the more ambiguous rule. These black figurines, utensils, and representations were at once agents of

Euro-American supremacy and icons of Euro-American identity; at once articles of "racial" alienation and of incorporation, of explicit hate and implicit desire. And if it is true that they horribly dehumanized, it is equally true that they subversively humanized, in much the same way that the wearing of black masks by Euro-American minstrels covertly expressed a deep envy of and desire for the Afro-American male body. Ironically, Goings, a proud and very conscious Afro-American scholar, gives the game away with a confession at the end of the preface to his book. He tells us that after collecting and studying these household objects for seven years, he has been seduced by them. "When I see Aunt Jemima and Uncle Mose resting on my shelves," he writes, "I think of them as people. I try to imagine what their lives were like, and who they would be if they were alive today. In my imagination, I see Aunt Jemima not as a cook but as a fighter for freedom in the mold of Angela Davis or Shirley Chisholm. Uncle Mose I imagine not as a faithful butler but as an activist and orator in the mold of Malcolm X, or of Medgar Wiley Evers."[63]

Hmmm. Whatever. It is a fact that middle-class Afro-Americans have been greatly taken with these collectibles for reasons astutely discussed by Gerald Early.[64] The point *I* wish to make, however, is that if a modern Afro-American scholar could in seven years come to "personify the collectibles" of overt Afro-American debasement, how much more likely is it that the "tens of thousands of such items" that swamped the American everyday consciousness from the 1880s to the late 1950s subverted their manifest racist function in American "racial" symbology, at the very least imprinting upon the consciousness of the dominant Euro-American majority a contradictory, obsessive engagement with the image and reality of "blackness"?

The tar-baby lore, if this is not already as obvious as pitch, is nothing other than the folk and cultural version of Hegel's dialectics of domination, in which the master becomes totally dependent for his own honor, being, and support on the slave he dishonors and pretends to support.[65] The master, living in the relative languor of his great house by means of his parasitism on the slave, shamelessly camouflages that parasitism by calling the slave a parasite, hides his inhumanity behind the image of the slave and his descendants as inhuman brutes, wraps himself with the rhetoric of honor and disguises the dishonor of his dastardly, slaveholding dependence by outwardly dishonoring, at every turn, the source of everything he is and owns and by libeling him in his minstrelsy.

It was simply not possible to get away with such an outrageous ploy. And they didn't. American cultural history, to use another revealing folk saying, is one long, heated case of the once-white pot calling the kettle black. As we have seen, it was never possible to completely smear and distort beyond recognition the images caricatured, whether because of the persistence of a fundamental element of Afro-Americanness, encoded within even the most virulent caricature; because of the concurrent presence of real, live Afro-American self-representations; or because of the intrusions on the dishonoring Euro-American stage of real live Afro-Americans such as the incredible cultural warrior William Henry Lane, with his mid-nineteenth-century imitations of imitations of Afro-American male bodily expressions.

The fact that Lane went on to demonstrate the real thing to the startled Charles Dickens and his coaudience that night points to the second and third reasons why simple Gramscian notions of cultural hegemony make no sense in any attempt to understand America. The second is that cultural productions are nonproprietary. I have followed Eric Lott in speaking of cultural robbery and theft, but I am sure he would be the first to agree with me that this is to use language more in its loosely emotive way. A people's image and creations can be appropriated, distorted, and used against them, but not monopolized, except in that admittedly nontrivial number of cases where folk, and sometimes written songs, are copyrighted by unscrupulous producers and collectors. Afro-Americans have always carried on with their own cultural creations.

What is more, and this is the third point, they never sought to isolate their productions from the rest of the nation. Indeed, they were proud to have their art, and their images, inserted into the national mainstream as long as these were authentically executed, preferably by Afro-Americans but, if necessary, by respectful Euro-Americans. Hearing the Mormon Tabernacle Choir delivering its heartfelt version of an Afro-American spiritual may elicit a wry smile from the typical Afro-American, but only the most boorish of Afrocentric chauvinist would consider this anything but another laudable instance of the ingrained Afro-Americanness of American civilization. And there is nothing to be even wry about in the art of the many Euro-American jazzmen of genius who have contributed to the civilization's most distinctive creation.

Up until the post–Second World War era, ordinary Afro-Americans reacted in several self-protective ways toward the centrality of their images and the use and misuse of their cultural productions in the broader society. Beyond vigorously contesting the misrepresentations and pursuing their own cultural agenda, they took care to insulate themselves from one important aspect of Afro-American art that few liberal and Afro-American intellectuals care to talk about. This is the fact that, with the exception of religious and literary creations, a major part of Afro-American cultural productions came out of the most troubled sections of their own communities, especially after the end of the nineteenth century.

There were few saints among the creators of the blues and its many cultural branches, from rhythm-and-blues to rap. The fact that the Afro-American church was one of its important musical sources only made the blues more threatening, as Lawrence Levine has pointed out: "Blues was threatening because its spokesmen and its ritual too frequently provided the expressive communal channels of relief that had been largely the province of religion in the past. . . . Like the spirituals of the nineteenth century the blues was a cry for release, an ode to movement and mobility, a blend of despair and hope."[66] Contrary to legend, jazz originated only partly in the "polite Creole music" of Downtown New Orleans, and even there its vital source was more the "rougher, blues-colored music of Uptown."[67] Elsewhere, in places like Chicago, Kansas City, and New York, jazz grew, socially, out of the speakeasies, riverboats, and other low-life entertainment joints.[68] Likewise, Afro-American dance, comedy, and athleticism are all in large part the creations of the group's most marginal, nonconforming, and unsettled individuals.[69] According to Charles Keil, hustling, entertaining, and storefront preaching constituted a "special domain to Negro culture wherein black men have proved and preserved their humanity. This domain or sphere of interest may be broadly defined as entertainment from the white or public point of view and as ritual, drama, or dialectical catharsis from the Negro or theoretical standpoint."[70]

It was precisely this trespassing between the sacred and the profane that made Afro-American entertainment so dangerous and Dionysian. And as Mary Douglas and other symbolic anthropologists have shown, every known human culture, while finding such crossings necessary, tends to symbolically protect the "normal" by ritually or socially isolating the trespassers, or at the very least symbolically bracketing them by magical beliefs and rituals.[71] Afro-American culture is no exception. Ordinary Afro-Americans all knew this, and while they were prepared to sponsor and enjoy the creations of this class of men and women in their midst, they also took great care not only to keep their distance morally and culturally from them, but to keep them in check. Up until the boom in "race records" of the 1920s, most middle-class Afro-Americans shunned the blues and the earlier, more authentic forms of jazz.[72] Even after that, most respectable and God-fearing Afro-Americans—the great majority—remained aloof. Nat Hentoff recalls how, years ago, upon visiting a predominantly Afro-American elementary school in Columbus, Ohio, where kids actually learned, he was proudly shown around the building by the Afro-American principal. On the walls hung portraits of many of the prominent leaders of Afro-American political and educational life, but there was not a single one of any of the great Afro-American musicians. When asked why, the "principal pursed her lips and looked at [Hentoff] with searing scorn: 'We do not put pictures of *entertainers* on our walls!'"[73] [emphasis in original]

All this was to change with the civil rights movement and the accompanying revolution in the representation of Afro-American athleticism and cultural productions. First, there was an explosive growth both of popular culture and of the centrality of Afro-American creations in that culture, whether in its mainstream or countercultural forms. Rock-and-roll in all its forms—including the so-called British invasion music—is all a mere variant of Afro-American swing and blues.[74] Spectator sports, the other leg of modern popular culture in America, has also become not only a major industry but the preeminent form of entertainment for most American men and a good number of women.[75]

Second, accompanying all this has been the rise of the Afro-American athletic and entertainment star. Not only are Afro-American images now represented by Afro-Americans,[76] but Afro-American men, as we have seen, are disproportionately present in major league sports and dominate several of them. Thus, by 1985, 80 percent of National Basketball Association players were Afro-American, as were 52 percent of National Football League players and 22 percent of major league baseball players.[77]

While this has been happening, the society has become less and less racist and has offered more and more openings to Afro-Americans. The result, which I examined in *The Ordeal of Integration*, has been the paradoxical economic integration and growth of the middle and stable working classes of Afro-Americans along with the growing segregation and isolation of the urban poor, who still make up between a quarter and 30 percent of the Afro-American population, as well as the small but nihilistic underclass.

Integration, urbanization, and ghettoization have also meant something else. The lower and underclasses still continue to generate the great majority of Afro-American entertainers and athletes, who retain their oppositional and self-destructive impulses. Only, now the traditional restraints of Afro-American communities upon the destructive tendencies of this creative class have nearly all evaporated. As we saw in the first essay, the influence of the church is waning rapidly among men in general, and young men in particular. And the end of segregation has meant the separation of the traditional moral and social leadership from the creative but Dionysian lowlife.[78]

Worse, it is precisely the cultural creations and athletic prowess of the Afro-American lumpen proletariat that most attract the broader mainstream culture in need of a Dionysian counterweight to the Apollonian demands of postindustrial schooling and workplace. Some two decades ago, Daniel Bell identified a double cultural contradiction in capitalism, wherein the work ethic that undergirded the system was subverted by the after-work behavior and attitudes of the capitalist classes. The rugged individualism and Apollonian discipline in the economic domain had become coupled with a modern culture that no longer celebrated disciplined purpose and moral unity of character, an adversarial culture that yearned for the "unrestrained self" of the liberated personality, that "emphasize[d] anti-cognitive and anti-intellectual modes which look[ed] longingly toward a return to instinctual sources of expression."[79] Bell saw the counterculture of the sixties as simply the latest version of the adversarial tradition of modernist culture. He was disdainful of its pretensions to originality, claiming that its ideas were merely a caricature of the codes "trampled" sixty years earlier by the Young Intellectuals. Perhaps. But Bell's emphasis on continuities in modernism prevented him from seeing what was radically new about developments in the sixties. This is the fact that postindustrial society had finally solved the problem of its contradictions at the very moment he was writing, and it had done so by using the oldest technique of capitalism—the division of labor—applied to the oldest symbolic resource in American culture—Afro-American male images and creations.

What has emerged is nothing other than a cultural division of labor[80] in which those images and creations have now become the specialized, Dionysian counterweight to the Apollonian discipline of the downsized, disciplined workplace. As I indicated earlier, one of the major achievements of the civil rights movement was to open to Afro-Americans the unfilled symbolic space of the Dionysian impulses of other Americans.

My argument is that while this has been wonderfully functional for Euro-Americans and the broader mainstream culture, it has been nothing short of a disaster for Afro-Americans. What so troubled Bell in the sixties and seventies—"that a corporation finds its people straight by day and swingers by night," and a society finds its children in rebellion during adolescence and early adulthood—no longer poses a threat to the corporation, the bourgeoisie, or their sustaining culture, for the simple reason that their members swing or drop out, when the mood takes them, to a different cultural drummer. In all the great sports stadiums of the nation, major corporations own exclusive box seats so that their most prized members can vent their deepest male instinctual urges by identifying with Afro-American gladiators. In boxing, as Gerald Early has so acutely argued, the "prizefighter enacts a drama of poor taste . . . that is in truth nothing more than an expression of resentment or a pantomime of rebellion totally devoid of any political content except ritualized male anger turned into a voyeuristic fetish."[81] What is true of boxing is equally true of other sports. And it is even more true of popular entertainment.

Contrary to Bell's predictions, the most fundamentalist wing of Protestantism is now experiencing yet another great revival, and every poll on the subject confirms that Americans of all faiths pray and go to church more often than the citizens of any other industrial nation. What is more, the Republican Party, corporate America's political arm, is now firmly in the grip of the Christian Coalition. At the same time, it is no longer ironical, but instead a fundamental principle of modern American culture, that hip-hop culture and its violent and orgiastic music, "gangsta rap," the most iconoclastic and self-consciously "black" of modern urban ghetto creations, should now find their largest audience among suburban Euro-American youth. Martha Bayles expresses understandable revulsion at "the spectacle of young black men who are not brutal criminals posing as such, in order to sell thrills to whites," and she cites a typical Capitol Records press release promising "mean-tempered diatribes on violent 'gangsta' lifestyles [that] challenge middle-class norms by rubbing their noses in the reality of contemporary urban jungle—a black place most suburbanites don't dare tread."[82] In rap, she rightly adds, Afro-American music has been reduced "to a minstrel version of grindcore."

But an even greater tragedy has befallen Afro-American music: it is the fact that while the mass of Afro-American music lovers have embraced the misogynistic, self-loathing noise of "gangsta" rap—now sponsored mainly by Euro-American companies—they have largely abandoned the authentic music of the blues and jazz.

I came face to face with the cultural division of labor in postindustrial America when I lived in Chicago during the early nineties. My wife and I chose to live in Lakeview, on the north shore of the great city, because of its diverse population and its famous blues and jazz clubs. Ardent lovers of the music, we planned to incorporate frequent visits to these clubs as a regular part of our lives. But it was not long before our visits ended. My wife and I are committed integrationists, but try as we might, we simply could not take the experience, night after night, of being the only people of color not on the stage, surrounded by an ecstatic audience letting it all hang out before returning to their gated havens in the segregated suburbs.

The concurrence of, on the one hand, the embrace of hip-hop and traditional Afro-American music by the various generations of Euro-Americans and, on the other, the reawakening of the mainstream culture's traditional Protestant religion is no contradiction. To the contrary, it is postindustrial America's final resolution of its "double contradiction." What Nietzsche wished for early industrial Germany has been perfectly realized in postindustrial America. Apollo reigns supreme in the domains of work and church and in the private schools where children still submit to the discipline of learning. Dionysus is given the free rein of the inner cities; the public enemy lurks undisturbed in what Ellison once vividly called "the seething vortex of those tensions generated by the most highly industrialized of Western nations," where "Negro music and dances are frenziedly erotic; Negro religious ceremonies violently ecstatic; Negro speech strongly rhythmical and weighted with image and gesture."[83] Here, the Dionysian impulse remains safely confined behind ghetto walls until the instinctual need for release from the Apollonian pressures of the workplace and the adolescent treadmill of college preparation calls for its tethered, darkened presence.

America's embrace of the outlaw culture of hip-hop is really only the culmination of what has long been in the making. Martha Bayles is surely correct in her observation that jazz, at its best, is "an extraordinary art, able to strike a new and wonderful balance between the Dionysian and the Apollonian. What other music tempers such primal rhythmic energy with such precisely controlled counterpoint?"[84] However, not all jazz achieves this sublime balance, and most blues candidly strives for the Dionysian. For this reason, it has been easy for Euro-Americans, from very early on in the history of the music, to adapt it to their Dionysian longings. This was already the case in the twenties—when jazz had yet to find the balance Bayles applauds—with the vogue of jazz during the Harlem Renaissance. The psychologist Norman Margolis was basically correct when he wrote during the mid-fifties: "As jazz progressed out of the specific areas of its birth, it ran into the American culture which places a high value on properness, control and restraint. In other words the general Puritan, Anglo-Saxon tradition, by this time solid in this country, dictated a rigid cultural conscience which required the repression of the objectionable impulses with which jazz had become associated and symbolized."[85] In line with this tradition, Norman Mailer's much cited and maligned screed on "the white Negro"[86] was merely one in a number of such Dionysian readings of jazz and the jazz aesthetic. In 1958, Whitney Balliett, the jazz critic for the *New Yorker,* was already complaining about a long line of Euro-American novelists and short-story writers, stretching back two decades, refashioning jazz in their own distorting image: "Jazz is notably unsentimental," he wrote, "as are, in main, the people who play it. Yet countless drooping, bleary novels and stories have appeared in which jazz musicians, postured in various awkward attitudes, like bad statuary, produce a homely, cathartic, semi-divine music. At the same time, jazz seems to provide a safety valve for these writers, who invariably let loose a thick, sticky spray of metaphor and simile that forms a bad counterpoint to the subject matter."[87]

What Balliett does not tell us is that there were more than a few jazz and blues musicians willing to cater to this counterpoint. And not all of it was bad. Consider, for example, Dinah Washington's 1954 "New Blowtop Blues," which John Corbett accurately describes as "a virtual topography of madness which connects it with both love and getting high":[88]

> I've got bad news baby/and you're the first to know.
> Well, I discovered this morning/that my wig is about to blow.
> I been rockin' on my feet/and I been talkin' all out of my head.
> And when I get through talkin'/I can't remember a thing I've said.
> Now I used to be a sharpie/all dressed in the latest styles
> But now I'm walkin' down Broadway/wearin' nothing but a smile.
> I see all kind of little men/although they're never there
> I tried to push a subway train/and poured whiskey in my hair.[89]

However thematically adapted to the Dionysian demands of an emerging postindustrial corporate culture, this is still the blues, and to hear Washington sing it is to know that it has been in no way culturally appropriated. Indeed, it is important to get clear that cultural appropriation is now no longer an issue. The dominant mainstream culture neither requires nor particularly desires to appropriate Afro-American culture from Afro-Americans. Its sociological objective is to integrate performer and performance into the mainstream as domesticated and innoculating cultural outlaws. And it has succeeded beyond measure. What has emerged is a new, lucrative industry of managed frenzy in which the preferred cultural workers are talented lower- and underclass Afro-Americans, in much the same way that Asians are the preferred workers in Silicon Valley—witness the rapid flameout of the faux rapper Rob Van Winkle, alias Vanilla Ice. But this new industry remains firmly under the control of the Euro-American corporate establishment—witness the eventual sellout of Motown, one of the most successful corporate enterprises in the history of Afro-America, to Boston Ventures in 1988 and its resale to Polygram in 1993.

With hip-hop, then, the blackface mask is now worn mainly by Afro-American performers who cater to the needs of mainstream youth when the time comes for them to go through their Dionysian rite of passage between the discipline of their suburban childhood and the discipline of the corporate life awaiting them. As "wiggers"—white "niggers"—these youths wear the black mask of the god, averting their eyes "from the love of the wise,"[90] living dangerously in the limbic sensuality of the ghetto's outlaw culture, savoring through rap, cocaine—in powdered form, for which, if caught, they are merely slapped on the wrist, in contrast with the crack form favored by Afro-American youth, for which they are locked away with hardened, raping criminals for the best part of their lives—and homeboy minstrel wear its antirational, antinomian, misogynistic, misanthropic, and matricidal moods. And through the very impurity of their wigger passage, they mentally and sociologically inoculate themselves against the wiles of Dionysus.

No great culture in the history of the world—not even Aeschylus's Athens, certainly not the one Euripides fled—has come anywhere close to so perfect a balance of its opposing primal impulses. But if America has ingeniously solved its cultural contradictions, it has done so, once again, at the tragic expense of Afro-Americans. Becoming the national culture's Dionysian counterweight has been detrimental to Afro-Americans in so many ways that a large volume would be needed to delineate them. I conclude by mentioning two of the most egregious.

First, there is the damage that is being done to the more authentic cultural creations of Afro-Americans. Tricia Rose is quite right in her view that "hip hop merely displays in phantasmagorical form the cultural logic of late capitalism," especially in the way it "replicates and reimagines the experiences of urban life and symbolically appropriates urban space through sampling, attitude, dance, style, and sound effects," but she falls into empty postmodernist rhetoric with talk about its "attempts to nego-tiate new economic and technological conditions as well as new patterns of race, class, and gender oppression in urban America."[91] I have no de-sire to join in the debate as to whether rap is musical junk or not.[92] What is certain is that this noise now overwhelms all other forms of music, both in production and audience, among Afro-Americans. And there is clear evidence that it has had distorting and regressive effects on all the other forms, including even jazz, the crown jewel of Afro-American creativity, as the final album of Miles Davis, *Doo-Bop,* produced in collaboration with rapper Eazy Mo Bee, so sadly demonstrates.[93]

Second, and even more disastrous, has been the permeation of the en-tire youth culture of Afro-America by the Dionysian ethos of its athletic and entertainment heroes. While I am not always in agreement with John Hoberman—especially his dated comments on cricket and colonial soci-ety—he is right on target in his views on the destructive impact on Afro-Americans of the fusion of the different images of the Afro-American male: "While it is assumed that sport has made important contribution to racial integration, this has been counterbalanced by the merger of the ath-lete, the gangster rapper, and the criminal into a single black male persona that the sports industry, the music industry, and the advertising industry have made into the predominant image of black masculinity in the United States and around the world."[94]

Athletes and entertainers are now the dominant exemplars of Afro-American achievement and the role models that set the tone, style, ideals, and moral standards of most Afro-American youth and young men. Alas, their way of life reflects the worst aspects of underclass Afro-American street culture, especially in relation to women. The behavior of Mike Tyson, the heavyweight boxer sent to prison for rape, and of Riddick Bowe, who was arrested in 1998 for wife abuse and kidnapping, is not un-typical. In May 1998, *Sports Illustrated* finally did a cover story on a sub-ject that everyone involved with sports knew about but had simply turned a blind eye to: that not only the fathering of children out of wedlock but paternal irresponsibility of the worst kind is epidemic among them. Patrick Ewing, Scottie Pippen, and Hakeem Olajuwon are among the many heroes who have faced paternity suits. Larry Johnson of the Knicks has five children by four women, two others by his wife; Shawn Kemp of the Cavaliers, who is unmarried, has seven children. Indeed, one top agent told *Sports Illustrated* that he spends more time on paternity suits than he does negotiating contracts.[95]

Another effect of this now pervasive influence is the near-complete rejection of intellectual achievement as a model to be strived for. Indeed, there is now such chronic anti-intellectualism among Afro-American youth that those few who, by some sociological miracle, become engaged with their studies and do well at school must find ways to camouflage their interests, either through clowning or through overcompensatory involvement in sports. Signithia Fordham and John Ogbu's widely cited study from the mid-eighties, which found that Afro-American students who did well academically were subjected to the taunt of "acting white,"[96] has been challenged by Philip Cook and Jens Ludwig, who argue that Euro-American students who excel are also taunted as "nerds" and "geeks." Moreover, Cook and Ludwig claim, academically successful Afro-American students gain more than they lose socially.[97] However, unpublished work I conducted with my graduate students on sports and academic culture in a large, ethnically mixed high school strongly supports the contention that involvement with sports is very negatively associated with academic performance, and others have replicated the "acting white" hypothesis.[98]

As if all this were not bad enough, most Afro-American intellectuals now celebrate the fusion of Afro-American male images, not only downplaying or excusing its worst excesses, but actually applauding its physicality, its anti-intellectualism, and the vitality of its "technological orality," or in other words, its illiteracy.[99] Only occasionally do we find a distinguished Afro-American intellectual with the courage and good sense to step back and express amazement at the self-destructive cultural role that Afro-Americans have burdened themselves with in postindustrial America. The late, great Ralph Ellison saw the danger with his prophetic eye: "We see that the Negro stereotype is really an image of the unorganized, irrational forces of American life, forces through which, by projecting them in forms or images of an easily dominated minority, the white individual seeks to be at home in the vast unknown world of America."[100] More recently, Gerald Early reflected insightfully at the end of his robust little study on Afro-American popular music: "Perhaps we black folk sometimes do not like the entrapment of sensuality we are forced to wear as a mask for the white imagination."[101]

But Early is one of the few exceptions among living Afro-American intellectuals to express ambivalence about the Dionysian entrapment of the group's youth and cultural heroes. And he, like Ellison, places the blame too squarely on one source. It is, to be sure, an entrapment that is partly the making of the nation's liberal Euro-American establishment, who, on the one hand, have come to expect too little from the left side of the Afro-American brain and, on the other hand, to expect and demand too much from its right side and its body. For it is they and their children who have mainly incited and sponsored the hip-hop culture and sports fixation for their own aesthetic, emotional, and economic needs, and for the greater integration and counterbalancing of the broader national culture.

However, the entrapment is also partly the making of America's conservative leadership, who dishonorably disclaim all responsibility for the unhealed injuries of the nation's shameful racist past during which Afro-Americans were forced into the miracle of making cultural bread out of stone, then saw their creations appropriated, cannibalized, caricatured, and used to enrich others. And it is this same leadership who, today, while preaching homilies on family values, eviscerate funds for infant and child care; who, while bemoaning the decline of national educational standards, undercut all serious attempts at establishing meaningful national curricula; and who, with their cynical and draconian law-and-order politics, have done much to promote the outlaw culture of hip-hop by placing one in three of all Afro-American male youths under the nation's prison and security system that simply makes criminals out of them.

But the entrapment is, above all else, the making of Afro-Americans themselves, a large proportion of whose men contemptibly *choose* to abandon their children to the welfare of the state, the authority of the streets, and the seductions of gang life and drugs; whose women *choose* to have more children than their emotional, economic, or social resources allow; and whose youth *choose* to reject literacy in favor of orality and *choose* to drop out of the educational system before achieving minimum levels of skills for survival in an advanced postindustrial society. And, too, it is the making of those overpaid, semiliterate, promiscuous culture heroes of Afro-America and of the nation's Euro-American youth—who condemn intellect, debase women, demonstrate by their fortunes and illiteracy the absurdity of ordinary work and pay, celebrate the physical and tasteless, and hypnotize the nation's Afro-American youth into the fantastic, all-or-nothing hope of one day slam-dunking the basketball net, a hope that has replaced Uncle Tom's cabin in the sky.

No, the warrior you see there dressed in drag is not King Pentheus, mesmerized by Dionysus into his final, cross-dressed walk to the orgiastic fields where his mother will tear his head from his body, imagining him to be a lion. For all we know it's Dennis Rodman, hero of Chicago, his panty-hosed legs astride his pink motorbike. Or is it O. J., the Trojan

champion wielding his ax, like "something out of antiquity," before playing his race card? Or perhaps it is the multimillionaire Ice-T, rapping in a
frenzy about dismembering his mother and setting her remains on fire? It
doesn't matter. Really. Afro-Americans at this dawning of the second millennium are now fully integrated into America's postindustrial *culture*,
even if they are still to be incorporated into its society and the higher
reaches of its economy. But the price they pay with their soaring, bacchanalian heroes, and with the hard bodies of their ensnared youth wearing
impassive, cool-pose masks beneath their shorn, dark heads, is such that
they might as well be denizens of Thebes at that fateful moment in the
dim distance of antiquity when Dionysus rapped his triumphant aside:

> Damsels, the lion walketh to the net!
> He finds his Bacchae now, and sees and dies,
> And pays for all his sins!—O Dionyse,
> This is thine hour and thou not far away.[102]

ACKNOWLEDGMENTS

A MUCH SHORTER, PRELIMINARY STATEMENT of the issues discussed in the first essay in this volume was published in my "Crisis of Gender Relations among Afro-Americans," in *Race, Gender, and Power in America,* ed. Anita Faye Hill and Emma Coleman Jordan (New York: Oxford University Press, 1995), 56–104. "Broken Bloodlines" is a very different study. Not only have my views shifted significantly on many critical issues, but the present essay surveys matters not considered in the earlier piece and is based largely on original data only recently available that I analyzed myself, in contrast with the secondary source materials of the preliminary essay. Two paragraphs from articles published in *Commentary Magazine* and the *Brookings Review* were incorporated in the text.

I would like to thank the two research teams that kindly made available the data for the first essay:

Professor Edward O. Laumann of the University of Chicago was a gracious and generous colleague during my year as a visiting professor in his department. He not only made the NHSLS data set available to me as soon as I requested it, but provided me with valuable background information about the study over lunch and gave me access to his research team, members of whom were always helpful on the occasions that I sought clarification about the data. I would also like to thank the

University of Chicago's computer lab for helping in the preliminary stages of my research on the data set, and its Department of Sociology for inviting and sponsoring me for a very productive year, during which I began work on all three essays in this volume. My first presentation on the findings included in the first essay was made at the workshop on gender at the university. It was a lively, stimulating evening, and the criticisms were valuable. A presentation of an early draft of the second essay to the culture seminar of Professor Wendy Griswold, now at Northwestern University, also drew useful comments.

I am extremely grateful also to the *Washington Post* and its research associates, the Harvard School of Public Health and the Kaiser Family Foundation, who made the survey data on women, work, and gender relations available to me for their first detailed statistical analysis. This, to a sociologist, was a gift from heaven—a major national survey conducted, at great expense, by an extremely skillful research team was made available to me simply for the asking. There should be more such kindnesses in the world. I hope the final results repay my debt in some way.

I am indebted to two friends and colleagues for their help. Professor Glenn Loury offered valuable criticisms of the manuscript, and Professor Jane Mansbridge very kindly sent me useful data from the General Social Survey that I had overlooked.

My editor, Ms. Sarah Flynn, was, as usual, a source of valuable advice and commentary on the various drafts of the text. This is a much better book as a result of her work with me. Ms. Karen Dalton, director of the Image of the Black in Western Art project at Harvard, was a valuable resource in the selection of images for this book.

Ms. Gabriella Gonzales, a graduate student in my department, was very helpful as a research assistant. My assistant, Ms. Dolores McGee, helped in innumerable ways during the preparation of the book, as did Ms. Nancy Williamson and Ms. Cheri Minton, computer consultants in the Department of Sociology at Harvard.

The modeling, graphing, analysis, and interpretation of these data sets, however, were entirely my responsibility, as are any methodological and substantive errors reported here.

Finally, I would like to thank my wife, Anita, who patiently acted as a gauge of how much technical information the proverbial educated reader can be expected to put up with, and who was always a valuable source of information and insights about her native culture, America, into which, by her, I have married.

NOTES

Introduction

1. Charles Keil, *Urban Blues* (Chicago: University of Chicago Press, 1966), 8–9.
2. Toni Cade Bambara, "On the Issue of Roles," in Toni Cade, ed., *The Black Woman: An Anthology* (New York: Signet, 1970), 101–110.
3. See Richard Wright's classic sociological novel, *Black Boy,* and Ralph Ellison's penetrating commentary on it in his "Richard Wright's Blues," in Ralph Ellison, *Shadow and Act* (New York: Vintage, 1964), 77–94.
4. Robert Goldberg, *Hooded Empire: The Ku Klux Klan in Colorado* (Urbana, IL: University of Illinois Press, 1981), 7.
5. Henry Mayer, *All on Fire: William Lloyd Garrison and the Abolition of American Slavery* (New York: St. Martin's Press, 1998).
6. Orlando Patterson, *Freedom in the Making of Western Culture* (New York: Basic Books, 1991).
7. Eric Lott, *Love and Theft: Blackface Minstrelsy and the American Working Class* (New York: Oxford University Press, 1993).
8. Edward O. Laumann, John H. Gagnon, Robert T. Michael, and Stuart Michaels, *The Social Organization of Sexuality: Sexual Practices in the United States* (Chicago: University of Chicago Press, 1994).

1. Broken Bloodlines: Gender Relations and the Crisis of Marriage and the Family among Afro-Americans

1. Emma Coleman Jordan, "The Power of False Racial Memory and the Metaphor of Lynching," in Anita Faye Hill and Emma Coleman Jordan, eds., *Race, Gender, and Power in America* (New York: Oxford University Press, 1995), 47.

2. Michele Wallace, *Black Macho and the Myth of the Superwoman* (New York: Dial Press, 1978). See also Robert Staples, "The Myth of Black Macho: A Response to Angry Black Feminists," *Black Scholar*, March-April 1979, 24–32; and the special issue of the *Black Scholar* on "Black Male/Female Relationships," May-June 1979, 14–67.

3. Patricia Hill Collins, *Black Feminist Thought* (New York: Routledge, 1991), 116.

4. Ibid., 186.

5. Noel A. Cazenave and Rita Smith, "Gender Differences in the Perception of Black Male-Female Relationships and Stereotypes," in Harold E. Cheatham and James B. Stewart, eds., *Black Families: Interdisciplinary Perspectives* (New Brunswick, NJ: Transaction Books, 1991).

6. Castellano Turner and Barbara Turner, "Black Families, Social Evaluations, and Future Marital Relations," in Constance Obudho, ed., *Black Marriage and Family Therapy* (Westport, CT: Greenwood Press, 1983), 23–37. This finding, however, has been contested by Lynette Smith and Jim Millham, "Sex Role Stereotypes amongst Blacks and Whites," *Journal of Black Psychology* 6: 1 (1979): 1–6.

7. Harriet Jacobs, *Incidents in the Life of a Slave Girl, Written by Herself* (Cambridge: Harvard University Press, 1987), 77.

8. Frances Beale, "Double Jeopardy: To Be Black and Female," in Toni Cade Bambara, ed., *The Black Woman* (New York: New American Library, 1970), 90–100.

9. See Orlando Patterson, *The Ordeal of Integration: Progress and Resentment in America's "Racial" Crisis* (Washington, DC: Civitas/Counterpoint, 1997), chap. 1; Rebecca M. Blank, *It Takes a Nation: A New Agenda for Fighting Poverty* (New York: Princeton University Press, 1997); Irwin Garfinkel and Sara S. McLanahan, *Single Mothers and Their Children: The New American Dilemma* (Washington, DC: Urban Institute Press, 1986); Diane Pearce, "The Feminization of Poverty: Women, Work, and Welfare," *Urban and Social Change Review* 11: 1/2 (1978), 28–36.

10. See "Blacks in the Economy," in Gerald D. Jaynes and Robin M. Williams Jr., eds., *A Common Destiny: Blacks and American Society* (Washington, DC: National Academy Press, 1989), chap. 6.

11. U.S. National Center for Health Statistics, *Life Tables, Actuarial Tables, and Vital Statistics for 1990* (Washington, DC: U.S. National Center for Health Statistics, 1998).

12. I refer to the French sociologist Emile Durkheim, whose classic study, *Suicide*, published in 1897, is a virtual foundation text of the discipline. Although most of Durkheim's empirical findings have been either rejected or sharply qualified, the theoretical issues he raised are still central to sociology.

13. J. T. Gibbs and A. M. Hines, "Factors Related to Sex Differences in Suicidal Behavior among African-American Youth," *Journal of Adolescent Research* 4: 2 (1989):152–72.

14. R. H. Seiden, "We're Driving Young Blacks to Suicide," *Psychology Today*, vol. 4 (1970): 24–28.

15. Collins, *Black Feminist Thought*, 118.

16. Fran Sanders, "Dear Black Man," in Cade Bambara, ed., *The Black Woman*, 73.

17. Jacqueline Jones, *Labor of Love, Labor of Sorrow: Black Women, Work, and Family from Slavery to the Present* (New York: Basic Books, 1985), 134.

18. Bonnie Thornton Dill, "'The Means to Put My Children Through': Child-Rearing Goals and Strategies among Black Female Domestic Servants," in La Frances Rodgers-Rose, ed., *The Black Woman* (Beverly Hills: Sage, 1980), 115.

19. See P. J. Bowman and C. Howard, "Race-Related Socialization, Motivation, and Academic Achievement: A Study of Black Youths in Three-Generation Families," *Journal of the American Academy of Child Psychiatry* 24: 2 (1985): 131–141. Diane K. Lewis admits that there was a strong preference for and greater tendency to promote girls in the past but speculates that, with growing economic opportunities for men, this should change: "The Black Family: Socialization and Sex Roles," *Phylon* 36: 3 (1975):221–231.

20. The relationship between income and attitude to child rearing was significant at the .03 probability level. It was not significant for other groups. Bear in mind though, that two-thirds of even the poorest group of Afro-Americans did hold that boys and girls should be raised alike.

21. For the classic exploration of such racist fears and fantasies about Afro-American men, see John Dollard, *Caste and Class in a Southern Town* (1937; reprint, New York: Doubleday Anchor, 1949), 160–163 and, more generally, chaps. 15–16.

22. Harry J. Holzer, *What Employers Want: Job Prospects for Less-Educated Workers* (New York: Russell Sage Foundation, 1996), 80–105.

23. Cynthia F. Epstein, "Positive Effects of the Multiple Negatives: Explaining the Success of Black Professional Women," *American Journal of Sociology* 78 (1973):912–935.

24. Philip Curtin, *The Atlantic Slave Trade* (Madison: University of Wisconsin Press, 1969); Paul Lovejoy, "The Volume of the Atlantic Slave Trade: A Synthesis," *Journal of African History* (1982), vol. 23: 473–501; Robert William Fogel, *Without Consent or Contract: The Rise and Fall of American Slavery* (New York: W. W. Norton, 1989), 19.

25. For a good discussion of this issue, see Sidney Mintz and Richard Price, *The Birth of African-American Culture* (Boston: Beacon Press, 1976), especially chaps. 1, 2, and 6. See also Claire Robertson, "Africa Into the Americas? Slavery and Women, the Family, and the Gender Division of Labor," in David Gaspar and Darlene Hine, eds., *More Than Chattel: Black Women and Slavery in the Americas* (Bloomington: Indiana University Press, 1996), 3–40.

26. A. R. Radcliffe-Brown and Daryll Forde, eds., *African Systems of Kinship and Marriage* (London: Oxford University Press, 1950).

27. Nancy Hafkin and Edna Bay, eds., *Women in Africa: Studies in Social and Economic Change* (Stanford: Stanford University Press, 1976); Sharon B. Stichter and J. Parpart, eds., *Patriarchy and Class: African Women in the Home and the Workforce* (Boulder: Westview, 1988).

28. Niara Sudarkasa, *Where Women Work: A Study of Yoruba Women in the Marketplace and in the Home* (Ann Arbor: University of Michigan Press, 1973); Paul Bohannan, ed., *Markets in Africa* (Evanston: Northwestern University Press, 1962).

29. J. Lorand Matory, *Sex and the Empire That is No More: Gender and the Politics of Metaphor in Oyo Yoruba Religion* (Minnesota: University of Minnesota Press, 1994); Kenneth Little, *African Women in Towns: An Aspect of Africa's Social Revolution* (Cambridge, U.K.: Cambridge University Press, 1973).

30. Orlando Patterson, *The Sociology of Slavery: An Analysis of the Origins, Structure, and Development of Negro Slave Society in Jamaica* (London: McGibbon and Kee, 1967), chap. 6.

31. The inheritance of slave status through the mother, what I have called elsewhere the Roman system, is not universal. In some slave systems, for example, slave status was inherited through the father's line, and in others (such as the ancient Chinese) through either the father's or the mother's line, depending on who had the lower status. See Orlando Patterson, *Slavery and Social Death* (Cambridge: Harvard University Press, 1982), chap. 5.

32. The classic interpretations emphasizing the destructive impact of slavery on Afro-American familial roles are W. E. B. Du Bois, *The Negro American Family* (1908; reprint, Cambridge: MIT Press, 1970); E. Franklin Frazier, *The Negro Family in the United States* (Chicago: University of Chicago Press, 1939). For the standard revisionist studies on the so-called slave family, see Robert William Fogel and Stanley Engerman, *Time on the Cross: The Economics of American Negro Slavery* (Boston: Little, Brown, 1974); Eugene Genovese, *Roll, Jordan Roll* (New York: Pantheon Books, 1974); Herbert G. Gutman, *The Black Family in Slavery and Freedom, 1750–1925* (New York: Pantheon, 1976); and Paul J. Lammermeier, "The Urban Black Family in the Nineteenth Century: A Study of Black Family Structure in the Ohio Valley, 1850–1880," *Journal of Marriage and the Family*, vol. 35 (August 1973): 440–456. Even so distinguished a scholar as the sociologist Frank Furstenberg Jr. has been misled by this revisionist literature. See F. Furstenberg Jr., Theodore Hershberg, and John Modell, "The Origins of the Female-Headed Black Family: The Impact of the Urban Experience," *Journal of Interdisciplinary History* 6: 2 (1975): 211–233.

33. Peter Parish, *Slavery: History and Historians* (New York: Harper and Row, 1989), 76; Kolchin, "Reevaluating the Antebellum Slave Community: A Comparative Perspective," *Journal of American History* 70: 3 (December 1983): 581.

34. The best critique of Fogel and Engerman's *Time on the Cross* is still the collection of critical studies edited by Paul A. David, Herbert Gutman, Richard Sutch, Peter Temin, and Gavin Wright, *Reckoning with Slavery: A Critical Study in the Quantitative History of American Negro Slavery* (New York: Oxford University Press, 1976). It is ironical that one of the best critiques of Fogel and Engerman's claim that the slaves had stable nuclear families was coauthored by Herbert Gutman in this volume. Gutman, as I have indicated, was to go on to construct his own misleading revisions. Among the best of the counterrevisionists, see Deborah Gray White, *Ar'n't I a Woman? Female Slaves in the Plantation South* (New York: Norton, 1985); Brenda Stevenson, "Distress and Discord in Virginia Slave Families, 1830–1860," in Carol

Blesser, ed., *In Joy and in Sorrow: Women, Family, and Marriage in the Victorian South, 1830–1900* (New York: Oxford University Press, 1991), 103–124; Ann Patton Malone, *Sweet Chariot* (Chapel Hill: University of North Carolina Press, 1992), especially chapters 7 and 8; Susan Lebsock, *The Free Women of Petersburg: Status and Culture in a Southern Town, 1784–1860* (New York: Norton, 1984); James Oliver Horton, "Freedom's Yoke: Gender Conventions among Antebellum Free Blacks," *Feminist Studies* 12: 1 (Spring 1986); and Elizabeth Fox-Genovese, *Within the Plantation Household: Black and White Women of the Old South* (Chapel Hill: University of North Carolina Press, 1989). See also the excellent review of Gutman's book by Stephen Gudeman: "Herbert Gutman's *The Black Family in Slavery and Freedom, 1750–1925*," *Social Science History,* vol. 3 (1979): 56–65.

35. Maria Coleta F. A. De Oliveira, "Family Change and Family Process: Implications for Research in Developing Countries," in Elza Berquo and Peter Xenos, eds., *Family Systems and Cultural Change* (Oxford: Clarendon Press, 1992), 201–214.

36. Ibid., 204.

37. Paul A. David and Peter Temin, "Capitalist Masters, Bourgeois Slaves," in David, Gutman, et al., *Reckoning with Slavery,* 48.

38. Ira Berlin, "Time, Space, and the Evolution of African-American Society," *The American Historical Review,* vol. 85 (1980): 44–78. Idem, *Many Thousands Gone: The First Two Centuries of Slavery in North America* (Cambridge: Harvard University Press, 1998).

39. Allan Kulikoff, *Tobacco and Slaves: The Development of Southern Cultures in the Chesapeake, 1680–1800* (Chapel Hill: University of North Carolina Press, 1986).

40. White, *Ar'n't I a Woman?* 118.

41. Ibid., 110. For further evidence on the matrifocality of the slave family, even where the two-parent pattern was technically present, see Cheryll Ann Cody, "Naming, Kinship, and Estate Dispersal: Notes on Slave Family Life on a South Carolina Plantation, 1786 to 1833," *William and Mary Quarterly,* vol. 39 (1982): especially 208–211; and Thomas Webber, *Deep Like the Rivers* (New York: Norton, 1978), 159–165.

42. White, *Ar'n't I a Woman?* 161.

43. See James Oliver Horton, "Freedom's Yoke: Gender Conventions among Antebellum Free Blacks," *Feminist Studies* 12: 1 (Spring, 1986): 53 (an otherwise excellent paper). Cf. Jacqueline Jones, "My Mother Was Much of a Woman: Black Women, Work, and the Family under Slavery," *Feminist Studies,* vol. 8 (Summer 1982):235–269. On the role of women in traditional West African societies and American slavery, see Melville J. Herskovits, *The Myth of the Negro Past* (Boston: Beacon Press, 1958), 167–186; and more recently, Claire Robertson, "Africa into the Americas? Slavery and Women, the Family, and the Gender Division of Labor," in David Barry Gaspar and Darlene Clark Hine, *More than Chattel: Black Women and Slavery in the Americas* (Bloomington: Indiana University Press, 1996), 3–40.

44. Paul D. Scott, *Slavery Remembered: A Record of Twentieth-Century Slave Narratives* (Chapel Hill: University of North Carolina Press, 1979), 44–53; Stephen

C. Crawford, "Quantified Memory: A Study of WPA and Fisk University Slave Narrative Collections" (Ph.D. diss., University of Chicago, 1980), chaps. 5–6.

45. Charles Wetherell, "Slave Kinship: A Case Study of the South Carolina Good Hope Plantation, 1835–1856," *Journal of Family History,* vol. 6 (Fall 1981): 294–308.

46. Stephen Gudeman, "Herbert Gutman's *The Black Family in Slavery and Freedom, 1750–1925*," 62.

47. For alternate views of slave kinship, see Charles Wetherell, "Slave Kinship," 294–308; and Cody, "Naming, Kinship, and Estate Dispersal," 192–211.

48. Cody, "Naming, Kinship, and Estate Dispersal," 192–211.

49. Orlando Patterson, "From Endo-Deme to Matri-Deme: An Interpretation of the Development of Kinship and Social Organization among the Slaves of Jamaica, 1655–1830," in Samual Proctor, ed., *Eighteenth-Century Florida and the Caribbean* (Gainesville: University Presses of Florida, 1976), 50–59.

50. See Stack, *All Our Kin,* chap. 4.

51. Stephen Gudeman, "Herbert Gutman's *The Black Family in Slavery and Freedom, 1750–1925*," 61.

52. On the role of chastity and "patterns of chaperonage of sexually mature unmarried girls and women" in human populations generally, see Alice S. Rossi, "Eros and Caritas: A Biopsychosocial Approach to Human Sexuality and Reproduction," 13–14.

53. For a good review of the historiography of slave sexual mores, see Robert William Fogel, *Without Consent or Contract: The Rise and Fall of American Slavery* (New York: W. W. Norton, 1989), 162–168.

54. Ibid., 183.

55. For a sobering account of what hardworking unattached men can do to a community, see Edith Clarke, *My Mother Who Fathered Me.* (London: Allen and Unwin, 1957). I grew up in the market towns of Lionel Town and May Pen, in Clarendon parish, Jamaica, which are located in the heart of the island's sugar-growing estates. Ask anyone from the region about the sexuality of cane cutters and they will tell you tales to make even the most jaded person of color blush crimson.

56. W. E. B. Du Bois, *The Negro American Family.* Interestingly, Fogel has offered qualified support for Du Bois's original position, in his most recent work, *Without Consent or Contract,* 164–186.

57. Malone, *Sweet Chariot,* 229.

58. On sexual violence among Euro-Americans and the incapacitation of Euro-American women in the slave South, see Bertram Wyatt Brown, *Southern Honor: Ethics and Behavior in the Old South* (New York: Oxford University Press, 1982).

59. White, *Ar'n't I a Woman?* 153.

60. Ibid., 159.

61. Ibid., 150.

62. Lebsock, *The Free Women of Petersburg,* 104–109.

63. Horton, "Freedom's Yoke," 67–68.

64. Richard H. Steckel, "The Slavery Period and Its Influence on Family Change in the United States," in Berquo and Xenos, eds., *Family Systems and Cultural Change,* 144–158.

65. Wilma King, *Stolen Childhood: Slave Youth in Nineteenth-Century America* (Bloomington: Indiana University Press, 1995), 13.

66. Ibid., 21.

67. See, in particular, Richard H. Steckel, "A Dreadful Childhood: The Excess Mortality of American Slaves," *Social Science History* 10:4 (1986): 427–465; and idem, "A Peculiar Population: The Nutrition, Health, and Mortality of American Slaves from Childhood to Maturity," *Journal of Interdisciplinary History* 46: 3 (1986): 721–741.

68. Steckel, "A Peculiar Population," 739.

69. King, *Stolen Childhood*, chap. 5.

70. Steven E. Brown states that "in no cases did slaves mention homosexual assaults" in their interviews and narratives, in his "Sexuality and the Slave Community," *Phylon* 42: 1 (Spring 1981): 1–10. This is hardly surprising, since it is only in recent years, with radically different attitudes toward sexual abuse, that men have been able to bring themselves to admit to having been sexually assaulted by older men when they were boys. I have two reasons for speculating that homosexual assaults took place. First, in every known human society, a small minority of men are homosexuals—between 3 and 6 percent—and in the highly probable event that homosexual Euro-Americans found themselves with total power, and no risk of arrest, over fine-looking slave boys, it is a reasonable assumption that they would have exploited them in some cases. If homosexual priests cannot resist the temptation to abuse their authority over boys in their charge, it is hard to see why slave-mongers, overseers, and owners would. My second reason is the fact that Southern culture was highly honorific, with a considerable degree of male bonding and homoerotic male play. We know from the literature on honorific societies that they tend to have a higher than normal proportion of homosexuals. See Jean G. Peristiany, ed., *Honor and Shame: The Values of Mediterranean Society* (London: Weidenfeld and Nicolson, 1966).

71. Willie Lee Rose, "Childhood in Bondage," in her *Slavery and Freedom* (New York: Oxford University Press, 1982), 37–48.

72. Ibid., 41.

73. Stevenson, "Distress and Discord in Virginia Slave Families," 115.

74. Webber, *Deep Like the Rivers*, 165–166. In Jamaica the pecking order of violence extended down to animals, the smallest slave children being notorious for their cruelty to young domestic animals. See Patterson, *The Sociology of Slavery*.

75. See King, *Stolen Childhood*, chaps. 3–4. King suggests that parents had more time with their children on the rice plantations of South Carolina and Georgia, where a task system allowed "a degree of autonomy" once their tasks had been completed. Ibid., 17.

76. Jane B. Lancaster, "Human Sexuality, Life Histories, and Evolutionary Ecology," in Rossi, ed., *Sexuality across the Life Course*, 39–62.

77. Ibid., 48–49.

78. King, *Stolen Childhood*, 60–65.

79. David Levine, *Family Formation in an Age of Nascent Capitalism* (New York: Academic Press, 1977).

80. Scott, *Slavery Remembered*, 44; Crawford, "Quantified Memory," chap. 5. Compare the most recent census data on types of unions and households among Afro-Americans. U.S. Bureau of the Census, "The Black Population of the United

States, 1996," unpublished on-line data, Internet release: 1997. See also Patterson, *The Ordeal of Integration,* chap. 1.

81. Furstenberg, Hershberg, and Modell, "The Origins of the Female-Headed Black Family," 211–233.

82. Herbert Gutman, "Persistent Myths about the Afro-American Family," *Journal of Interdisciplinary History* 6: 2 (1975): 181–210. For the same error, see Elizabeth Peck, "The Two-Parent Household: Black Family Structure in Late Nineteenth-Century Boston," *Journal of Social History,* vol. 5 (1971):183–209.

83. Frank Furstenberg, Hershberg, and Modell, "The Origins of the Female-Headed Black Family," 218 n.9.

84. Ibid., 221.

85. Samuel H. Preston, Suet Lim, and S. Philip Morgan, "African-American Marriage in 1910: Beneath the Surface of Census Data," *Demography* 29: 1 (1992):1–15.

86. Frazier, *The Negro Family in the United States.*

87. Preston, Lim, and Morgan, "African-American Marriage in 1910," 1–2.

88. Ibid., 11, especially table 8.

89. Ibid., 12–13.

90. Stewart E. Tolnay, "Black Family Formation and Tenancy in the Farm South, 1900," *American Journal of Sociology* 90: 2 (1984): 305–325.

91. Ibid., 309. See also Allison Davis, B. Gardner, and M. Gardner, *Deep South* (Chicago: University of Chicago Press, 1941), 240–241.

92. Ibid., 310.

93. Ibid., 320.

94. Gavin Wright, *Old South, New South: Revolutions in the Southern Economy Since the Civil War* (New York: Basic Books, 1986) 65, 93–96, and Table 4.1.

95. Dollard, *Caste and Class in a Southern Town,* 450–451. See also, Hortense Powdermaker, *After Freedom: A Cultural Study of the Deep South* (New York: Viking Press, 1939), 63–64.

96. On the South, see Florence Halpern, *Survival: Black/White* (Elmsford, NY: Pergamon, 1973), 126–136, 145; on the urban North, see Adelbert H. Jenkins, *The Psychology of the Afro-American* (New York: Pergamon, 1982), 158–159, 179–180.

97. Dollard, *Caste and Class in a Southern Town,* 420. In the mid-thirties, when Dollard carried out his research, a great number of his middle-aged respondents would have been children of persons born in slavery; Powdermaker, *After Freedom,* 67–69 and chap. 8.

98. Paul H. Ornstein, ed., *The Search for the Self: Selected Writings of Heinz Kohut: 1950–1978* (New York: International Universities Press, 1978), 1: 201–203.

99. Horton, "Freedom's Yoke," 70.

100. Paul R. Amato and Alan Booth, *A Generation at Risk: Growing Up in an Era of Family Upheaval* (Cambridge: Harvard University Press, 1997), 84.

101. Andrew J. Cherlin, *Marriage, Divorce, Remarriage* (Cambridge: Harvard Uiversity Press, 1992), 3.

102. Willard L. Rodgers and Arland Thornton, "Changing Patterns of First Marriage in the United States," *Demography* 22: 2 (1985): 265–279. The authors

conclude their analysis of marriage patterns among Americans over the present century by noting: "The basic similarity in the timing of changes in marriage rates across age levels and for both men and women, blacks and whites, is a striking characteristic of these marriage curves. There are also, however, important differences among these groups with respect to the magnitude and slopes of the shifts."

103. See Cherlin, *Marriage, Divorce, Remarriage*, 92–94.

104. This paragraph is based on figures calculated by Robert Mare and Christopher Winship, "Socioeconomic Change and the Decline of Marriage for Blacks and Whites," in Christopher Jencks and Paul Peterson, eds., *The Urban Underclass* (Washington, D.C.: Brookings, 1991), 182–184, table 1. The marriage rate they use is "the annual number of first marriages per 100 never-married persons in age, sex and race group."

105. Ibid., 182–184.

106. Thomas Espenshade, "The Recent Decline of American Marriage: Blacks and Whites in Comparative Perspective," in Kingsley Davis and Amyra Grossbard-Schechtman, eds., *Contemporary Marriage* (New York: Russell Sage Foundation, 1986), 53–90, cited in Cherlin, *Marriage, Divorce, Remarriage*, 95.

107. Cherlin, *Marriage, Divorce, Remarriage*, 95.

108. Mare and Winship, "Socioeconomic Change and the Decline of Marriage for Blacks and Whites," 176.

109. William Julius Wilson, *The Truly Disadvantaged: The Inner City, the Underclass, and Public Policy* (Chicago: University of Chicago Press, 1987); and, more recently, idem, *When Work Disappears: The World of the New Urban Poor* (New York: Knopf, 1996). See also Neil G. Bennett, David Bloom, and Patricia Craig, "The Divergence of Black and White Marriage Patterns," *American Journal of Sociology* 95: 3 (1989): 692–722.

110. See Thomas Espenshade, "Marriage Trends in America: Estimates, Implications, and Underlying Causes," *Population and Development Review*, vol. 11 (1985): 193–245; Cherlin, *Marriage, Divorce, Remarriage*, 48–57, 99–107.

111. Mare and Winship, "Socioeconomic Change and the Decline of Marriage for Blacks and Whites, 193–194.

112. Ibid., 194.

113. See Ronald Inglehart, *Culture Shift in Advanced Industrial Society* (Princeton: Princeton University Press, 1990), chap. 6.

114. R. N. Anderson, K. D. Kochanek, S. L. Murphy, "Report of Final Mortality Statistics, 1995," *Monthly Vital Statistics Report* 11, Supp. 2.

115. Robert Schoen and James R. Kluegel, "The Widening Gap in Black and White Marriage Rates: The Impact of Population Composition and Differential Marriage Propensities," *American Sociological Review*, vol. 53 (1988): 895–907.

116. Ibid., 904.

117. Shirley J. Hatchett, "Women and Men," in James S. Jackson, ed., *Life in Black America* (Newbury Park, CA: Sage Publications, 1991), 84–104; Scott J. South, "For Love or Money? Sociodemographic Determinants of the Expected Benefits from Marriage," in Scott J. South and Stewart E. Tolnay, eds., *The*

Changing American Family: Sociological and Demographic Perspectives (Boulder: Westview Press, 1992), 171–194.

118. Ibid., 99.

119. Scott South, "For Love or Money?" 183–188.

120. Ibid., 188–189.

121. Robert Schoen and Dawn Owens, "A Further Look at First Unions and First Mariages," in South and Tolnay, eds., *The Changing American Family,* 109–117.

122. See ibid., tables 6.1–67.4.

123. Bennett, Bloom, and Craig, "The Divergence of Black and White Marriage Patterns."

124. Neil G. Bennett, David E. Bloom, Cynthia K. Miller, "The Influence of Nonmarital Childbearing on the Formation of First Marriages," *Demography* 32: 1 (1995): 47–62.

125. See, for example, Marcia Guttentag and Paul F. Secord, *Too Many Women? The Sex Ratio Question* (Beverly Hills: Sage, 1983).

126. Bennett, Bloom, and Miller, "The Influence of Nonmarital Childbearing on the Formation of First Marriages," 7.

127. Ibid., 57–58.

128. Sara McLanahan and Gary Sandefur, *Growing Up with a Single Parent* (Cambridge: Harvard University Press, 1994), 54.

129. Ibid., 60.

130. Ronald Rindfuss and Audrey VandenHeuvel, "Cohabitation: A Precursor to Marriage or an Alternative to Being Single?" in South and Tolnay, eds., *The Changing American Family,* 118–142.

131. James Sweet and Larry Bumpass, "Young Adults' Views of Marriage, Cohabitation, and Family," in South and Tolnay, eds., *The Changing American Family,* 143–170.

132. A.T. Geronimus and S. Korenman, "The Socioeconomic Consequences of Teen Childbearing Reconsidered," *Quarterly Journal of Economics,* vol. 107 (1992): 1187–1214.

133. Alice S. Rossi, "Eros and Caritas: A Biopsychological Approach to Human Sexuality and Reproduction," in her *Sexuality across the Life Course* (Chicago: University of Chicago Press, 1994), 3–36.

134. G. Elder, "Family History and the Life Course," *Journal of Family History,* vol. 2 (1977): 279–304.

135. McLanahan and Sandefur, *Growing Up with A Single Parent,* 36–38, 51–63.

136. Ibid., 61.

137. Ibid., 76–77.

138. Inglehart, *Culture Shift in Advanced Industrial Society,* chap 6.

139. Arland Thornton, "Changing Attitudes toward the Family Issues in the United States," *Journal of Marriage and the Family,* vol. 51 (1989): 873–893.

140. Myron Magnet, *The Dream and the Nightmare: The Sixties' Legacy to the Underclass* (New York: W. Morrow, 1993).

141. For what it is worth, though, these statistically nonsignificant odds were always positive and moderately high.

142. The chi2 test has a probability level of (p) .019.

143. Elijah Anderson, *Streetwise: Race, Class, and Change in an Urban Community* (Chicago: University of Chicago Press, 1990), 3.

144. Marc Mauer and Tracy Huling, *Young Black Americans and the Criminal Justice System: Five Years Later* (Washington, D.C.: Sentencing Project, 1995).

145. Andrew J. Cherlin, *Marriage, Divorce, Remarriage*, 47.

146. Scott South, "Do You Need to Shop Around? Age at Marriage, Spousal Alternatives, and Marital Dissolution," *Journal of Family Issues*, vol. 6 (1995): 432–449.

147. Larry Bumpass, Teresa Martin, and James Sweet, "The Impact of Family Background and Early Marital Factors on Marital Disruption," *Journal of Family Issues*, vol. 12 (1991): 22–42.

148. Amato and Booth, *A Generation at Risk*, 97–98. The authors came up with inconsistent findings about the mediating effects of offsprings' education and earned income.

149. Paul Amato and Alan Booth, "Consequences of Parental Divorce and Marital Unhappiness for Adult Well-Being," *Social Forces*, vol. 69 (1991): 895–914. Jerold Heiss, "On the transmission of marital instability in black families," *American Sociological Review*, vol. 37 (1972): 82–92.

150. Amato and Booth, *A Generation at Risk*, 111–115.

151. Ibid., 104–105, 219.

152. The p-level of the chi2 is under .0000.

153. For the difference between Afro-American and Euro-American women the p-level is over .30. However, the greater faithfulness of Latinas is significant.

154. Guttentag and Secord, *Too Many Women?*

155. *Essence*, August 1993, 30. I found it odd that Dr. Grant, in her response, addressed only the woman's jealousy and advised her to fix herself, with the aid of professional help if necessary. The problem causing the jealousy was assumed to be either a fantasy or a fact of life over which the woman had no control.

156. U.S. Bureau of the Census, "Marital Status of Persons 15 Years Old and Over, by Age, Sex, Region, and Race: March 1996," unpublished on-line data, Internet release, June 26, 1997.

157. Richard A. Posner, *Sex and Reason* (Cambridge: Harvard University Press, 1992), 140.

158. Rindfuss and VandenHeuvel, "Cohabitation: A Precursor to Marriage or an Alternative to Being Single?" 137.

159. Amato and Booth, *A Generation at Risk*, 113–116. See also Sara McLanahan and Larry L. Bumpass, "Intergenerational Consequences of Family Disruption," *American Journal of Sociology*, vol. 94 (1988): 130–152.

160. Amato and Booth, *A Generation at Risk*, 115. The authors did find, however, that nontraditional gender attitudes among parents increased the odds of divorce among daughters.

161. Bumpass, Martin, and Sweet, "The Impact of Family Background and Early Marital Factors on Marital Disruption," 22–42.

162. Amato and Booth, *A Generation at Risk*, 97.

163. South, "For Love or Money?" 178–190.

164. See ibid., figures 9.1–9.6.

165. A. Rosenbaum and D. O'Leary, "Marital Violence: Characteristics of Abusive Couples," *Journal of Consulting and Clinical Psychology,* vol. 49 (1981): 63–71.

166. Indeed, one study came up with the disturbing finding that there is actually a negative relationship between Afro-American ego development and Afro-American racial identity, a finding that so distressed the researcher, who had been expecting just the opposite, that she promptly turned on her own fundamental concepts, condemning them as the racist product of a "white frame of reference"! See Jacqueline Looney, "Ego Development and Black Identity," *Journal of Black Psychology* 5: 1 (1988): 52.

167. hooks, *Yearning: Race, Gender and Cultural Politics* (Boston: South End Press, 1990), 58.

168. Shahrazadi Ali, *The Blackman's Guide to Understanding the Blackwoman* (Philadelphia: Civilized Publications, 1989).

169. H. Edward Ransford and Jon Miller, "Race, Sex, and Feminist Outlooks," *American Sociological Review,* vol. 48 (1983): 46–59.

170. Ibid., 57–58.

171. Emily W. Kane, "Race, Gender, and Attitudes toward Gender Stratification," *Social Psychology Quarterly* 55: 3 (1992): 311–320.

172. Ibid., 316.

173. See, for example, Joyce A. Ladner, *Tomorrow's Tomorrow: The Black Woman* (Garden City, NY: Doubleday, 1971); Charles Willie, "The Black Family and Social Class," in Robert Staples, ed., *The Black Family: Essays and Studies* (Belmont, CA: Wadsworth, 1978), 240; Hatchett, "Women and Men," 90.

174. Sandra DeJarnett and Bertram H. Raven, "The Balance, Bases, and Modes of Interpersonal Power in Black Couples: The Role of Sex and Socio-Economic Circumstances," *Journal of Black Psychology* 7: 2 (1981): 51–66.

175. Hatchett, "Women and Men," 103.

176. Wade C. Mackey, *Fathering Behaviors: The Dynamics of the Man-Child Bond* (New York: Plenum Press, 1985), 153.

177. Ibid., 180.

178. Lee Rainwater, *Behind Ghetto Walls* (Chicago: Aldine, 1970).

179. Each increase in a six-category income scale raises the odds of agreeing by about 12 percent. Each decade of life after eighteen years of age reduces them by 31 percent, other factors held constant. As one would expect, defining oneself as a political conservative substantially reduces the odds of agreeing—by over 60 percent in my model.

180. Among Euro-Americans, 83 percent of men versus 89 percent women agree that it has become harder (p=.005); among Latinos, the difference is 77 versus 91 percent (p=.09). The difference between Afro-American men and women (72 versus 78 percent) is not significant (p=.339).

181. Women, 71 percent; men 66 percent (p=.086).

182. P=.019.

183. Sixty-seven percent of Afro-American women, 72 percent of Euro-American women, and 78 percent of Latinas think so. These differences are not significant.

184. The difference between Afro-American men and women is significant at the .07 level. There is also a significant difference between Latino men and Latinas, 61

versus 78 percent (p=.069), but that is because so many more Latinas think that working has made it harder for marriages to succeed. Latino men are no different from Euro-American men on this score.

185. The 12-percentage-point difference between Afro-American men and women is not significant (p=.224), although one should bear in mind the much lower likelihood of obtaining acceptable p-values for chi square tests with small *N*s. The stark differences between Latino men and Latinas were significant at the .009 p-level.

186. Forty-seven percent of Euro-American men and women say it is harder; 50 percent of Afro-American men and 41 percent Afro-American women say it is; and 45 percent of Latino men, compared with 55 percent of Latinas, also say this. The Afro-American and Latino differences are not significant.

187. Sixty percent of Euro-American women and 69 percent of Afro-American women rejected this statement, a nonsignificant difference. However, 80 percent of Latinas rejected it, 67 percent of them strongly, and in this they differed importantly from other women (p=.09).

188. Fifty-nine percent of Euro-American men, 55 percent of Afro-American men, and 81 percent of Latino men rejected the statement. In spite of these percentile differences, we cannot infer that there is any difference among men in the population at large in their responses to this question.

189. Seventy-five percent of women agreed, versus 69 percent of men (p=.10).

190. Sixty-seven percent of Euro-American men, 72 percent of Afro-American men, and 77 percent of Latino men agreed that a woman can do both.

191. The 21-percentage-point difference in their responses is significant at the .05 probability level.

192. For an early dissent, see Marjorie Hershey, "Racial Differences in Sex-Role Identities and Sex Stereotyping: Evidence against a Common Assumption," *Social Science Quarterly*, vol. 58 (1978): 583–596.

193. Jim Millham and Lynette Smith, "Sex-Role Differentiation among Black and White Americans: A Comparative Study," *Journal of Black Psychology* 7: 2 (1981): 77–79.

194. The gender difference is significant at the .000 probability level.

195. Another 5 percent would like both genders to change (p=.000).

196. The gender difference between Afro-American men and women is significant at the .072 level. The difference between Latino men and Latinas is not statistically important on this question.

197. Sixty-eight percent of Euro-American women and 69 percent of Latinas were of this view. The differences between Afro-American women and other women, as well as those between Afro-American men and women, were all significant at below the .05 level, as were the gender differences between Euro-Americans. However, the gender differences between Latino men and Latinas were not important.

198. Sixty-one percent of Afro-Americans said upbringing was the main factor, compared with 50 percent of Euro-Americans and Latinos (p was under .05).

199. Seventy-two percent of women said both good and bad, compared with 63 percent of men; nearly the same percentages of men and women, 14 and 13 respectively, thought that these changes were bad, and almost no one thought that they had made no difference.

200. Thirty percent of Euro-American men think it would be better for the country, and a third that it would be worse; the respective percentages of Latino men are 42 and 31. The male ethnic differences are not significant.

201. The gender differences in all ethnic groups were significant at below the .005 p-level. On this issue, Latinos had the widest gender discrepancy, 86 percent of women saying it is wrong, compared with 67 percent of men.

202. Thus the odds of disapproving are increased by only 22 percent with Euro-American female respondents and are decreased by only 18 percent with Euro-American male respondents.

203. Compared with 57 percent of Euro-American women and 61 percent Latinas (p=.000).

204. The odds are increased by 48 percent among Euro-Americans and by 295 percent among Latinos.

205. Ninety-one percent of Euro-Americans and 93 percent of Latinos think it is wrong, compared with 87 percent of Afro-Americans. The differences are significant at the .010 p=level.

206. The gender gap between Euro-American men and women (3 percentage points) is significant at the .006 level; that between Afro-American men and women is significant at the .000 level. The 6-percent difference between Latino men and Latinas is not statistically significant.

207. Seventy-seven percent of Afro-American and Euro-American women agreed, along with 79 percent of Latinas.

208. The gap between Euro-American men and women was 23 points and, like that between Afro-Americans, was significant at under .000. That between Latino men and Latinas was 18 points, significant at the .012 level.

209. For Euro-Americans, being molested as a child decreases the odds of agreeing that love and sex should go together by 60 percent; among Latinos, by 72 percent; and among Afro-Americans, by 32 percent.

210. Edward O. Laumann, John H. Gagnon, Robert T. Michael, and Stuart Michaels, *The Social Organization of Sexuality: Sexual Practices in the United States* (Chicago: University of Chicago Press, 1994), 161–171.

211. I calculate the probability of a match simply by multiplying the probability of the woman liking the practice by that of the man liking it. Likewise, the probability of neither liking the practice will be the probability of one party disliking it multiplied by the probability of the other party disliking it. After calculating these two probabilities, the probability of the pair disagreeing with each other will simply be the sum of these two probabilities subtracted from 1.

212. For the mathematical foundation of the model upon which these calculations are based, see Laumann et al., *The Social Organization of Sexuality*, 166 n6.

213. Claire Sterk-Elifson, "Sexuality among African-American Women," in Rossi, ed., *Sexuality across the Life Course*, 112.

214. Among Afro-American women who were poor 15 percent reported having sex by age fourteen and 25.5 percent by age fifteen, not that much different from the mean for all Afro-American women. Among Latinas who were poor, a quarter reported they had had sex by age fourteen and 32 percent by age fifteen.

215. Again, there is not a large difference between the mean for the poor and that for other classes of respondents; 41 percent of people with poor incomes reported having had sex by age fourteen and 52 percent by age fifteen. The class difference for Latino men is much greater; 37 percent of poor Latino men had had sex by age fourteen and almost 60 percent by fifteen.

216. For Latinos, 40 percent of boys and 28 percent of girls had had sex by age fifteen, and the respective percentages for age fourteen are 27 and 17.

217. Affection for partner; peer pressure; curious/ready for sex; wanted to have a baby; physical pleasure; under the influence of drugs or alcohol; wedding night; and other.

218. Thirty-seven percent of Euro-Americans and 30 percent of Latinos did it because of curiosity or because they felt the time had come; 14 percent of Euro-Americans and 13 percent of Latinos were virgins on their wedding night, compared with 4 percent of Afro-Americans. Only 1 percent of Afro- and Euro-Americans engaged in sex for the first time because they wanted a baby; 2 percent of Latinos did.

219. Thirteen percent of Afro-American men gave the "physical pleasure" of sex as their main reason, compared with 3 percent of Afro-American women, and 5 percent of Afro-American women were virgins when they got married, compared with less than 1 percent of Afro-American men. These differences were similar to those between Euro-American men and women, only more extreme, especially in regard to affection as the main reason for first sex. The differences between Latino men and Latinas were striking: 59 percent of women said they did it first for affection, while only 23 percent of men did; 50 percent of men said they did it because they were curious, compared with 12 percent of women; 21 percent of men cited physical pleasure as the main reason and no Latina did; and only 2 percent of Latino men were virgins when they got married, compared with 22.4 percent of Latinas.

220. Among Euro-Americans, lower-class men cited affection more often than middle-class men (32 versus 25 percent), and lower-class women cited curiosity more frequently than their middle-class counterparts (30 versus 24 percent). The main class difference among Latinos was the somewhat greater tendency for lower-class women to give wanting a baby as a main reason for first sex (6 percent).

221. Thirty-nine percent of Afro-American poor women said they had lost interest at some time during the previous twelve months, compared with 43 percent of Afro-American middle-class women. In contrast, significantly more poor Euro-American women had been turned off of sex during the previous twelve months than had middle-class Euro-American women (41 versus 32 percent), while just the opposite was true of Latinas—22 percent of poor Latinas had experienced lack of interest, compared with 31 percent of middle-class Latinas.

222. By *multiple,* I mean two or more partners. Twenty-seven percent of poor Euro-American men had multiple partners, compared with 18 percent of middle- and upper-class Euro-American men; 18 percent of poor Euro-American women had multiple partners compared with 9 percent of middle- or upper-class women. For Afro-American women, the respective percentages are 20 for the poor and 16 for the middle class.

223. Compared with 44 percent of Euro-American men and 40 percent of Latinos (p=.08).

224. Forty-three percent of Euro-American women said they had done so, compared with 33 percent of men. However, the difference is not statistically significant.

225. Fifty-eight percent of Afro-American middle-class men said they had done so, compared with 41 percent of Euro-American men and 33 percent of Latino men.

226. Apart from the greater tendency to have two rather than one orgasm, the sexual functioning of Afro-American women is strikingly similar to that of Euro-American women. It is Latinas who stand out, a relatively high proportion of them failing to achieve any orgasm. On another indicator of sexual functioning—the duration of the last sex act—there was virtually no difference between women from the various ethnic groups.

227. Among the Euro-American middle classes, 91 percent of men and 86 percent of women fell in the category of very or extremely satisfied; among Latinos, 87.5 percent of men and 92 percent of women did.

228. Millham and Smith, "Sex-Role Differentiation," 85 (emphasis added).

229. See J. Garbarino, "The Human Ecology of Child Maltreatment: A Conceptual Model for Research," *Journal of Marriage and the Family,* 39 (1977): 721–727; Jay Belsky, "Child Maltreatment: An Ecological Integration," *American Psychologist* 35: 4 (1980): 320–335; Joan I. Vondra, "The Community Context of Child Abuse and Neglect," in *Families in Community Settings: Interdisciplinary Perspectives* (1990): 19–38.

230. Joan I. Vondra, "The Community Context of Child Abuse and Neglect," *Marriage and Family Review,* vol. 15 (1990): 19–38.

231. Carl H. Nightingale, *On the Edge: A History of Poor Black Children and Their American Dreams* (New York: Basic Books, 1993), 76.

232. Ibid., 77.

233. See Jessica H. Daniel, Robert Hampton, and Eli Newberger, "Child Abuse and Accidents in Black Families: A Controlled Comparative Study," *American Journal of Orthopsychiatry* 53: 4 (1983): 645–653; Robert L. Hampton, ed., *Violence in the Black Family: Correlates and Consequences* (Lexington, MA: Lexington Books, 1987); Richard Dembo, "Delinquency and Black Male Youth," in Jewelle T. Gibbs, ed., *Young, Black, and Male in America* (Dover, MA: Auburn House Pub., 1988), 140–142, 152–153. See also E. M. Kinard and L. V. Klerman, "Teenage Parenting and Child Abuse: Are They Related?" *American Journal of Orthopsychiatry* 50: 3 (1980): 481–488.

234. E. J. Smith, "The Black Female Adolescent: A Review of the Education, Career, and Psychological Literature," *Psychology of Women Quarterly* 6:3 (1982): 261–288.

235. Rainwater, *Behind Ghetto Walls,* 221.

236. Natalie Pardo, "Sex Abuse Cases Decline, but Blacks Still Main Victims," *Chicago Reporter,* January 1998.

237. Anderson, Kocherek, and Murphy, "Report of Final Monthly Mortality Statistics, 1995."

238. National Research Council, 1993.

239. Richard J. Gelles, "Poverty and Violence toward Children," *American Behavioral Scientist* 35: 3 (1992): 258–274.

240. U.S. Department of Health and Human Services, *Child Maltreatment 1996: Reports from the States to the National Center on Child Abuse and Neglect* (Washington, D.C.: National Center on Child Abuse and Neglect, 1997).

241. Robert Hampton, "Race, Class, and Child Maltreatment," *Journal of Comparative Family Studies* 18: 1 (1987): 113–126. These estimates are not very different from those given in the most recent study by the U.S. government, mentioned in the previous note.

242. Daniel, Hampton, and Newberger, "Child Abuse and Accidents in Black Families," 645–653.

243. Hampton, "Race, Class, and Child Maltreatment," 118–120.

244. James Gaudin, Norman Polansky, Allie Kilpatrick, Paula Shilton, "Loneliness, Depression, Stress, and Social Supports in Neglectful Families," *American Journal of Orthopsychiatry* 63: 4 (1993): 597–605.

245. See, especially, Gibbs, *Young, Black, and Male in America*, chapters 4 and 8.

246. Jo-Ellen Asbury reports that the incidence of wife abuse among Afro-Americans is four times greater than for any other ethnic group, although she correctly points out that poverty explains a good deal of this abuse: "Black Women in Violent Relationships," in Hampton, ed., *Violence in the Black Family*, 89–105.

247. On the cool-pose culture today, see Richard Majors and Janet Billson, *Cool Pose*, (Lexington, MA: D.C. Heath, 1992), especially chaps. 2–3; and Anderson, *Streetwise*, chap. 5. On the history of underclass violence, see Roger Lane, *Roots of Violence in Black Philadelphia, 1860–1900* (Cambridge: Harvard University Press, 1986), especially chaps. 4–6. On the tradition of "bad men and bandits" in lower-class Afro-American culture, see Lawrence Levine, *Black Culture and Black Consciousness* (New York: Oxford University Press, 1977), 407–420.

248. Paul E. Peterson, "The Urban Underclass and the Poverty Paradox," in Jencks and Peterson, eds., *The Urban Underclass*, 19.

249. Nightingale, *On the Edge*, especially chaps. 5–6. The point is also made in Mitchell Dunier, *Slim's Table: Race, Respectability, and Masculinity* (Chicago: University of Chicago Press, 1992), 127.

250. Belsky, "Child Maltreatment," 320–335.

251. David A. Schulz, *Coming Up Black* (Englewood Cliffs, NJ: Prentice Hall, 1969), 64.

252. Ibid., 175–180.

253. Carol B. Stack, *All Our Kin: Strategies for Survival in a Black Community* (New York: Harper and Row, 1974), 111.

254. Charles Willie, "The Black Family and Social Class," 240.

255. G. I. Joseph, "Black Mothers and Daughters: Traditional and New Populations," *SAGE: A Scholarly Journal on Black Women* 1: 2 (1984): 17–21.

256. Alex Kotlowitz, *There Are No Children Here* (New York: Doubleday, 1991), 85.

257. John M. Hagedorn, *People and Folks: Gangs, Crime, and the Underclass in a Rustbelt City* (Chicago: Lakeview Press, 1988), 131.

258. Bruce R. Hare, "Reexamining the Achievement Central Tendency: Sex Differences within Race and Class Differences within Sex," in Harriette Pipes McAdoo and John McAdoo, eds., *Black Children: Social, Educational, and Parental Environments* (Beverly Hills: Sage, 1985), 139–155.

259. Ibid.

260. See F. F. Furstenberg Jr., "Burden and Benefit: The Impact of Early Childbearing on the Family," *Journal of Social Issues* 36: 1 (1980): 64–87. Cf. C. J. Poole, M. S. Smith, and M. Hoffman, "Mothers of Adolescent Mothers," *Journal of Adolescent Health,* vol. 3 (1982): 28–31.

261. Roger Rubin's work carefully demonstrates that while the lower-class single-mother Afro-American family can be very supportive for the child under certain circumstances, the crowding of the household with too many family members has immediate damaging effects on the personality development of younger children. See his *Matricentric Family Structure and the Self-Attributes of Negro Children* (San Francisco: R and E Research Associates, 1976).

262. National Research Council, *Risking the Future: Adolescent Sexuality, Pregnancy, and Childbearing* (Washington, D.C.: National Academy Press, 1987), 134–138.

263. Let me be clear on this matter. The issue is *not* high fertility, for if anything, the fertility rate is stable generally, and declining precipitously among middle-class Afro-Americans. Nor is the issue that of out-of-wedlock marriages, since the increasing proportion of out-of-wedlock births in the Afro-American population is accounted for almost entirely by the decline in birth rate among married Afro-Americans and the increase among Afro-Americans in the category of "never married" women.

264. Phyllis Harrison-Ross and Barbara Wyden, *The Black Child: A Parent's Guide* (New York: Peter Wyden, 1973), 237.

265. Belsky, "Child Maltreatment," 326.

266. Thomas Kochman, "Toward an Ethnography of Black American Speech Behavior," in Thomas Kochman, ed., *Rappin' and Stylin' Out: Communication in Urban Black America* (Urbana: University of Illinois Press, 1972), 243.

267. Majors and Billson, *Cool Pose,* 43.

268. Ibid.

269. Nightingale, *On the Edge,* 31. See also, Wilson, *When Work Disappears,* 99–100; Ulf Hannerz, *Soulside* (New York: Columbia University Press, 1969), chap. 4.

270. Claudia Mitchell-Kernan, "Signifying, Loud-Talking, and Marking," in Kochman, ed., *Rappin' and Stylin' Out,* 315–335. See also the classic study of Roger D. Williams, *Deep Down in the Jungle: Negro Narrative Folklore from the Streets of Philadelphia* (Hartboro, PA: Folklore Associates, 1964).

271. Henry Louis Gates, *The Signifying Monkey: A Theory of African American Literary Criticism* (New York: Oxford University Press, 1988), 80–81.

272. See Roger Abrahams, "Joking: The Training of the Man of Words in Talking Broad," in Kochman, ed., *Rappin' and Stylin' Out,* 215–240.

273. Gates, *The Signifying Monkey,* 66.

274. Levine, *Black Culture and Black Consciousness*, 347. Levine notes that the mother is "a favorite though not invariable target."

275. Quoted in Rainwater, *Behind Ghetto Walls*, 278. Majors and Billson, who also cite this rhyme, fail to note that it was "joaned" to the researcher by a girl. However, this is consistent with the second kind of double message I have discussed, which they themselves report.

276. Not all students of the subject have buckled under the pressure to conform to the dogma that father-absence means nothing. See, for example, J. Badaines, "Identification, Imitation, and Sex-Role Preference in Father-Present and Father-Absent Black and Chicano Boys," *Journal of Psychology*, vol. 92 (1976): 15–24; L. L. Hunt and J. G. Hunt, "Race and Father-Son Connection: The Conditional Relevance of Father Absence for the Identity of Adolescent Boys," *Social Problems* 23: 1 (1975): 35–52.

277. Peter Blos, "Freud and the Father Complex," *Psychoanalytic Study of the Child*, vol. 42 (1978): 425–441.

278. Kosuke Yamazaki et al., "Self Expression, Interpersonal Relations, and Juvenile Delinquency in Japan," in Charles M. Super, ed., *The Role of Culture in Developmental Disorder* (New York: Academic Press, 1987), 197–201.

279. Stack, *All Our Kin*, 52–53.

280. John H. Scanzoni, *The Black Family in Modern Society* (Boston: Allyn and Bacon, 1971), 93.

281. Dale R. Meers, "Psychoanalytic Research and Intellectual Functioning of Ghetto-reared Black Children," *Psychoanalytic Study of the Child* 28 (1973): 411 (emphasis added).

282. Nightingale, *On the Edge*, 15–49. Elijah Anderson, "The Code of the Streets," *Atlantic Monthly*, May (1994): 80–94.

283. There is a long tradition of studies of these distinctions. See Allison Davis, *Children of Bondage* (New York: Harper and Row, 1940); Charles Willie, *A New Look at Black Families* (Bayside, NY: General Hall, 1976). On the vexed question of the size of the underclass and its relation to the larger Afro-American lower and working classes, see Wilson, *The Truly Disadvantaged;* Jencks and Peterson, *The Urban Underclass*, especially the chapters by Jencks, Peterson, and Duncan.

284. Scanzoni, *The Black Family in Modern Society*, 36–39; Harriette Pipes McAdoo, "Upward Mobility and Parenting in Middle-Income Black Families," *Journal of Black Psychology* 8: 1 (1981): 12.

285. Andrew Billingsley, *Black Families in White America* (Englewood Cliffs, NJ: Prentice Hall, 1968).

286. Scanzoni, *The Black Family in Modern Society*, 93–98.

287. John L. McAdoo, "Parenting Styles: Mother-Child Interactions and Self-Esteem in Young Black Children," in Obudho, ed., *Black Marriage and Family Therapy*, 135–150.

288. Walter Allen, "Race, Income, and Family Dynamics," in M. B. Spencer et al., eds., *Beginnings: The Social and Psychological Development of Black Children* (Hillsdale, NJ: L. Erlbaum, 1985).

289. John McAdoo, "The Roles of Black Fathers in the Socialization of Black Children," in Harriette Pipes McAdoo, ed., *Black Families* (Newbury Park, CA: Sage, 1988), 257–269.

290. Sterk-Elifson, "Sexuality among African-American Women," 113.

291. Annie S. Banes, "Black Husbands and Wives: An Account of Marital Roles in a Middle-Class Neighborhood," in Obudho, *Black Marriage and Family Therapy*, 55–73.

292. Sterk-Elifson, "Sexuality among African-American Women," 120.

293. See Patricia Voydanoff, "Economic Distress and Family Relations: A Review of the Eighties," in Alan Booth, ed., *Contemporary Families: Looking Forward, Looking Back* (Minneapolis: National Council on Family Relations, 1991): 429–445.

294. For readers not familiar with statistics, the Pearson correlation coefficient used here is a measure of co-relation, or association, that ranges between –1 (a perfect negative relationship) and +1 (a perfect positive relationship). A coefficient of 0 means that there is no relationship between the two variables.

295. Scanzoni, *The Black Family in Modern Society*, 176–190; see also chap. 4.

296. Mark Granovetter, "The Strength of Weak Ties," *American Journal of Sociology*, vol. 78 (1973): 1360–1380.

297. Mark Granovetter, *Getting A Job* (Cambridge, MA: Harvard University Press, 1974), 133.

298. A limitation of the question is that it is somewhat biased toward eliciting information on the density rather than the range of ties. However, it yielded a wealth of information on Americans' network patterns and, in view of its built-in bias, the results on Afro-Americans are all the more remarkable. If the popular view that Afro-Americans and others have about the group is true—that there is a compensatory emphasis on friendship, camaraderie and soulful bonding, what I am calling the myth of the 'hood—the question should have exaggerated such ties.

299. The measure of density used was the mean tie among the five people the respondent mentioned. For Afro-Americans it was .462, for Euro-Americans .40, and for other Americans .448.

300. Educational levels ranged from below high school graduate, through high school graduate, some college education, to college graduate. The gamma coefficient for the relationship with categorized density of ties was –.3185 with a standard error of 0.039.

301. Gamma = –.0382 with a standard error of 0.152.

302. Sixty-two percent of Euro-Americans still in the labor market fell in the category of persons with the lowest network densities (measuring between 0 and .34) in contrast with only 46 percent of retirees. Among Afro-Americans, the retirees and those still in the labor market had statistically similar percentages of persons in the low density category of networks: between 50 and 54 percent.

303. Stanley Lieberson and Mary Waters, *From Many Strands: Ethnic and Racial Groups in Contemporary America* (New York: Russell Sage, 1988), 171–175.

304. It is the odds-ratio derived from the ratios of Afro-American to non-Afro-American women's marital choices, or the ratio of column 3 to column 4.

305. See Joycelin Massiah, ed., "Women in the Caribbean, Parts 1 and 2," in *Social and Economic Studies*, 35:2 and 3 (1986); Errol Miller, *Marginalization of the*

Black Male: Insights from the Development of the Teaching Profession (Mona, Jamaica: Canoe Press, 1994).

306. Orlando Patterson, "Persistence, Continuity and Change in the Jamaican Working Class Family," *Journal of Family History,* vol. 7 (1982): 135–161; B. Edward Pierce, "The Historical Context of Nengre Kinship and Residence: Ethnohistory of the Family Organization of Lower Status Creoles in Paramaribo," in Ann M. Pescatello, ed., *Old Roots in New Lands* (Westport, CT: Greenwood Press, 1977): 107–131. Raymond T. Smith, *Kinship and Class in the West Indies* (New York: Cambridge University Press, 1990).

307. Preston, Lim, and Morgan, "African-American Marriage in 1910," 12–13.

308. Patterson, *The Ordeal of Integration,* chap. 1.

309. Toni Cade Bambara, "On the Issue of Roles," in Bambara, ed., *The Black Woman,* 109.

2. The Feast of Blood: "Race," Religion, and Human Sacrifice in the Postbellum South

1. Bruce Nichols and Chris Lee, "A Town Divided but Civil," *Dallas Morning News,* June 14, 1998.

2. W. E. B Du Bois, *Black Reconstruction in America, 1860–1880* (1935; reprint, New York: Atheneum, 1962), 678.

3. Ralph Ellison, "Twentieth Century Fiction and the Black Mask of Humanity," in his *Shadow and Act* (New York: Vintage, 1953) 24–44.

4. Trudier Harris, *Exorcising Blackness: Historical and Literary Lynching and Burning Rituals* (Bloomington: Indiana University Press, 1984), especially chap. 2.

5. Nancy MacLean, *Behind the Mask of Chivalry: The Making of the Second Ku Klux Klan* (New York: Oxford University Press, 1994), especially chap. 5; Leon F. Litwack, *Trouble in Mind: Black Southerners in the Age of Jim Crow* (New York: Alfred A. Knopf, 1998), 212–216, 343–352.

6. Forrest G. Wood, *Black Scare: The Racist Response to Emancipation and Reconstruction* (Berkeley: University of California Press, 1970), 145 and, more generally, 53–79 and 130–155.

7. W. Fitzhugh Brundage, *Lynching in the New South: Georgia and Virginia, 1880–1930* (Urbana: University of Illinois Press, 1993), 58. See also Martha Hodes, "The Sexualization of Reconstruction Politics: White Women and Black Men in the South after the Civil War," *Journal of the History of Sexuality,* vol. 3 (1993).

8. Victor Turner, "Sacrifice as Quintessential Process: Prophylaxis or Abandonment?" *History of Religions,* vol. 16 (1977): 189–215; Mary Douglas, *Purity and Danger* (London: Routledge, 1966). For a fascinating recent interpretation of the ways in which the emerging social science and literary thought of British and American writers of the late nineteenth and early twentieth century were influenced by narratives of sacrifice in ancient and primitive societies, see Susan L. Mizruchi, *The Science of Sacrifice: American Literature and Modern Social Theory* (Princeton: Princeton University Press, 1998), especially chap. 3.

9. There are several published collections of eyewitness reports on lynching based mainly on newspaper accounts of the events. I have drawn on the following:

NAACP, *Thirty Years of Lynching in the United States 1889–1918* (New York: Arno Press and *New York Times*, 1969); Ida B. Wells, *Southern Horrors: Lynch Law in all its Phases* (New York: Age Print, 1892; reprinted by Arno Press and *New York Times*, 1969); Ralph Ginzburg, *100 Years of Lynching* (Baltimore: Black Classic Press, 1962). The two classic analyses and interpretations of the killings, both of which provide additional eyewitness accounts, are Walter White, *Rope and Faggot* (New York: Arno Press and *New York Times*, 1969); and James Elbert Cutler, *Lynch Law: An Investigation into the History of Lynching in the United States* (London: Longmans, Green, 1905). There have been several modern case and regional studies of lynching, of which the most important are Brundage, *Lynching in the New South;* James R. McGovern, *Anatomy of a Lynching: The Killing of Claude Neal* (Baton Rouge: Louisiana State University Press, 1982); Howard Smead, *Blood Justice: The Lynching of Mack Charles Parker* (New York: Oxford University Press, 1986); Dennis Downey and Raymond Hyser, *No Crooked Death: Coatesville, Pennsylvania and the Lynching of Zachariah Walker* (Urbana: University of Illinois Press, 1991). An additional work of special interest is Jacquelyn D. Hall, *Revolt Against Chivalry: Jesse Daniel Ames and the Women's Campaign against Lynching* (New York: Columbia University Press, 1979). On the sources of interracial violence in South Carolina during Reconstruction, see Joel Williamson, *After Slavery: The Negro in South Carolina During Reconstruction, 1861–1877* (Chapel Hill: University of North Carolina Press, 1965), 240–273.

10. On the lynching of Afro-Americans during slavery and in direct response to the Union victory, see Thomas G. Dyer, "A Most Unexampled Exhibition of Madness and Brutality: Judge Lynch in Saline County, Missouri, 1959," and Joan E. Cashin, "A Lynching in Wartime Carolina: The Death of Saxe Joiner," in W. Fitzhugh Brundage, ed., *Under Sentence of Death: Lynching in the South* (Chapel Hill: University of North Carolina Press, 1997), 81–108; 109–131.

11. The figures upon which the ensuing calculations are based are given in Daniel T. Williams, "The Lynching Records at Tuskegee Institute," in his compilation, *Eight Negro Bibliographies*, no. 7 (New York: Kraus Reprint, 1970). It should be noted that the data given by race and year do not quite tally with those given by state and race, although the discrepancy is minor. More serious criticisms have been leveled at these data by Tolnay and Beck, who, among other criticisms, claim that there is some double-counting (see note 13). However, these are still the only data available on lynching throughout the nation.

12. Litwack, *Trouble in Mind*, 303.

13. Stewart E. Tolnay and E. M. Beck, *A Festival of Violence: An Analysis of Southern Lynchings, 1882–1930* (Urbana: University of Illinois Press, 1992), 271–272, table C–3.

14. E. M. Beck and Stewart E. Tolnay, "When Race Didn't Matter: Black and White Mob Violence against Their Own Color," in Brundage, ed., *Under Sentence of Death*, 132–154.

15. Brundage, *Lynching in the New South*, 36.

16. Williams, "The Lynching Records at Tuskegee Institute," 15.

17. Tolnay and Beck, *A Festival of Violence*, 269, table C–1.

18. Litwack, *Trouble in Mind*, 288–289.

19. E. M. Beck and Stewart E. Tolnay, "The Killing Fields of the Deep South: The Market for Cotton and the Lynching of Blacks, 1882–1930," *The American Sociological Review*, vol. 55 (1990): 526.

20. Cutler, *Lynch Law*, 187–191. For the raw data on the relationship between fundamentalist membership and lynching, see White, *Rope and Faggot*, 247–248. In fact, these data do not stand up to modern statistical analysis. At the same time, modern studies have demonstrated that fundamentalism and fundamentalist clergymen were disproportionately involved with the Ku Klux Klan. See MacLean, *Behind the Mask of Chivalry*, 91–97.

21. James M. Inverarity, "Populism and Lynching in Louisiana, 1889–1896: A Test of Erikson's Theory of the Relationship between Boundary Crisis and Repressive Justice," *American Sociological Review*, vol. 41 (1976): 262–280.

22. Larry J. Griffin, Paula Clark, and Joanne Sandberg, "Narrative and Event: Lynching and Historical Sociology," in Brundage, ed., *Under Sentence of Death*, 24–47.

23. Roberta Senechal de la Roche, "The Sociogenesis of Lynching," in Brundage, ed., *Under Sentence of Death*, 48–76. The author's theoretical claims are not supported and are vitiated by other work such as Litwack's *Trouble in Mind*, chap. 6, which demonstrates the often gratuitous nature of the killings and the tendency to select successful Afro-Americans as victims, and the data presented by Tolnay and Beck's *A Festival of Violence*, chap. 4.

24. Erle Fiske Young, "The Relations of Lynching to the Size of Political Areas," *Sociology and Social Research*, vol. 12 (1927–28): 348–353; John S. Reed, "Percent Black and Lynching: A Test of Blalock's Theory," *Social Forces*, vol. 50 (1972): 356–360; J. Corzine et al., "Black Concentration and Lynchings in the South: Testing Blalock's Power-Threat Hypothesis," *Social Forces*, vol. 61 (1983): 774–796.

25. S. Tolnay, E. Beck, and J. Massey, "Black Lynchings: The Power Threat Hypothesis Revisited," *Social Forces*, vol. 67 (1989): 605–623.

26. J. Corzine, L. Corzine, and J. Creech, "The Tenant Labor Market and Lynching in the South: A Test of the Split Labor Market Theory," *Sociological Inquiry*, vol. 58 (1988): 261–278; Susan Olzak, "The Political Context of Competition: Lynching and Urban Racial Violence, 1882–1914," *Social Forces*, 69: 2 (1990): 395–421.

27. Arthur Raper, *The Tragedy of Lynching* (Chapel Hill: University of North Carolina Press, 1933); Carl Hovland and R. R. Sears, "Minor Studies of Aggression: Correlations of Economic Indices with Lynchings," *Journal of Psychology*, vol. 9 (1940): 301–310. The last is sharply criticized by A. Mintz, "A Re-Examination of Correlations between Lynchings and Economic Indices," *Journal of Abnormal Social Psychology*, vol. 41 (1946): 154–160. See, more recently, J. Reed, G. Doss, and J. Hurlbert, "Too Good to be False: An Essay in the Folklore of Social Science," *Sociological Inquiry*, vol. 57 (1987): 1–11.

28. Tolnay and Beck, *A Festival of Violence*. For a briefer statement, see their paper, "The Killing Fields of the Deep South."

29. See Alberto R. Green, *The Role of Human Sacrifice in the Ancient Near East* (Missoula, MT: Scholars Press, 1975). For the classic comparative study on sacri-

fice, still worth reading for all its evolutionary biases, see William Robertson Smith, *Lectures on the Religion of the Semites: The Fundamental Institutions* (1889; reprint, New York: Ktav, 1969). For a vast compendium on the role of sacrifice in early Europe and other areas see Sir James Frazier, *The Golden Bough: A Study in Magic and Religion* (London: Macmillan, 1911), especially vols. 3 and 9.

30. For comparative references, see Orlando Patterson, *Slavery and Social Death* (Cambridge, MA: Harvard University Press, 1982), 107, 190–193, 224.

31. E. O. James, *Comparative Religion* (London: Methuen, 1938), 248.

32. Patterson, *Slavery and Social Death*, 221, 223.

33. Edwin Loeb, "The Blood Sacrifice Complex," *Memoirs of the American Anthropological Association*, no. 30 (1923): 23–24.

34. On the nature of sacrifice, see M. F. C. Bourdillon, ed., *Sacrifice* (New York: Academic Press, 1980); Douglas, *Purity and Danger;* Godfrey Ashby, *Sacrifice: Its Nature and Purpose* (London: SCM Press, 1988); and the classic work by Henri Hubert and Marcel Mauss, trans. W. D. Halls, *Sacrifice: Its Nature and Function* (Chicago: University of Chicago Press, 1964).

35. Hubert and Mauss, *Sacrifice*, 28.

36. Meyer Fortes, Preface to Bourdillon, ed., *Sacrifice*, ix.

37. Friedrich Nietzsche, *On the Genealogy of Morals* (New York: Vintage Books, 1989), 213.

38. The ethical aspect of sacrifice is closely related to its cathartic element, as Nietzsche himself saw. On this, see Beattie, "On Understanding Sacrifice," in Bourdillon, ed., *Sacrifice*, 36, 42–43.

39. Edward Norbeck, "Religion and Human Play," in A. Bharati, ed., *The Realm of the Extra-Human: AgenPublisherssherts and Audiences* (The Hague and Paris: Mouton, 1976), 95–104, especially 95–96, 98.

40. Girard, "La violence et le vrai savoir de l'homme," *Corporation Canadienne des Sciences Religieuses*, vol. 10 (1981): 1.

41. Ashby, *Sacrifice*, 18.

42. A. Metraux, "The Tupinamba," in J. Steward, ed., *Handbook of the South American Indians*, vol. 3, Bulletin No. 143 (Washington, D.C.: Bureau of American Ethnology, 1948): 95–133.

43. Ibid.

44. Florestan Fernandes, "La guerre et le sacrifice humain chex les Tupinamba," *Société des Americanistes, Journal* (Paris), vol. 41 (1952): 139–220.

45. A. Metraux, "The Tupinamba," 125–126.

46. *Weekly Republican*, April 28, 1899, quoted in Ginzburg, ed., *100 Years of Lynchings*, 19.

47. Quoted in Ralph E. Luker, *The Social Gospel in Black and White* (Chapel Hill: University of North Carolina Press, 1991), 105.

48. Lewis Hervie Blair, "Lynching as a Fine Art," *Our Day*, July-August 13, 1884, quoted in Luker, *The Social Gospel in Black and White*, 106.

49. Eugene D. Genovese, *Roll, Jordan, Roll* (New York: Pantheon, 1974), 32.

50. John Hope Franklin, *The Militant South* (Boston: Beacon Press, 1964); Bertram Wyatt-Brown, *Southern Honor: Ethics and Behavior in the Old South* (New

York: Oxford University Press, 1982). See my review of Wyatt-Brown's book, "The Code of Honor in the Old South," *Reviews in American History* (Spring 1984).

51. Richard E. Nisbett and Dov Cohen, *The Culture of Honor: The Psychology of Violence in the South* (Boulder: Westview Press, 1966), xvii–xviii.

52. Ibid., chaps. 1 and 6. Among historians, the best support for this argument is found in D. H. Fischer, *Albion's Seed: Four British Folkways in America* (New York: Oxford University Press, 1989).

53. Du Bois, *Black Reconstruction*, 52–53.

54. Quoted in Franklin, *The Militant South*, 76.

55. Ira Berlin, *Slaves without Masters* (New York: Vintage Books, 1974), 338.

56. Wood, *Black Scare*, 17–39.

57. Eyewitness accounts of this sacrifice are reported in Wells, ed., *Southern Horrors*, 25–32.

58. Ibid.

59. Ibid.

60. *Chicago Record-Herald*, August 8, 1901, quoted in Ginzburg, ed., *100 Years of Lynching*, 41.

61. *New York World*, April 20, 1923, quoted in Ginzburg, ed., *100 Years of Lynching*, 169.

62. *New York Tribune*, April 24, 1899, quoted in NAACP, ed., *Thirty Years of Lynching*, 12–13.

63. *New York World*, December 7, 1899, quoted in Ginzburg, ed., *100 Years of Lynching*, 28.

64. *Crisis*, June 1912, quoted in Ginzburg, ed., *100 Years of Lynching*, 21–22.

65. Larry Griffin, "Narrative, Event-Structure Analysis, and Causal Interpretation in Historical Sociology," *American Journal of Sociology*, 98: 5 (1993): 1119. This is the only substantive point made in what is primarily a paper demonstrating a sociological method and ethnographic computer program. One cannot help wondering what the response would be to a paper that uses the most painful details of the Nazi death camp to illustrate a new computer program.

66. White, *Rope and Faggot*, 3.

67. NAACP, ed., *Thirty Years of Lynching*, 26.

68. Quoted in McGovern, *Anatomy of a Lynching*, 22.

69. McGovern, *Anatomy of a Lynching*, 85.

70. Claire Murphy, "Olfactory Psychophysics," in Thomas E. Finger and Wayne Silver, eds., *Neurobiology of Taste and Smell* (New York: John Wiley and Sons, 1987), 251–273.

71. *New York Negro World*, August 22, 1920, quoted in Ginzburg, ed., *100 Years of Lynching*, 139.

72. Exodus 30:34–38.

73. Leviticus 9:24.

74. Leviticus 8:21.

75. Thomas E. Finger and Wayne Silver, "Overview and Introduction," in Finger and Silver, eds., *Neurobiology of Taste and Smell*, 3–10.

76. Trygg Engen, *Odor Sensation and Memory* (New York: Praeger, 1991), 66–67.

77. Claude Levi-Strauss, "The Culinary Triangle," *Partisan Review* (1966), 33: 586–595.

78. Judith Goode, "Food," in Richard Bauman, ed., *Folklore, Cultural Performances, and Popular Entertainments* (New York: Oxford University Press, 1992), 233–245.

79. Engen, *Odor Sensation and Memory,* 27.

80. Ibid., 81.

81. Ibid., 86–87.

82. Ibid., 86–87.

83. Quoted in White, *Rope and Faggot,* 26

84. Wyn C. Wade, *The Fiery Cross: The Ku Klux Klan in America* (New York: Touchstone Books, 1987), 172.

85. Ibid., 169. See also Nancy MacLean, *Behind the Mask of Chivalry,* 91–97. On the early history of this homo-sacrificial cult, see Cutler, *Lynch Law,* 139–154.

86. Howard Smead, *Blood Justice,* 35–36.

87. *Chicago Record-Herald,* June 24, 1903, quoted in Ginzburg, *100 Years of Lynching,* 53.

88. Ibid., 53–54.

89. Ibid.

90. *Kissimmee Valley (Florida) Gazette,* April 28, 1899, quoted in Ginzburg, ed., *100 Years of Lynching,* 11.

91. *Baltimore Afro-American,* June 24, 1921, quoted in Ginzburg, ed., *100 Years of Lynching,* 151.

92. Downey and Hyser, *No Crooked Death,* chap. 1. Although strictly in the North of the United States, Coatesville, Pennsylvania, was only twenty miles from the Maryland border, and many of its residents, including the victim, Zachariah Walker, were migrants from the South.

93. *Atlanta Constitution,* September 30, 1916, quoted in Ginzburg, ed., *100 Years of Lynching,* 109.

94. Alan W. Watts, *Myth and Ritual in Christianity* (Boston: Beacon Press, 1968), 160–161.

95. *New York World,* December 7, 1899, quoted in Ginzburg, ed., *100 Years of Lynching,* 25.

96. *Cleveland Gazette,* December 13, 1914, quoted in Ginzburg, ed., *100 Years of Lynching,* 93.

97. *New York Times,* October 19, 1933, quoted in Ginzburg, ed. *100 Years of Lynching,* 201–202.

98. *Chicago Record,* February 27, 1901, quoted in Ginzburg, ed., *100 Years of Lynching,* 37.

99. *New York World,* April 20, 1923, quoted in Ginzburg, ed., *100 Years of Lynching,* 102–103.

100. *New York World,* May 16, 1916, quoted in Ginzburg, *100 Years of Lynching,* 103.

101. *Memphis Press*, January 27, 1921, quoted in Ginzburg, *100 Years of Lynching*, 145.

102. James Sellers, *The South and Christian Ethics* (New York: Association Press, 1962), 118–119.

103. Ibid., 120. For more on the theology of segregation, especially the conceptions of God, Christ, and Man, see 121–128.

104. Ashby, *Sacrifice*, 22.

105. For a probing analysis of the genuinely sacrificial interpretation of Jesus' execution by early Christians and the continuation of this interpretation in Christianity, see S. W. Sykes, "Sacrifice in the New Testament and Christian Theology," in Bourdillon, ed., *Sacrifice*, 61–83. On sacrifice in the Old Testament, which obviously influenced early and later Christian thought, see J. W. Rogerson, "Sacrifice in the Old Testament: Problems of Method and Approach," in Bourdillon, *Sacrifice*, 45–59.

106. Charles Reagan Wilson, *Baptized in Blood: The Religion of the Lost Cause, 1865–1920* (Athens: University of Georgia Press, 1980), 36.

107. George M. Fredrickson, *The Black Image in the White Mind: The Debate on Afro-American Character and Destiny, 1817–1914* (Hanover: Wesleyan University Press, 1971), 259 and chap. 9, passim.

108. MacLean, *Behind the Mask of Chivalry*, 91.

109. Ibid., 93.

110. Wade, *The Fiery Cross*, 169.

111. Ibid., 178.

112. Wilson, *Baptized in Blood*, 27.

113. On the role of slavery in the social life and emerging theology of the early church, see Orlando Patterson, *Freedom in the Making of Western Culture* (New York: Basic Books, 1991).

114. David Brion Davis, *The Problem of Slavery in Western Culture* (Ithaca, NY: Cornell University Press, 1966), 90.

115. H. Shelton Smith, *In His Image But . . . Racism in Southern Religion, 1780–1910* (Durham, NC: Duke University Press, 1972), 188.

116. Clement Eaton, *The Waning of the Old South Civilization, 1860–1880's* (Athens: University of Georgia Press, 1968), 113.

117. Winthrop D. Jordan, *White over Black: American Attitudes toward the Negro, 1550–1812* (Baltimore: Penguin Books, 1969) 257–258.

118. Ibid., 233.

119. Victor Turner, *The Forest of Symbols: Aspects of Ndembu Ritual* (Ithaca, NY: Cornell University Press, 1967), 105.

120. A. T. Smythe to his mother, December 12, 1865, quoted in Williamson, *After Slavery: The Negro in South Carolina During Reconstruction*, 251.

121. Eric Foner, *A Short History of Reconstruction* (New York: Harper and Row, 1990), 5.

122. Ibid., chap. 4.

123. Quoted in Eaton, *The Waning of the Old South Civilization*, 113.

124. William H. Trescot quoted in Foner, *A Short History of Reconstruction*, 56.

125. Smith, *In His Image But*, 201.

126. Wilson, *Baptized in Blood,* chap. 3, passim.

127. On the paternalist "racial" tradition in the New South between 1877 and 1890, see Fredrickson, *The Black Image in the White Mind,* chap. 7.

128. For a good summary of these "rituals of white nostalgia," as he calls them, see Litwack, *Trouble in Mind,* 185–197.

129. Du Bois, *Black Reconstruction,* 139.

130. Litwack, *Trouble in Mind,* 197–198.

131. Wilson, *Baptized in Blood,* 107, 114.

132. Fortes, Preface to Bourdillon, ed., *Sacrifice,* xiv.

133. Alberto R. Green, *The Role of Human Sacrifice in the Ancient Near East,* 88.

134. Thomas Bailey, Southern educator, quoted in Litwack, *Trouble in Mind,* 181.

135. Keith Thomas, *Religion and the Decline of Magic* (New York: Scribner, 1971), 475, 493ff.

136. Thomas, *Religion and the Decline of Magic,* 520–521.

137. Michael and Judy Ann Newton, *The Ku Klux Klan: An Encyclopedia* (New York: Garland Publishers, 1991), 145–146.

138. Wade, *The Fiery Cross,* 185.

139. J. Pelikan, *Jesus through the Centuries* (New Haven: Yale University Press, 1988), 47.

140. Frances Young, *Sacrifice and the Death of Christ* (London: SPCK, 1975), 91.

141. Sykes, "Sacrifice in the New Testament and Christian Theology," 61–83.

142. See my discussion of the social origins of Christian symbolism in the primitive church in my *Freedom in the Making of Western Culture,* part 4.

143. Deuteronomy 21:23.

144. Leviticus 16:1–22.

145. Young, *Sacrifice and the Death of Christ,* 29.

146. John Dominic Crossan, *Jesus: A Revolutionary Biography* (San Francisco: Harper, 1995), 146–152. I have, nonetheless, found Crossan's work of great value.

147. For the classic study of the emergence of this tradition in the early centuries of Christianity, especially after its attempt to assimilate the pagans, see G. Aulen, *Christus Victor* (New York: Macmillan, 1951).

148. Young, *Sacrifice and the Death of Christ,* 56.

149. Genesis 22:1–19. See also Chrysostom, *Homilies on Hebrews,* XXV.

150. Quoted in Crossan, *Jesus,* 149. Crossan argues ingeniously that the sacrificial meanings of the two goats were fused in this early tradition. This certainly appears to be going on in *Barnabas,* and there can be no doubt that then, as now, both traditions were simply held together without much thought for their consistency. However, in Christian theology there are clearly two traditions of interpretations, the source of much exegetical conflict throughout the ages of Christian thought.

151. David Bastone, *From Conquest to Struggle: Jesus of Nazareth in Latin America* (Albany: State University of New York Press, 1991), 17.

152. John McKay, *The Other Spanish Christ* (New York: Macmillan, 1933), 110–111.

153. Bastone, *From Conquest to Struggle,* 17, summarizing Casalis.

154. Wilson, *Baptized in Blood,* 52–53.

155. C. Vann Woodward, *The Strange Career of Jim Crow* (New York: Oxford University Press, 1966), 4 n.

156. Woodward, 31 and chap. 2, passim.

157. See, in addition to Woodward, Fredrickson, *The Black Image in the White Mind,* chap. 7.

158. Quoted in Wade, *The Fiery Cross,* 172.

159. Leslie Dunbar, *A Republic of Equals* (Ann Arbor: University of Michigan Press, 1966), 32–33.

160. Sterling A. Brown, *The Collected Poems of Sterling A. Brown,* ed. by Michael S. Harper (Chicago: Tri Quarterly Books, 1987).

161. *Chicago Record-Herald,* June 29, 1903.

162. James Weldon Johnson, *The Autobiography of an Ex-colored Man* (1927), in John Hope Franklin, ed., *Three Negro Classics* (New York: Avon Books, 1965), 497–498.

163. Benjamin Mays, *The Negro's God As Reflected in His Literature* (New York: Russell and Russell, 1938), chapter 8.

164. Countee Cullen, *My Soul's High Song: The Collected Poems of Countee Cullen,* ed. by Gerald Early (New York: Doubleday, 1991).

165. W. E. B. DuBois, *Darkwater: Voices from within the Veil* (Millwood, N.Y.: Kraus-Thomson Organization, 1975 [1920]).

166. Langston Hughes, *The Collected Poems of Langston Hughes,* ed. by Arnold Rampersad (New York: Knopf, 1994).

167. Booker T. Washington, Letter to *Birmingham Age Herald,* February 29, 1904, quoted in Ginzburg, ed., *100 Years of Lynching,* 64–65.

168. G. S. Wilmore, *Black Religion and Black Radicalism* (Maryknoll, New York: Orbis Books, 1986), chap. 4.

169. C. Eric Lincoln, "The Black Heritage in Religion in the South," in Charles R. Wilson, ed., *Religion in the South* (Jackson: University Press of Mississippi, 1985), 53.

170. Mays, *The Negro's God,* 14.

171. Wilmore, *Black Religion and Black Radicalism,* 122–135 and chap. 6, passim. For a nuanced interpretation of the tension between universalism and particularism in the Afro-American church, and the ways in which this tension related to radicalism and accommodation, see George M. Fredrickson's valuable study, *Black Liberation: A Comparative History of Black Ideologies in the United States and South Africa* (New York: Oxford University Press, 1995), especially chap. 2.

172. Adam Fairclough, *To Redeem the Soul of America: The Southern Christian Leadership Conference and Martin Luther King, Jr.* (Athens: University of Georgia Press, 1987), 14.

173. Crossan, *Jesus,* 121.

174. Peter Blickle, *The Revolution of 1525: The German Peasants' War from a New Perspective,* trans. T. Brady Jr. and H. C. Erik Midelfort (Baltimore: Johns Hopkins University Press, 1981).

175. Christopher Hill, *The World Turned Upside Down: Radical Ideas during the English Revolution* (New York: Penguin, 1991).

176. See David J. Garrow, *Bearing the Cross: Martin Luther King and the Southern Leadership Christian Conference* (New York: William Morrow, 1986); Taylor Branch with Eugene M. Proppo, *Parting the Waters: America in the King Years, 1954–63* (New York: Simon and Shuster, 1989).

177. Dunbar, *A Republic of Equals,* 39.

3. American Dionysus: Images of Afro-American Men at the Dawn of the Twenty-first Century

1. *Chicago Tribune,* March 19, 1995.

2. Ibid.

3. *Chicago Tribune,* March 20, 1995.

4. The Los Angeles Times Staff, *In Pursuit of Justice: The People vs. Orenthal James Simpson* (Los Angeles: Los Angeles Times, 1995), 73.

5. Stephen Miller, introduction to his *Arete: Greek Sports from Ancient Sources* (Berkeley: University of California Press, 1991).

6. Ralph Ellison, "Twentieth Century Fiction and the Black Mask of Humanity," in his *Shadow and Act* (New York: Vintage, 1953), 28.

7. Edmund Morgan, *American Slavery, American Freedom: The Ordeal of Colonial Virginia* (New York: Norton, 1975).

8. Mechal Sobel, *The World They Made Together: Black and White Values in Eighteenth-Century Virginia* (Princeton: Princeton University Press, 1987), 5.

9. Ibid., 3.

10. J. L. Dillard, *Black English* (New York: Vintage, 1972), 217.

11. See Orlando Patterson, *Slavery and Social Death* (Cambridge: Harvard University Press, 1982), chap. 12.

12. Ellison, "Twentieth Century Fiction and the Black Mask of Humanity," 29.

13. Winthrop D. Jordan, *White over Black: American Attitudes toward the Negro, 1550–1812* (Chapel Hill: University of North Carolina Press, 1968); George M. Frederickson, *The Black Image in the White Mind: The Debate on Afro-American Character and Density, 1817–1914* (New York: Harper and Row, 1971); Forrest G. Wood, *Black Scare: The Racist Response to Emancipation and Reconstruction* (Berkeley: University of California Press, 1968); Stanley Elkins, *Slavery* (Chicago: University of Chicago Press, 1959); Alexander Saxton, *The Rise and Fall of the White Republic* (London: Verso, 1990).

14. Orlando Patterson, *The Sociology of Slavery: Jamaica, 1655–1838* (London: McGibbon and Kee, 1967); idem, *Slavery and Social Death.*

15. United States Kerner Commission, Report of the National Advisory Commission on Civil Disorders (Washington, D.C.: Government Printing Office, 1968); Stephen Goode, *Violence in America* (New York: Mesner, 1984).

16. On the realities and romanticization of Southern and frontier violence, see David Fischer, *Albion's Seed: Four British Folkways in America* (New York: Oxford University Press, 1989); Bertram Wyatt-Brown, *Southern Honor: Ethics and Behavior in the Old South* (New York: Oxford University Press, 1982); Jon Tuska, ed., *The American West in Fiction* (New York: New American Library, 1982); and

idem, *The American West in Film: Critical Approaches to the Western* (Westport, CT: Greenwood Press, 1985).

17. David O. Friedrichs, *Trusted Criminals: White Collar Crime in Contemporary Society* (Belmont: Wadsworth Publishing Co., 1996); Murray Strauss, Richard Gelles, and Susan Steinmetz, *Behind Closed Doors: Physical Violence in American Families* (Garden City, N.Y.: Anchor, 1981).

18. Joseph Campbell, *The Hero with a Thousand Faces* (Princeton: Princeton University Press, 1949), 30–40.

19. Campbell, *Hero with a Thousand Faces*, 147.

20. Terry Armour, "He's Back, All Right—Back on Top," *Chicago Tribune*, March 17, 1996.

21. Campbell, *Hero with a Thousand Faces*, 193.

22. Cory Johnson, "Zen and the Art of Basketball," *Swing* 2: 3 (March 1996): 37–45.

23. Phil Jackson, *Sacred Hoops: Spiritual Lessons of a Hardwood Warrior* (New York: Hyperion, 1995).

24. Friedrich Nietzsche, *The Birth of Tragedy and the Case of Wagner* (New York: Vintage Books 1967).

25. Charles Segal, *Dionysiac Poetics and Euripides' Bacchae* (Princeton: Princeton University Press, 1982).

26. For an excellent modern overview, see Albert Henrichs, "'He Has a God in Him': Human and Divine in the Modern Perception of Dionysus," in Thomas H. Carpenter and Christopher A. Faraone, eds., *Masks of Dionysus* (Ithaca, NY: Cornell University Press, 1993), 13–43.

27. Ibid., 15.

28. Martha Nussbaum, introduction to *The Bacchae of Euripides: A New Version*, translated by C. K. Williams (New York: Farrar Straus Giroux, 1990), xv.

29. Eric Lott, *Love and Theft: Blackface Minstrelsy and the American Working Class* (New York: Oxford University Press, 1993), 4.

30. For accounts of the nature of minstrelsy, see Lott, *Love and Theft*, chap. 1; and Robert C. Toll, *Blacking Up: The Minstrel Show in Nineteenth-Century America* (New York: Oxford University Press, 1974). For a fascinating account of the brief period of inter-"racial" proletarian camaraderie in New York during the first two decades of the nineteenth century, when blackface, the prototype of minstrelsy, emerged, see W. T. Lhamon Jr., *Raising Cain: Blackface Performance from Jim Crow to Hip Hop* (Cambridge: Harvard University Press, 1988), chap. 1.

31. Alexander Saxton, "Blackface Minstrelsy and Jacksonian Ideology," *American Quarterly* 33: 4 (1981): 437–458; idem, *The Rise and Fall of the White Republic*; David Roediger, *The Wages of Whiteness: Race and the Making of the American Working Class* (London: Verso, 1991).

32. Ralph Ellison, "Change the Joke and Slip the Yoke," in his *Shadow and Act*.

33. Lhamon, *Raising Cain*, 12.

34. Ibid., 45–46.

35. See, for example, ibid., 134.

36. Victor Turner, *The Forest of Symbols: Aspects of Ndembo Ritual* (Ithaca, NY: Cornell University Press, 1967).

37. Eric Lott, *Love and Theft*, 115–116.

38. Note that this argument, however superficially similar, is different from Lhamon's claim that Afro-American reality was somehow "encoded" in the minstrelsy act. Lott is saying that the concurrent presence of real Afro-American persons, real Afro-American theatrical representations, and occasionally real Afro-Americans imitating Euro-Americans imitating Afro-Americans in minstrelsy performances is the source of the unmasking and potential subversiveness of minstrelsy. Lhamon, on the other hand, is suggesting an autonomous cultural process maintaining the reality of "blackness" beneath the unreality of minstrel caricature. There may be something to this, but Lott's argument carries far greater weight.

39. Dickens celebrated Henry William Lane (a.k.a. Juba) in his *American Notes*, published in 1842, on which see Lott, *Love and Theft*, 112–115.

40. Lott, *Love and Theft*, 113.

41. Lott, *Love and Theft*, 9

42. See Martha Bayles, *Hole in Our Soul: The Loss of Beauty and Meaning in American Popular Music* (New York: Free Press, 1994), chap. 4.

43. See Noel Ignatiev, *How the Irish Became White* (New York: Routledge, 1995).

44. See Karen Sacks, "How Did the Jews Become White Folks?" in Steven Gregory and Roger Sanjek, eds., *Race* (New Brunswick: Rutgers University Press, 1994).

45. Euripides, *The Bacchae,* translated by Gilbert Murray, in *Nine Greek Dramas* (New York: P. F. Collier and Son, Harvard Classics, 1909).

46. See John Corbett, *Extended Play: Sounding Off from John Cage to Dr. Funkenstein* (Durham, NC: Duke University Press, 1994).

47. Michael Jameson, "The Asexuality of Dionysus," in Carpenter and Faraone, eds., *Masks of Dionysus*, 63–64.

48. See the rather fetching account by Evelyn Nieves of Tyson's relationship with his "adoptive mother," Camile Ewald, the ninety-three-year-old former companion of his late trainer and father figure, Cus D'Amato. Tyson not only views Ewald as his mother but retreats to her place in Catskill, New York, which he calls his "real home," whenever his Dionysian antics get him in too much trouble. "Far from Ring and Headlines, a Corner Tyson Calls Home," *New York Times,* August 2, 1998.

49. Dennis Rodman (with Tim Keown), *Bad As I Wanna Be* (New York: Delacorte Press, 1996), 8. To my pleasant surprise, I found this to be one of the most moving, unsparingly honest, and provocative autobiograpies by a popular figure I have ever read. It will almost certainly become a classic of the pop-autobiography genre.

50. Ibid., 31.

51. Ibid., 134.

52. Mike Royko, "Answer to Rodman Riddle Is in Mind of the Beholder," *Chicago Tribune,* May 7, 1996.

53. Marc Cerasini, *O. J. Simpson: American Hero, American Tragedy* (New York: Pinnacle Books, 1994), 191–192.

54. Ibid., 191.

55. Ibid., 137.

56. Albert Henrichs, "'He Has a God in Him,'" 19.

57. The Los Angeles Times Staff, *In Pursuit of Justice: The People vs. Orenthal James Simpson*, 8.

58. Ibid., 15.

59. Ibid., 23–24.

60. Jannette L. Dates and William Barlow, "A War of Images," in Dates and Barlow, eds., *Split Image: African Americans in the Mass Media* (Washington, D.C.: Howard University Press, 1993), 3.

61. Kenneth W. Goings, *Mammy and Uncle Mose: Black Collectibles and American Stereotyping* (Bloomington: Indiana University Press, 1994), plates 1–29.

62. Ibid., 13.

63. Ibid., xxiv.

64. Gerald Early, *The Culture of Bruising* (Hopewell, NJ: Ecco Press, 1994), 155–162.

65. Georg Hegel, *Phenomenology of Spirit,* trans. by A. V. Miller (Oxford, U.K.: Clarendon, 1977), chap. 5. See also my critique of Hegel and reinterpretation of what he tried to say, and might indeed have said correctly had he known more about the real nature of slavery, in *Slavery and Social Death,* chap. 12.

66. Lawrence Levine, *Black Culture and Black Consciousness* (New York: Oxford University Press, 1977), 237.

67. Gunther Schuller, *Early Jazz: Its Roots and Musical Development* (New York: Oxford University Press, 1968), 70.

68. Samuel A. Floyd Jr., *The Power of Black Music* (New York: Oxford University Press, 1995), especially chaps. 3 and 6. Gerald Early has emphasized the lower-class and proletarian Afro-American subcultures of the Midwest as the main sources of much of Afro-American music. See his *One Nation under a Groove: Motown and American Culture* (Hopewell, NJ: Ecco Press, 1995), 68–79.

69. On Afro-American dance, see Lynne Fauley Emery, *Black Dance: From 1619 to Today* (Princeton, NJ: Princeton Book Company, 1988), especially chaps. 5, 6, and 10. On humor, see Levine, *Black Culture and Black Consciousness,* chaps. 5. And on the antihero and hero in Afro-American popular culture, see ibid., 407–440. Levine contrasts Joe Louis and Jack Johnson, but as Early recently reminds us, Joe Louis, for all the veneration he enjoyed among both Euro-Americans and Afro-Americans, was no saint. He was a rotten father and husband, and his last years were spent fraternizing with Mafia hoodlums and killers. See Early, *The Culture of Bruising,* 61–63.

70. Charles Keil, *Urban Blues* (Chicago: University of Chicago Press, 1966), 15.

71. Mary Douglas, *Purity and Danger* (London: Routledge and Kegan Paul, 1966); Victor Turner, "Symbolic Studies," *Annual Review of Anthropology,* vol. 4 (1975): 145–161.

72. Schuller, *Early Jazz,* 71.

73. Nat Hentoff, *Listen to the Stories: Nat Hentoff on Jazz and Country Music* (New York: Harper Collins, 1995), 40–41.

74. See Dates and Barlow, eds., *Split Image,* chaps. 1 and 2; Floyd, *The Power of Black Music,* chaps. 6–8; and Early, *One Nation under a Groove: Motown and American Culture.*

75. See D. S. Eitzen and G. H. Sage, *The Sociology of American Sport* (Dubuque, IA: W. C. Brown, 1978).

76. See Gina Dent, ed., *Black Popular Culture* (Seattle: Bay Press, 1992); and Dates and Barlow, eds., *Split Image,* especially parts 1–4.

77. See National Research Council, "Black Participation in American Society," in Gerald D. Jaynes and Robin M. Williams Jr., eds., *A Common Destiny: Blacks and American Society* (Washington, D.C.: National Academy Press, 1989), 95–98; John Hoberman, *Darwin's Athletes: How Sports Has Damaged Black America and Preserved the Myth of Race* (Boston: Houghton Mifflin, 1997); Jeffrey Sammons, "'Race' and Sport: A Critical, Historical Examination," *Journal of Sport History,* vol. 21 (Fall 1994); Gerald Early, *The Culture of Bruising,* part 1.

78. William Julius Wilson, *The Truly Disadvantaged* (Chicago: University of Chicago Press, 1987); Elijah Anderson, *Streetwise: Race, Class, and Change in an Urban Community* (Chicago: University of Chicago Press, 1990).

79. Daniel Bell, *The Cultural Contradictions of Capitalism* (New York: Basic Books, 1978), foreword and 33–84.

80. The term was first used by Michael Hechter in a very different context—British ethnic relations. See his *Internal Colonialism: The Celtic Fringe in British National Development* (Berkeley: University of California Press, 1975).

81. Early, *The Culture of Bruising,* xiv.

82. Bayles, *Hole in Our Soul,* 356.

83. Ralph Ellison, "Richard Wright's Blues," in his *Shadow and Act,* 88.

84. Bayles, *Hole in Our Soul,* 62.

85. Norman M. Margolis, "A Theory of the Psychology of Jazz," *The American Imago,* 2: 3 (Fall 1954), quoted in Marshall Stearns, *The Story of Jazz* (New York: New American Library, 1958), 210.

86. Norman Mailer, "The White Negro," in his *The Time of Our Time* (New York: Random House, 1998): 211–230.

87. Whitney Balliett, *The Sound of Surprise* (Harmondsworth, England: Penguin Books, 1959), 29.

88. John Corbett, *Extended Play,* 15.

89. Dinah Washington, "New Blowtop Blues," quoted in Corbett, *Extended Play,* 15.

90. Euripides, *The Bacchae,* trans. by Gilbert Murray.

91. Tricia Rose, *Black Noise: Rap Music and Black Culture in Contemporary America* (Hanover, NH: Wesleyan University Press, 1994), 22.

92. See Professor Rose's vigorous defense of rap in *Black Noise,* chap. 3, where she argues that it "is a complex fusion of orality and postmodern technology." Cf. Bayles, *Hole in Our Soul,* chap. 18. On the influence of Jamaican reggae music on the few technical aspects of rap worthy of any attention, see Dick Hebdige, *Cut 'n' Mix: Culture, Identity, and Caribbean Music* (London: Comedia, 1987), chap. 17. Unfortunately, reggae, having provided rap with its technical foundation, was then polluted by rap. It is generally agreed among students of Jamaican music that rap's influence on the lyrics of the dance-hall genre of reggae has been an unmitigated disaster, given the fact that reggae, in the works of lyricists such as Bob Marley,

Toots Hibbert, and Bunny Wailer, had achieved in the seventies the high point of all modern popular songwriting.

93. On the generally disastrous efforts at fusion between rap and other Afro-American musical forms, see Bayles, *Hole in Our Soul*, chap. 20. For a more detailed and sympathetic, if not uncritical, analysis of the fusion movement see Mark C. Gridley, *Jazz Styles: History and Analysis*, 5th ed. (Englewood Cliffs, NJ: Prentice Hall, 1994), chap. 16.

94. Hoberman, *Darwin's Athletes*, xviii.

95. "Where's Daddy?" cover story in *Sports Illustrated*, May 4, 1998.

96. Signithia Fordham and John Ogbu, "Black Students' School Success: Coping with the Burden of 'Acting White,'" *Urban Review* 18: 3 (1986): 176–206. And, more recently, see John Ogbu, "Racial Stratification in the United States: Why Inequality Persists," *Teachers College Record* 96: 2 (1994): 264–298.

97. Philip J. Cook and Jens Ludwig, "The Burden of 'Acting White': Do Black Adolescents Disparage Academic Achievement?" in Christopher Jencks and Meredith Phillips, eds., *The Black-White Test Score Gap* (Washington, D.C.: Brookings Institution Press, 1988), chap. 10. The main problem with this study is that it is based mainly on self-reported questionnaire data, which is simply not appropriate for the kind of deeply cultural and social-psychological processes involved in the rejection of intellectual effort. There is a long-established tradition of valuing education in Afro-American culture, going back to the postemancipation days of the Freedmen's Bureau. All little Afro-American children will tell interviewers that they intend to become brain surgeons and corporate lawyers. The question is whether they know or value the mental and social commitments and discipline necessary to achieve these goals. Cook and Ludwig fail to recognize that profound anti-intellectualism and a strong practical desire for education can go together. Note also that the taunt of being a "nerd" is in no way similar to that of "acting white." The former does not involve an assault on one's ethnic identity and may even be taken as cute and unwittingly flattering. After all, the richest man in the history of the nation, Bill Gates, has been, still is, and from all accounts, always will be a nerd.

98. L. Steinberg, S. Dornbusch, and B. Brown, "Ethnic Differences in Adolescent Achievement: An Ecological Perspective," 47: 6 (1992): 723–729.

99. Hoberman, *Darwin's Athletes*, chap. 5; Tricia Rose, *Black Noise*, 85–96 and chap. 5. Cf. Sherley Ann Williams, "Two Words on Music: Black Community," in Dent, ed., *Black Popular Culture*, 164–172.

100. Ellison, "Twentieth Century Fiction and the Black Mask of Humanity," 41.

101. Early, *One Nation under a Groove: Motown and American Culture*, 134.

102. Euripides, *The Bacchae*, trans. by Gilbert Murray.

Index

in single-parent households, 4,
    45–46, 47, 55, 69, 133, 162
as slaves, *see* slavery; slaves
sons of, 140–45, 146
anal sex, 122
Apollonian principle, 250–51, 272, 274
Aqedah, 220
Arthur, Irving and Herman, 199
Artist Formerly Known As Prince, 256
autocannibalism, 197
aversion, rituals of, 218
Aztecs, human sacrifice of, 197

Bacchae (Euripides), 249–50, 251, 280
Baldwin, James, 174
blood
    feasting on, 231
    ritual shedding of, 175, 181–82
    ritual significance of, 182; *see also*
        ritual
    South's compact of, 215
    see also human sacrifice; sacrifice
bloodletting, 182
blood ties, 34, 35
Bowe, Riddick, 277
bridges, symbolism of, 206–7, 209–10
Bush, George, 242, 243, 244
Byrd, James, 171–72, 173

Campbell, Joseph, 245–46, 247
cannibalism, 183, 187, 195–202
    and autocannibalism, 197
    as blood-sacrifice, 182, 188
    olfaction in, 198–202
Caribbean archipelago
    matri-deme in, 34
    slavery in, 28, 32, 34
castration, 174, 184
Celtic culture, 190–91, 209
child abuse
    and divorce, 91–92
    forms of, 136
    and sexual morality, 120
    in single-parent households, 162
    slavery and, 40–41
    and social class, 133–37

children
    day-care programs for, 166
    expectations for, 22
    force-ripe socialization of, 135
    in the ghetto, 137–45, 271, 274
    illiteracy of, 279
    as marriage benefit, 69–70
    mortality rate of, 42–43
    out of wedlock, 72–77, 86–87, 119,
        124
    parental influence on, 133
    responsibility for care of, 102–5,
        165, 166
    in sharecropping families, 48
    in slavery, 35, 39–41, 42–43
    socialization of, 39–41, 135–46, 161
    teenage parents of, 76–77
    of working parents, 105
Christianity
    Christian Coalition, 273, 274
    contradictions of, 227
    crucifixion in, 189, 205, 208, 214,
        216–17, 218–23, 231
    Eucharist in, 218
    human sacrifice in, 208, 214,
        216–17, 220, 224–32
    Jews persecuted in, 245
    olfaction in, 199
    redemption in, 221–22
    resiliency of, 220
    resurrection in, 221, 223
    rituals of, 209, 218, 220
    scapegoats in, 219–20, 222
    of slaves, 221
    slaves as symbols in, 210–11
    in the South, 188–89, 218–24
    Sunday activities in, 204–5
    trees as symbols in, 205–6, 219
    see also religion
circumcision, 182
civil rights movement, 255, 271, 272
Civil War
    and religion of the Lost Cause, 208–18
    and resurrection, 221–22
    and slavery, 192, 212
    and violence, 192